ISBN 978-1-333-59435-0
PIBN 10524058

AFRICA

AND THE

DISCOVERY *of* AMERICA

VOLUME III

By LEO WIENER

PROFESSOR OF SLAVIC LANGUAGES AND LITERATURES AT
HARVARD UNIVERSITY; AUTHOR OF "A COMMENTARY TO
THE GERMANIC LAWS AND MEDIAEVAL DOCUMENTS,"
"CONTRIBUTIONS TOWARD A HISTORY OF ARABICO-
GOTHIC CULTURE," "HISTORY OF YIDDISH LITERATURE,"
"HISTORY OF THE CONTEMPORARY RUSSIAN DRAMA,"
"ANTHOLOGY OF RUSSIAN LITERATURE," "INTERPRETA-
TION OF THE RUSSIAN PEOPLE," TRANSLATOR OF THE
WORKS OF TOLSTOY; CONTRIBUTOR TO GERMAN, RUSSIAN,
FRENCH, ENGLISH, AND AMERICAN PHILOLOGICAL
PERIODICALS, ETC., ETC.

INNES & SONS
129-135 N. TWELFTH ST., PHILADELPHIA, PA.
MCMXXII

TABLE OF CONTENTS

LIST OF ILLUSTRATIONS

FOREWORD.

No archaeologist, no historian, no philologist will be more startled by the data collected in this book than I have been in their discovery.   While I to a certain extent foresaw the end toward which the presence of Africans in America before Columbus must ultimately lead in the social and religious orders, I did not allow myself in my first two volumes to be influenced by any such considerations, but confined myself to an analysis of the documentary evidence as to the American origin of cotton, tobacco, the bread roots, and wampum.

When it became necessary similarly to subject the spiritual culture of the New World to a comparative study, it turned out that the difficulties in the way were far more serious than when I undertook to brush aside the accumulated misconceptions in regard to the material civilization of pre-Columbian times.   Not only was the documentary proof scanty for America and frequently distorted by the monks and later by those who had theories to defend, but the parallel material for Africa, especially for the Western Sudan, turned out to be in a more fragmentary condition and even more distorted by investigators totally unacquainted with the Arabic antecedents of the Sudanic beliefs and customs. With the exception of the more or less objective attitude and cautious work of Delafosse and a very few others, the African material bearing on fetishism and kindred subjects is a mass of extravagances of which it is not possible to avail oneself seriously.   In archaeology the Sudan represents almost a blank.   Except for the commendable field work of Frobenius and Desplagnes, whose conclusions are unfortunately impossible, as has been pointed out by Arabicists, the whole region, in which a dozen powerful states have arisen within the last millennium, might as well be off the map,—it certainly furnishes to the student almost nothing whatsoever for a proper comprehension of fetishism, totemism, the social structure, the mediaeval trade routes, the organization of the state.

The task seemed hopeless.   But it soon became clear that the prospect was brighter than it had appeared, when the Sudanic languages were examined for the Arabic element contained in them.   This foreign intrusion, as regards Moslem conceptions, had long been known and studied, but there was a residue of cultural ideas in nearly every intimate relation in life which had not even been suspected.   Steinthal, in his study of the Mande languages, pointed out the fact that the "all-devouring" tendency of the Negro languages often completely obliterated the borrowed prototype; but, by including a study of the Arabic influence through the oases and in the Berber languages, especially in Zenaga, in the languages of the Niger Bend, such as Songay and Peul, down to the furthest outposts of the Arabic trader and magician, among the Yoruba, Asante, Dahome tribes, and even further, to the Congo, it was possible to overcome this "all-devouring" tendency and lay the foundation for an African philology and then to trace the religious conceptions of the greatest part of Northern Africa back to Islamic religion and magic.

This study cast a new aspect upon the religious ideas of the Negroes, heretofore contemptuously denominated as fetishism, and the delusive totemism, which has led to a prolixity of theories, became simple and intelligible. In fact, the spiritual culture of the Sudan appears not very different from the popular undercurrent of belief and practice among Europeans or Asiatics, while its connection with the Moslem folk religion is still closer.

The powerful Moslem interpenetration in spiritual matters among the pagan Negroes became as clear as it had been in the case of the Moslem Negroes, hence the thought suggested itself that the caste system of the Blacks, with their contempt for the blacksmith, which they share with the Arabs, might itself be of Arabic origin. In the attempt to solve this question the discovery was made that the treatment of the blacksmiths was due to the analogous Moslem treatment of the nomad Gypsies, who found their way to the Niger valley possibly as early as the VII. century. While pursuing the status of the Hindu metal-workers, the history of iron expanded into a longer chapter than was originally intended, but it serves to accentuate the fact that the westward movement through Africa of Asiatic culture, with its cotton and steel, did not take place on any appreciable scale before the Arabic occupation.

With these necessary preliminary studies, the task of coördinating the American religious, social, and political orders with the Mandingo civilization became simple, although the fragmentary condition of information seemed to preclude any definite deduction. The two civilizations are not merely similar,—they are identical, in concept, in form, in ritualistic observances, in nomenclature, and in the Arabic origin of the terms employed. The matter of chance is mathematically excluded. If chance can play such pranks, then all historical, archaeological, and philological conclusions are null and void, and the respective science must be relegated to the lumber-room.

Only the surface has been scratched. Many more analogies and identities are known to me, but it has seemed best to spurn any data which are capable of further elaborations and need the long patient labor of many men. The Peruvian civilization has barely been touched upon, because that of Mexico more easily furnished the direct evidence of the Mandingo origin.   The archaeologist will be disappointed not to find a nicely worked out chronology, but this is impossible at the present stage of our knowledge.   Only this much is certain,—the civilization so far investigated cannot be earlier than of the XII. century, and in all probability is not older than of the XIV. century.

It will be asked whether an older civilization for America is denied.   It is neither denied nor affirmed, because it is beyond the scope of the present investigation.   All that is attempted is the separation of late accretions from what may have existed before.   When the top layer has been thoroughly worked over, there will be time to work the archaeological ground with a subsoil plow, without danger of destroying its fertility.

The reader will want to know how to account for the stone structures and hieroglyphic writing in America, which do not seem to exist in Africa.   To this the answer is that we know almost nothing of the archaeology of Africa, that recent excavations have revealed monoliths and inscriptions on stone, that amazing sculptures have been unearthed in Yoruba-land, that the remarkable Benin culture is still a puzzle.   When the Western Sudan has received the thorough attention from explorers and archaeologists which it richly deserves, and we have coördinated all the Sudanic cultures, we shall be able to answer the questions which are now baffling us.   Such work can be done only by the coöperation of many men, men free from the virus of specific "schools," free from academic arrogance, free to follow the dictates of reason, no matter where it may lead,— seekers of the truth, indeed.

The Author.

SOURCES QUOTED.

[Abiven].   Dictionnaire français-malinké et malinké-fran-
                                 çais, Conakry 1906.
Acta sanctorum, July IV.
Alldridge, T. J.   A Transformed Colony, London 1910.
Allen, W. and   A Narrative of the Expedition to the River Niger,
   Thomson, T. R. H.   vol. I, London 1848.
Annual of the British School at Athens, The, vol. VIII.
Arevalo, F.   M. Avreli Clementis Prvdenti V. C. Carmina,
                                 vols. I, II, Romae 1788.
Artin Pacha, Yacoub   Contribution à l'étude du blason en Orient, Lon-
                                 dres 1902.
Avelot, R.   Note sur les pratiques religieuses de Ba-Kalé, in
                                 Bulletins et ˉmémoires de la Société d'An-
                                 thropologie de Paris, series VI, vol. II.

Bacon, R.   See Brewer.
Baron, R.   See Sibree.
Basset, R.   Mission au Sénégal, vol. I, part I, in Publications de
                                 l'École des Lettres d'Alger, vol. XXXIX.
Beck, L.   Die Geschichte des Eisens, vol. I, Braunschweig
                                 1884.
Becker, C. H.   Der Islam, vol. IV, Strassburg 1913.
Berend, W.   See Lepsius.
Bérenger-Féraud, L.   Les peuplades de la Sénégambie, Paris 1879.
Berthelot, M.   Collection des anciens alchimistes grecs, vols.
                                 I-III, Paris 1887-1888.
                               La chimie au moyen âge, vol. I, Paris 1893.
Bezold, C.   Die Schatzhöhle, aus dem syrischen Texte dreier
                                 unedierten Handschriften in's Deutsche über-
                                 setzt, Leipzig 1883.
Black, G. F.   A Gypsy Bibliography, London 1914.
Blaydes, F.   Aristophanis comoediae, Halis Saxonum 1886.
Bork, F.   Tierkreise auf westafrikanischen Kalebassen, in
                                 Mitteilungen der vorderasiatischen Gesellschaft,
                                 vol. XXI.
Bosman, W.   A New and Accurate Description of the Coast of
                                 Guinea, London 1721.
Bostock, J. and   The Natural History of Pliny, London 1855-1857.
   Riley, H. T.
Bosworth, J.   A Compendious Anglo-Saxon and English Dic-
                                 tionary, London 1852.
Breton, R.   Dictionaire caraibe-français, Leipzig 1892.
Brewer, J. S.   Fr. Rogeri Bacon opera inedita, vol. I, London 1859.
Bricchetti, R.   Somalia e Benadir, Milano 1899.
Brinton, D. G.   A Primer of Mayan Hieroglyphics, [Philadelphia]
                                 1895.

Nagualism, Philadelphia 1894.

Brugsch, H.   Hieroglyphisch-demotisches Wörterbuch, vol. II, Leipzig 1868.

Brun, J.   Le totémisme chez quelques peuples du Soudan Occidentale, in Anthropos, vol. V.

Brun, S.   Schiffarten, Basel 1624, reprinted in Werken uitgegeven door de Linschoten-Vereeniging, vol. VI, 's-Gravenhage 1913.

Brunet, L. et   Dahomey et dépendances, Paris 1901.
  Giethlen, L.

Burnam, J. M.   Recipes from Codex Matritensis A 16, in University of Cincinnati Studies, vol. VIII.

Burton, R.   A Mission to Gelele, King of Dahome, London 1864.
                      See Tootal.

Cardinall, A.W.   The Natives of the Northern Territories of the Gold Coast, London, New York.

Carra de Vaux, B.   See Tannery.

Caspari, C. P.   Kirchenhistorische Anecdota, vol. I, Christiania 1883.

Chéron, G.   La société noire de l'Afrique Occidentale Française, Paris 1908.

Christaller, J. G.   A Dictionary of the Asante and Fante Language, Basel 1881.

Clavigero, D. F. S.   The History of Mexico, trans. by C. Cullen, London 1787.

Clément-Mullet, M.   Essai sur la minéralogie arabe, in Journal Asiatique, series VI, vol. XI.

Colección de documentos inéditos de Ultramar, series II, vol. V, series I, vol. I.

Colección de documentos inéditos relativos al descubrimiento, conquista y colonizacion de las posesiones españolas en América y Occeanía, series I, vols. I, III.

Colección de libros y documentos referentes á la historia del Perú, vol. III.

Coppolani, X.   See Depont.

Corpus scriptorum historiae Byzantinae, vols. VIII, X, XIV, XXV, XXVI, XXXVIII.

Crowther, S.   See Schön.

Cullen, C.   See Clavigero.

Cumont, F.   Textes et monuments figurés relatifs aux mystères de Mithra, vol. I, Bruxelles 1899.

Defrémery, C. and   Voyages d'Ibn Batoutah, vol. IV, Paris 1879.
  Sanguinetti, B.

Deherme, G.   L'Afrique Occidentale Française, Paris 1908.

Delafosse, M.   Haut-Sénégal-Niger, series I, vols. I, III, Paris 1912.
                      Manuel dahoméen, Paris 1894.
                      Vocabulaires comparatifs de plus de 60 langues ou dialectes parlés à la Côte d'Ivoire, Paris 1904.

Depont, O. et
Coppolani, X.
: Les confréries religieuses musulmanes, Alger 1897.

Desplagnes, L. : Le plateau central nigérien, Paris 1907.

Destaing, E : Fêtes et coutumes saisonnières chez les Beni Snoùs, in Revue Africaine, vol. L.

Diemer, J. : Genesis und Exodus nach der Milstäter Handschrift, vol. I, Wien 1862.

Dindorf, G. : Harpocrationis lexicon in decem oratores atticos, vol. I, Oxonii 1853.

Doughty, C. : Travels in Arabia Deserta, vol. I, Cambridge 1888.

Doutté, E. : Magie et religion dans l'Afrique du Nord, Alger 1909.
Merrākech, Paris 1905.

Dozy, R. : Dictionnaire détaillé des noms des vêtements chez les Arabes, Amsterdam 1845.
Supplément aux dictionnaires arabes, vol. I, Leyde 1881.

Dübner, F. : Scholia graeca in Aristophanem, Parisiis 1843.

Ducange. : Glossarium mediae et infimae latinitatis, Niort 1883-1887.

Duchesne, L. : Le liber pontificalis, vol. II, Paris 1892.

Duran, D. : Historia de las Indias de Nueva España, vol. II, México 1880.

Duveyrier, H. : Les Touareg du Nord, Paris 1864.

Ellis, A. B. : The Tshi-Speaking Peoples of the Gold Coast of West Africa, London 1887.
The Yoruba-Speaking Peoples of the Slave Coast of West Africa, London 1894.

España sagrada, vols. XXXVI, XXXVII.

Ewald, P. : Gregorii I Papae registrum epistolarum, vol. I, part I, Berolini 1887.

Ferrand, G. : Les Musulmans à Madagascar, vol. I, Paris 1891.

Foà, E. : Le Dahomey, Paris 1895.

Forcellini. : Totius latinitatis lexicon, Patavii 1771.

Förstermann, E. : Altdeutsches Namenbuch, vol. I, Bonn 1900.

Fühner, H. : Bezoarsteine, in Janus, vol. VI.

García Icazbalceta, J. : Memoriales de Fray Toribio de Motolinia, Méjico 1903.

Gennep, A. van : L'état actuel du problème totémique, Paris 1920.

Gibson, M. : Apocrypha arabica, in Studia sinaitica, vol. VIII.

Giethlen, L. : See Brunet.

Goeje, M. de : Mémoire sur les migrations des Tsiganes à travers l'Asie, Leide 1903.

Goetz, G. : Corpus glossariorum latinorum, vols. II-V, Lipsiae 1888-1894.

Gómara, F. Lopez de : La historia general delas Indias, Anvers 1554.

Graff, E. G. : Althochdeutscher Sprachschatz, vol. VI, Berlin 1842.

Granada, D.   Vocabulario rioplatense razonado, Montevideo 1890.
Gregory the Great.   See Ewald.
Grimm, J.   Teutonic Mythology, vol. II, London 1883.

Hall, H.   See King.
Harpocration.   See Dindorf.
Harris, J. R.   The Cult of the Heavenly Twins, Cambridge 1906.
Hatzidakis, G. N.   Zur Wortbildungslehre des Mittel- und Neugriech-
ischen, in Byzantinische Zeitschrift, vol. II.
Haywood, A.   Through Timbuctu and across the Great Sahara,
London 1912.
Hefele, C. J. von   Conciliengeschichte, vol. III, Freiburg im Breis-
gau, 1877.
Henry, J.   Les Bambara, Münster 1910.
Herodotus.
Herrera, A. de   Historia de las Indias, Madrid 1730.
Hessels, J. H.   A Latin-Anglo-Saxon Glossary, Cambridge 1906.
Hilprecht, H. V.   Zur Lapislazuli-Frage im Babylonischen, in
Zeitschrift für Assyriologie und verwandte
Gebiete, vol. VIII, Berlin 1893.
Hofmann, K.   Archiv für lateinische Lexikographie, vol. II,
Leipzig 1885.
Holmes, W. H.   Art in Shell of the Ancient Americans, in Second
Annual Report of the Bureau of Ethnology to
the Secretary of the Smithsonian Institution,
1880-'81, Washington 1883.
Horstmann, C.   The Three Kings of Cologne, London 1886.
Houtsma, M. Th., etc.   The Encyclopaedia of Islam, Leyden, London
1913.
Hughes, T. P.   A Dictionary of Islam, London 1885.
Hutton, W.   A Voyage to Africa, London 1821.

Ibn-al-Baitār.   See Leclerc.
Ibn-Batutah.   See Defrémery.
Isidore.

Jaubert, H. F.   Glossaire du centre de la France, Paris 1864.
Jayakar, A. S. G.   Ad-Damîrî's Ḥayât Al-Ḥayawân, vol. I, London
1906.
Jewish Encyclopedia, The
Jobson, R.   The Golden Trade: or, A Discouery of the Riuer
Gambra, and the Golden Trade of the Aethiop-
ians, London 1623.
Johnston, H.   A Comparative Study of the Bantu and Semi-
Bantu Languages, Oxford 1919.
Juynboll, Th. W.   Handbuch des islamischen Gesetzes, Leiden,
Leipzig 1910.

Kersaint-Gilly, F. de — Le Nama, in Bulletin du Comité d'Études historiques et scientifiques, No. 4, Paris 1919.
King, L. and Hall, H. — Egypt and Western Asia in the Light of Recent Discoveries, London 1907.
Kingsborough, E. K. — Antiquities of Mexico, vol. II, London 1830.
Koelle, S. W. — Polyglotta africana, London 1854.

Lane, E. W. — An Account of the Manners and Customs of the Modern Egyptians, London 1837.
An Arabic-English Lexicon, book I, part V, London 1874.
Laoust, E. — Mots et choses berbères, Paris 1920.
Largeau, V. — Encyclopédie pahouine, Paris 1901.
Las Casas, B. de — Historia de las Indias, vol. III, Madrid 1875.
Laufer, B. — Die Sage von den goldgrabenden Ameisen, in T'oung Pao, series II, vol. IX.
Leclerc, L. — Traité des simples par Ibn El- Beïthar, in Notices et extraits des manuscrits de la Bibliothèque Nationale, vol. XXIII.
Leonard, A. G. — The Lower Niger and its Tribes, London 1906.
Lepsius, C. R. and Berend, W. — Les métaux dans les inscriptions égyptiennes, in Bibliothèque de l'École des hautes Études, part XXX.
Léry, J. de — Histoire d'un voyage faict en la terre du Brésil, vol. II, Paris 1880.
Lippmann, E. O. von — Entstehung und Ausbreitung der Alchemie, Berlin 1919.
Lucan. — Pharsalia.
Lüring, H. — Die uber die medicinischen Kenntnisse der alten Ägypter berichtenden Papyri, Leipzig 1888.

Mabillonii, D. Joannis Praefationes, Venetiis 1740.
MacDonald, G. — The Gold Coast, London, New York, Bombay 1898.
Mannhardt, W. — Wald- und Feldkulte, vol. I, Berlin 1904.
Mappae Clavicula, in Archaeologia, vol. XXXII.
Marees, P. de — Beschryvinghe ende historische verhael van het Gout Koninckrijck van Gunea, 's-Gravenhage 1912.
Meyer, L. — Handbuch der griechischen Etymologie, vol. III, Leipzig 1901.
Migne, J. P. — Patrologia graeca, vol. LXXXVI.1.
Patrologia latina, vol. CLXXVII.
Miklosich, F. — Über die Mundarten und die Wanderungen der Zigeuner Europa's, part VI, Wien 1876.
Modi, J. J. — The Game of Ball-Bat among the Ancient Persians, as Described in the Epic of Firdousi, in The Journal of the Bombay Branch of the Royal Asiatic Society, vol. XVIII.
Molina, A. de — Vocabulario de la lengua mexicana, Leipzig 1880.
Montgomery, J. A. — The Samaritans, Philadelphia 1907.
Monumenta Germaniae historica, Capitularia, Concilia, vol. I.

Morley, S. G.   The Inscriptions at Copan, Washington 1920.
Morton, J.   The Ancren Riwle, London 1853.
Muratori, L. A.   Antiquitates italicae medii aevi, vol. II, Mediolani 1739.

Nasmith, J.   Itinerarium Symonis Simeonis, et Hugonis Illuminatoris ad Terram Sanctam, Cambridge 1778.
Newbold, Capt.   The Gypsies of Egypt, in The Journal of the Royal Asiatic Society of Great Britain and Ireland, vol. XVI, part II.
Nicholson, R. A.   The kitáb al-luma' fi 'l-taṣawwuf, in "E. J. W. Gibb Memorial" Series, vol. XXII.
Nicole, J.   L'édit de l'empereur Léon le Sage, in Mémoires de l'Institut national genevois, vol. XVIII.

Oppenheim, M.   Vom Mittelmeer zum Persischen Golf, vol. I, Berlin 1899.
Orozco y Berra, M.   Historia antigua y de la conquista de México, vol. I, México 1880.
Oviedo, F. de   Historia general y natural de las Indias, vols. I-IV, Madrid 1851-1855.

Palmer, H. R.   Notes on the Kororofawa and Jukon, in Journal of the African Society, vol. XI.
Parkhurst, J.   An Hebrew and English Lexicon, London 1813.
Pelly, L.   A Visit to the Wahabee Capital, Central Arabia, in The Journal of the Royal Geographical Society, vol. XXXV.
Perregaux, E.   Chez les Achanti, in Bulletin de la Société neuchâteloise de Géographie, vol. XVII.
Pliny.   Historia Naturalis.
    See Bostock.
Portugaliae monumenta diplomatica, vol. I.
Proceedings of the Society of Biblical Archaeology, vol. XIII.
Purchas, S.   Hakluytus Posthumus or Purchas His Pilgrimes, vol. VI, Glasgow 1905.

Quatremère, M.   Histoire des sultans mamlouks, vol. I, parts I, II, vol. II, part I, Paris 1837.

Raccolta di documenti dalla R. Commissione Colombiana, part I, vol. I, Roma 1892, part III, vol. II, Roma 1893.
Radčenko, K.   Einige Bemerkungen zur neugefundenen Abschrift des Lebens des heil. Barbar in bulgarischer Übersetzung, in Archiv für slavische Philologie, vol. XXII.
Raffenel, A.   Nouveau voyage dans le pays des Nègres, vol. I, Paris 1856.
Rheinisches Museum, vol. XLV.

Riley, H. T.   See Bostock.
Robert, A.   L'Arabe tel qu'il est, Alger 1900.
Rochefort, C. de   Histoire naturelle et morale des Isles Antilles de
                                l'Amérique, Roterdam 1658.
Roger, F. E.   La Terre Saincte, Paris 1646.
Roth, H. L.   Great Benin, its Customs, Art and Horrors, Hal-
                                ifax 1903.
Ruelle, E.   Notes anthropologiques, ethnographiques et soc-
                                iologiques sur quelques populations noires du
                                2e territoire militaire de l'Afrique Occidentale
                                Française, in L'Anthropologie, vol. XV.
Ruska, J.   Untersuchungen über das Steinbuch des Aristoteles,
                                Heidelberg 1911.
Rymer, T.   Foedera, vol. I, London 1727.

Sachau, E.   Muhammedanisches Recht, in Lehrbücher des
                                Seminars für orientalische Sprachen zu Berlin,
                                vol. XVII.
Sahagun, B. de   Histoire générale des choses de la Nouvelle-
                                Espagne, Paris 1880.
Saint Lo, A. de   Relation dv voyage dv Cap-Verd, Paris 1637.
Sanguinetti, B.   See Defrémery.
Sauvant, P.   Grammaire bambara, Maison-Carrée (Alger) 1913.
Scheepstra, T.   Van den heilighen drien coninghen, Groningen
                                1914.
Schellhas, P.   Representation of Deities of the Maya Manu-
                                scripts, in Papers of the Peabody Museum of
                                American Archaeology and Ethnology, Harvard
                                University, vol. IV, No. I.
Schön, J. F. and   Journals of the Expedition up the Niger, London
  Crowther, S.   1842.
Schwarzlose, F. W.   Die Waffen der alten Araber aus ihren Dichtern
                                dargestellt, Leipzig 1886.
Scriptores rerum merovingicarum, vols. III, IV.
Seler, E.   Codex Borgia, vols. I-III, Berlin 1904-1909.
                                Gesammelte Abhandlungen zur amerikanischen
                                Sprach- und Alterthumskunde, vol. II, Berlin
                                1904.
Seybold, C.   Glossarium latino-arabicum, Berolini 1900.
Sibree, J. and   The Antananarivo Annual and Madagascar Mag-
  Baron, R.   azine, vol. IX.
Sievers, E.   See Steinmeyer.
Simeon, R.   Dictionnaire de la langue nahuatl, Paris 1885.
Smith, R. P.   Thesaurus syriacus, Oxonii 1868-1879.
Smith, T. B.   Relation of Alvar Nuñez Cabeça de Vaca, New
                                York 1871.
Spiess, C.   Fabeln über die Spinne bei den Ewe am Unterlauf
                                des Volta in Westafrika, and Fortsetzung der
                                Fabeln über die Spinne bei den Ewe am Unter-
                                lauf des Volta in Westafrika, in Mitteilungen des
                                Seminars für orientalische Sprachen, vol. XXI,
                                part III, vol. XXII, part III.
Stade, H.   See Tootal.

Steinen, K. von den	Unter den Naturvölkern Zentral-Brasiliens, Berlin 1894.
Steinmeyer, E. und Sievers, E.	Die althochdeutschen Glossen, vols. I-IV, Berlin 1879-1899.
Steinschneider, M.	Die „Skidy" oder geomantischen Figuren, in Zeitschrift der deutschen morgenländischen Gesellschaft, vol. XXXI.
Steinthal, H.	Die Mande-Neger-Sprachen, Berlin 1867.
Strabo.	
Sudheim, L. de	De itinere Terre Sancte, in Archives de l'Orient latin, vol. II.
Tafel, G. L. Fr. und Thomas, G. M.	Urkunden zur älteren Handels- und Staatsgeschichte der Republik Venedig, vol. I, Wien 1856.
Tannery, P. and Carra de Vaux, B.	Le Rabolion, in Mémoires scientifiques, published by J. L. Heiberg, vol. IV, Toulouse, Paris 1920.
Terrien de Lacouperie, A.	Western Origin of the Early Chinese Civilization, London 1894.
Theophilus.	Schedula diversarum artium, in Quellenschriften für Kunstgeschichte und Kunsttechnik des Mittelalters und der Renaissance, vol. VII.
Thevet, A.	La cosmographie universelle, vol. II, Paris 1575.
Thomas, C.	Notes on Certain Maya and Mexican Manuscripts, in Third Annual Report of the Bureau of Ethnology to the Secretary of the Smithsonian Institution, 1881-'82, Washington 1884.
Thomas, G. M.	See Tafel.
Thomas, N. W.	Timne-English Dictionary, in Anthropological Report on Sierra Leone, part II, London 1916.
Thomson, T. R. H.	See Allen.
Tootal, A. and Burton, R.	The Captivity of Hans Stade of Hesse (The Hakluyt Society), London 1874.
Tremearne, A. J. N.	Hausa Superstitions and Customs, London 1913. The Ban of the Bori, London 1914.
Trilles, H.	Le totémisme chez les Fan, Münster 1912.
Torquemada, J. de	De la monarquia indiana, vol. II, Madrid 1723.
Vámbéry, H.	Etymologisches Wörterbuch der turko-tatarischen Sprachen, Leipzig 1878.
Vincent of Beauvais.	Speculum doctrinale, Venetiis 1494. Speculum naturale, Venetiis 1494.
Wallis, C. B.	The Advance of our West African Empire, London 1903.
Wellhausen, J.	Skizzen und Vorarbeiten, vol. III, Berlin 1887.
Westermann, D.	Wörterbuch der Ewe-Sprache, Berlin 1905.
Westermarck, E.	Ceremonies and Beliefs Connected with Agriculture, Certain Dates of the Solar Year, and the Weather, in Morocco, Helsingfors 1913. The Magic Origin of Moorish Designs, in The Journal of the Anthropological Institute of Great Britain and Ireland, vol. XXXIV.

Wherry, E. M.   A Comprehensive Commentary on the Quran, vols. I-IV, London 1882-1886.

Wiener, L.   Africa and the Discovery of America, vols. I, II, Philadelphia 1920, 1922.

Commentary to the Germanic Laws and Mediaeval Documents, Cambridge 1915.

Contributions toward a History of Arabico-Gothic Culture, vol. I, New York 1917, vol. IV, Philadelphia 1921.

Gypsies as Fortune-Tellers and as Blacksmiths, in Journal of the Gypsy Lore Society, new series, vol. III, Nos. I, IV.

Ismaelites, in Journal of the Gypsy Lore Society, new series, vol. IV, No. II.

Wilson, C. W.   On the Tribes of the Nile valley, North of Khartûm, in The Journal of the Anthropological Institute of Great Britain and Ireland, vol. XVII.

Wright, T. and Wülcker, R.   Anglo-Saxon and Old English Vocabularies, vol. I, London 1884.

Wülcker, R.   See Wright.

Wylde, A.   Modern Abyssinia, London 1901.

Zayas y Alfonso, A.   Lexicografía antillana, Habana 1914.

Zeitschrift der deutschen morgenländischen Gesellschaft, vol. XXXIII.

Zeitschrift für die Geschichte des Oberrheins, vol. IV, Karlsruhe 1853.

Zimmermann, J.   A Grammatical Sketch of the Akra- or Gã-Language, vol. II, Stuttgart 1858.

CHAPTER I.

The History of Copper and Iron.

(a) Sumerian *urudu*.

The Assyrian name for "copper" or "bronze" is *erū*, for which the Sumerian equivalent is *urudu*. Related to the first is Assyrian *erū* "to engrave, carve, be strong," but this is, no doubt, derived from the connotation "bronze," since the root is absent from the other Semitic languages. Sumerian *urudu* is unquestionably a development of the root *ur*, which in Sumerian seems to have had the original connotation "to be strong," to judge from *ur* "lion, man, dog, enemy, bone, enclose." Unfortunately the fragmentary condition of the Sumerian vocabulary does not permit to determine positively the connotational value of the roots. This may, however, be accomplished by consulting the Dravidian languages, which are nearest related to the ancient Sumerian.

The Dravidian languages have preserved the "bronze" word in the sense of "iron, steel," a confusion which is universal in India, due to the fact that the two metals were interchangeable in common use. Thus Sanskrit *lohas* means both "copper" and "iron." For "iron" we have Tamil *irumbu*, Malayalam *irimba*, Telugu *inumu*. But we also have Kannada *urku, ukku*, Tamil, Malayalam *urukku* "wootz, steel," which cannot be separated from Kannada *urku, ukku* "to rise, swell, be greatly increased, boil excessively, be elated, pride, power," that is, we have in *urku* "steel" a "strong" word. Other derivatives, such as Kannada *urbu, urbu* "to be elated, become full of effort, energy, firmness or joy," *uṟuvu* "mass, excess, bigness, excellence," show that the original root is *ūṟu* "to fix, stick in the ground, to settle one's abode, stop, reside, stay, penetrate, exist, be," *uṟu* "to be, stay, stop," which are all derived from the original meaning "to be strong" and, if we go further back, "to enclose," hence both Tamil, Malayalam, Kannada *ura* "exertion, great effort, to be strong, to be violent as the wind" and *ūr* "an inhabited place, village, town" belong here. Similarly we have Sumerian *ur* "enclosure, to surround," *uru* "to found, plant, town, settlement, dwelling," *uru* "whirlwind," all derived from the same root. Even Sanskrit possesses this root in all these connotations. We have *uru* "wide, spacious, extended, large, much, excessive, precious, space, room," etc., and Sanskrit *ūru* "the thigh" is the same as Sumerian *ur* "foundation, lower part, leg." It is not my purpose here to trace the enormous ramifications of this root in the Indo-European, Semitic, and other families of languages,[1] but only to show that Sumerian *urudu* is a derivative of the root *ur* "to be strong."

This is also borne out by Assyrian *erū*, for we have the corresponding Dravidian words, all of them derived from the "strong" root. The Tamil *irumbu* "iron," etc. is obviously derived from *ir* "to be, exist, stay, hesitate," a variation of *uṟu*. From the same root come Kannada *iṟa* "the state of being compressed, confined," *iṟi* "to beat, strike, butt, kill." But we have also Kannada *ēṟu* "to become more or much, mount, climb," *ēṟ* "the state of being fit, to meet in battle, a wound," *ĕṟĕ* "master, fitness for being poured, to cast metals," hence *ĕraka* "any metal infusion." Here again the Sanskrit has corresponding forms, such as *irya* "active, powerful, destroying

---

[1] Such a work is in preparation.

parāsu "to divide," *paršigu* "band," *šupparuru* "to spread out" are ultimately derived from Sumerian *bar*, so is Assyrian *siparru* "copper" ultimately to be referred to Sumerian *za-bar*, and Latin *cuprum* is, no doubt, originally of a similar origin. Sumerian *an-bar* "iron," literally "sky-bright," refers to the blue color of the iron or steel, as generally represented on Egyptian monuments, hence Egyptian *bàa-en-pet* "metal of heaven, iron" does not refer to meteoric iron, as sometimes assumed, but only to the color of the iron imple ments. The Assyrian term *parzillu* "iron" is obviously a compound of Sumerian *bar*, and the second part is presumably Sumerian *sil* "to cut," or *gal* "to divide." This word is also found in the other Semitic languages, Hebrew *barzĕl* "iron," Arabic *farzala* "he put on fetters," etc. This term is distributed over an enormous territory, for we have Malay *besi*, Javanese *wesi*, Čam *pasĕi*, *basĕi*, *sĕi*, Carolinian *wasei*, Malagassy *wy*, Maori *wi* etc. There can be little doubt that Latin *ferrum* is derived from the same source, through a form *fers*.

The Sumerian *sil*, which, as we see, led to the meaning "iron" is represented in a large number of languages. We have Chinese *t'ieh*, old pronunciation *t'it*, but, since the ideogram is composed of two parts which mean "foreign metal," it follows that China is not the original country of iron manufacture. This Chinese word is found in Annamese as *thiēt* or *săt*, in Tibeto-Burman as Lalung *sar*, Dhima *shēr*, Garo *ser*, *sil*, Tipura *sor*, Bara *shurr*, Mech *shoora*, Andro *sēn*, Sengmai *sēl*, Chairel *thīr*, Khougzai *thi*, Sairang *thih*, Siyin *chī*, *khī*, Lai *tirh*, Shonshe *tīr*, Taungtha *shi*, Shö *n'thi*. In Tibetan we have *ča*, while Japanese *tetsu* is directly borrowed from the Chinese. In the Philippine languages we have apparently a borrowing from Chinese *bak t'ieh* "white iron,"[1] which is most likely a parallel to Assyrian *parzillu*. Such are Igorot *patachim*, Bontok *patatjĭm*, Bagobo *puto*, Moro *pūtaū*, Bisaya *pothao*, Tagalog *bakal*.

By the side of Chinese *t'ieh* "iron" we have *ts'ieh*, old pronunciation *ts'it*, "to cut," and this makes it possible once more to locate the origin of the word. We have Sanskrit *chedas* "a cut, piece," *chidram* "hole," *chinātti* "he cuts off," to which are related Avestan *saed*, Greek σχίζω, Latin *scindo* "I split." But these are not specifically Indo-European words, for we find them on a bewildering scale in the Dravidian languages. The Kannada "little" words, *kiṛi*, *giḍḍu*, *činna*, *čini*, *čiṭi*, *siḍi*, are *i* ablauts of the root *kaṭi* "to cut a stone with a chisel," *kadi* "a cut, piece, bit," already discussed. These at once show that Sumerian *kid* "to do, to split, to enclose" are all derived from the same root and are identical with *kar*, *kaḍ*, which has the same meanings in the Dravidian and Sumerian. This is further shown by Assyrian *garāšu* "to split," *kalū* "to enclose," by which Sumerian *kid* is translated, where we get the original roots *kar*, *kal*.

But this Sumerian *kid* "to split" is also translated by Assyrian *gallabu*, a development of the root *kar*, *gal*, already discussed. We have Assyrian *galbu* "cut, torn," *galabu* "to cut, castrate," found also in Syriac *galâbâ*, Talmudic *gĕlābā* "a sharp tool, razor," which show that Greek γλύπτειν "to chisel," γλαφυρός "smooth," Latin *glaber* "bald," etc. are all borrowings from the east, where the sharp-cutting tool, that is, steel, was first invented. But Assyrian *galbu* is a derivative of Sumerian *ǵal* "to divide," that is, we once more come back to our "cut" words.

Avestan *sidara* "rift, hole," *sinā* "destruction" are derived from the root *saēd*, of which the participial

---

[1] A reference to white iron is given in the Pi-tan.   See L. Beck, *Die Geschichte des Eisens*, Braunschweig 1884, vol. I, p. 295.

form *çastrām* means "a cutting metal, iron," hence one would expect somewhere in the Indo-European languages a form *sidara* for "iron," which is found in Greek σίδηρος. But this root is found in many languages. Etruscan *Sethlans* "Vulcan" is apparently derived from an Indo-European language. For Egypt we have Plutarch's statement, from Manetho, that iron was called "the bone of Seth," and *Seṭ* means not only "the god Seth," but also "to cut, pierce." The metal *teḥaset*, which has been variously taken for "copper" or "iron" is, in all probability, popularly derived from such a combination and originally refers to iron.

The cumulative evidence of the preceding investigation confirms the assumption that the metals were at first worked in Central Asia, whence, before the first pre-Christian millennium, the knowledge of copper and iron had spread in all directions.

(c) Assyrian *haçinnu*.

It is now well established that much of the Egyptian religion, especially the sun-worship, is of Sumerian origin.[1] The sky-god of Edfu was surrounded by his *mesniu* or smiths, but *mesen* originally means "the place where metallic work is done," then "the adytum consecrated to Horus," and only in the last instance "smith." As a verb it means "to protect." This shows that we are dealing here with an *m* derivative of a verb, which should mean "to work in metals" and "to protect," and this leads us to Assyrian *haçanu* "to protect," *huçannu* "sharp sword," *haçinnu* "axe," which are derivatives of *haçaçu* "to break, cut off." The same connotations of "to protect" and "axe" are found in Arabic حصن *haṣn* "he preserved or guarded

[1] L. King and H. Hall, *Egypt and Western Asia in the Light of Recent Discoveries*, London 1907, p. 39 ff.

it," ﺣﺴﻴﻦ *ḥaṣīn* "axe." The relation of the two words
is made clear from some Egyptian words, *aghu* "carpenter's adze, axe" and *aghau* "axe-men, soldiers,"
which are from the root *geḥ* "a kind of stone, flint,"
geḥgeḥ "to cut stone, carve, engrave." The Egyptian
root *geḥ* is, no doubt, identical with the "cut" roots so
far discussed. It is certainly not an accident that Assyrian *ḥaçinnu* is found in Sanskrit as *kaṭhiṇas* "hard,
sharp," and in Greek as ἀξίνη "axe." The latter are
borrowings from the source that first developed the
"axe" words. But this is certainly not a Semitic word,
since the regularity of the ending -*in*, attached to the
root *ḥaṣ*, as also in Talmudic חָצִינָא *ḥaçīnā*, חָזִינָא
ḥazīnā, Syriac *ḥaçinâ*, points to a common borrowing.
The simpler Arabic ﺣﺎﺩ *ḥāḍ* "sharp" produced
ﺣﺪﻳﺪ *ḥaḍīḍ* "iron," but the Assyrian *ḥaçinnu* has remained an unrelated word in all the Semitic languages,
hence it is an intrusion from without.

The Sanskrit and Dravidian languages have derivatives meaning "a cutting tool" from *kaṭi* "to cut with a
chisel," such as Sanskrit *kaṭṭāra* "a dagger," *kuṭhāra*,
Kannada *kŏḍali* "axe," hence, just as these are related
to Sanskrit *kaṭhōra*, Kannada *kaṭura* "hard," so are the
other "axe" words related to Sanskrit *kaṭhiṇas*, but
this is not of necessity originally Sanskrit. All these
words are more likely Sumerian derivatives, or compounds, of *gaz*, *ǵaš*, *ǵaz* "to break, crush." Ethiopic
ḥasin, ḥaṣin, hatin, Chamir *açin* more commonly mean
"iron, steel," and before the VII. century A. D. this
passed into Pehlevi as *āsin* "iron," and is found also in
Kurd *hāsin, hesin, awsin*, Persian *āhen*, Ossetic *äfsān*,
Afghan *ōspanah, ōspīna* "iron," while Gypsy *abčin*,
apsin has preserved the meaning "steel." In Egypt the
old *masent* "smith" has led to Coptic *basnet, besnat*
(that is, *vasnet, vesnat*) "blacksmith."

(d) Arabic 'atr.

Vincent of Beauvais, quoting Avicenna, says: "There are four kinds of iron. The first is of Spain,—it is hard; from it hammers, wedges, and such like things are made, but it is not good for cutting, and does not enter the science of alchemy. Another kind is *alidena*,—it is coarse and is not good to work with. The third kind is steel (*acerium*), which can sharpen Spanish iron. The fourth is Hindu iron,—it cuts better than any of these." "There is another kind of iron in the Orient,—it is commonly called *alidena*. It is good for incisions, and is malleable like copper or silver, but is not ductile."[1] Roger Bacon, also quoting Avicenna, says: "Iron, according to the universal opinion, is of the nature of Mars. . .The kinds and operations of iron are expounded in the Fifth Book of Avicenna's *De Anima*. There are three plainly different kinds. One kind of iron is good to sustain and give blows and forgings, and to be cast into any form desired by strong blows and fire, as in the case of hammers and anvils. This kind of iron is good for striking and warding off blows, not for cutting. Another is commonly called 'iron' (ferrum), from which are made iron tools that have to sustain percussions. Another kind is better for sharpening and cutting, such as steel (chalybs), and is purer than common iron, and it has more of heat and so is better adapted for cutting and sharpening, according to Avicenna, because it is not so ductile nor so malleable, nor fit for striking or sustaining blows. And a third kind is called *andena*, which is less common among the Latins. It differs from common iron, in that common iron cannot be drawn out or beaten except when greatly heated, whereas *andena* needs be heated only like silver, and it is not so fit for cutting as steel. But it is better for

---

[1] *Speculum naturale*, viii. 52 ff.; *Speculum doctrinale*, xi. 114.

sustaining and giving blows than steel, while common
iron surpasses both in this."[1]

Avicenna unquestionably referred to "male" and
"female" iron, in addition to the common iron. The
poet Ibn Errūmī says, "Which weapon is best? Only
a sharp sword with male edge and female blade,"[2] and
the alchemical writings make it clear that Avicenna's
definition, as given by Roger Bacon, is correct, even as
Ibn Haukal, in the middle of the X. century, referred to
the two kinds of iron.[3] The hard "male" iron was called
ذكر *dzakar*, while the soft was known as انثى *ānīt*
"female." *Dkar* is still the expression for "steel"
among the Berbers. In the Spanish-Arabic dictionary
of Alcalá *azero* is translated by *daquir* and *hind*, that is,
by "male" and "female," but the latter has been confused with هندي *hindī* "Indian," because the best steel
actually came from India.

For ذكر *dzakar* "male" another Arabic word gained
recognition, namely اثر *'atr*, *'itr*, *'utr*, originally "the
diversified wavy marks of a sword and its luster and
glitter," hence ماثور *ma'tūr* "a sword having in its
blade diversified wavy marks, or luster, or glitter, or
having its blade of female, or soft iron, and its edge of
male iron, or steel, or that is said to be of the fabric of
the jinn, or genii." Thus *atr* came to mean "steel"
par excellence. This word was in Spain confused with
اسر *'asr* "strength of make or form," اسر *'asara* "he
bound, braced, or tied," through a series of formal
blunders.

[1] *Fr. Rogeri Bacon opera inedita*, ed. by J. S. Brewer, London 1859, vol. I,
p. 382 f.
[2] F. W. Schwarzlose, *Die Waffen der alten Araber aus ihren Dichtern
dargestellt*, Leipzig 1886, p. 142.
[3] E. O. von Lippmann, *Entstehung und Ausbreitung der Alchemie*, Berlin
1919, p. 403.

In the *Affatim* glosses[1] we have "*calips* ferrum uel fornax," where "fornax" is a contamination with the succeeding gloss "caminus fornax." In the *Codex Vaticanus 1468*[2] we read "*calips* fornax ferri uel furca penalis," where to the blunder in the *Affatim* gloss is added an unusual explanation, and where steel is made equal to "gallows." The earliest reference to this is in *Codex Sangallensis 912*.[3] The addition can be understood only through the gloss in the Latin-Arabic vocabulary,[4] where we have "*calips* ferrum," and, immediately preceding it, "calibum" غل, كبل, that is, "a ring, or collar, of iron, which is put upon the neck, a shackle with which the Arabs used to confine a captive when they took him, made of thongs." This is precisely a "furca poenalis" of the Latin glosses, but the reading *calibum* at once indicates that we have here a gloss to Lucan's *Pharsalia*, VI. 797, "aeternis *Chalybum* nodis," which has obviously the meaning "vinculum, fetters."

Five years ago I wrote: "If the Gothic Bible is based on a Greek text, then *eisarn* never means 'iron,' but only 'chains, irons,' for it is the translation of Greek ἁλύσεις and πέδαι. As the corresponding passages in the Vulgate have each time 'catenae' for *eisarn*, there cannot be the slightest doubt that *eisarn* did not mean 'iron' in Gothic. It is generally supposed that Goth. *eisarn* means 'iron' and is derived from the Celtic, because of the specific statement in the *Vita Eugendi* (+510), that in the Gallic language *Ysarnodorus* means 'ferrei ostii.' But as it has been conclusively shown that the *Vita* was written after 800, the explanation is valueless, as are similar other attempts of the mediaeval author.

---

[1] G. Goetz, *Corpus glossariorum latinorum*, Lipsiae 1894, vol. IV, p. 491.
[2] *Ibid.*, vol. V, p. 493.
[3] *Ibid.*, vol. IV, p. 252.
[4] C. Seybold, *Glossarium latino-arabicum*, Berolini 1900.

"As Goth. *eisarn* means 'catena, ἄλυσις,' it is absurd to begin with the meaning 'iron.' Now Arab. اسار *īsār-un* means 'a thing with which one binds, a thong of untanned hide, a rope or cord, with which a captive is bound, a pair of shackles.' Obviously the other Germanic languages borrowed this Arabic word through the Gothic, where it had a leaning toward the meaning 'iron chain.' In OHG., *īsarn* means 'iron,' and very early we get here the corruption *īsen, īsin*, leading to Ger. *Eisen*. Similarly AS. *īsern* deteriorates early to *īsen, īren*, producing Eng. 'iron,' while in ONorse *īsarn* occurs only in poetry and popularly changes to *earn, járn*. From the ASaxon the word passed into OIrish as *iarn, hiarn*, and spread to the other Celtic languages."[1]

The discovery I have now made confirms my former assumption to a nicety rarely to be hoped for in philological investigations, and the lateness of the Gothic Bible is once more vindicated beyond any possibility of cavil, except by the mentally blind. Again, in a Hebrew translation of Ibn-al-Gezzar's work on stones, there is a quotation from the *Lapidary of Aristotle*, a IX. century forgery, where it says, among other things, that the magnet attracts אסיר *āsīr*. Ruska[2] thinks that this is a miswritten اسرب or اﺑﺮ, but he is certainly mistaken. It can be only اﺗﺮ *'atr* or اﺳﺮ *'asr* "steel" or "iron."

The Germanic "iron" words could not have arisen before the VIII. century. But the Romance languages, too, have them. The Arabic word for "steel" is found in the *Glossae nominum*, which is of Anglo-Saxon origin.

[1] *Contributions toward a History of Arabico-Gothic Culture*, New York 1917, vol. I, p. xxvi f.
[2] J. Ruska, *Untersuchungen über das Steinbuch des Aristoteles*, Heidelberg 1911, p. 36.

Here we read "ferumen *acer.*"[1] As the Graeco-Latin glosses give "ferrumen στόμωμα,"[2] and for στόμωμα also stands "ferrum durum,"[3] it follows that the unusual gloss in the *Codex Sangallensis 912*, namely "*acer durus,*"[4] is due to an abbreviation for "ferrum durum," the glossator having naturally taken *acer* to mean "hard." The early Anglo-Saxon glosses give "*accearium steli,*" which concludes the proof that we are dealing here with an Arabic word. Outside the Anglo-Saxon glosses, the word is found only in Graeco-Latin vocabularies and in the *Liber glossarum* where it is given as *aciare* and is glossed "ferrum durum,"[5] whence it also found its way into the *Codex Vaticanus 3321.*[6] Thus we find that French *acier*, Spanish *acero* "steel" are of Arabic origin.[7]

---

[1] Goetz, *op. cit.*, vol. II, p. 580.

[2] *Ibid.*, pp. 71, 438.

[3] *Ibid.*, vol. III, pp. 204, 368.

[4] *Ibid.*, vol. IV, p. 202.

[5] *Ibid.*, vol. V, p. 162.

[6] *Ibid.*, vol. IV, p. 6.

[7] As K. Hofmann (*Archiv für lateinische Lexikographie*, vol. II, p. 275) assumed that the Romance word for "steel" came from the Festus gloss for *acieris*, it is necessary to point out the fact that *acieris* is a ghost word.   In Festus there is an entry "acerra ara, quae ante mortuum poni solebat, in qua odores incendebant.   Alii dicunt arculam esse turariam, scilicet ubi tus reponebant." Here *ara* is unquestionably a miswritten *arca*, which Paulus found in a bad copy of Festus, and so doubled up the lemma, for it does not appear from any source that altars called "acerra" were placed before the dead.   In the glosses we have only "arca turaria" or "uas (far) quod sacrificiis adhibetur." *Acerra* is generally misspelled *accersa, acersa*.   Some gloss must have had "*accersa* arca quae sacrificiis adhibetur," which was read "*accersa* aerea," etc., and gave rise to an interpolation in Festus, "*acceris* securis aerea, qua in sacrificiis utebantur sacerdotes."   In the *AA* glosses (G. Goetz, vol. V, p. 436) the two glosses follow each other:
Acerra alcolatoria uel turibulu.
Acersu securis quam flāmines aut pontifices habent.
The two glosses are also in *Codex Sangallensis 912* (G. Goetz, vol. IV, p. 202):
Acerlis securis quam flaminei subpontificis habebant
Acersa arculatoreania,
and the gloss agrees with Festus' lemma for *acceris*, and the Graeco-Latin gloss "ἀξίνη ἱεροφάντου, ὡς Πλαῦτος" (*ibid.*, vol. II, p. 13), where the latter, most likely, should have been "ὡς Παῦλος." When the glossator found in a

We have Arabic انت 'ānīt, اسى 'unṯa, with the nominative ending 'ānītun, for the soft iron of the sword blade. Although not so good for the edge as the "male" iron, it was better than iron and became more popular in the East, hence we have Votyak *andan*, Ossetic *andun*, Beduye *enti* "iron, steel." In LLatin it became *andanicum*, the *ondanique* of Marco Polo. In Beauvais' *alidena*, Bacon's *andena* we have still earlier forms. We have already seen that in Spain *hindī* became substituted for انت 'ānīt, hence Spanish *alinde*, *alfinde*, *alhinde* is used for "steel."

We have seen that the Anglo-Saxon gloss for "accearium" is *steli*. The OHGerman glosses have for this *stahal*, *stahel*, *stahl*, and that these are borrowings follows from the fact that we have also Coptic *stali* "steel." To trace the history of this word we shall begin with its Sumerian prototype. We have Sumerian *za-gin* "shining, lapis lazuli," literally "shining stone." We have also the uncompounded *gin* "shining." That *gin* is an original root follows from its Dravidian correspondent, where *kan* has the fundamental meaning of "shining," hence Kannada *kani* "glow," *kan* "the eye," *kannaḍi* "mirror," Tamil *kanja* "mirror, a pane of glass " The Assyrian borrowed the root *gin* in its *ugnū*, *uknū* "shining, precious stone, crystal,

copy of Festus "acerra *aerea*," he hunted through the vocabularies for an explanation of the word, and found it in the *Placidus* glosses, where the etymology of "heros" is given, namely:

"Heroes. dicuntur. . . . . . *aerii* uel celo digni. id uel fortes uel sapientes. ab area. id iunonem. quam aerem dicunt esse ubi regnum. et sedes. animarum est. ut aeris in campis latis. et cicero. in sommio. scipionis. ergo hic heros huius herois. huic. hero. hunc. heroem. ab hac heroem. mulier uero. heroin. e. uel heroadas. aut eroas. ut. lemnias

"Hec securis dicimus. huius securis. huic securi. hanc securem. o securis. ab hac securi. et pluraliter. secures. o secures. ab his securibus. secur. nusquam legimus," (*ibid.*, vol. V, p. 108, and again, p. 24 f.).

The sequence "hero" and "haec securis" made the stupid glossator assume that the axe had something to do with "aeree," which he took to be "made of brass," and thus arose the interpolated gloss in Festus, where *accersa*, *accersu*, *accerlis* of the glosses at last become *acceris* and *accieris*.

glass,"[1] and we find it in Chinese as *king* "metallic mirror, to shine." The Dravidian word led to Sanskrit *kāñc, kac* "to shine," *kācas* "crystal, glass."

The Sumerian word *za-gin* must also have existed as *za-gagin* or *za-gigin*, for it is a peculiarity of Sumerian "bright" words that they appear reduplicated, such as *babara, dadaga*. The Sumerian word entered early into the Semitic languages, for we have Hebrew זָג *zāg* "the transparent grape-skin," זכה *zkh* "to be pure," זכו *zakkū* "pure, shining." The Sumerian *šag, sig, dag* "shining" words may themselves be apocopated *za-gin*; the Hebrew words and the Aramaic זכא *zka*, דכא *dka* may be derived from the apocopated forms rather than from *za-gin*. But Arabic زجاج *ziĝāĝ, zaĝāĝ, zuĝāĝ* "glass," سجنجل *saĝanĝal*, زجنجل *zaĝanĝal* "mirror" are obviously derived from the Sumerian. As may be expected these Arabic words are found in Gothic and OHGerman. In Gothic we have *skuggwa*, in OHGerman *scuchar* "mirror."

It has been suggested that the Arabic *saĝanĝal* may have been a corruption of Latin *speculum*. While the above discussion shows that we have to go back to the Sumerian for the origin of the word, a contamination with the Latin word is not excluded. We have the Arabic صقل *ṣaqala* "he furbished, polished," which may well have arisen from صفقل *ṣfaqala*, misread *ṣqaqala*, since the diacritical marks were often confused, and reduced to *ṣaqala*. This word is also found in Syriac and in the Talmud as סִיקְלִי *sīqlī* "a furbisher," but here it is a ἅπαξ λεγόμενον and not reliable. That there was also an Arabic form *staqla* or *stala* appears from the languages that have borrowed from the

---

[1] H. V. Hilprecht, *Zur Lapislazuli-Frage im Babylonischen*, in *Zeitschrift für Assyriologie und verwandte Gebiete*, Berlin 1893, vol. VIII, p. 188.

Arabic. We have not only Hindustani *sakelā* "a kind of steel," but also Coptic *stelli* "to shine," by the side of *stali* "steel," and neither is explicable from its own language. But we have also Gothic *stikls* "beaker," OHGerman *stahel*, OPrussian *stakla* "steel," OBulgarian *stĭklo* "glass," Russian *stakan* "beaker."

(e) Greek πλάνης.

Arabic ‫فلز‬ *filizz*, *filazz*, *fuluzz* means "white copper, whereof are made cooking pots of large size, and mortars in which substances are pounded," and the Persian dictionary adds "ore, metal in general, dross, scoria, a stone." The plural ‫فلزّات‬ *filizzātu* signifies "the seven metals, gold, silver, copper, iron, lead, tin, and tutenag."[1] The relation of "white copper" to the seven elementary metals would not appear clearly, if we did not have the explanation in the earliest Arabic lapidary. This copper alloy is called in Persian *haftǧauš*, that is, "prepared from the seven metals."[2] This establishes the relation of the two, and at the same time makes it possible to identify the Arabic word *flzz*. In the Greek alchemy the seven metals were identified with the seven planets, the signs of which are the alchemist's expressions for these metals, hence Greek πλάνης, πλάνητες must have come to mean "metal, ore, stone." In Arabic it would appear as ‫بلنس‬ *blns*, or ‫بلنز‬ *blnz*, or ‫فلنز‬ *flnz*. The early transcriptions into Arabic are so bad that almost anything may be expected there.[3] The Arabic ‫فلنز‬ has

----

[1] Ruska (*op. cit.*, p. 61) identifies this metal called ‫حار صيني‬ *ḥār ṣīniy* as a kind of red copper alloy imported from China.

[2] *Ibid.*, p. 60 f.

[3] *Ibid.*, p. 55.

degenerated to فلزز, written ̈فلزّ *flzz*, which, pronounced *felizz*, etc., became the appellation *par excellence* of "ore, metal in general."

In the Hrabanian-Keronian glosses we have "berillus genus saxi candidi (*pisleht*) *pilent* chunni *felises* scinandi." This corresponds exactly to the Arabic definition of بلور *balaur*, *balur*, etc., which, however, is not "the beryl," but "crystal" or "flint." Taifāšī says that the *balur* is a kind of white borax, which has become a white transparent stone.[1] In the OHGerman gloss the "stone" or "ore" is *felis*, a precise rendering of Arabic فلزّ *felizz*. *Felis* is almost entirely absent from the other Germanic languages, except as ONorse *fjall* "mountain," where the very apocopation shows that it is not a native word.

OHGerman *pilent* is the same Arabic word but in a different form. We have Arabic بلنط *balant* "a stone resembling marble, but inferior to it in softness." This is, of course, again our Greek πλάνητες. The reason for applying this name to crystal or flint is obvious. According to Taifāšī the crystal could be melted like glass. Taifāšī here quotes Theophrastus, who says that the best glass was produced from crystal or flint mixed with copper,[2] and it is well known that the famous green glass was produced by a mixture with copper compounds.[3] But crystal or glass was frequently indentified with the moon, which usually stood for silver, or with Jupiter, which usually stood for bronze or tin. It was the shining "metal" *par excellence*, the "fire-stone," which originally did not mean "flint," but a shining substance, that is, crystal. That

---

[1] M. Clément-Mullet, *Essai sur la minéralogie arabe*, in *Journal Asiatique*, Paris 1868, series VI, vol. XI, p. 231.

[2] *Ibid.*, p. 235.

[3] Von Lippmann, *op. cit.*, p. 102.

the Arabic بلنط. *balant* is only a variation of a form بلنط *flnt* or فلنز *flnz*, is shown by the early ASaxon gloss "petrafocaria *flinta*," and the OHGerman gloss "silex *flins*." Hence OHG. *pilent* is only a variation of Arabic بلنط. *balant*, and has the meaning of "crystal" or "flint."

The natural crystal was supposed to be defective, and already Pliny called it a "blind" stone,[1] because it did not reflect the sun's rays, and he said that the eyes of certain animals, such as the panther, emitted a bright light not unlike that of the beryl. According to him also the beryl, that is, the crystal or flint, was good for diseases of the eye. This conception is contained in a highly interesting series of Germanic glosses. The Keronian glosses read "hyena bestia cuius pupille lapideae sunt *staraplint* des seha augono stani sint."[2] This is a slight change of Isidore's "hyaenia lapis in oculis hyaenae bestiae invenitur,"[3] which is also in Pliny: "hyaeniae, ex oculis hyaenae lapides."[4] The Latin source is based on a blunder. In Egyptian medicine the eye-salve *ḥetem* is frequently referred to. This *ḥetem* is identical with Greek καδμία, the eye-salve *par excellence*,[5] but Egyptian *hetem* also means "hyaena," hence the assumption of the hyaena stone found in its eye. In the *Cassel* glosses of the IX. century we read "albios oculos *staraplinter*," where *staraplint* obviously means some kind of blindness— "white eyes." The Latin *albios oculos* produced the French *aveugle*, and *staraplint* led to German *Staar* "cataract of the eyes," but it can be shown that this is

---

[1] See my discussion of the beryl in *Contributions*, vol. IV, p. 114 ff.

[2] E. Steinmeyer und E. Sievers, *Die althochdeutschen Glossen*, Berlin 1879, vol. I, p. 170.

[3] XVI. 15. 25.

[4] XXXVII. 168.

[5] H. Lüring, *Die über die medicinischen Kenntnisse der alten Ägypter berichtenden Papyri*, Leipzig 1888, p. 91.

a mere misunderstanding of the particular disease which produces blindness, for in the ASaxon *Corpus* glosses we have "scotomaticus *staerblind*," and Greek σκότωμα is a blindness produced by vertigo, hence ASaxon *staerblind*, OHGerman *starplint*, which means "hyaenia lapis," is really "the vertigo stone." We have already seen that the white stone is *pilent*, from the Arabic. Similarly OHG. *star* is Arabic سدر *saḍar* "vertigo." Just as *albios oculos* has led to French *aveugle*, the *blint* of OHGerman *staraplint*, ASaxon *staerblind* has produced Germanic *blind* "blind," while OHG. *starblind* assumed the meaning "glaucoma" instead of "scotoma," leading to German *Staar* "cataract of the eye."

Just as the beryl was the "shining stone," so bronze was the "shining metal" *par excellence*, hence Arabic فلزّ *filizz* referred more particularly to "white copper." But by the side of this we have found Arabic بلنط *balant*, and in Armenian we actually have *plindž* "copper, brass." In Persian we have, side by side, *birindž, beredž, piring* "brass, copper." In reality, however, this is not the origin of the name for "bronze." Copper was in Greek alchemy called by the planet Venus, namely ἀφροδίτη. This became in the Syriac alchemy *afrodīṭī, frodīṭī*, which also referred to "bronze," but for this more usually the Syriac name *bilaṭi* was used. The accidental resemblance of the triliterals *blṭ, frd* with the derivatives from Greek πλάνης led to the identification of "bronze" as the "chief" planet, hence we have Arabic فلزّ *flzz* by the side of Armenian *pirindž*, etc. At the same time Coptic *barot*, Ethiopic *bert* "copper, brass" bear witness to the "Venus" origin of the metal.

After discussing the silver mirrors, Pliny says: "However, to finish our description of mirrors on the

present occasion—the best, in the times of our ancestors, were those of Brundisium, composed of a mixture
of stannum and copper."[1]   That is clearly an interpolation, since there is no reference before to mirrors
made of tin and copper.   Further on, while speaking of
tin, the following passage occurs: "Stagnum inlitum
aereis vasis saporem facit gratiorem ac compescit virus
aeruginis, mirumque, pondus non auget. specula etiam
ex eo laudatissima, ut diximus, Brundisi temperabantur,
donec argenteis uti coepere et ancillae."[2]   This runs
in Isidore as follows· "Stagnum inlitum aereis vasis
saporem facit gratiorem et conpescit virus aeruginis.
Specula etiam ex eo temperantur."[3]   Here again the
interpolation is seen from the fact that Isidore, who
quoted just before Pliny's account of lead in full, has
nothing whatsoever about the *Brundisian* mirrors
which *were* manufactured, but speaks only of mirrors
which *are* manufactured.   Not a word is found about
such a composition until the end of the VIII. century
when "compositio *Brandisii*" or "*Brindisii*" is found
in two metallurgical recipes.[4]   As this alloy is composed of copper, tin, lead, and glass, in somewhat the
manner mentioned in Pliny, there can be little doubt
that we have here a *haftǧauš*, hence a confusion with
Greek πλάνης; hence we get, originally through the
Arabic, Greek βροντήσιον, English *bronze*, etc.

Förstemann[5] has observed that derivatives of
berhta in names hardly occur among Goths, Vandals,
Frisians and Normans, are rare among Saxons, but very
common among Anglo-Saxons, Langobards, Franks and
Bavarians.   He also notices that the name does not seem
to occur at all before the VI. century.   When we now

[1] "Atque ut omnia de speculis peragantur in hoc loco, optima aput maiores fuerant Brundisina, stagno et aere mixtis," XXXIII. 130.
[2] XXXIV. 160.
[3] XVI. 23. 2.
[4] Von Lippmann, *op. cit.*, p. 561.
[5] *Altdeutsches Namenbuch*, Bonn 1900, vol. I, col. 277.

further observe that Goth. *bairhts* "bright, shining" is used only very rarely as an adjective in OHGerman, namely *peraht* "clarus," and has survived only in Ger. *pracht* "splendor," while ONorse *bjartr* "clarus," *birta* "to illuminate," like Goth. *bairhtjan* "to reveal," are only derivatives of the Goth. *bairhts* or OHG. *peraht*, and ASaxon *beorht* does not even occur in the early vocabularies, the suspicion is at once roused that *berht* is not a common Germanic word, but due to some borrowing.   It is useless to adduce a Sanskrit *bhraç* "to shine" as the prototype of this word, because Semitic *braq* is much nearer, and the same root may be discovered elsewhere, but particularly because the word appears in the Germanic languages exclusively in the form *berht*, and not *berh*.

Brattea, originally *bractea*,[1] was a thin gold lamina, which was variously used as an ornament.   Pliny tells of jewels made of such laminae stuffed with a lighter material,[2] and of a cheap imitation of such *bratteae*, made of brass or bronze, generally used for actors' crowns.[3]   The vast number of bracteates in Scandinavia and on the continent, the rich garments adorned with gold and bronze laminae, found in the south of Russia, bear witness to the fact that *bractea* was identical with "rich adornment, splendor."   This at once shows that the Latin word is derived from the Semitic, most probably from Phoenician.   We have Hebrew בָּרַק *bāraq*, Syriac ܒܪܩ *braq*, Arabic بَرَقَ *baraqa* "to

---

[1] See *Rheinisches Museum*, vol. XLV, p. 495.

[2] "Alii bratteas infercire leviore materia propter casum tutius gemmarum sollicitudini putant," XXXIII. 25.

[3] "Nunc praevertemur ad differentias aeris et mixturas. in Cyprio [coronarium et regulare est utrumque ductile] coronarium tenuatur in lamnas taurorumque felle tinctum speciem auri in coronis histrionum praebet, idemque in uncias additis auri scripulis senis praetenui pyropi brattea ignescit. regulare et in aliis fit metallis, itemque caldarium. differentia quod caldarium funditur tantum, malleis fragile, quibus regulare obsequitur ab aliis ductile appellatum, quale omne Cyprium est," XXXIV. 94.

shine, glitter," Talmudic בַּרְקָא *barqṭā*, Syriac ܒܪܩ
bârqâ "emerald," and the Romans were acquainted
with the word at least through Hamilcar's name,
Barcus "the lightning."

The Romans already had identified *bractea* with
"splendor," more especially "tinsel splendor," hence
while Prudentius used *brattealis* for "gilt," others
employed *bratteatus* for "beautiful, superb," but also
"tinsel, simulated." The glossaries[1] wrote *brattea*,
bratthea, *brattanea*, *brantia*, *branzia* and glossed these
words with "lamina aurea." The forms *brantia*,
branzia arose from a confusion with *brando* "torch,
flashing sword."

There is a common gloss "*vibrantia* iacula ful-
gentia,"[2] which in the *Corpus*, *Vatican 3321*, *Abavus*,
and *Asbestos* glosses reads *bibrantia*, while the *Abactor
Anglonianus II* glosses read for it *brantia*. Here the
"flashing weapon" was once more confused with *brando*
"torch, flashing sword." The earliest reference
to *brand* is found in Gregory the Great, who says
that the Latins were not in the habit of using parts of a
saint's body as a relic, but the shroud, *brandeum*, in
which he was buried,[3] and from the Merovingian
writers we learn that the saint's shroud was red.[4]
At a later time *brandeum* also referred to a belt or other
garment, and from the *Edict of Leo the Wise* we learn
that the πρανδιοπρᾱται were Syrian cloth merchants who

---

[1] Goetz, *op. cit.*, sub *brattea*.

[2] *Ibid.*, sub *vibrantia*.

[3] "Romanis consuetudo non est, quando sanctorum reliquias dant, ut
quicquam tangere praesumant de corpore. Sed tantummodo in buxide
brandeum mittitur, atque ad sacratissima corpora sanctorum ponitur,"
Epistolae, IV. 30.

[4] "Involutum est corpus illius integrum, sed exsiccatum, de *brandeo*
rubeo," *Scriptores rerum merovingicarum*, vol. III, p. 321; "ipsum corpus
sanctissimum, sicut et in anteriori translatione, ab episcopis Remorum
dioceseos integrum inventum est et *brandeo* rubeo involutum," *ibid.*, p. 326.

imported garments from Syria, silk stuffs from Selencia, and Saracenic and Bagdad cloth.[1]

We are, therefore, sure that *brandeum* was some cloth from the east. Indeed, we have Persian *parand* "the glittering surface of a polished sword, a kind of fine figured, painted silk, plain silk," but also "a bird," which makes it sure that we have here a popular etymology, a participial derivative from *par* "a wing," from which we also get *pari magas*, literally "fly's wing," but now "the brilliancy of the sword, a delicate kind of silk stuff." It is clear that Greek πράνδιον, LLatin *brandeum* are derived from the Persian, but the Persian *parand* is itself a corruption of *parniyān* "a kind of fine painted China silk, also garments made of it, shroud for a royal corpse," and this is from Chinese *pin-lien* "to bury in a shroud," which brings us back to the beginning of the Christian era, when, according to Pliny, Chinese silks were introduced into Rome.

The silk, to judge from the connotation this *brandeum* took, was "watered" or "shot," and therefore led to the designation of "undulating surface," as in a sword, besides "torch" and "flame," on account of the prevailing red color of this silk Hence the Persian *parand*, *barand*, read in Arabic as *firind*, *barand*, became the name of Damaskeen steel, the best of which came from India, but more especially from China.[2]

In Anglo-Saxon we find early *brand* "sword," which is obviously the Persian and Arabic word. But in Persian and Arabic it means "the glittering, flashing sword," hence both in Anglo-Saxon and Old High German *brand* means "torch, flame," even as we have side by side Italian *brando* "sword," OFrench *brandir* "to brandish," that is, "to flash." How very much the Arabic or, possibly, somewhat earlier, the Persian

---

[1] J. Nicole, *L'édit de l'empereur Léon le Sage*, in *Mémoires de l'Institut national genevois*, vol. XVIII, p. 29 f.
[2] Von Lippmann, *op. cit.*, p. 399.

word influenced the connotation of the word in the Germanic languages, is seen from the ASaxon gloss "rubigo *brond om*," where "rubigo" means either "rust" or "erysipelas," for we have also the ASaxon glosses "*ōman, hōman* erysipelas," *ōmig* "rusty, inflammatory," *ōmiht* "full of inflammation," ONorse *ámr* "loathsome, black," *áma* "erysipelas," all of which are from Arabic ‏حمرة‎ *humrah* "erysipelas, a certain disease which attacks human beings, in consequence of which the place thereof becomes red," ‏حمر‎ *humar* "redness, anthrax, erysipelas." Similarly the Arabic *barand* "flashing sword" has led to ASaxon *brand* "erysipelas." And thus was evolved the idea of "burning" in connection with *brand*, which entered all the Germanic languages.   By the side of Arabic ‏برند‎ *barand* we have also ‏فرند‎ *firind*, hence there must also have existed a form *birind*, and this is preserved in Gothic *brinnō* "fever," from which the verb *brinnan* "to burn" is formed.   The variant ASaxon *beornan, byrnan*, ONorse *brenna* "to burn" further show that the verb is not originally Germanic.

(f) OHGerman aruz.

The Mahābhārata, Herodotus, and the Mongols and Tibetans tell of gold which was mined by ants,[1] and Laufer has shown that the reference is to gold mined in the Altai region by Tatar or Mongol tribes, bearing the name of "ants" in the Tatar language.   It is not necessary to subscribe to Laufer's philological identification, but there cannot be the slightest doubt that the Indians and Greeks distinctly referred to a kind of gold

---

[1] B. Laufer, *Die Sage von den goldgrabenden Ameisen*, in *T'oung Pao*, series II, vol. IX, p. 429 ff.

which came from the mountains of the interior of Asia. Now the Assyrians have a word *ḫurāçu* "gold," while *hariçu* means "ditch," *ḫaraçu* "to dig." *Hurāçu* is not the usual word for "gold" in the Semitic languages, but the Hebrew has חָרוּץ *hāruç* "dug up, gold," and there is also recorded Phoenician *haraç* "gold."

It is obvious that Greek χρυσός refers to the same mined gold and is of Semitic origin. Strabo quotes Polybius to the effect that "mined gold," χρυσὸς ὀρυκτός, was found in mines, ὀρύγματα, and that this differed from wash gold in being partly impure and containing useful mineral ingredients.[1] It has long been suspected that Greek ὀρύσσω is no other than Assyrian *ḫarāçu*,[2] and this makes the expression χρυσὸς ὀρυκτός merely a tautology. The Assyrian *ḫaraçu* "to dig" is merely an extension of the root *ḫar*, for we find also *ḫurru* "hole, ravine, cave," *ḫarru* "canal," *ḫarū, ḫirū* "to dig," *ḫaraku* "to engrave, cut," *ḫiritu* "ditch, canal."

Ball has pointed out that the Sumerian ideogram for "gold" is identical with that of the Chinese, which was pronounced *kin*.[3] De Lacouperie thinks that the identity of the two ideograms is, among others, a proof of the derivation of the Chinese civilization from the Sumerian.[4] But in Sumerian we have a compound *guškin*, whereas in Chinese *kin* merely means "metal," so that a denominative, apparently meaning "yellow," must have dropped out in Chinese. In Japanese we have *ko-gane*, literally "yellow metal," and Sumerian *guš-kin* stands for *ku-kin*, literally "shining metal."

[1] IV. 6. 12.
[2] J. Parkhurst, *An Hebrew and English Lexicon*, London 1813, p. 242; L. Meyer, *Handbuch der griechischen Etymologie*, Leipzig 1901, vol. III, p. 323; *Zeitschrift der deutschen morgenländischen Gesellschaft*, vol. XXXIII, p. 327; *The Annual of the British School at Athens*, vol. VIII, p. 144.
[3] *Proceedings of the Society of Biblical Archaeology*, vol. XIII, p. 84 f.
[4] *Western Origin of the Early Chinese Civilisation*, London 1894, p. 85.

Chinese *hwang* "yellow" was originally *kung* or *gung*, and this, with Sumerian *ku*, *guš*, indicates an original *kur*, that is, we come back to a form resembling Assyrian *hur* "to dig." That *hwang* "yellow" in Chinese had something to do with "to dig," follows from the composition of its ideogram, one part of which was "a field."

From the Assyrian or another Central Asiatic language the word for gold spread into all directions. We have Sanskrit *hiranyam* "gold," *haris* "yellow," etc., and similarly Avestan *zaranya*, *zarōna* "gold," *zaray* "golden, yellow," Persian *zer*, *zerīn* "gold," *zerīr*, *zirīr* "yellow dye wood," *zerd* "yellow." The derivations in the other Indo-European languages are well understood. In Tibetan "gold" is *gser*, possibly borrowed from the Persian. In the Turkish languages we have forms like *altun*, *alcin*, but *al* means "yellow" and is a variation of *jal*, *zil*, *kil*, *čil* "yellow," also represented by *jar*, *sar*, *žar*,[1] hence we have here once more relationships to Assyrian *har*.

Pliny has the following account of the mining of gold: "Gold is found in our own part of the world; not to mention the gold extracted from the earth in India by the ants, and in Scythia by the Griffins. Among us it is procured in three different ways; the first of which is, in the shape of dust, found in running streams, the Tagus in Spain, for instance, the Padus in Italy, the Hebrus in Thracia, the Pactolus in Asia, and the Ganges in India; indeed, there is no gold found in a more perfect state than this, thoroughly polished as it is by the continual attrition of the current.

"A second mode of obtaining gold is by sinking shafts or seeking it among the debris of mountains; both of which methods it will be as well to describe. The

---

[1] H. Vámbéry, *Etymologisches Wörterbuch der turko-tatarischen Sprachen*, Leipzig 1878, pp. 11, 114, 117.

persons in search of gold in the first place remove the 'segutilum,' such being the name of the earth which gives indication of the presence of gold.   This done, a bed is made, the sand of which is washed, and, according to the residue found after washing, a conjecture is formed as to the richness of the vein.   Sometimes, indeed, gold is found at once in the surface earth, a success, however, but rarely experienced.   Recently, for instance, in the reign of Nero, a vein was discovered in Dalmatia, which yielded daily as much as fifty pounds' weight of gold.   The gold that is thus found in the surface crust is known as 'talutium,' in cases where there is auriferous earth beneath.   The mountains of Spain, in other respects arid and sterile, and productive of nothing whatever, are thus constrained by man to be fertile, in supplying him with this precious commodity.

"The gold that is extracted from shafts is known by some persons as 'canalicium,' and by others as 'canaliense;' it is found adhering to the gritty crust of marble, and, altogether different from the form in which it sparkles in the sapphirus of the East, and in the stone of Thebais and other gems, it is seen interlaced with the molecules of the marble.   The channels of these veins are found running in various directions along the sides of the shafts, and hence the name of the gold they yield—'canalicium.'   In these shafts, too, the superincumbent earth is kept from falling in by means of wooden pillars.   The substance that is extracted is first broken up, and then washed; after which it is subjected to the action of fire, and ground to a fine powder.   This powder is known as 'apitascudes,' while the silver which becomes disengaged in the furnace has the name of 'sudor' given to it.   The impurities that escape by the chimney, as in the case of all other metals, are known by the name of 'scoria.'   In the case of gold, this scoria is broken up a second time, and melted over again.   The crucibles used for this purpose are made of 'tasconium,' a white earth similar to potter's clay in appearance; there being no other substance capable of withstanding the strong current of air, the action of the fire, and the intense heat of the melted metal.

"The third method of obtaining gold surpasses the labours of the Giants even: by the aid of galleries driven to a long distance, mountains are excavated by the light of torches, the duration of which forms the set times for work, the workmen never seeing the light of day for many months together.   These mines are known as 'arrugiae;' and not unfrequently clefts are formed on a sudden, the earth sinks in, and the workmen are crushed beneath; so that it would really appear less rash to go in search of pearls and purples at the bottom of the sea, so much more dangerous to ourselves have we made the earth than the water!   Hence it is, that in this kind of mining, arches are left at frequent intervals for the purpose of supporting the weight of the mountain above.   In mining either by shaft or by gallery, barriers of silex are met with, which have to be driven asunder by the aid of fire and vinegar; or more frequently, as this method fills the galleries with suffocating vapours and smoke, to be broken to pieces with bruising-machines shod with pieces of iron weighing one hundred and fifty pounds: which done, the fragments are carried out on the workmen's shoulders, night and day, each man passing them on to his neighbour in the dark, it being only those at the pit's mouth that ever see the light.   In cases where the bed of silex appears too thick to admit of being penetrated, the miner traces along the sides of it, and so turns it.   And yet, after all, the labour entailed by this silex is looked upon as comparatively easy, there being an earth—a kind of potter's clay mixed with gravel, 'gangadia' by name, which it is almost impossible to overcome.   This earth has to be attacked with iron wedges and hammers like those previously mentioned, and it is generally considered that there is nothing more stubborn in existence —except indeed the greed for gold, which is the most stubborn of all things.

'When these operations are all completed, beginning at the last, they cut away the wooden pillars at the point where they support the roof: the coming downfall gives warning, which is instantly perceived by the sentinel, and by him only, who is set to watch upon a peak of the same mountain.   By voice as well as by signals, he orders the workmen to be immediately summoned from their labours, and at the same moment takes to flight himself.   The mountain, rent to pieces, is cleft asunder, hurling its debris to a distance with a crash which it is impossible for the human imagination to conceive; and from the midst of a cloud of dust, of a density quite incredible, the victorious miners gaze upon this downfall of Nature.   Nor yet even then are they sure of gold, nor indeed were they by any means certain that there was any to be found where they first began to excavate, it being quite sufficient, as an inducement to undergo such perils and to incur such vast expense, to entertain the hope that they shall obtain what they so eagerly desire.

"Another labour, too, quite equal to this, and one which entails even greater expense, is that of bringing rivers from the more elevated mountain heights, a distance in many instances of one hundred miles perhaps, for the purpose of washing these debris.   The channels thus formed are called 'corrugi,' from our word 'corrivatio,' I suppose; and even when these are once made, they entail a thousand fresh labours.   The fall, for instance, must be steep, that the water may be precipitated, so to say, rather than flow; and it is in this manner that it is brought from the most elevated points. Then, too, vallies and crevasses have to be united by the aid of aqueducts, and in another place impassable rocks have to be hewn away, and forced to make room for hollowed troughs of wood; the person hewing them hanging suspended all the time with ropes, so that to a spectator who views the operations from a distance, the workmen have all the appearance, not so much of wild beasts, as of birds upon the wing.   Hanging thus suspended in most instances, they take the levels, and trace with lines the course the water is to take; and thus where there is no room even for man to plant a foot-step, are rivers traced out by the hand of man.   The water, too, is considered in an unfit state for washing, if the current of the river carries any mud along with it. The kind of earth that yields this mud is known as 'urium;' and hence it is that in tracing out these channels, they carry the water over beds of silex or pebbles, and carefully avoid this urium.   When they have reached the head of the fall, at the very brow of the mountain, reservoirs are hollowed out, a couple of hundred feet in length and breadth, and some ten feet in depth.   In these reservoirs there are generally five sluices left, about three feet square; so that, the moment the reservoir is filled, the floodgates are struck away, and the torrent bursts forth with such a degree of violence as to roll onwards any fragments of rock which may obstruct its passage.

"When they have reached the level ground, too, there is still another labour that awaits them.   Trenches— known as 'agogae'—have to be dug for the passage of the water; and these, at regular intervals, have a layer of ulex placed at the bottom.   This ulex is a plant like rosemary in appearance, rough and prickly, and well-adapted for arresting any pieces of gold that may be carried along.   The sides, too, are closed in with planks, and are supported by arches when carried over steep and precipitous spots   The earth, carried onwards in the stream, arrives at the sea at last, and thus is the shattered mountain washed away; causes which have greatly tended to extend the shores of Spain by these encroachments upon the deep.   It is also by the agency of canals of this description that the material, excavated at the cost of such immense labour by the process previously described, is washed and carried away; for otherwise the shafts would soon be choked up by it.

"The gold found by excavating with galleries does not require to be melted, but is pure gold at once.   In these excavations, too, it is found in lumps, as also in the shafts which are sunk, sometimes exceeding ten pounds even.   The names given to these lumps are 'palagae,' and 'palacurnae,' while the gold found in small grains is known as 'baluce.'   The ulex that is used for the above purpose is dried and burnt, after which the ashes of it are washed upon a bed of grassy turf, in order that the gold may be deposited thereupon.

"Asturia, Gallaecia, and Lusitania furnish in this manner, yearly, according to some authorities, twenty thousand pounds' weight of gold, the produce of Asturia forming the major part.   Indeed, there is no part of the world that for centuries has maintained such a continuous fertility in gold."[1]

Here at least the majority of the technical terms are interpolated.   In Spanish mining the terms *segullo*, *alutación* (for *alutium* or *talutium*), *sudor*, *tasconio*, *arrugia*, *ganga*, *palaca* are used just as in Pliny, but they

[1] XXXIII. 66-78.

are unquestionably late borrowings and so are of no avail for the determination of the corresponding terms. Similarly *baluce* "gold in small grains" is of no avail, since it had long been in use among the Romans, having originally been borrowed from a Semitic language. The Greek gloss "χρύσαμμος *balluca*" shows that the original meaning was "gold-bearing sand." We have Sanskrit *vālukā* "sand, gravel," which cannot be explained from the Sanskrit. But Arabic بلوقة *balūqah* "sandy desert" is the same as Assyrian *balaqu* "to lay waste," and this is but an extension of the Semitic *bal* "destroy" root. From the Latin text of Pliny "*palagas*, alii *palacurnas*, iidem quod minutum est *balucem* vocant," it does not clearly appear whether the first two are the same as the third or refer to larger nuggets, but in any case they seem to be mere variations of *balux* or *baluce*.

Segutilum appears in some manuscripts as *segullum*. This is unquestionably Latin *sigillum*, which in the Arabic form in the Koran assumed the meaning of "book," and also means "judgment, transcript." As the verb سجل *saǵala* also means "to verify," it is clear that the noun also meant "verification," hence, as we find in Pliny, "indicium."

Gold found on the surface is in Pliny called *talutium*, for which some manuscripts read *alutatium, alutationem, alutiatum*, which produced Spanish *alutación*. In XXXIV. 157 the gold mines in which lead is also found are called *alutiae*. Here we fortunately can see that the word is an interpolation, because the sentence in Pliny is distinctly an elaboration of the corresponding passage in Isidore, where neither *alutiae*, nor *eluente*, to explain the word, are to be found:

"Lavant eas harenas, metallici et, quod subsedit, cocunt in fornacibus. invenitur et in aurariis metallis, quae alutias vocant, aqua inmissa eluente calculos nigros paullum candore variatos, quibus eadem gravitas quae auro, et ideo in calathis, quibus aurum colligitur, cum eo remanent; postea caminis separantur conflatique in plumbum album resolvuntur," Pliny, XXXIV.157.

"Lavant eas arenas, et quod subsidit, quoquunt in fornacibus. Inveniuntur et in aurariis metallis aqua missa calculi nigri et graves, et dum aurum colligitur, cum eo remanent; postea separati conflantur et in plumbum album resolvuntur," Isidore, XVI. 22.1.

The Spanish term *alutación* "a bed of gold nuggets" shows that *alutiae, talutium* mean "pure gold, as it comes from the gold bed," that is, that we have here Arabic خالص *ḫāliṣ* "pure, refined (gold)," تخليص *taḫlīṣ* "to refine (gold)," خلوص *ḫalūṣ* "genuineness," etc. The term seems to occur in a X. century Portuguese document as the denomination of a pall, which is mentioned by the side of "Greek" garments,[1] which are distinctly mentioned as being made with gold thread.[2] However, this particular *aluz* may be a different spelling of *alguexi, alvexi, alveice*, from Arabic وشى *wašī* "a delicate silk fabric, generally embroidered with gold thread."

[1] "Palae greciscas, duas palas de *aluz*. omnique casula piscina, glisissas, tres de *aluz*," (959), *Portugaliae monumenta diplomatica*, vol. I, p. 47.

[2] "Dono etiam frontales, pallas, acitaras auro textas, grecirias varias," (812), *España sagrada*, vol. XXXVII, p. 317; "pallas lineas greciscas II, cum auro porto paratas. item palla linea I polimita, et ipsa cum auro porto parata," (IX. c.), *Zeitschrift für die Geschichte des Oberrheins*, vol. IV, p. 250; "mantos duos auri frissos, alio alquexi auro texto, cum alio *gricisco* in dimisso cardeno: casulla aurifrissa, cum dalmaticis duabus aurofrissis: et alia alvexi auro texta," (1063), *España sagrada*, vol. XXXVI, p. clxxxix.

Pliny's *gangadia* "gravelly earth, a kind of potter's clay mixed with gravel" is written in some manuscripts *gandadia, gandeda, candida*, and is Arabic فضَّة *qaddaṭ* "land in which are pebbles." It has been adopted into Spanish as *ganga*, whence it passed into French and English as *gangue* "the earthy or stony matter in a mineral deposit."

Urium is given as "the land which carries mud." This is Arabic خور *ḥaur*, plural خوور *ḥu'wūr*, "low or depressed ground, the part in which the water flows from the two sides of a valley."

Arrugia is "mine," while *corrugium* is given as "artificial rivers." They are clearly the same word and un questionably from Arabic خرق *ḥarq* "aqueduct," خريقة *ḥarīqah*, plural خرق *ḥuruq*, "a channel of water, a low or depressed tract of land," words in use in the Arabic documents in Sicily. In the Spanish documents, beginning with the VIII. century, we frequently find *arrogium* for "water-course, brook," which leads to Spanish *arroyo* "brook," *arroyar* "to water, inundate." No doubt, Provençal *arrozar*, French *arroser* "to water" are formed from the same Spanish word which in Provençal was popularly etymologized as from *ros* "dew."

Iso Magister, who died in 871 at St. Gall, glossing Prudentius' *Apotheosis*, I. 724 f., "non sicut sculptor ab aeris rudere decoctam consuescit viuere massam,"[1] says "rudere = *mina* a terra, vbi aes tollitur," that is, he identifies "rudus, ore" with *mina*, which he etymologizes as being derived from *minare* "to lead away," because the ore is taken away from the earth. This etymology is as useless as Isidore's "aurum ab aura,"

[1] F. Arevalo, *M. Avreli Clementis Prvdenti V. C. Carmina*, Romae 1788, vol. I, p. 465.

"ferrum dictum quod farra, id est semina frugum terrae condat," but it shows that *mina* "mine," hence *minerale* "mineral" were already known in 871.   The origin of this *mina* takes us back to dim antiquity.   In the old Egyptian texts we often find *menà*, *menàt*, *menit* "an amulet worn to give physical happiness, an ornament worn on ceremonial occasions," which was made of turquoise, malachite, emeralds, or other similar gems, and was in the form of a necklace, obviously because it was worn about the neck, especially by nurses.[1] This Egyptian amulet, in the form of a necklace, was early in use in the east and the west.   To this bear witness Latin *monīle*, OIrish *muinde*, *muince*, OWelsh *minci*, Greek μάννος, μόννος, ONorse *men*, ASaxon *mene*, OHGerman *menni*, OBulgarian *monisto*, Avestan *minuš* "necklace."   In Persian, *mīnā* has assumed the meaning of the gems from which the necklace was composed, "a glass globule or bead, a false gem of blue color, bluestone, caustic, a stone resembling lapis lazuli with which silver is tinged, vitriol, enamel, concha veneris, a goblet, glass," and has coincided with *mīnā* "heaven, sky," which is from Avestan *mēnōī* "spirit, heaven."   In Arabic it has chiefly the meaning of "enamel, alchemy," hence we get in the IX. century LLatin *mina* "mine, shaft," as in Iso Magister, whence we get later *minerale* "ore, mineral."

Iso Magister confuses, as others do, "mine" with "mineral," hence we should expect *arrugia* "mine," in the sense of "ore," to get into Iso's gloss to Prudentius' *Peristephanon*, II. 190, "effossa gignunt rudere," where we get the equation "rudere = *arizzi*, vel stercora, rudera dicunt maceriam ruinae."[2]   The two words, *mina* and *arizzi*, run through all the Germanic glosses of

---

[1] See H. Brugsch, *Hieroglyphisch-demotisches Wörterbuch*, Leipzig 1867, p. 645, where a representation of it is given.

[2] Arevalo, *op. cit.*, vol. II, p. 905.

Prudentius.[1] In reality Iso, who obviously quoted from an Arabic source, correctly rendered "stercora" by Arabic روت *raut̲*, plural اروات *'arwāt̲*, "dung." *Aruz* later produced German *Erz* "ore."

This Arabic root had before that entered into the Germanic languages. Arabic روتﺔ *rautah* means not only "dung," but also "tip of the human nose," unquestionably from its discharge of mucus, while Ibn-al-Awam regularly used روت *'rawat̲a* in the sense of "to manure," so that it is clear that "rot" was one of the connotations of the word in Arabic. This is well brought out in one of the Prudentius glosses, "mucculentis i. sordidis a mucca i. *rotz*,"[2] where "mucculentus" is given as "filthy," hence related to the Arabic word. But the lemma "a mucca" produced the OHGerman *roz* "snot." We have a still closer Arabic form in the Keronian glosses, where "aerugo," that is, "rust, rot," is given as *rost*, in the *Corpus* glosses as *rust*. In the Gothic Bible this word does not occur, but, instead, we have *nidwa*, which is from the Arabic ندوﻩ *naḍwah* "dampness," in Alcalá, "liento por unidad, rocio *nedve*."

Now we come to the most interesting word in Pliny— *tasconium* "a white earth from which pots are made." In Greek medicine ξήριον was a desiccating powder used for the cure of wounds and ulcers. In Greek alchemy it very early designated a powder used in the

---

[1] Steinmeyer und Sievers, *op. cit.*, vol. II, "rudere. stercore. al *mina* .i. *aruz*," p. 383; "stercorc al: *nama aruz*," p. 385; "*mina* .i. *aruz*," p. 386; "*arize*," p. 396; "*ris* .i. *molt*," p. 402; "*aruzi*," p. 405; "*ris* .i. *molta, ari zin*," p. 432; "*arize* l *molto*," p. 458; "*ruris* .i. *molt*," p. 480; "*arvzze*," p. 482; "*aruz* l. *stercora*," p. 491; "*mina. aruze*," p. 493; "*aruzz, arutz*," p. 496; "*aerizze, arici* stercora l *molta*," p. 505; "*aerizze, arizce*," p. 513; "*aruzze*," p. 526; "*arice*," p. 535; "*arizzae*," p. 555; "*arizze*," p. 560; "*mina* dicitur, *arize*," p. 565; "*arvt*," p. 572; "*mina* dicitur. *arize*," p. 574; "*aruze*," p. 578; "*arutos. rudus mist*," p. 586; "*aruz*," vol. IV, p. 93; "metalli *aruzzes*," vol. II, p. 420; "*aruzzin*," p. 432; "*ariz*," p. 505; and "massam .i. *mina. ariz*," p. 578.

[2] *Ibid.*, vol. II, p. 382.

transmutation of metals, hence it became the philosopher's stone, in Arabic الاكسير al-'iksir, the elixir of life. In Arabic medicine and alchemy the chief ingredient of such a cure-all was طلق talq "a sort of medicament which, when one is anointed therewith, prevents the burning of fire," which was also taken to mean "a plant that is used in dyes." The word is unquestionably taken from the Coptic where talčo, also pronounced talgo, means "medicine, cure." This talq referred to a number of substances, gypsum, mica, but especially talc, which was supposed to be well adapted for pots, because it withstood fire, as, indeed, such vessels were often made of soapstone, a variety of talc, so called from its greasy feeling. Pliny's tasconium is clearly this Arabic talq.

Talq was readily etymologized as of Arabic origin, since the root طلق talaqa means "to become cheerful, be freed from slavery or impediment," in which sense it is already found in the Koran. The Arabic word was early adopted by the Germanic peoples. We have in the *Corpus* glossary "fucus faex *taelg*," where *taelg* has the meaning of "dye" and "sediment." The first meaning was retained in ASaxon, while the second is due to the fact that "the art employed in dissolving it consists in putting it into a piece of rag with some pebbles and immersing it in tepid water, then moving it about gently until it becomes dissolved and comes forth from the piece of rag into the water, whereupon the water is strained from it, and it is put in the sun to dry."[1] We also find in the *Corpus* glossary "rediua *aet-taelg*," where "redina" stands for "rediviva," and *aet-taelg* literally means "again made cheerful," and "propensior *tylg*," that is, "more cheerful, more readily inclined."

[1] E. W. Lane, *An Arabic-English Lexicon*, London 1874, sub طلق.

In the Gothic Bible we have similarly *tulgjan* "to make safe, fortify," which corresponds to Arabic طلق *tuluq* "not shackled."[1]

From the above investigation it follows that with the appearance of the Arabs in Europe the metals assumed a far greater importance in life than they had held heretofore. The intensive working of the gold mines, the improved methods in the alloys of the metals, especially of bronze, and the universal use of welded steel according to the Indian method revolutionized metallurgy in Europe. It cannot be said that the Arabs discovered any new paths in this direction. They were rather the popularizers of the Greek alchemy which heretofore had been restricted to Byzantium and Egypt and to a small number of men initiated in the mysteries of the craft. The most surprising thing in the dissemination of the Arabic metallurgy is the enormous Arabic technical vocabulary which has left its impress upon the Romance and Germanic peoples, even upon the Goths, whose contact with the Arabs in the VIII. century was of the closest. It behooves us now to investigate the type of smiths that the Arabic invasion brought in its wake into Europe and Africa, but, before doing so, we shall study the history of the smith in Europe shortly before the arrival of the Arabs, as it is revealed in language. The Greek ἤλεκτρος, OHGerman *smaidar*, was the classical name of the Egyptian *asem*, a natural mixture of gold and silver.[2] This word, like Greek ἠλέκτωρ "the sun," is related to Sanskrit *arkas* "the sun," *arcati* "to shine," which are taken from the Dravidian, Kannada *arka*, *akka*, etc. "the sun," which is from the root "to shine," preserved in Kannada *ulku* "to shine," Tamil *ūl* "sunshine," etc. In Sumerian we have the

---

[1] See my *Contributions*, vol. IV, p. 233.
[2] See C. R. Lepsius and W. Berend, *Les métaux dans les inscriptions égyptiennes*, in *Bibliothèque de l'École des hautes Études*, part XXX, p. 12 ff.

root *el* "clear, pure," which in Assyrian is found as *ellu* "to shine." We are, therefore, once more in the basic group which produced Tatar *alcin* "gold," hence it must be assumed that the *electrum* proceeded from somewhere in the center of Asia.

The *electrum* was more brilliant than gold, and resembled brass,[1] hence it led to an artificial alloy in which the alchemists did not necessarily employ the native *electrum*.[2] They manufactured it from two parts of silver, one part of copper and one of gold,[3] and produced it of even inferior quality.[4] This composition is as frequently called *elidrium*[5] and *lato*,[6] and it hardly needs any proof that these words are corruptions of *electrum*. We may, however, follow the degeneration of this group through the vocabularies.

The Greek alchemists used ἐλύδριον as an equivalent for the plant *chelidonium*[7] and also for a certain yellow mineral, and Berthelot has shown that among the alchemists writing in Latin *elidrium* has similarly this double meaning; but in this case the yellow metal is definitely the *electrum*.[8] Apparently there is here a confusion of ἤλεκτρος and χελιδονία, which has produced this

---

[1] *Ibid.*, p. 15.

[2] "Quod ex urina pueri et auricalco fit aurum optimum: quod intelligendum est in colore, non in substantia; hoc auricalcum frequentis scripturae vocatur *electrum*," Vincent of Beauvais, *Speculum naturale*, lib. VIII. 36, and M. Berthelot, *La chimie au moyen âge*, Paris 1893, vol. I, p. 83.

[3] *Ibid.*, pp. 78 and 218; also in *Mappae Clavicula*, in *Archaeologia*, vol. XXXII, p. 215.

[4] "Eris partes. iij. argenti pars. i. simul confla et adicies auripigmenti non usti partes. iij. Et cum valde calefeceris, sinito ut refrigeret et mitte in patina, et obline argilla, et assa donec fiat cerussa; tolle et confla, et invenies argentum. Si autem multum assaveris, fiet *electrum*, cui, si pars. i. auri addideris, fiet aurum optimum," Berthelot, *op. cit.*, p. 218.

[5] *Ibid.*, in Index, sub *elidrium*.

[6] *Ibid.*, p. 83.

[7] "Χελιδονία ἐστὶ τὸ ἐλύδριον," Berthelot, *Collection des anciens alchimistes grecs*, vol. I, Paris 1877, p. 16. See also vol. III, pp. 306 and 310.

[8] Berthelot, *La chimie au moyen âge*, vol. I, p. 31. See also pp. 213, 218, 220, and *Archaeologia*, vol. XXXII, pp. 193, 194, 195, 196, 200, 203, 227. Also J. M. Burnam, *Recipes from Codex Matritensis A 16*, in *University of Cincinnati Studies*, vol. VIII, p. 16.

elidrium.   In the Anglo-Saxon vocabularies we find the forms *elotr, elothr,*[1] *electre, elehtre,* which show intermediate stages between *electrum* and *elidrium,* and also betray a form *elotrium,* which, however, is not recorded. But we find early the form *lato* in the Romance languages, which is apparently a corrupt form, in which *chelidonium* affected *electrum* and *elidrium.* Indeed, we possess intermediate stages which show how *electrum* developed into *lato.* In the *Dissertationes* printed by Muratori, we have the two forms *eletarum* and *letarum,*[2] from which there is but a step to *letanum* and *latonum,* recorded by Ducange. It is, however, not unlikely that we have here a confusion with χαλϰὸς ἐλατός,[3] the ductile brass of the Greek alchemists.

The ASaxon vocabularies have for Latin *electrum* also the glosses *smylting,*[4] *smelting.*[5] This is identical with the OHGerman gloss for *electrum,* which is *gismelze,*[6] but this word is also employed for pure gold, *obryzum.*[7] In the tenth century the Germans well knew that this was of Italian origin,[8] and, indeed, the earliest reference to it is to be found in Anastasius' *Life of Leo IV,* of the end of the IX. century, where we learn that the enamel, for this is meant here by *smaltum,* was carried out on a background of pure gold.[9]

---

[1] J. H. Hessels, *A Latin-Anglo-Saxon Glossary,* Cambridge 1906, p. 102.
[2] "Ad cluttan auream de *Letarum. Eletarum* comodo fiet? Pones duas partes argenti, et eramenti tres, et auri tres," *Antiquitates italicae medii aevi,* Mediolani 1739, vol. II, col. 384.
[3] Berthelot, *Collection,* vol. II, p. 313.
[4] T. Wright and R. Wülcker, *Anglo-Saxon and Old English Vocabularies,* London 1884, vol. I, cols. 141 and 334.
[5] *Ibid.,* col. 148.
[6] Steinmeyer und Sievers, *op. cit.,* vol. I, p. 641, vol. II, pp. 399, 463, 523, 533, 546, 593, vol. III, pp. 121, 192, etc.
[7] "*Gismelcit,*" *ibid.,* vol. I, p. 509; "*smelzigolt, smalzgolt,*" *ibid.,* vol. II, p. 14; "*smelzigold,*" p. 18.
[8] "*Electrum* heizet in uualescun *smaldum,*" E. G. Graff, *Althochdeutscher Sprachschatz,* Berlin 1842, vol. VI, sub *smelzi.*
[9] "Fecit denique tabulam de *smalto,* opus ducentas sexdecim auri obrizi pensan. libras," *Acta sanctorum,* July IV, p. 314.

As the foundation was more frequently of composition than of gold, *electrum* came to have not only the meaning of a substitute for gold, but also of the whole enamel work as well, hence "to adorn with *electra*" was tantamount to "to adorn with enamel work."[1] Theophilus has devoted a chapter to the manner in which the *electra* were to be laid on,[2] and from this it is again evident that the enamel was laid on by means of a composition called *electrum*.   In the *Liber pontificalis* we have mention, under Benedict III (855-858), of a reticule made of gems and golden pendants, which had in it pieces of gold enamel, where, for *electra*, we have "*petias exmaltitas.*"[3]   Toward the end of the century we hear, in the same *Liber pontificalis*, of enamel work under the name of *smaltum*.[4]

Theophilus gives, in the chapter on *enamel*, a careful description of the manner in which the *electrum* has to be melted down evenly and smoothly[5]   The *electrum* itself, that is, the gold composition, was, besides, very carefully polished until it shone brilliantly.[6] It is, therefore, clear that the confusion between *electrum* and *smaltum* is due to the employment of the alloy, or of pure gold, in the enamel work, and that *smaltum* meant

---

[1] "Ornare lapidibus et *electris* atque margaritis," Theophilus, *Schedula diversarum artium*, lib. III, cap. 50, in *Quellenschriften fur Kunstgeschichte und Kunsttechnik des Mittelalters und der Renaissance*, vol. VII, p. 223.

[2] *Ibid.*, p. 235 ff.

[3] "Benedictus praesul pulcherrimi decoris retem factam miro opera totam gemmis ex alva veris et bullulis aureis, conclusas etiam auri petias in se habentem *exmaltitas*. . . . . .praecepit fieri," L. Duchesne, *Le liber pontificalis*, Paris 1892, vol. II, p. 147.

[4] "Posuit cantram auream I, cum pretiosis margaritis et gemmis ac *smalto*," (885-891), *ibid.*, p. 194; "obtulit in ea crucem auream super altare cum gemmis et *smalto*," *ibid.*, p. 195.

[5] "Aperiens vero tolles *electrum* et lavabis, rursumque implebis et fundes sicut prius, sicque facies donec liquefactum aequaliter per omnia plenum sit," Theophilus, *op. cit.*, p. 239.

[6] "Super quod polies ipsum *electrum* donec omnino fulgeat, ita ut si dimidia pars ejus humida fiat et dimidia sicca sit, nullus possit considerare, quae pars sicca, quae humida sit," *ibid.*, p. 241.

"enamel work made with molten electrum carefully and smoothly distributed over the plate."

We can now proceed to trace the history of *smaltum*. The Semitic languages have the root *mlt* "to smear over," from which they derive their word for "cement, paste." Thus we have Syriac ܡܠܬ *mlat* "he smeared over, put on, meditated," ܡܠܝܬ *mlīt* "smeared over, wise," hence ܡܠܬܐ ܡܠܬܐ *mlāt, mlātā* "cement, mud," Hebrew מֶלֶט *melet* "mortar, cement," Arabic ملط *malita* "smooth," ملط *malata* "he smeared over," ملط *milāt* "cement," Ethiopic *malāč* "to rub off, make bald." But there are also the forms, Syriac ܡܪܛ *mrat* "to make bald," and Hebrew derivatives of the root מרט *mrt* which mean "to pull out the hair, smooth down, make bald, polish," Arabic *marata* "he plucked out the hair," which are related to this group. The enormous mass of words in all the languages of Europe and Asia that are related to this group cannot be discussed here. All that is necessary is to keep in mind the specific meaning of "cement, mortar," which the Semitic nouns have evolved. Related to these, or directly derived from one of them, are Latin *mortarium* "mortar," that is, "cement" and "pounding instrument, pan in which cement is made," Greek μάλθα "calking pitch, wax smeared on writing-tablets." The Latin *mortarium* shows at once that we have here the same root as in Sanskrit *marda* "crushing, grinding, rubbing."

The word which directly concerns us is Latin *maltha*, the very writing of which shows its borrowing from Greek. Pliny calls by this name a natural cement, found in the Syrian city of Samosata,[1] and an artificial

---

[1] "In urbe Commagenes Samosata stagnum est emittens limum—*maltham* vocant—flagrantem. cum quid attigit solidi, adhaeret," II. 235.

hard cement made chiefly from chalk.[1] He also used the verb *malthare* "to lay on a cement, enamel,"[2] and an old gloss to Juvenal reads "Sulphure solent vitrum solidare, id est *malthare*,"[3] but *solidare* means not only "to solder," but also "to cement, enamel."   In Italian we have side by side *malta* "cement, mortar," *maltare* "to cement," and *smalto* "cement, mortar, enamel," *smaltare* "to enamel," *smaltire* "to digest," *smaltito* "digested, clear, intelligible, easy."

Thus we see that the Semitic word, still noticeable in Pliny's *maltha*, as referred to the natural *asphaltum*, and the Greek word, which gives Latin *maltha* "cement," have in Italy produced the two forms *malt-* and *smalt-*, both of them of late origin, although the Latin *mortarium*, Sanskrit *marda*, and the endless number of related words are widely diffused and go back to prehistoric times.   Now the Greek has already a verb μέλδειν "to melt," but it is an extremely rare word, and has left no trace behind in either Latin or the other Indo-European languages.   In Modern Greek we have, indeed, a number of similar verbs, but it can be shown that they all are newly formed from μίλτος, σμάλτος, that is, that they owe their origin to the employment of μάλθα in the enamel work of the Middle Ages.

In Modern Greek we have σμάλθη, σμάλτος, σμάγδος "enamel," σμαλτώνω, σμαγδώνω "I enamel," and μίλτος "enamel," μιλτόω "I enamel."   Here there is a confusion between Italian *smalto* and Greek μίλτος "rubric." Modern Greek σμάγδος is found at an earlier time as σμάρδος,[4] where there is apparently a confusion with σμάραγδος "emerald," for we find σμάραγδος mentioned among the metals.

[1] "*Maltha* e calce fit recenti. glaeba vino restinguitur, mox tunditur cum adipe suillo et fico, duplici lenimento. quae res omnium tenacissima et duritiam lapidis antecedens," XXXVI. 181.
[2] "Quod *malthatur*, oleo perfricatur ante," *ibid.*
[3] In Forcellini.
[4] Berthelot, *Collection*, vol. III, pp. 323, 329.

The alchemists of the early Middle Ages, according to Berthelot,[1] confused a large number of red substances of mineral origin under the name of μίλτος, namely oxides of iron, lead, and mercury, and protoxide of copper, so that rubric (μίλτος), minium, cinnabar, vermilion are frequently synonyms. But the metallic oxides are also known under the name of ἰός *virus.* The Latin glosses give *rubrica* for μίλτος and *aerugo* for ἰός. Another word for the oxide is *rubigo,* and, as ἰός indicates, the spoiled or poisonous product of the metal is meant by this word. The Germanic glosses have *rubigo*[2] and *erugo,*[3] *miltow, milcdov, milidou,* etc., and distinctly identify *rubigo* with *erugo*[4] and also with *metalla.*[5] This is also the case with the ASaxon glosses, where we read "*erugo,* i. uitium frumenti, uel ferri."[6] OHGerman *miltou* has, however, lost the meaning of "metallic rust," and refers only to "plant rust," while ASaxon *mildeaw,* unrecorded before the XI. century, is popularly connected with Latin *mel* "honey," and at first meant "nectar."[7] The ASaxon glosses give for *rubigo* and *erugo* the words *brand* and *om,* the latter of Arabic origin, as has already been discussed.

In a similar, if not identical, way has arisen the confusion in Syriac for the words denoting "metal" and "mine." The Talmud has already מְטַלְיָה *mĕtālyāh,* מְטָלִין *mĕtālōn* "mine, quarry," which is borrowed directly from the Latin, since the reference is invariably to the Latin "damnare in metallum." But the He-

[1] *Ibid.,* p. 261.
[2] Steinmeyer und Sievers, *op. cit.,* vol. I, pp. 290, 430, 438, 669, 819, vol. II, pp. 473, 683, vol. III, pp. 307, 343.
[3] *Ibid.,* vol. I, pp. 443, 445, 519, 524, 669, vol. III, pp. 234, 334.
[4] *Ibid.,* vol. I, pp. 242, 669.
[5] *Ibid.,* p. 710.
[6] Wright and Wülcker, *op. cit.,* vol. I, col. 229.
[7] *Ibid.,* col. 455.

brew מְטִיל *mĕtīl*, Talmudic מְטָל *metāl* "iron rod" are older, and with Arabic *matala* "he forged, extended" seem to point to a root with the original meaning "to forge." The Semitic word is not universal and so is itself a borrowing, together with the Greek, from some other source. The Syriac has ܡܛܠܘܢ *metalōn*, obviously Greek μέταλλον "mine," and, side by side with it, ܡܠܛܘܢ *melatōn* "mine," which is supposed to be a corruption of the first. It is more likely a confusion with Greek μίλτος.

The Arabic has معدن *maʿdin* "mine, mineral, metal," but in some places, as in Morocco, it generally signifies "brass" or "bronze." This is referred to the root عدن *ʿadana* "to stay," but that is mere popular etymology, for not only is "metal, mine" only forcedly deduced from it, but we have also derivatives from معدن *maʿdin*, namely معدن *maʿdana* "to mine," معدن *mumaʿdan* "metallic," where any ultimate origin from عدن *ʿadana* is not suspected. The word is utterly unrelated to any Semitic word, and is unquestionably a borrowing. As the Syriac shows a confusion with Greek μίλτος, due to the Greek alchemists' vocabulary, Arabic معدن *maʿdin* is without doubt due to the same confusion which in Modern Greek produces σμάλτος, σμάγδος, μίλτος for "fusible metal." Indeed, Arabic *maʿdin* must be due to a popular borrowing, from Greek σμάγδον or μίλτον, from which a form μίγδον, although unrecorded, is to be presupposed from the form σμάγδος for σμάλτος. Such a popular borrowing would have to take place in a territory where Greek and Arabic met on intimate terms. Such a place would be Sicily, and it is here, indeed, that we learn of the intermediate forms of the unrecorded μάγδον, μίγδον. Here we have in Sicilian *mauta, smauto* for Italian *malta, smalto*. Similarly, we have Neapolitan *smardire, smantire, smautire* for Italian *smaltire*, and *smardare* for Italian *smaltare*. In like manner, the Provençal dialects have *esmaut, esmalt, esmart* for "enamel," and even the LLatin records *esmaudus* by the side of *smaltus*. As Italian *smalto* and *malta* have the same meaning, "cement, mortar," the Arabic *ma'din* cannot be separated from Syriac *melatōn* or *maltōn* (for the vocalization is not given), and both must be considered as contaminations of the same type as MGr. σμαγδώνω and μιλτόω. Indeed, the most likely direct derivation of Arabic ملعن is from the Syriac ܡܠܬܘܢ *mltōn*, read as ܡܥܬܘܢ *m'tōn* and popularly derived from عدن *'adana* "to stay."

The Prudentius glosses several times gloss "rudera" by "stercora," and this by *molta*, that is, *molta* is equal to "waste, dirt."[1]   In the Keronian and Hrabanian glosses *molta* is the translation of "humus"[2] and "telus."[3]   Similarly the ASaxon glosses give *molde* for "sablo, sabulum, humus, rus, aruum," and the Gothic has *mulda* "dust," *muldeins* "earthly."   All these words are borrowed directly from LLatin *molta*, a variation of *malta*.   "Cementum est *molta* ex quo conjunguntur lapides," says the *Liber sacerdotum*,[4] and from the *Ordo Romanus* we learn that in the dedication of a Catholic church the relics of the saint were deposited at the altar in mortar, and that this mortar, *malta*, was made of chalk and holy water.[5]   But in the beginning of the XII. century this deposition of the

---

[1] See p. 38.
[2] Steinmeyer und Sievers, *op. cit.*, vol. I, p. 168.
[3] *Ibid.*, p. 8.
[4] Berthelot, *La chimie au moyen âge*, vol. I, p. 217.
[5] "Tunc faciat *maltam* de calce et tegula cum ipsa aqua benedicta ad occludendas sanctorum reliquias loco altaris," in Ducange, sub *malta*.

relics had become purely symbolical, for the mortar was made of holy water mixed with salt and ashes,[1] and this mortar, called *molta* or *mola*, was, after the ceremony of dedication, scattered on the ground.[2]   Thus *molta* or *mola* are synonymous with "dust, earthly relics," and thus the Germanic words are directly derived from the Latin.[3]

The Greek μάλαγμα "poultice, plaster" was accepted by the Romans as a medical term, but the mediaeval alchemy extended the meaning of *malagma*, with its corruptions *magma*, *mulmus*, so as to include the meaning "any finely-ground substance," more especially "a wet, macerated mineral compound,"[4] that is, we get here a synonym for *molta*.   Most of the recipes in which *malagma*, *magma* occur, refer to the making of liquid gold, or, rather, a composition that should pass for gold, hence μαλαγματίζειν came in Greek alchemy to mean "to amalgamate with mercury,"[5] and μάλαγμα, μάλαμα in Modern Greek very early was synonymous with "gold."   At a later time the alchemists used *amalgama* for this reduction of gold or silver by mercury.   This *amalgama* is Arabic الملجمة *almalǧamah*

---

[1] "Post haec benedicitur aqua, cui admiscentur sal et cinis, et ad ultimum vinum. . .cinis vero significat reliquias," J. P. Migne, *Patrologia latina*, vol. CLXXVII, col. 386.

[2] "De residuo *moltae* seu *molae* ad basim altaris condendo. . . .Et quod remanet de *molta* qua conditae sunt sanctorum reliquiae, fundit ad basim altaris," *ibid.*, col. 387.

[3] *Mola* is the *mola salsa* of the Romans, salted meal used, just as in the Catholic church, for sacrificial purposes; but *molta* is our *malta*, apparently influenced by *molita* "ground (grain)," so that, after many vicissitudes, *malta* has returned to the original root form, represented in Latin *molere*.

[4] "Conteres limaturas, adiciens aceti acerimi salisque modicum, donec argentum combibat limaturam, et fiet *malagma*," *Liber sacerdotum*, in Berthelot, *La chimie*, vol. I, p. 193; *Mappae Clavicula*, in *Archaeologia*, vol. XXXII, p. 195; "et commisce guatum cum coctione *magmatis*; et tere diligenter donec pulvis fiat," *ibid.*, p. 219; also Muratori, *Antiquitates*, vol. II, col. 378; "fungus est rotundus, pagani vocant amanita. desiccatum ubicunque percusseris pulverem levat *mulmum*," *Mappae Clavicula*, in *Archaeologia*, vol. XXXII, p. 239.

[5] Berthelot, *Collection*, vol. II, p. 164.

"amalgam,"[1] of which the popular form was مرهم المرهم
almaraham, marham "poultice." The amalgamation
of the metals consisted in a calcination of the metals by
a drying process after treatment with mercury, hence
ἀφροσέληνος, the usual term for "chalky substance,
fine powder,"[2] became in Syriac the usual word for
"amalgam." Thus *malagma* in alchemy meant both
"amalgam" and "fine, chalky substance, powder."
This is represented in the Germanic languages in the
shorter forms, Gothic *malma* "sand," ASaxon *mealms-
tan* "sandstone," ASaxon, OHGerman *melm* "dust,"
but is also found in Italian as *melma* "fine, pasty mud
at the bottom of rivers and pits."

The Arabic word for "metal" is found in all the languages that have borrowed directly from the Arabic.
In the Slavic languages we have OBulgarian *mēd'*
"brass," *mēden* "of brass," but Slovenian *medina* "ore,
metal," by the side of *med* "ore, metal, copper, brass,"
and *medinar, medar* "coppersmith," Serbian *mjedenica*
"brass kettle, bell" make it certain that we have in
OBulgarian *mēd'* a backformation of *mēden*, that is,
that we have borrowings from the Arabic. In the
German *Messing* we have a totally different origin.
ASaxon *maestling* is given as the translation of "electrum" and "aurichalcum." The first means, as we
have seen, "a metal mixed from gold and silver," and is
generally given in the vocabularies as "aurum et argentum *mixtum*," hence ASaxon *maestling* is an ASaxon
transformation of Latin *mixtum*. Indeed, in Ducange
there is recorded a form *mestallum*, as though transformed from "metallum," for "copper" or "brass,"
even as a mixture of grains is found in the form *mestal-
lium*, which leads to OFrench *métail*. When "aurichalcum" came to mean "a mixture of metals known as

---

[1] R. P. Smith, *Thesaurus syriacus*, p. 351, sub *afrōselīnōn*.
[2] Berthelot, *La chimie au moyen âge*, vol. I, pp. 31, 203.

bronze or brass," the ASaxon *maestling* assumed the meaning of "brass," and a similar form is found in German *Messing* "brass."

The Germanic languages have borrowed either the Latin *malta* or the Italian *smalto* for words to denote the art of enamelling. In the Gothic Bible we have once *gamalteinais*, as a side gloss to "diswissais," which is the translation of Greek ἀναλύσεως. But ἀνάλυσις is an alchemical term for dissolution of a body by melting, hence the Gothic glossator has chosen the root *malt-* with which to explain the less common "diswissais." There is no way of determining whether Gothic possessed any derivatives from *smalto*. We have already seen that in OHGerman the usual translation for "electrum" is *gismelze*. The earliest references to *smelzan* show that the enamel was understood to be produced by liquefaction of the metal, hence we get in the Keronian glosses the meanings "liquefieri, mulcere" for it,[1] and we have even the unmutated form *smultar* "liquidus, serenus."[2] The *electrum* was generally confused with the purest gold, the *obryzum*, hence we find *electrum* glossed by "obrizum ubarguldi,"[3] where *ubar* is unquestionably the abbreviation OBR,[4] for *obryzum;* but more frequently *electrum* was identified with quicksilver,[5] or even with glass,[6] while the Keronian gloss translated *electrum* by "uueralttiurida," that is, "natural glory."

---

[1] "Mulcet *smilcit*, mulcendus *smelzendi*," Steinmeyer und Sievers, *op. cit.*, vol. I, p. 207; "liquore *smelzi*," ibid., vol. II, p. 450; "liquido *smelzindimo*," ibid., p. 516; "liquitur *smalz*," ibid., p. 555; "*smalt*," ibid., p. 584; "liquatur *smilcit*," ibid., p. 680; "sagimen *smalz*," ibid., vol. III, p. 259.

[2] Graff, *op. cit.*, vol. VI, col. 830.

[3] Steinmeyer und Sievers, *op. cit.*, vol. II, p. 499; see also vol. I, p. 508.

[4] See my *Commentary to the Germanic Laws and Mediaeval Documents*, Cambridge 1915, p. 185.

[5] Steinmeyer und Sievers, *op. cit.*, vols. I, p. 134, II, pp. 384, 386, 390, 411, 499, 530.

[6] *Ibid.*, vol. I, p. 653.

In the ASaxon glosses we have *smelting, smilting*
"electrum," where there is possible a confusion between
"electrum" and "amber," but the transferred meanings
survived in *smolt* "serene, quiet, peaceful," *smylte*
"quiet, tranquil, calm, serene;" but we also have *meltan*
"to melt, become liquid," and, like Italian *smaltire*,
"to digest." Curiously, while the OHGerman glosses
several times translate "obryzum" by *smelzigold*, the
ASaxon glosses have *ymaeti gold* and *smāēte gold*.[1]
The assumption that *smāēte* comes from *smiton* "to
beat," is inadmissible, because "obryzum" is not leaf-
gold in particular, but any pure gold. We have here
simply a form without the *l*, such as we have already
met in the languages discussed above. Indeed,
smāēte did not survive in Anglo-Saxon, except in the
connection *smāēte-gold*, and that, too, not for any
length of time. By the side of *smolt, smylte* "serene,"
we have, in the early vocabularies, also the ASaxon
smoeđum "politis," *smođ* "smooth," *smeđe* "lenis,"
smeđie "polio." Thus we have here as large a variety
of derivatives from the original, which means "to enamel, make a smooth surface," as we have in the
Romance languages or in the Greek. There cannot be
the slightest doubt as to the philological identity of
Gothic *smiþa* "smith," *gesmiþon* "to forge," OHGerman *smid, smitha* "smith," *smidon, smithon* "to forge,"
and AS. *smiđian* "to forge" with this group, because
OHGerman *smeidar* "a worker in metal" and *smida*
"metal," *smidaziereda* "necklace" show that we proceed
to "smith" from the idea "metal, precious metal."

The peculiar vocalization and the whole form of
OHGerman *smid*, Gothic *smiþa* is apparently due to a
confusion with Arabic ـمـ *smīđ* "finely ground, smooth,
white flour." We have also Syriac *smīda*, Hebrew

---

[1] Hessels, *op. cit.*, p. 156, sub *obrizum*.

סְמִידָא *smīdā*, Coptic *samit*, related to or derived from Greek σεμίδαλις, from which also comes Latin *simila*, *similago*.   This word is, in all likelihood, derived from Egyptian χma, Coptic *šma* "to grind fine," even as the other Coptic word for "fine wheat flour," *noeit*, *nōit*, is derived from *nout* "to grind," and Greek ἄλευρον "flour" is related to ἀλήϑειν "to grind." Such a confusion is the more probable, since in ASaxon we have direct derivatives from the Arabic *samīḍ* or *samīḍun* in ASaxon *smeduma*.[1]

We can now show how *smidan* has really arisen from *smaltarius* "metal-worker *par excellence*."   The Keronian glosses, text Pa., has "Dedalus *smaidar*," and, under "opifex," in texts Gl.K. and Ra., "artifex *smeidar*." Text Gl.K. has also here "fabricat *smid*," but it is clear that the regular VIII. century word for "smith" was *smaidar*, *smeidar*, which is a Germanized form of *smagdarius* for *smaltarius*, even as *maistar* for "opifex" is a popular, Germanized form of *magister*.

---

[1] "Polenta .i. subtilissima farina .i. *sineduma*; uel gisistit melo," Steinmeyer und Sievers, *op. cit.*, vol. I, p. 375; "simila *smĕtuma*," *ibid.*, vol. II, p. 341; and in the Leiden Glossary, and in Bosworth.

CHAPTER II.

THE GYPSIES IN EUROPE.[1]

In 789 Charlemagne issued at Aix-la-Chapelle a general admonition to the clerical and secular authorities of his realm, in which the following decree is contained: "Item ut isti mangones et cotiones qui sine omni lege vagabundi vadunt per istam terram, non sinantur vagare et deceptiones hominibus agere, nec isti nudi cum ferro, qui dicunt se data sibi poenitentia ire vagantes: melius videtur, ut si aliquid inconsuetum et capitale crimen conmiserint, ut in uno loco permaneant laborantes et servientes et paenitentiam agentes secundum quod sibi canonice inpositum sit."[2] As it stands, this decree says: "Let those cheats who travel about this land without any law be stopped from running around and cheating people, and those naked ones with iron, who say that they are roving on account of a vow of penance. It seems best that, if they have committed any unusual and capital crime, they should stay in one place working and serving and doing penance according to ecclesiastic law."

Hefele[3] thinks that this law was directed against a class of cheats called "mangones" and "cotiones," who were no longer to wander about freely, and the naked people with chains, who pretended to wander about for penance' sake, were to stay in one place and there do penance, if they had committed a grievous

---

[1] See my contributions in the *Journal of the Gypsy Lore Society* for July, 1909, April, 1910, and October, 1910.

[2] *Monumenta Germaniae historica, Capitularia*, vol. I, p. 60 f.

[3] *Conciliengeschichte*, Freiburg im Breisgau 1877, vol. III, p. 670.

crime. Mabillon[1] tried to explain this penancing with iron by adducing two or three cases from the VII. century where men, having committed murder on their relatives, took the vow of penance by carrying bonds made of the iron with which the crime had been committed upon their necks and arms until, by a miracle, they burst open. Even assuming that these cases of penancing for parricide are typical, they cannot have occurred in such large numbers as to demand special and oft-repeated legislation. Besides, if this penance were sincere, why should those who did penance wander about and deceive people? There is nowhere any mention of "naked men" doing penance with iron, and Canciani[2] uses this passage as a proof of such a practice, just as Mabillon and others had adduced other cases of penancing with iron, in order to prove it.

The mistake made by the authors who have analyzed this passage is due to the fact that they have misunderstood the phrase "nudi cum ferro" and thus have created two or three classes of people to whom the decree is supposed to refer. But "nudi cum ferro" is a mere lemma taken by Charlemagne out of Vergil and Servius. To *Georgica* I.58 "At Chalybes nudi ferrum," Servius writes: "Chalybes populi sunt, apud quos nascitur ferrum, unde abusive dicitur chalybs ipsa materies, ut vulnificusque chalybs. 'Nudi' autem aut apud quos arbores non sunt: aut vere nudi propter ferri caedendi studium; nam legimus Brontesque Steropesque et nudus membra Pyracmon." The *Brevis Expositio* writes: "Chalybes gens in Ponto inventrix ferri, dicti a Chalybio, Euboiae vico, quod hinc coloni sunt. 'Nudi' ad hoc expediti, vel quod ita operantur, cum fodiunt ferrum." In the Commentary of Probius

---

[1] D. Joannis Mabillonii *Praefationes*, Venetiis 1740, p. 69.

[2] F. P. Canciani, *Barbarorum leges antiquae*, Venetiis 1785, vol. III, p. 209.

we read: "Chalybes natio Pontica, in qua sunt ferri-
fodinae: ibi autem a nudis ferrum quaeritur."

It follows from these glosses that Charlemagne, in
using "nudi cum ferro," had in mind the Chalybes, that
is, iron-workers, who were in his day roving over the
country, on the plea that they were doing penance.
It was they that were the cheats, the "mangones" and
"cotiones," against whom he was legislating. In other
words we are dealing here with Gypsies, although we
are not yet in a position to ascertain whether they belonged to the same linguistic family as the modern
Gypsies.   All we know so far is that they worked in
iron and at the same time cheated the people.   Heretofore we heard only of smiths who were respected for
their art and who often were supposed to be endowed
with supernatural powers, while here we are informed
that they were cheats and vagabonds.   What was the
cause of this sudden change in attitude towards the
very important class of iron-workers?

We are able to ascertain this from the identical relation that the Arabs bear to the blacksmiths.[1]   The
best proof of the contempt they have for the Gypsies
appears from the study of a series of words applied to
them.

Aristophanes several times uses the term κόβαλος,
which obviously means "trickster, cheat."   The word
is otherwise totally unknown in Greek literature, except in annotations of the scholiasts, as in Harpocration, where the word is also quoted as found in the
second 'Ατθίς of Philochorus, where Bacchus is mentioned as being a κόβαλος, a cheat.   Yet the large
Greek dictionaries, from Stephanus to Liddell and Scott,
and Pope, aver that κόβαλοι "were also a set of mischievous goblins, invoked by rogues."   This erroneous
statement is due to an interpolation in the scholia to

---

[1] A. Robert, L'Arabe tel qu'il est, Alger 1900, p. 99.

Harpocration,[1] which Maussacus unfortunately attached to the word κοβαλεία, although it is absent from the oldest scholia of the *Codex Venetus* and *Ravennates*,[2] and is not found earlier than the XII., possibly not earlier than the XIV., century.[3] This interpolation reads: "*κόβαλοι, δαιμονές εἰσί τινες σκληροὶ περὶ τὸν Διόνυσον,*" "the *cobaloi* are certain malicious spirits about Bacchus." The scholiast confused the reference to Bacchus as a cheat with the mediaeval *covali, cobali* "goblins," and thus created for Aristophanes the impossible imps. Neither Hesychius, nor Suidas, nor any other mediaeval Greek lexicon knows anything about this reference, although the rest of Harpocration's note is quoted in full. It appears clearly that κόβαλος was an Attic slang expression, otherwise unknown to the Greeks, hence apparently not of Greek origin. It can easily be shown that it was borrowed from a Semitic tongue, most likely from Phoenician. The root *ḥbl* is found in all the Semitic languages. We have Assyrian *ḥabalu* "injury, ruin," *ḥabbilu* "wicked rascal," Syriac *ḥabâlâ* "corrupter, pederast," *ḥubâlâ* "corruption, destruction," Ethiopic *ḥĕbûl* "tricky, perverse," Arabic حبول *ḥabûl*, حوّل *ḥuwwal* "tricky, agile," خبل *ḥabl* "corruptness," Hebrew *ḥâbal* "to hurt, destroy, corrupt." Among the Hebrews the evil angels were called angels of חבלא *ḥabbâlâ* "destruction," and from this generic term there developed the specific Arabic evil jinn. We have Arabic خبل *ḥabal*, plural خبّل *ḥubbal*, "the jinn, devil." This specific meaning does not occur in the other Semitic languages.

[1] G. Dindorf, *Harpocrationis lexicon in decem oratores atticos*, Oxonii 1853, vol. I, pp. 180, 183.

[2] F. Blaydes, *Aristophanis comoediae*, Halis Saxonum 1886, vol. VI, p. 192.

[3] F. Dübner, *Scholia graeca in Aristophanem*, Parisiis 1843, p. iii ff.

The Semitic root is an amplification of a root represented in Egyptian *ḥeb* "to grieve, mourn," *ḥebau* "miserable man, wretched," *ḥeben* "one who is dejected, cast down," which in their turn are related to *kheb* "to diminish, pilfer, destroy, deceive, defraud," *khebt, khebent* "moral obliquity, deceit, fraud, sin, wickedness," *khebenti* "offender, sinner, criminal," all developing from an original meaning "to lay low," Coptic *hobe* "to humble."

The Arabs also possess these words in جبان *ġabān* "coward," خ *ḥab, ḥib, ḥub* "a great deceiver, wicked, deceitful, mischief-maker," خون *ḥaun* "diminution, weakness," غبن *gabn* "to cheat, defraud, be unmindful or inadvertent, to pass by inclining, to elude observation." These Arabic words became immensely popular throughout Europe, and are found in most of its languages. Arabic خون *ḥaun*, خائن *ḥā'in* "treacherous, unfaithful, looking treacherously or clandestinely at a thing at which it is not allowable to look" is found in Gothic *hauns* "low, humble," ASaxon *héan* "low, contemptible, miserable," OHGerman *hōnen* "to scorn," hence French *honnir* "to scold," *honte* "shame," Italian, Provençal, Catalan *onta*, OSpanish *fonta* "shame." Arabic خ *ḥab* "a great deceiver, mischief-maker" has similarly entered into the Germanic and Romance languages, producing ONorse *gabb* "scorn," ASaxon *gabban* "to mock, delude, jest," Italian *gabbo* "jest," OFrench *gab* "mocker, deceit," Portuguese *gabar* "to praise." Arabic غبان *gabān* "coward" is derived from the verb غبن *gabn* "to cheat, to pass by inclining so as to elude observation." The great variety of phonetic changes in the Arabic at once indicates a foreign origin. Egyptian *khebent* has also left behind the Arabic خوّار *ḥawwār*, خوّور *ḥawwūr* "feeble, cowardly," of which the plurals are خوّارون *ḥuwwārūn*, خوّرة *ḥuwwaraṭ*, of which the first is preserved in Venetian *cabalone* "trickster, cheat," while the second is found over an enormous territory. We have French *couard*, Spanish *cobarde*, Italian *codardo* "coward," while in the Balkan Peninsula we get Albanian *gabarde*, *kabarde* "barbarian," OBulgarian *kovarĭnŭ* "tricky," Turkish *ḥor* "vile, abject," *ḥoriat* "barbarian, rustic." The Turkish is, however, borrowed from the Persian, where the Arabic word was popularly related to the native *ḥwar* "light, easy," which only in Modern Persian assumes the meaning "vile, abject."

The derivatives from the Arabic in the Albanian and Slavic languages are instructive. We have Albanian *gabel* "Gypsy, horse dealer," *gabe* "lie," *gabim* "deception," *gaboj* "I deceive, cheat," *kobe* "theft," *kobon* "I steal secretly," *kobim* "deception," *kobe* "I tell fortunes." The same group is found in the Slavic languages. We have OBulgarian *kovalĭ* "blacksmith," *kovalĭnya* "anvil," *kovŭ* "deception," and similarly in the other Slavic languages. The Albanian *kobe* "I tell fortunes" by the side of *kobe* "theft," etc. shows that OBulgarian *kobĭ* "augury," Rumanian *kobi* "to tell fortunes" belong to the same group. The Celtic languages use the Arabic غبن *gabn* to designate a smith, namely OIrish *goba*, Armorican, Welsh *gof*, but we also have OIrish *gau*, Cornish *gow*, Welsh *gau* "a falsehood, a lie."

In the XII. century German *kobolt*, OFrench *gobelin* make their appearance, the first obviously in the sense of "puppet of the pantomime,"[1] for the sources speak

---

[1] J. Grimm, *Teutonic Mythology*, London 1883, vol. II, p. 500 ff.

of being struck dumb like a *kobolt*, speaking like a *kobolt*, that is, in silence or whispering.   The *kobolt* was carried by the juggler or showman under his mantle, and he is often associated with the *taterman*, another kind of puppet.   The latter makes it possible to show that the particular puppet-show mentioned by the mediaeval German authors was derived from Spain and ultimately from the Arabs.   *Taterman* is derived from Spanish *titere* "puppet," and this from Arabic ترتر *tartar* "to shake, tremble."   This Spanish word produced ONorse *titra*, OHGerman *zitaron* "to tremble," while in *taterman* the phonetic change did not take place.   German *kobolt*, OFrench *gobelin* are from Arabic حبّل *hubbal* "mischievous spirit, devil."

From Charlemagne's decree it follows that he had before him an Arabic law directed against the Gypsies, where they were called حبل *habal*, a name as we shall later see, by which they have been known throughout Africa.   It may be that this Arabic word is a mere transformation of the classical *Chalybes*, but in any case it served to indicate the cheating diviners, who also were blacksmiths, as which the Gypsies have ever been known.   Charlemagne divided the lemma of *habal* into "mangones et cotiones," that is, "cheating traders," and "nudi cum ferro," that is, "blacksmiths," and thus gave us the first definite reference to the despised smiths found in literature.

Charlemagne's reference to the penance of the Gypsies is not spontaneous, but is based on a legend long current in the Christian world.   In the pre-Christian apocryphal book of *Jannes and Jambres*,[1] unfortunately lost to science, the two wizards who withstood Moses, according to *Midrash Yelammedenu, Ki Tissa* (Ex. XXXII),

---

[1] See *The Jewish Encyclopedia.*

were "among the mixed multitude that went up with Israel from Egypt" and aided in the making of the golden calf. A Greek tale on the subject is mentioned in Gelasius' *Decretum* under the name of *Poenitentia Jannis et Mambre*, and the title shows that the Egyptian magicians were supposed to have done some penance.

Jambres, Mambre has survived in the Koran as *Sāmirī:* "And we spake by revelation unto Moses, saying, Go forth with my servants out of Egypt by night; and smite the waters with thy rod, and make them a dry path through the sea: be not apprehensive of Pharaoh's overtaking thee; neither be thou afraid. And when Moses had done so, Pharaoh followed them with his forces; and the waters of the sea overwhelmed them. And Pharaoh caused his people to err, neither did he direct them aright. Thus, O children of Israel, we delivered you from your enemy; and we appointed you the right side of Mount Sinai to discourse with Moses and to give him the law; and we caused manna and quails to descend upon you, saying, Eat of the good things which we have given you for food; and transgress not therein, lest my indignation fall on you; and on whomsoever my indignation shall fall, he shall go down headlong into perdition. But I will be gracious unto him who shall repent and believe, and shall do that which is right, and who shall be rightly directed. What hath caused thee to hasten from thy people, O Moses, to receive the law? He answered, These follow close on my footsteps; but I have hastened unto thee, O Lord, that thou mightest be well pleased with me. God said, We have already made a trial of thy people, since thy departure; and al Sāmirī hath seduced them to idolatry. Wherefore Moses returned unto his people in great wrath, and exceedingly afflicted. And he said, O my people, had not your Lord promised you a most excellent promise? Did the time of my absence

seem long unto you?   Or did ye desire that indignation
from your Lord should fall on you, and therefore failed
to keep the promise which ye made me?   They answered, We have not failed in what we promised thee of our
own authority; but we were made to carry in several
loads of gold and silver, of the ornaments of the people,
and we cast them into the fire; and in like manner al
Sāmirī also cast in what he had collected, and he produced unto them a corporeal calf, which lowed.   And
al Sāmirī and his companions said, This is your god,
and the god of Moses; but he hath forgotten him, and is
gone to seek some other.   Did they not therefore see
that their idol returned them no answer, and was not
able to cause them either hurt or profit?   And Aaron
had said unto them before, O my people, verily ye are
only proved by this calf; for your Lord is the Merciful,
wherefore follow me, and obey my command.   They
answered, We will by no means cease to be devoted to
its worship, until Moses return unto us.   And when
Moses was returned, he said, O Aaron, what hindered
thee, when thou sawest that they went astray, that
thou didst not follow me?   Hast thou therefore been
disobedient to my command?   Aaron answered, O son
of my mother, drag me not by the beard, nor by the
hair of my head.   Verily I feared lest thou shouldest
say, Thou hast made a division among the children of
Israel, and thou hast not observed my saying.   Moses
said unto al Sāmirī, What was thy design, O Sāmirī?
He answered, I saw that which they saw not; wherefore
I took a handful of dust from the footsteps of the
messenger of God, and I cast it into the molten calf; for
so did my mind direct me.   Moses said, Get thee gone;
for thy punishment in this life shall be, that thou shalt
say unto those who shall meet thee, *Touch me not*, and
a threat is denounced against thee of more terrible
pains, in the life to come, which thou shalt by no

means escape. And behold now thy god, to whose worship thou hast continued assiduously devoted; verily we will burn it; and we will reduce it to powder, and scatter it in the sea."[1] The accidental resemblance of Sāmirī with Samaritan has led to the identification of the Samaritans by the Arabs with the "Touch-me-nots," which was the more easy, since the Samaritans actually washed themselves after having touched a stranger.[2] However, while the Samaritans purified themselves, the "Touch-me-not" of al-Sāmirī was included as a curse.

The real identification of the Gypsy fortune-tellers with the Egyptian magicians is found in the Syriac versions of the *Cave of Treasures*, of not earlier than the VI. century. Noah, upon awakening from his intoxication, cursed Ham and his race: "He was very angry at his son, Ham, and said: 'Cursed be Canaan, let him be the slave of the slaves of his brothers!' And why was Canaan cursed on account of Ham's guilt? When he was a tall youth and had reached discretion, Satan flew into him and became his teacher in sinning. And he renewed the work of the house of Cain and manufactured flutes and zithers; and the demons and devils flew in and settled in them, and every time the wind blew through them, the demons sang from them and uttered a mighty voice. And when Noah heard that Canaan had done so, he was grieved that the work of error had been renewed, which had brought about the fall of the children of Seth, for with the singing and playing and raging of the children of Cain Satan had overthrown the giants, the 'children of God,' and with the playing of the flutes and zithers sin had grown in the older generation, until God in his anger brought about the flood. And because Canaan had dared to

[1] Chapter XX, 79-97.
[2] J. A. Montgomery, *The Samaritans*, Philadelphia 1907, p. 319.

do so, he was cursed, and his seed became the slaves of slaves, who are the Egyptians, and the Cushites, (and the Indians), and the Mysians.   And because Ham had been bold and had scorned his father, he has been called 'the unclean one' until the present day.   But Noah, by his sleep of intoxication, indicates the cross of the Messiah, as the pious David has sung of him and said, 'The Master awoke as a sleeper and a man whom his wine had shaken.'   The heretics are mad who say, 'God was crucified,' for he calls him here 'Master,' as the apostle Peter says, 'God has made him for a Master and Messiah,' namely this Jesus whom you have crucified.   And he does not say 'God' but 'Master,' for he means the oneness of the two hypostases, that are united in one sonhood.   And when Noah awoke from his sleep, he cursed Canaan and humbled his seed unto an enslavement and scattered his seed among the nations.   But the seed of Canaan, as I said, were the Egyptians, and, behold, they were scattered over the whole earth, and served as slaves of slaves.   And what is 'the slavery of slavery?'   Behold, these Egyptians are driven about in the whole land and carry burdens on their backs.   But those who were brought under the yoke of subjection travel, when they are sent out upon journeys by their masters, not on foot and do not carry burdens, but ride in honor upon beasts, like their masters.   But the seed of Ham are the Egyptians, who carry burdens and travel on foot, while their backs are bent under their burdens, and who wander about at the doors of their brothers' children.   This punish ment was sent down upon them on account of Canaan's foolishness, so that they became the slaves of slaves."[1]

Another Arabic version of the story runs as follows: "When Noah awoke from his drunken sleep, he cursed

[1] C. Bezold, *Die Schatzhöhle, aus dem syrischen Texte dreier unedierten Handschriften in's Deutsche übersetzt*, Leipzig 1883, p. 25 f.

Canaan and made his posterity slaves. Likewise when the Christ arose from the grave He cursed the Devil and destroyed those who had crucified Him and scattered them among the nations. The sons of Canaan became slaves for ever, carrying burdens upon their necks. Every proprietor negotiates riding about on his business, but the children of Canaan negotiate about the affairs of their masters, as poor men on foot, and they are called the slaves of slaves."[1]

In these apocryphal works we learn that the Gypsies were wandering about on account of the crime of magic, and that they were called "the unclean ones," even as al-Sāmirī was a "Touch-me-not," but we still have to show that the appellation *Egyptians* actually refers to our Hindu Gypsies, as they are known to us since the XV. century. That the Gypsies actually passed through Egypt, before scattering over Europe, follows from the presence of at least one Coptic word in the Gypsy vocabulary and one Gypsy word in the Coptic vocabulary. We have Greek Gypsy *bilanó* "melted," *bilañov* "to melt," etc. Miklosich was unable to find a Sanskrit root for it, but it is found in Hindustani *bilānā, pighlānā* "to melt," and is from Sanskrit *pragalanīyam* "melting, fusion." This is found in Coptic *bēl, bōl* "to melt," for which there is no Egyptian antecedent. Here we have a direct proof of the introduction of Indian metallurgy into Egypt, which has been established historically from the Arabian manufacture from Indian steel. But the Copts have supplied the Gypsies with their very word for "Gypsy." We have Gypsy *rom* "man, husband, Gypsy," which is Coptic *rōme* "man," *rem* "man, native," hence *rm-n-kēme* "Egyptian." As the Gypsy language indicates no presence of Arabic words in its vocabulary, the Gypsies must have started from Egypt on their

[1] M. Gibson, *Apocrypha arabica,* in *Studia sinaitica,* vol. VIII, p. 30 f.

European and Asiatic pilgrimages before the arrival of
the Arabs in Egypt, that is, before the middle of the
VII. century.   This agrees with the account in the
Cave of Treasures, where they are first mentioned.

In the *Cave of Treasures* we have a distinct reference
to Melchizedek, the high priest of God, whose altar was
at the center of the earth, where Adam was buried, and
where was the tree that was the precursor of holy rood.[1]
To those who considered the sect of the Melchizedekites
to be an abomination, it was therefore natural to identify the "unclean" Egyptians with Melchizedekites.
We find the earliest mention of these in Timotheus
Presbyter, of whom we only know that the latest date
mentioned by him is the year 622,[2] who, therefore,
must have written in that year or later.   He says:
"The Melchizedekites are those who now are called
Athinganoi.   They worship Melchizedek, whence they
received their name.   They live in Phrygia, and are
neither Jews nor pagans.   They seem to keep the
Sabbath, and do not circumcise.   They do not allow
anyone to touch them, and, if someone gives them bread
or water or some other article, they do not dare to take
it from their hands, but call out to the giver to put it on
the ground, and then they walk up and take it, and they
do similarly when they give something to others.   For
this reason they are called *Athinganoi*, because they do
not allow anyone to touch them."[3]

It is clear that we have here a vague recollection of
the *Jannes and Mambre* story and the *Cave of Treasures*,
where the important point is that the cursed race of
magicians were called "Touch-me-nots."   The very
fact that now the Melchizedekites, now the Samaritans

[1] Bezold, *op. cit.*, p. 35.
[2] J. P. Migne, *Patrologia graeca*, vol. LXXXVI. 1, p. 9.
[3] For the later references to *Athinganoi*, see F. Miklosich, *Über die Mundarten und die Wanderungen der Zigeuner Europa's*, Wien 1876, part VI,
p. 58 ff.

are called "Touch-me-nots" indicates that the importance lies in the name, which had to be explained. There can be no doubt that the appearance of the Gypsies in the Byzantine Empire under the Pehlevi Persian name of *ātsīngār, āsīngār*, literally "iron-workers," immediately suggested the Greek etymology 'Αθίγγανοι "Touch-me-nots," for which the name "Egyptians" attached to the Gypsies gave no explanation, whereas the hated sectarian Melchizedekites, or the Samaritans, at once suggested such an explanation. Gelasius' *Decretum* is, to say the least, full of interpolations, hence it cannot be adduced for the settlement of the date when the "Touch-me-not" story arose. We are left for this only with Timotheus Presbyter and Mohammed, both of whom lived in the first quarter of the VII. century. We are, therefore, not far from locating the arrival of the Gypsy *ātsīngār* from a Persian region into Byzantine territory, which gave rise to the 'Αθίγγανοι, the "Touch-me-nots," whence they passed into the Arabic and Syriac versions of the *Jannes and Mambre* story and into the *Cave of Treasures*.

But the Gypsies, from their association with the Egyptians and their scant borrowing of one word from the Coptic vocabulary, must have passed through Egypt and out of it immediately before the arrival of the Arabs. We have, therefore, narrowed down their Egyptian sojourn to a very short period, and the history of their origin can be written with definite dates. The *Jannes and Mambre* story and the Koran refer to the "Touch-me-nots," but, although the reference is to the Egyptian magicians, the Egyptians are not yet singled out as "slaves of slaves." Therefore, the Greek 'Αθίγγανοι arose either in the time of Mohammed, who died in 632, or earlier. In 616 the Persian, Chosroës, conquered Egypt. Unquestionably he brought with his army Gypsy smiths, for we shall soon see that the

Greeks later also carried Gypsies in the army, a custom which they inherited from the Persians.   In 626 Egypt was restored to Rome, and in 636 the Arabs swooped down upon the country.   Some of the Gypsies were carried back to Greece by the retreating Greeks, who settled them in various parts of the Balkan Peninsula in localities that became known as Γυπτοχάστρα or "Little Egypt."   Hence the versions of the *Cave of Treasures* which contain definite references to the "Egyptians" who became "slaves of slaves" must have arisen after 626, when the Egyptian magicians upon whom there rested a curse were definitely identified with the Indian Gypsies, the smiths, fortune-tellers, and vagabonds, as which they have been known ever since.

The Gypsy name for "a Greek" in Greece is *balamo*, while in Egyptian Gypsy *balamu* means "Christian." The word does not seem to occur elsewhere and Miklosich was unable to explain it.   It obviously cannot come from a Greek source, and must have arisen in Egypt, or before the Gypsy settlement in Egypt, to have been preserved in the two countries.   We have the rare Hebrew בלם *blm* "to bind, tame," *bĕlīm* "dumb," Syriac *blam* "to check a heresy," *balīm* "one whose mouth has been tied up, mute," expressions used in regard to the silencing of a heretic.   In Arabic, اﻹﻻم *'iblām* "to be silent" occurs and is unquestionably a borrowing from the Syriac.   The application of Syriac *blam, belim* to "a Greek," as in the Gypsy language, can have arisen only in a Christian country, among the non-orthodox people, that is, in or near Syria itself, and must have gotten into the Gypsy language from the Pehlevi, which also supplied *āsīngār* "iron-worker."   We are, therefore, once more in the presence of the Persian conquest of Egypt, when *balamo* was by the Gypsies applied to the Greeks in

Egypt and, later, to the Greeks in Greece. Had the Gypsies received the word later, they would have been obliged to apply the word to other nations as well, which is not the case.

We have already seen that the Syriac *Cave of Treasures* forced upon the Gypsies the appellation of "Egyptian," hence of the Coptic *rom* "man." But the Coptic word for "Egypt," *Kēmi*, must equally have been current among the Gypsies, hence their full name, in Gypsy, would have been *Kemeno-rom*, or some such form. Indeed both *rom* and *Kemeno-rom*, as applied to the Gypsies, are recorded. *Kemeno-rom* is found Hellenized as χομοδρόμος or χωμοδρόμος, as though it meant "village-rover." The word χωμοδρομεῖν occurs already in Pollux, but the work of this author is so badly interpolated that no conclusion can be drawn as to the age of the word. We next find it in Malalas, who tells of an Italian wizard, who came to Greece, showing his magical art, χωμοδρομῶν, in presenting a blind dog that could return property to their owners and do other wonderful things.[1] Malalas places the event early in the VI. century, but, of course, this does not prove that the word was already in use then, although such may have been the case. Theophanes places this event in 536 and calls the wizard χωμοδρόμος (χομοδρόμος).[2] Constantinus Porphyrogenitus, who wrote in the X. century, says that each bandum, or cohort, contained one χομόδρομος, that is, blacksmith,[3] and there was a "vicariatus" called "that of the χομοδρόμος."[4] We have a form of χομόδρομοι in the XI. century, when we read in a glossary, "*gallodromi* sunt mangones discurrentes et fraude decipientes,"[5] where

---

[1] *Corpus scriptorum historiae Byzantinae*, vol. XIV, p. 453.
[2] *Ibid.*, vol. XXXVIII, p. 347. The same story is also told by Glycas, *ibid.*, vol. XXVI, p. 501.
[3] *Ibid.*, vol. VIII, p. 494.
[4] *Ibid.*, vol. X, p. 225.
[5] Goetz, *op. cit.*, vol. V, p. 620.

we for the first time have the Gypsies mentioned as cheats. In Modern Greek, κομοδρόμος is given as "blacksmith," while κομοδρομεύω is "I forge."

The statement made in Constantinus Porphyrogenitus that a Gypsy was attached to each cohort is of extraordinary importance in determining the early settlements of the Gypsies in the Balkan Peninsula, because we find them later in military or administrative divisions in connection with blacksmithing. In 1204 the Greek possessions were divided among the Emperor, the Venetians, and the Crusaders. To the share of the Venetians fell, among other provinces, the east coast of the Adriatic, from Lacedaemon to Venice. In the enumeration of the lands[1] ceded to them, we find "*prouintia Dirachii et Arbani, cum chartolaratis de Glauiniza, de Bagenetia.*" Arbani is the modern Albania, and *Bagenetia* is thus indicated as being in its neighborhood. A footnote gives the variants *Bagenatia, Vagnetia*, and quotes from Anna Comnena, 5, 4 (ed. Bonn, T. I, p. 236), "κατaλαμβάνει διὰ τῆς Βαγενητίας τὰ 'Iωάννινα," from Eustathius (Op. p. 282, 20) "ἔκ ποθεν Βαγεντίας," from *Chronicon Moreae* (ed. Buchon, v. 7819), "τὰ μέρη τῆς Βαγενετίας, τὰ ἦσαν πρὸς τῆς θαλάσσης," and several other passages, one from *Le livre de la conqueste* (ed. Buchon, pp. 314, 324), where the form *Vagenetie* is given. From all this we conclude that *Vagenetia* was the strip of land opposite Corfu. In the Greek text of the convention, the passage runs as follows:—[2] "Τὸ θέμα Δυρραχίου καὶ 'Αλβάνου, σὺν τοῖς χαρτουλαράτοις τῆς τε Γλαβινίτζης καὶ Βαγενετίας.'

The next year the Podestà of the Venetians in Romania clearly defined the territorial division thus acquired:[3] "In nomine domini Dei et saluatoris nostri Jhesu Cristi. Anno domini millesimo ducentesimo quinto,

[1] G. L. Fr. Tafel und G. M. Thomas, *Urkunden zur älteren Handels- und Staatsgeschichte der Republik Venedig*, Wien 1856, vol. I, p. 472.
[2] *Ibid.*, p. 491.
[3] *Ibid.*, p. 569 f.

mense Octobris, indictione nona. Constantinopoli. Cum aliquid a principibus terre communiter ordinatur, oportet, ut scripture uinculo anodetur, qua possit ordo rei oportuno tempore manifestius recognosci. Igitur nos Marinus Geno, Venetorum in Romania Potestas eiusdemque Imperij quarte partis et dimidie dominator, cum judicibus et sapientibus conscilij et populi con- laudacione, decreuimus, in scripturis publicis hoc esse corroboratum: videlicet quod in diuisione iam dicte nostre quarte partis et dimidie eiusdemque Imperij Romanie, que nobis nostroque comuni habere contin- gebat tempore, quo diuidebamus inter nos Venetos et alios homines, qui uenerant in fidelitate et seruitio domini Venecie Ducis, iam dictam quartam partem et dimidiam tocius dicti Imperij—dimisimus comuni Venecie prouinciam Dirrachij cum chartolarato Glauen- izi, et prouinciam Vagenecie, et Corfu cum tota eius insula   Hec sunt enim sub Dirrachio, uidelicet Sfinarsa, [cum] chartolarato de Glauenitis, quod chart- olaratum potest esse cum tribus uel quatuor casalibus, et Ablona: est catepanikium Vagenetie, et habet unum chartola[ra]tum de Gliki cum alijs duabus uillis et duobus agridijs, idem (*id est?*) paruis casalibus.   Hec autem omnia suprascripta comuni Venecie dimissimus, ut superius est denotatum, et uolumus, quod supra- scriptum comune Venecie plenissimam imperpetuum habeat potestatem ad faciendum de his suprascriptis o'mnibus, quicquid sibi placuerit; et hec confirmatio carte maneat in sua firmitate.''

What is a *chartolaratum?* The editors of the text are not sure about it. Proceeding from the assumption[1] that Macedonia, Thessaly, and the Epirus were well fitted for the raising of horses (*seminaria equina*), they assume that the *chartolarata* were territories set aside

[1] *Ibid.*, p. 267.

for such a purpose. In another place[1] they quote a
gloss "quae Constantinopolitani Imperii strategiae er-
ant," and again assume that *strategiae equorum* were
meant.   It looks as though they had merely been
guessing at the context, but they guessed well.   In
Ducange we find χαρτουλάριος, among other things,
with the meaning of "attendant upon horses."   The
μέγας χαρτουλάριος was an important dignitary in the
immediate service of the Emperor, and χαρτουλάρης
is given as equivalent to "equiso, groom."   In the long
list of geographical names mentioned in the above
quoted documents *chartolarata* are given but three
times—once on the Adriatic coast, once in Thessaly,
once in Macedonia.   Now, we do know that Gypsies in
the thirteenth or fourteenth centuries migrated from
Vagenetia to Corfu and were there called *Vageniti
homines.*   These apparently came from the chartularatum de Gliki in Vagenetia, where, if horses were raised
there, they would have naturally been employed.   We
are fortunate to be able to show that there were also
Gypsies in the chartularatum de Glauenitis, near
Dyrrhachium, the modern Durazzo, on the Adriatic
shore, and that they were known there as Egyptians.

There is a *Life of St. Barbaros the Egyptian,*[2] in
Greek and in Bulgarian.   St. Barbaros was an Egyptian of black color.   At twenty years of age he lost his
parents and joined a piratical band, by which he was
chosen leader on account of his bodily strength.   At
one time he set out to Durazzo on a piratical expedition.
A storm broke out, and Barbaros, who was a Christian,
began to pray to God, and he vowed that in case of
being saved he would devote his life to the service of the

---

[1] *Ibid.*, p. 472.
[2] In the account of his life, and in the conclusions drawn from it, I follow
K. Radčenko, *Einige Bemerkungen zur neugefundenen Abschrift des Lebens
des heil. Barbar in bulgarischer Uebersetzung,* in *Archiv für slavische Philologie,*
vol. XXII (1900), p. 575 ff.

Lord. The ship with all its men was lost, but St. Barbaros was saved. With the fantastic episodes in his life we are here not concerned. What is interesting to us is the fact that the Bulgarian author of the *Life* says that there were many Egyptians near Durazzo, and that by means of them St. Barbaros made himself understood to others. In the Greek version St. Barbaros was called an African, but the Bulgarian author transferred the scene to Durazzo, where he knew of the existence of Gypsies who, as Egyptians, were to him real Africans.

In some parts of Greece μάντις means both "fortune-teller" and "blacksmith."[1] Another Greek word for this is μαντιπόλος, and this was, between 1364 and 1379, used by a Cologne clerical, presumably Joannes of Hildesheim, in regard to the Gypsies in the Orient: "In the Orient and in all the parts across the sea there are especial men, called *Mandapolos* (*Mandopoli*). They keep no especial rite nor heresy, nor have they any priests among them. They travel about in large crowds with their wives and children and asses, and they do not sow nor reap, nor do they sleep in houses, neither in winter, nor in summer, in the rain, or cold, or heat of the sun, in daytime or at night, nor do their wives bear children in a house, but they roam the whole year from place to place, from one town to another; and when they stay in one place, they manufacture sieves or similar household utensils. They cannot stay in one place more than three days, and it has frequently been

---

[1] "Μαντιὲς μυρίζει Cypern, wie ein Schmied riechen, da daselbst μάντις sowohl den χαλκεύς (= Schmied) als auch den μάντις (= Wahrsager) bedeutet," G. N. Hatzidakis, *Zur Wortbildungslehre des Mittel- und Neugriechischen*, in *Byzantinische Zeitschrift*, vol. II, p. 266. Χαλκεύς is not merely smith,—it generally means "Gypsy:" "χαλκιάς, χαρκιάς, σιδεράς, ἀτζίγκανος, fabbro, ferraro," A. da Somavera, *Tesoro della lingua greca-volgare ed italiana*, Parigi 1709; in Chios the Gypsy blacksmith is called χαρτζάς: "'Εκει χαρτζᾶς τοὺς ἀπαντᾷ, χαρτζιὰς μὲ τὰ παιδιά του, χαρτζᾶς μὲ τὴν γυναῖκά του κί ἡ μαυροφαμηλιά του," Α. Γ. Πασπάτης, *τὸ Χιακὸν Γλωσσάριον*, ἐν 'Αθήναις 1888, p. 383 f.

found that if they remained three days in one place, or slept in a house or under a roof, they immediately died. And they have among themselves a special language which no one but themselves can understand or learn, whereas they understand many tongues.   They never have any discord among themselves, whether in words or deeds, but if anyone steals from another, as is the custom with them, or if anyone finds another man with his wife or daughters in adultery, he does not become angry, but retaliates as well as he can.   And these men, coming to a place of the Christians or heretics or Saracens, so long as they are among them, they live according to their rites, manners and customs, and wherever people fast, celebrate, eat, drink, work, lament, weep, or rejoice, these people do likewise.   Nor have they any priest, nor any especial rite, nor law, but in whatsoever place of the Christians or heretics their wives bear children, they baptize the children according to their rites, and in whatsoever place of the Christians or heretics they become ill, they confess and receive communion according to their rite, and the dead are consigned to earth according to the rite of their church. And in whatsoever place of the Christians or heretics they happen to be on a Sunday, there they go in the morning to church with trumpets and musical instruments, with their wives and their children, from the youngest to the oldest, and attend church while still at fast, and similarly adore God in great humility, and there cause a Mass to be sung of the Three Kings, that God for their deserts may lead them safely all the week through the deserts, fields and mountains, and preserve them from all the danger of worms and animals."[1]

This famous book is found in innumerable versions, where the name of the Gypsies is written *mandopoli*,

[1] C. Horstmann, *The Three Kings of Cologne*, London 1886, p. 287 ff.

mandopolijn, mandeopolos, mandropolos.[1] The passage on the *Mandopoli* occurs in Sudheim's *De itinere Terre Sancte*, written about the year 1340, but in a somewhat abbreviated form: "The *Mandopolini* or *Mandindes* live according to no law, but they call themselves Egyptians and say that they are of the race of Pharaoh. They are first-class thieves, travel with their wives from place to place, making sieves and similar things, and paying no attention to the heat of the sun. With the Greeks they are Greeks, with the Saracens, Saracens, and thus with others. And if one is caught with his wife, he does not get angry, but, if he can, he retaliates in a similar way."[2]

In 1322 Symon Simeonis saw Gypsies in Crete: "We saw here a people that was living outside of the town according to the Greek rite and that professed to be of the race of Chaym, who rarely or never remained more than thirty days in one place but, as though cursed by God, roved after thirty days from field to field with their small oblong black tents, in the manner of the Arabs, and from cavern to cavern, because the place which has been occupied by them for the above mentioned time becomes full of worms and other uncleanliness, with which it is impossible to stay."[3]

To this identification of the Gypsies with Ham, as in the *Cave of Treasures*, must be added a quotation from the XII. century German Bible paraphrase, in which the Gypsy blacksmiths are identified with the Ismaelites: "Hagar bore a son from which came the blacksmiths (*chaltsmide*). When Hagar bore the child, she called him Ismael, whence came the Ismaelites who travel far over the land, and whom we call *chaltsmide.*

[1] T. Scheepstra, *Van den heilighen drien coninghen*, Groningen 1914, p. 278.
[2] L. de Sudheim, *De itinere Terre Sancte*, in *Archives de l'Orient latin*, Paris 1884, vol. II, part II, p. 375.
[3] J. Nasmith, *Itinerarium Symonis Simeonis, et Hugonis Illuminatoris ad Terram Sanctam*, Cambridge 1778, p. 17.

Woe to them!   Everything which they have for sale
has always some fault.   Let him buy anything well or ill,
he always wants something to boot.   They deceive the
people with whom they have dealings.   They have
neither house nor home, and they are everywhere
equally at home.   They roam over the land and
oppress the people.   They deceive the people, and
never rob them openly."[1]   These Gypsies are here
called *chaltsmide* from their occupation as smiths.   It
is generally assumed that the word means "cold-
smiths," that is, "hammerers of cold metal," but this is
not very certain.   It is far more likely that the first
part of the word is identical with German *Kälte* "a
tumbler" or "dish" of some kind, or Italian *caldaia* "a
vase" or "pot," and that thus the whole means "tin-
ker."   This is the more likely since we not only have
Italian *calderaio*, French *chaudronnier*, who are sometimes identified with the Gypsies, but Modern Greek
κατζίβελος "Gypsy" is similarly derived from κατζίβελα
"dishes," and this from Italian *cazzuola* "ladle, trowel."

From the above discussion it follows that, with the
exception of the last reference, every other mention of
the Gypsies, from Charlemagne in 789 to *The Three
Kings of Cologne*, at the end of the XIV. century, goes
back to the magicians of *Jannes and Mambre* and to
Ham and the Egyptians in the *Cave of Treasures*.   It
does not appear that the Gypsies were found in any
considerable numbers in the west, since all the accounts
locate them in the Byzantine Empire.   They were, however, settled in the northern part of the Balkan Peninsula, and in the XIV. century sedentary Gypsies are
frequently recorded in Hungary,[2] whence they began
their westward movement in 1417, unquestionably

---

[1] J. Diemer, *Genesis und Exodus nach der Milstäter Handschrift*, Wien 1862,
vol. I, p. 36.
[2] See my article *Ismaelites*, in *Journal of the Gypsy Lore Society*, new series,
vol. IV, p. 83 ff.

under the pressure of the Turkish invasions, which had been begun in the previous century. The later history of the Gypsies[1] is of no interest to us here, except that it shows that in a thousand years the Gypsies have changed little from their original state. Their influence upon social conditions in Europe has upon the whole been small, since they had nothing to add to the store of European civilization.

[1] For a full bibliography on the subject, see G. F. Black, *A Gypsy Bibliography*, London 1914.

CHAPTER III.

THE GYPSIES IN AFRICA.

The Gypsies of Persia are known by several names, among which are the *āhingar* "blacksmiths, tinkers," and *gerbal-band*[1] "sieve-makers," with whom we have become acquainted in the European sources. *Ahingar* is the Modern Persian form of Pehlevi *āsīngār*, itself for *ātsīngār*, hence in the Modern Syriac *jingānih* "Gypsy" we see a corrupted Pehlevi *āsīngār*, even as the European Gypsy words, such as German *Zigeuner*, are similar corruptions of the original Pehlevi word. The Syrians also have the designation *rūmeli* and *kurbāt* for the Gypsies. The first is unquestionably derived from the Gypsy *romani* "Gypsy."

The most common word in the early Arabic authors of Egypt for Gypsy is زعر , ذعر , دعر *da'r, dza'r, za'r*, also ذعار *dzu'ār*.[2] The first means "vile," but the great variety of forms indicates that this is merely a popular etymology and that the original form was more nearly *dzigar*, that is, a word derived from *ātsīngār*. A Modern Arabic form is عجر *gaǵar*, no doubt another transformation of the same word. Al-Maqrīzī frequently refers to a class of people with Gypsy characteristics as رمضيه *ramaḍīah* or *rumaḍiah*, and Quatremère is unquestionably right when he identifies them with

---

[1] Capt. Newbold, *The Gypsies of Egypt*, in *The Journal of the Royal Asiatic Society of Great Britain and Ireland*, vol. XVI, part II, p. 310.

[1] R. Dozy, *Dictionnaire détaillé des noms des vêtements chez les Arabes*, Amsterdam 1845, p. 259.

our Gypsies.[1] The word, like Syriac *rūmeli*, is again our Gypsy *romani*.

The Egyptian *gaǧars* are conscious of their relationship to the Hungarian Gypsies. They are tinkers and blacksmiths, vend earrings, amulets, bracelets and instruments of iron and brass, and, above all, are thieves.[2] There is also a class of Gypsies known as *Nūris* or *Nāwars*, which Quatremère takes to be from Arabic نور *nūr* "light," since among the XIII. century writers on Egypt we frequently hear of مشعليه *maš'alīah* "executioners," whose name was derived from Arabic مشعل *maš'al* "a lantern," which they carried before them.[3] The scanty vocabulary of the Nāwars, as recorded by Newbold,[4] shows Gaǧar affinities.

The greater number of the Egyptian Gypsies belong to the حلبي *ḥelebī*, who, like the rest, "are looked down upon with almost the same horror as the Pariahs of India by the Brahmans."[5] "The male Helebis are chiefly ostensible dealers in donkeys, horses, camels, cattle, &c., and pretend to great skill in the veterinary art; but their character for common honesty does not stand very high in the estimation of those who know them best. With their women, they lead a vagabond life, but return to the towns at stated periods. Their wanderings are confined to the Rif, or valley of the Nile, and to the Delta, rarely extending far into the desert, except when they go forth to meet the *Hájj*, on its return from Mecca, in order to cheat the way-sick pilgrims out of their jaded beasts, or to sell cattle-medicines. Some few accompany the *Hájj* all the way to

[1] M. Quatremère, *Histoire des sultans mamlouks*, Paris 1837, vol. I, part II, p. 5 f.
[2] Newbold, *op. cit.*, p. 292 ff.
[3] *Op. cit.*, p. 4 f.
[4] *Op. cit.*, p. 295 ff.
[5] *Ibid.*, p. 285.

Mecca; and, having performed the pilgrimage, are proud of prefixing *Hájji* to their names—a title, however, which among the more experienced Cairenes is supposed to add but little to a man's credit in the ordinary dealings of life 'If your neighbour,' say they, 'has performed *one hájj*, be suspicious of him; if *two*, avoid him; but if *three*, then by all means give up your house immediately, and seek another in some remote quarter.'

"The Helebis usually live in tents or *kheish* (portable huts), which they pitch on the outskirts of some large village or town.   Near Cairo they are to be found at certain seasons (chiefly during the winter and spring), near a village on the right of the road from Cairo to Shúbra.   They are expert in disguises, and hardly yield the palm to their brethren in Europe in cunning and deception."[1] "The female Helebis (the Fehemis), as before stated, practice palmistry and divination. During their halts on the outskirts of towns and villages, and in roaming about the streets, bazars, and coffee-houses, in different disguises, they contrive to pick up, with wonderful tact and accuracy, the information necessary to their vocation, regarding the private history and prospects of persons with whom they are thrown in contact.   In this secret intelligence department they are also assisted by their male relations, who, it is said, are to be found in every official department in Egypt, though not known to be gypsies; and, at all events, mingle much both with residents on the spot, and with strangers in the coffee-houses and caravanserais.

"Practice of Palmistry and Divination.—In practising the art of palmistry, the Fehemi takes the right hand of the inquirer into the book of destiny into her own, holding it by the tips of the fingers, which she

[1] *Ibid.*, p. 286 f.

often bends gently back, so as to render the lines on the palm more distinct. Muttering some spell, she looks gravely and earnestly into these lines for a moment or two; and then raising her penetrating eyes, fixes them steadily on those of the fortune seeker, gazing into them as if reading his destiny, written in large characters, at the bottom. She then unfolds to him the result with much decision and emphasis. The tale she tells is very much like what the gypsy women impart to the nursery maids and young lads on Blackheath. There are the different dangers and felicities awaiting them at different epochs of life—the dark or light lady, or gentleman, who is to love and be loved—the jealous enemy of whom they are to beware—the number of children they are to have, &c. It is almost unnecessary to add that in most cases the weight of the silver coin, with which the sybil's hand must be crossed, exerts a corresponding influence over the future (silvery or coppery, as the case may be) aspect of the aspirant's fortunes.

"In divination, the Fehemi seats herself on a mat or carpet at the foot of the divan, or on the floor, and empties her gazelle-skin bag of a portion of its contents, viz., small shells, broken bits of glass, small coloured stones of agate, jasper, basalt, &c.; coloured bits of wax, &c. She throws the shells repeatedly on the carpet, after much jugglery, grimace, repeating spells, &c.; and from the position they chance to lie in she draws her inferences, much in the same way as the servant girls in England tell their fortunes from the arrangement of the grounds of tea at the bottom of their cups.

"On one occasion the shell, which is supposed to represent the person whose fortune is being told, happened to fall in the centre of a circle formed by the other shells being accidently ranged round it. This answer to the question, which was: 'Will his friends prove faithful in the hour of need?' was interpreted as highly favourable.

"Thus the Fehemi goes on casting the shells and divining from them.   Money is required at various stages of the operation, and the farce usually concludes with the gypsy's presenting a few bits of coloured stone or wax to her employer as charms.

"I witnessed a curious trick played by one of the Fehemi women near Cairo in this sort of divination. She put one of the shells—a small cowry—into a basin of clear water, which was placed on the carpet of the floor, at the foot of the divan where a friend and myself were seated, enjoying our chibouqes and coffee.   She then covered the basin with a cloth, and directed me to repeat after her an invocation in Arabic, and, while doing so, retired a few feet from the basin, after taking off the cloth, to the edge of the carpet.   The shell was seen lying under the water, at the bottom of the basin as before; but no sooner was the invocation finished than the water bubbled up, and the shell was shot out to the distance of several feet, with some of the water, with a slight explosion, like that of a percussion-cap thrown into the fire.

"This, doubtless, was the effect of some chemical substance, placed probably in the shell itself; but whether the secret of its preparation be a remnant of the art of ancient Egypt, or vended to the gypsies by some itinerant charlatan from Europe, is doubtful.   The last appears the more reasonable hypothesis.

"The Fehemi women, as well as the men, have a family resemblance to the Kurbáts of Syria.   They are noted for their chastity, in contradistinction to the Ghagar women.   Intrigues, however, have happened, but, if discovered, they are punished with death; the woman being usually thrown into the Nile, with a bag of stones tied to her neck.

"Until their marriage the young Fehemi females wear a cincture of silk or cotton thread round their loins, in token of virginity. They never intermarry with the Arabs, Copts, or other inhabitants of Egypt. In this respect they are as rigid as the Hindus. They are not remarkable for cleanliness either of person or apparel; in this respect, and their passion for trinkets of brass, silver, and ivory, they remind one of the Brinjári women of India.

"They are remarkably intelligent, quick in gaining information, and would make capital spies in an enemy's camp. An instance of their shrewdness in this respect fell under my own observation. Passing their encampment one day, I persuaded my companion to stop and have his fortune told; to which, after some demur, he at last consented. While the gypsy woman was looking at the lines of his hand, I took the opportunity of inspecting the interior of their tents. They resembled those of the common Bedouin of the desert, and contained little beyond some wretched horse and donkey furniture, pots, pans, &c. Everything externally denoted the most squalid poverty, excepting only an enormous mess of fowls, mutton, and savoury vegetables, seething in a large iron cauldron over a wood fire; and which proved, to more senses than one, that the care of the flesh-pots of ancient Egypt had not devolved on a race insensible to their charms. On return, I found my companion still in the hands of the gypsy, now listening to her tale with as much seriousness in his face as there was merriment and mockery before.

"When she had finished, he told me that he had been perfectly astounded in hearing from her lips a circumstance which, to the best of his recollection, he had never divulged to any person; but which, no doubt, must have on some occasion inadvertently escaped him."[1] "The Helebis do not give their daughters in

[1] *Ibid.*, p. 287 ff.

marriage to the Ghagars, though they occasionally marry Ghagar damsels.   The *húg* or *dilk* (zone of chastity) is often made of plaited leather, like the waist-covering of the women of Soudan, and is cut off on the wedding night.

"The Helebi females, though chaste themselves, occasionally do not scruple to act as procuresses of Gentile or *Husno* women, and will even sometimes expose their own persons for a reward.   The Arabs and Copts charge them with kidnapping children; but this they strenuously deny, as well as the common accusation of their eating cats and dogs, and other animals held in abhorrence by Moslems.

"They bury their dead, but have no fixed places of interment."[1]

The collective name of the *helebī* is محلباش *maḥlibāš*, which at once leads to Greek Χάλυβες, the word which we found glossed in Charlemagne's law of 789 as "nudi cum ferro," hence the Gypsies in Egypt go back at least to the Greek occupation, after the Persians, as we have already found from other considerations.   The lengthening of حلبى to حلباش is universal in Arabic and shows its un-Arabic origin.   We have Arabic خليبى *ḥillība* "deceit, guile," خالب *ḥālib*, خلوب *ḥalūb* "deceitful," خلا ه *ḥallābah* "enchanter," and, at the same time, خلبوص *ḥalbūṣ* "servant of the almeh, buffoon," that is, we come back to our Gypsies.   "The Helebis pretend to derive their origin from Yemen or the Hadramāt; and assert that the early history of their race is chronicled in a written record, called the *Tariḥ az-Zīr*, which, as far as I can glean, is an obscure and unsatisfactory document.   From Yemen, they say, their tribes were expelled by the persecutions of Zīr, a king of the Tūba

[1] *Ibid.*, p. 293.

race; and wandered over Syria, Egypt, Persia, and Europe. The seven brother chiefs of the tribes which migrated into Egypt obtained from its sovereign the privilege of exemption from taxes, and of wandering about the country without molestation. The tombs of these seven chiefs are regarded by the Helebis as holy places to this day. Two of them are said to be in the Bahriyeh district, one in the Kelyubiyeh, and the rest in the Syud."[1]

The Helebis, Gaǧars, and Nāwars, no doubt, represent different migrations of the Gypsies, and there is no reason to cast any doubt on the assertion of the Helebis that they came from Arabia. Indeed, the Helebis are found in Arabia under the name of صليب Ṣlēb, a slightly changed form of the Egyptian name. Oppenheim saw them in northern Arabia: "Not far from the Hufne there were encamped about twenty Ṣlēb, who belong to a remarkable tribe, who in their appearance and manner of life in many ways differ from the Arab Bedouins. Generally less tall than these, they subsist chiefly on the chase of gazelles, the skins of which they often wear as clothing. The women, to begin with, are remarkable for their wonderful beauty. I saw in Ruḥbe a Ṣlēbīye of moderate height, with a tawny complexion, small face, melancholy, but flashing eyes beneath long lashes, superb, straight, black hair, and magnificent teeth. The Ṣlēb seldom own horses or camels, and generally ride on small donkeys of great endurance, and occasionally keep a few sheep and goats. The Ṣlēb live in peace with nearly all the desert tribes, and, in exchange for the hospitality which they receive on all sides, and for the immunity to their scanty property, they everywhere offer their services as guides, for no one knows the desert so well as the Ṣlēbī. At certain

[1] *Ibid.*, p. 291.

occasions the Ṣlēb men and women dance for the Bedouins, for which they receive presents.   The ethnographical origin of Ṣlēb has not yet been fully established, but in all probability they are not Semites, but of Hindu origin.   It is said that the later Khalifs had Indian musicians sent to their court at Bardād, who, upon the arrival of Tamurlan, wandered into the desert.   I have heard the opinion that the modern Ṣlēb are descendants of those musicians.   At the present time the Ṣlēb are to be found from Aleppo to the Persian Gulf, south of the Euphrates.   Whereas the Bedouins wander about by tribes, the Ṣlēb roam only by families, sometimes only by twos or threes, and occasionally even without tents, but they bury their dead, if possible, only in large common cemeteries.   They to a certain extent may rightfully be called 'the Gypsies of the desert.' "[1]

Pelly[2] gives other current notions about the Ṣlēb, from which we only learn that they were held in contempt by the Bedouins: "A few miscellaneous remarks on the Selabah or Selaib tribe, based on information collected among themselves, may be interesting.

"The caste is called Seleb or Selaib, because on certain festivals, and particularly on occasions of marriage and circumcision, they fix a wooden cross, dressed in red cloth and adorned at the top with feathers, at the door of the person married or circumcised.   At this signal the people collect and dance round the cross.   They have a particular dance.   The young men stand opposite their female partners, each advances, and the youth slightly kisses the shoulder of the maiden: anything like touch of the hand or waist is out of etiquette.

[1] M. Oppenheim, *Vom Mittelmeer zum Persischen Golf*, Berlin 1899, vol. I, p. 220 f.

[2] L. Pelly, *A Visit to the Wahabee Capital, Central Arabia*, in *The Journal of the Royal Geographical Society*, vol. XXXV, p. 189 ff.

"The word Seleeb means a cross.   But some of the
caste derive their name from As-Solb-Al-Arab, *i.e.*, from
the back of the Arabs—meaning to assert that they are
pure descendants of aboriginal Arabs.   The Mohammedans, on the other hand, stigmatise them as out-
castes.   The tradition is that, when Nimrod was about
to cast Abraham into the fire, some angels appeared and
protected him.   Eblis or Satan then made his appearance and pointed out to the bystanders that if someone
would only commit a shameful crime, the angels would
be obliged to depart, and thus Abraham would be left
unprotected.   Upon this one of the Arabs lay with his
own mother, and forthwith the angels fled.   Upon this
the angel Gabriel came to the rescue, and changed the
spot where the fire was kindled into a garden.   The descendants of the man who lay with his mother were,
thenceforward, called As-Selaib.

"The Selaib who have emigrated into Nejd and other
Mohammedan settlements conform outwardly to the
religious rites and ceremonies of the dominant creed.
But in their own tents, or when alone, they do not so
conform.

"No intermarriage takes place between the Selaib and
the Arabs.   Even a Bedouin will not stop to plunder a
Selaib, nor to revenge a blood feud against him.   The
Selaib are capital sportsmen.   They live largely on
deer's flesh, and wear a long shirt of deerskin coming
down to the feet.   Their common diet is locusts, and
dates when procurable; but they will eat anything.
They tend their sheep and camels, wander for pasturage
during eight months of the year, and for the remainder
seek some town or village where to exchange their produce for necessaries of life.   Their tents are black, of
goat's hair, and are pitched separate from those of the
Arabs.   The Selaib are filthy in appearance; but the

Arabs confess that, in point of features, the Selaib
women are the most beautiful among them.

"Forty days after birth a child must be washed, being
dipped seven times in water.

"Marriage is contracted by mutual consent of the
parties.   The assent of the father, or failing him, of the
nearest of kin, must also be obtained.   The father of
the girl receives some sort of payment, according to the
ability of the bridegroom.   The parties go before a
mollah, or an elder of the tribe, who asks them three
several times if they freely consent to the union.
The parties replying in the affirmative, the mollah takes
his fee, and they cohabit.   The neighbours then collect
at the tent, sheep are killed for them, and they dance.
The only invitation is the sign of the cross fixed outside
the tent.

"The Selaib wash their dead, cover the body with a
white shroud, and inter it with a prayer.   Failing a
white shroud, they use a new shirt of deer-skin.

"They profess to reverence Mecca, but state that
their own proper place of pilgrimage is Haran, in Irak
or Mesopotamia.   They say also that their principal
people have some psalms and other books written in
Chaldean or Assyrian.   They respect the Polar star,
which they call Jah, as the one immovable point which
directs all travellers by sea and land.   They reverence
also a star in the constellation, called Jeddy, corresponding with Aries.   In adoring either of these
heavenly bodies the Selaib stands with his face towards
it, and stretches out his arms so as to represent a cross
with his own body.   They believe in one God.   Some
of them pretend to believe in Mohammed.   Others
deny the prophet, but trust in certain intermediate
beings, who are called the confidants of God.   They
pray three times a day: first, as the sun rises, so as to
finish the prayer just when the entire disc is above the

horizon; secondly, before the sun begins to decline from the meridian; and thirdly, so as to finish the prayer as the sun sets. It is asserted, however, that the Selaib of Haran have pure forms of prayer, in the Assyrian or Chaldean. They fast three times a year: for thirty days in Ramadan; for four or seven days in Shāban, and for five or nine days in a summer month. They are peaceful, and are undisturbed by the Arabs, who hold them below injury. They are markedly hospitable, like all people who have nothing to give. They assert themselves to be a tribe of the Sabians emigrated to Nejd. The Mohammedans deny this. The Selaib eat carrion and profess themselves to be the chosen people of God, who pay no tribute or tax, since no one will deign to receive it from them."

The fullest account of these Arabic Gypsies is given by Doughty:[1] "As we went by to the mejlis, 'Yonder (said Zeyd) I shall show thee some of a people of antiquity.' This was a family which then arrived of poor wanderers, *Solubba*. I admired the full-faced shining flesh-beauty of their ragged children, and have always remarked the like as well of the Heteym nomads. These alien and outcast kindreds are of fairer looks than the hunger-bitten Beduw. The Heteym, rich in small cattle, have food enough in the desert, and the Solubba of their hunting and gipsy labour: for they are tinkers of kettles and menders of arms, in the Beduin menzils. They batter out upon the anvil hatchets, *jedûm*, (with which shepherds lop down the sweet acacia boughs, to feed their flocks,) and grass-hooks for cutting forage, and steels for striking fire with the flint, and the like. They are besides woodworkers, in the desert acacia timber, of rude saddle-trees for the burden-camels, and of the thelûl saddle-frames, of pulley reels, (*máhal*) for drawing at any deeper wells of the desert, also of rude

---

[1] C. Doughty, *Travels in Arabia Deserta*, Cambridge 1888, vol. I, p. 280 ff.

milk vessels, and other such husbandry: besides, they are cattle surgeons, and in all their trade (only ruder of skill) like the smiths' caste or *Sunna*.   The Solubba obey the precept of their patriarch, who forbade them to be cattle-keepers, and bade them live of their hunting in the wilderness, and alight before the Beduin booths, that they might become their guests, and to labour as smiths in the tribes for their living.   Having no milch beasts, whereso they ask it at a Beduin tent, the house-wife will pour out léban from her semîla, but it is in their own bowl, to the poor Solubba: for Beduins, otherwise little nice, will not willingly drink after Solubbies, that might have eaten of some *futîs*, or the thing that is dead of itself.   Also the Beduw say of them, 'they eat of vile insects and worms:' the last is fable, they eat no such vermin.   Rashly the evil tongue of the Beduin rates them as 'kuffâr', because only few Solubbies can say the formal prayers, the Beduins are themselves not better esteemed in the towns.   The Solubba show a good humble zeal for the country religion in which they were born, and have no notice of any other; they are tolerant and, in their wretched manner, humane, as they themselves are despised and oppressed persons.

"In summer, when the Beduw have no more milk, loading their light tents and household stuff, with what they have gained, upon asses, which are their only cattle, they forsake the Aarab encampment, and hold on their journey through the wide khála.   The Solubby house-hold go then to settle themselves remotely, upon a good well of water, in some unfrequented wilderness, where there is game.   They only (of all men) are free of the Arabian deserts to travel whithersoever they would; paying to all men a petty tribute, they are molested by none of them.   Home-born, yet have they no citizen-ship in the Peninsula.   No Beduwy, they say, will rob a Solubby, although he met him alone, in the deep of the wilderness, and with the skin of an ostrich in his hand, that is worth a thelûl. But the wayfaring Beduwy would be well content to espy, pitched upon some lone watering, the booth of a Solubby, and hope to eat there of his hunter's pot; and the poor Solubby will make the man good cheer of his venison. They ride even hunting upon ass-back. It is also on these weak brutes, which must drink every second day, (but otherwise the ass is hardly less than the camel a beast of the desert,) that they journey with their families through great waterless regions, where the Beduwy upon his swift and puissant thelûl, three days patient of thirst, may not lightly pass. This dispersed kindred of desert men in Arabia, outgo the herdsmen Beduw in all land-craft, as much as these go before the tardy oases villagers. The Solubba (in all else ignorant wretches,) have inherited a land-lore from sire to son, of the least finding-places of water. They wander upon the immense face of Arabia, from the height of Syria to el-Yémen, beyond *et-Tâif*, and I know not how much further!—and for things within their rat-like understanding, Arabians tell me, it were of them that a man may best enquire.

"They must be masters in hunting, that can nourish themselves in a dead land; and where other men may hardly see a footprint of venison, there oftentimes, the poor Solubbies are seething sweet flesh of gazelles and bedûn, and, in certain sand districts, of the antelope; everywhere they know their quarries' paths and flight. It is the Beduw who tell these wonders of them; they say, 'the S'lubba are like herdsmen of the wild game, for when they see a troop they can break them and choose of them as it were a flock, and say, "These will we have to-day, as for those other heads there, we can take them after to-morrow". '—It is human to magnify, and find a pleasant wonder, this kind of large speaking is a magnanimity of the Arabs; but out of

doubt, the Solubba are admirable wayfarers and hardy
men, keen, as living of their two hands, and the best
sighted of them are very excellent hunters.   The Solubba or *Slèyb*, besides this proper name of their nation,
have some others which are epithets.   West of Hâyil
they are more often called *el-Khlûa* or *Kheluîy*, 'the
desolate,' because they dwell apart from the *Kabâil*,
having no cattle nor fellowship;—a word which the
Beduw say of themselves, when in a journey, finding no
menzil of the Aarab, they must lie down to sleep
'solitaries' in the empty khála.   They are called as well
in the despiteful tongue of this country, Kilâb el-Khála,
'hounds of the wilderness.'   *El-Ghrúnemy* is the name
of another kindred of the Slèyb in East Nejd; and it is
said, they marry not with the former   The Arabians
commonly suppose them all to be come of some old
kafir kind, or Nasâra.

"—Neither are the Sherarát and Heteym nomads
(which are of one blood) reckoned to the Beduin tribes.
The dispersed kindreds of Sunna are other home-born
aliens living amongst the Aarab, and there is no marry-
ing between any of them.   *Mâ li-hum asl*, say the
Beduw, 'They are not of lineage,' which can be understood to signify that 'not descended of Kahtân, neither
of the stock of Ishmael, they are not of the Arabs.'
And if any Arabians be asked, What then are they?
they answer: 'Wellah, we cannot tell but they come
of evil kin, be it Yahûd or Nasâra' (this is, of the
Ancients which were in the land before Mohammed, and
of whom they have hardly any confused tradition).
As often as I met with any Solubba I have asked of
their lineage: but they commonly said again, wonder-
ing, 'What is this to enquire of us *mesquins* dwelling in
these deserts? we have no books nor memory of
things past: but read thou, and if anything of this be
written, tell us.'   Some said the name of their an-

cestor is *M'aibî*; the Beduw also tell of them, that which is read in Arabic authors, how they were the *Aarab Jessàs*, once Beduins: being destroyed in their controversy with the *Aarab K'leyb* and bereaved of all their cattle, they for their livelihood took up this trade of the hammer, and became Solubba. Later in the summer I found some Solubba families pitched under the kella at el-Héjr, who were come over the Harra and the Teháma from Wejh, their own station. At that season they make a circuit; last year they had wandered very far to the south, and I saw their women grinding a minute wheaten grain, which they had brought from a wady near Mecca! They (as coast and Hejâz dwellers) were of more civil understanding than the uplandish Solubba. To my questions the best of them answered, 'We are Aarab K'fâ, of old time possessors of camels and flocks, as the Beduw: those were our villages, now ruins, in the mountains southward of el-Ally, as *Skeirát* in *Wady Sódr*; but at last our people became too weak to maintain themselves in an open country, and for their more quietness, they fell to this trade of the Solubba. Said one of them, 'We are all *Beny Murra*, and fellowship of *Sâlim Ibn ez-Zîr*, from the hill *Jemla*, a day on the east side of Medina; we are called *Motullij* and *Derrûby*.' Haj Nejm laughed as I came again, at 'this strange fantasy of Khalîl, always to be enquiring somewhat, even of such poor folk. Khalîl! these are the *Beny Morr*, they are dogs, and what is there besides to say of them?'

"When Beduins asked me if I could not tell them by book-craft what were the Solubba, it displeased them when I answered, 'A remnant, I suppose, of some ancient Aarab;' they would not grant that Solubbies might be of the right Arabian kindred. All who are born in the Arabs' tongue are curious etymologers; a negro, hearing our discourse, exclaimed, 'Well, this is likely that

Khalîl says; is not Solubba to say *Sulb el-Arab*, the Arab's stock?' The poor soul (who had spoken a little in malice, out of his black skin, for which he was dispraised among the white Arabs) was cried down by the other etymologers, which were all the rest of the company, and with great reason, for they would not have it so. 'The Solubba are rich (say the Arabs), for they take our money, and little or nothing comes forth again; they need spend for no victuals. They have corn and dates enough, besides samn and mereesy, for their smith's labour.' The Solubby has need of a little silver in his metal craft, to buy him solder and iron; the rest, increased to a bundle of money, he will, they say, bury in the desert sooner than carry it along with him, and return perhaps after years to take it up again, having occasion it may be to buy him an ass. Yet there are said to be certain Solubba, keepers of a few cattle, towards Mesopotamia; living under their own sheukh, and riders upon dromedaries. I have seen a sheykhly northern man, honourably clad, at Hâyil, who was a Solubby; he invited me (I think at the great Emir's bidding) to ride with him in the next mountains, seeking for metals. I asked, 'Upon what beast?' He said I should ride upon an ass, 'we have no other.' I would gladly have ridden out of Hâyil into the free air; but I thought a man's life was not to trust with abjects, men not of the Beduin tradition in faithful fellowship. Even the Solubba hold to circuits, and lodge by their tribes and oases. There are Solubby families which have their home station, at some settlement, as Teyma; but the most remain in the desert. The Sunna are some settled in the villages, and some are wandering men with the tribes, leading their lives as nomads, and possessors of cattle. The Solubba outcast from the commonwealth of mankind, and in disgrace of the world, their looks are of destitute humility. Their ragged hareem, in what encampment they alight, will beg somewhat, with a lamentable voice, from beyt to beyt, of the poor tolerant Beduw: yet other (as those from Wejh) are too well clad, and wellfaring honest persons, that their wives should go a-mumming. I have seen young men, which were Slèyb, in the Syrian wilderness, clad in coats of gazelle-skins. The small Solubby booth is mostly very well stored, and they have daily meat to put under their teeth, which have not the most poor Beduins."

Leaving out all conjectures by the different authors, and the Ṣlēb varying accounts of their origin, we are left only with the positive fact that the Ṣlēb are either a pure or mixed race of Gypsies. What a pity that no study of their dialect has been made! It would be interesting to know whether any Gypsy words are left among them. Considering the fact that the Egyptian Gypsies, especially the Nāwars, have but a few words of Indian origin left in their vocabulary, it is not at all impossible that no such words would be preserved in Arabia, even as Gypsies may be found in Europe who no longer speak Romani.

Gypsies are found as far south as Abyssinia, but unfortunately the information about them is scanty: "I saw here the first gipsy encampment in Abyssinia, curious people with a red brown complexion, long straight black hair with regular gipsy features. The Abyssinians dislike them and believe they are capable of doing all sorts of mischief by magic and other means. They had with them a lot of waterproof grass baskets and wooden bowls and platters, which they manufacture and sell at the markets. . .they live by catching animals and they have the reputation of being great thieves, helping themselves at night time to the growing crops; in habits therefore they resemble the English gipsies. There are only a few bands of them left in the country, and I regret that Hailou would not allow me to enter into conversation with them; he pulled out his crucifix from the inside of his shirt and held it between himself and them until he got out of their sight."[1]

It cannot always be said that these pariahs are of Hindu origin, because intermixtures have taken place in the past, and even where totally unrelated races have been reduced to abject servility, it is remarkable that under Arabic influence the profession of the blacksmith has been connected with this low estate.   Such is the case with at least some of the low caste Somalis: "The great Somali social order is divided in two large ethnic groups distinctly separated in the two component races. The pure Somali race, called *Gob*, consists of various tribes, which, although tradition assigns to them different origins, differ very little in their social organization, and the impure race of the pariahs, *Gum*, consists of the proscribed and rejected people, known under the name of *Tumal*, *Midgan*, and *Yibir*.   The population of the first group, *Gob*, may conveniently be divided into three classes, namely: 1)Sedentary Somalis, a small class that lives in the coast villages, or nearby, or connected with confraternities (the most civilized); 2) People occupied in trade, who take large caravans from the interior to the coast, during the commercial period of cool weather, and *vice versa* (merchants, hence few in number, but real vehicles of progress); 3)Nomad Somalis, who keep cattle, goats, sheep, and camels, and raise horses and oxen, and lead the lives of Bedouins, roaming through the bush according to the rainy season in search of pasturage for their beasts (shepherds, naturally the most restive).   In the second group, the *Gum*, the origin of the subcastes is unknown. They are easily distinguished from the true Somalis by their ignoble appearance, their less proud and bold

[1] A. Wylde, *Modern Abyssinia*, London 1901, p. 338 f.

aspect, their coarse features, but they are not slaves. They are not organized, and live by families, confusedly scattered in the whole country amidst the known tribes. The *Tumal* (also known under the name of *Tum-tum*) are exclusively blacksmiths, manufacturers, and manipulators of all kinds of weapons, such as arrows, lances, knives, horse bits, hooks, daggers, and all kinds of small utensils for the people. The *Midgan*, who resemble the Somalis, but are of smaller stature, are the most numerous among the proscribed class, and have no especial occupation, and usually enter service, drive cattle, and do similar things. They are armed with a bow and poisoned arrows, which they carry in a quiver, and a small knife, and generally live by the chase. Some of them raise certain wild dogs, which they train for the chase. Their chief game is the oryx, a large ox-like antelope, which is provided with horns of half to a whole meter in length. These two classes intermarry, and they marry occasionally, but very rarely, some low caste Somali. The *Midgan* are often used in the tribal wars as messengers, explorers, ambushers and excellent spies. The *Yiber*, the lowest class, are considered even more abject than the poor and despised *Tumal* and *Midgan*. These *Yiber*, avoided and despised by all, live by themselves, begging here and there for a miserable bit, living on anything that they find, often on the flesh of animals fallen dead on the road. For garment they wear a skin rag over their loins, and another very small one which serves them for a mantle over their shoulders. They bear neither lance nor shield and, like the *Midgan*, always walk armed with a bow and poisonous arrows and a long double-edged knife, which they carry tied to the waist by a strap. They are leather-workers and make saddles, sheaths, bags, straps, amulets, etc. They are nearly always charlatans and mystifiers by profession, act as buffoons

on holidays, weddings and other solemn occasions.   It
is said that often they sell their children, and that they
are not allowed to follow the Somalis to war.   It is
customary for the first *Yiber* who arrives in a kraal,
where a boy is born, to receive from the family of the
new-born child a small present, which may be a piece of
cotton ware or a kid, or lamb, or other small thing.
Such a customary present in these circumstances is
called *samanyo*, and he who receives it gives to the
donor in return, as a proof of such a receipt, an amulet,
called *macran*, which consists of a small piece of wood
or bark of a certain tree, enclosed in a bit of kid leather,
which is placed about the neck of the child, so that
when another *Yiber* passes he may see that the *samanyo*
has been paid and the *macran* received.   If the new-
born child is a girl, no present is given.   Similarly the
Yiber receive the same kind of present from every
youth who gets married, when they give another small
macran of the same kind, which the bride keeps in the
house for a whole year, after which it is thrown away.
The families of the *Yiber*, now small in number, are
steadily disappearing."[1]

The structure of society in the Western Sudan is in
essence identical with that of the Somalis just studied.
Among the Malinkes, of whom the majority are Moslems, the tribe is divided into two portions, those who
are free, and those who are captives, while the free
portion is again subdivided into five castes:

"(1) The *Horos*, who are citizens.
(2) The *Sohrés*, weavers.
(3) The *Garangis*, or shoemakers.
(4) The *Hrabis*, or blacksmiths.
(5) The *Yellimanis*, or jesters.

[1] R. Bricchetti, *Somalia e Benadir*, Milano 1899, p. 214 ff.

"The *Horos* are the only class from which chiefs and headmen can be selected. They are the predominant caste, and all the others are their menials.

"*Horos* can only marry in their own class. The other people can marry amongst themselves as they please.

"The *Hrabis* are looked on with great contempt, corresponding in caste to the sweeper class of India. It is uncertain what was the origin of this, but there is a story connected with Mohammed and a blacksmith which probably accounts for it. It is said that the Prophet was once pursued by some infidels, and concealed himself in the trunk of a tree near the spot where a blacksmith was at work. The latter was on the point of betraying Mohammed's hiding-place when he was struck blind by God. Mohammed, when he issued from the tree, is supposed to have cursed the blacksmith and all his kind.

"The *Yellimanis* are a very obnoxious class. They spend their time in abusing those who do not give them any money, while they sing the praises of their patrons. Every chief has an entourage of these jesters. They are often equipped with musical instruments, and form a sort of band which precedes him wherever he goes."[1]

For *horo* the Malinke dictionary[2] gives *foro*, and translates it by "free man." This is Arabic ﺣﺮ *hurr* "free," which indicates that the borrowing of the divisions is from the Arabs.

Delafosse[3] more justly classes Sudanese society in three castes, of which the first, the *Horos*, busy themselves with occupations that do not demand any special training, such as agriculture, fishing, cattle raising, hunting, war. The second category includes the pro-

[1] A. Haywood, *Through Timbuctu and across the Great Sahara*, London 1912, p. 57 f.
[2] [Abiven], *Dictionnaire français-malinké et malinké-français*, Conakry 1906.
[3] M. Delafosse, *Haut-Sénégal-Niger*, Paris 1912, series I, vol. III, p. 115 ff.

fessions of religion and commerce, that is, the occupations of the merchant, tailor, weaver, painter, or Moslem preacher or teacher.   The third category comprises the true castes, and here one finds the workers in wood, clay, leather, and the metals.   Each one of these forms a special caste, and to these must be added the two castes of the *griots*, kinds of buffoons, musicians, bards and professional dancers, who attach themselves to kings and famous warriors and extol their exploits. To these must be added the caste of magicians, doctors, sorcerers, manufacturers and merchants of talismans, fortune-tellers, etc.

The oldest reference we possess to the Mandingo bards is contained in Ibn-Batutah's account of his voyage to the African kingdom of Malli: "On the holiday, after the Sultan Dūgā has finished his games, the poets come, who are called *ǵulā*, in the singular *ǵālī*.   They make their entrance, every one of them in the hollow of a figure formed by feathers, which resembles a *šigšāg*, or a kind of sparrow, to which a wooden head has been attached with a red beak, to imitate the head of this bird.   They stand before the Sovereign in this ridiculous make-up, and recite their poetry to him.   I have been informed that it consists of a kind of admonition and that they say to the Sultan: 'This *penpi* on which you are now seated was occupied by such and such a king, who has done such and such generous deeds; another has done such and such noble acts, etc.   So you, in your turn, do likewise that you may be remembered after death.'   Then the chief of the bards climbs the steps of the *penpi* and places his head in the Sultan's lap; then he ascends the *penpi* itself and places his head on the right shoulder, then on the left shoulder of the Sovereign, all the time speaking in the language of the country.   Finally he descends. I have been assured that this is a very old custom, pre-

"GRIOTS."

From Reeve's *The Gambia*

vious to the introduction of Islam among these people, in which they have always persisted."[1]

A fuller account of them was given by Jobson, in 1623: "There is, without doubt, no people on the earth more naturally affected to the sound of musicke than these people; which the principall persons do hold as an ornament of their state, so as when wee come to see them, their musicke will seldome be wanting, wherein they haue a perfect resemblance to the Irish Rimer sitting in the same maner as they doe vpon the ground, somewhat remote from the company; and as they vse singing of Songs vnto their musicke, the ground and effect whereof is the rehearsall of the auncient stocke of the King, exalting his antientry, and recounting ouer all the worthy and famous acts by him or them hath been atchieued: singing likewise *extempore* vpon any occasion is offered, whereby the principall may bee pleased; wherein diuerse times they will not forget in our presence to sing in the praise of vs white men, for which he will expect from vs some manner of gratification. Also, if at any time the Kings or principall persons come vnto vs trading in the Riner, they will haue their musicke playing before them, and will follow in order after their manner, presenting a shew of State. They haue little varietie of instruments, that which is most common in vse, is made of a great gourd, and a necke thereunto fastned, resembling, in some sort, our Bandora; but they haue no manner of fret, and the strings they are either such as the place yeeldes or their inuention can attaine to make, being very vnapt to yeeld a sweete and musicall sound, notwithstanding with pinnes they winde and bring to agree in tunable notes, hauing not aboue sixe strings vpon their greatest instrument: In consortship with this they haue many times another

[1] C. Defrémery and B. Sanguinetti, *Voyages d'Ibn Batoutah*, Paris 1879, vol. IV, p. 413 f.

who playes vpon a little drumme which he holds vnder
his left arme, and with a crooked sticke in his right
hand, and his naked fingers on the left he strikes the
drumme, & with his mouth gaping open, makes a rude
noyse, resembling much the manner and countenance
of those kinde of distressed people which amongst vs
are called Changelings; I do the rather recite this that
it may please you to marke, what opinion the people
haue of the men of this profession, and how they dispose
of them after they are dead: but first I would acquaint
you of their most principall instrument, which is called
Ballards made to stand a foot aboue the ground, hollow
vnder, and hath vppon the top some seuenteene wood-
den keyes standing like the Organ, vpon which hee that
playes sitting vpon the ground, iust against the middle
of the instrument, strikes with a sticke in either hand,
about a foote long, at the end whereof is made fast a
round ball, couered with some soft stuffe, to auoyd the
clattering noyse the bare stickes would make: and vpon
either arme hee hath great rings of Iron: out of which
are wrought pretty hansomly smaller Irons to stand out,
who hold vpon them smaller rings and iuggling toyes,
which as hee stirreth his armes, makes a kinde of musicall
sound agreeing to their barbarous content: the sound
that proceeds from this instrument is worth the ob-
seruing, for we can heare it a good English mile, the
making of this instrument being one of the most ingenious things amongst them: for to euery one of these
keyes there belongs a small Iron the bignesse of a quill,
and is a foote long, the breadth of the instrument,
vpon which hangs two gourdes vnder the hollow, like
bottles, who receiues the sound, and returnes it againe
with that extraordinary loudnesse; there are not many of
these, as we can perceiue, because they are not common,
but when they doe come to any place, the resort vnto
them is to be admired; for both day and night, more

especially all the night the people continue dauncing, vntill he that playes be quite tyred out; the most desirous of dancing are the women, who dance without men, and but one alone, with crooked knees and bended bodies they foot it nimbly, while the standers by seeme to grace the dancer, by clapping their hands together after the manner of keeping time; and when the men dance they doe it with their swords naked in their hands, with which they vse some action, and both men and women when they haue ended their first dance, do giue somewhat vnto the player: whereby they are held and esteemed amongst them to be rich; and their wiues haue more Cristall blew stones and beades about them, then the Kings wiues: but if there be any licentious libertie, it is vnto these women, whose outward carriage is such wee may well conceit it: and this one especiall note, howsoeuer the people affect musicke, yet so basely doe they esteeme of the player, that when any of them die, they doe not vouchsafe them buriall, as other people haue, but set his dead corps vpright in a hollow tree, where hee is left to consume: when they haue beene demanded a reason for so doing, they will answer, they are a people, who haue alwayes a familiar conuersation with their diuell *Ho-re*: and therefore they doe so dispose of them: which opinion of theirs caused vs to neglect and especially in their hearing to play vpon any Lute or Instrument which some of vs for our priuate exercise did carry with vs, in regard if they had hapned to see vs, they would in a manner of scorne say, hee that played was a *Iuddy*: The greatest resort of people, with the most aboundance of these *Iuddies*, is at their times of Circumcision."[1]

The best modern description of the *griots*, summarizing a number of earlier authors, is that by Chéron:

[1] R. Jobson, *The Golden Trade: or, A Discouery of the Riuer Gambra, and the Golden Trade of the Aethiopians*, London 1623, p. 105 ff.

"The *griots* form the most degraded portion of the people, an abject, useless caste.   They are parasites who produce nothing whatsoever, because they are not allowed to do any manual labor.   They gain all their livelihood by exploiting the Blacks' chief fault, vanity, and impose themselves on the great and small alike. The *griot* proceeds in the most ingenious manner.   He begins by showering praises upon him from whom he wishes to obtain a present, glorifying his and his ancestors' generosity, bravery, nobility.   If he does not succeed, he will make a disadvantageous comparison between his liberality and that of one of his ancestors or of a well-known citizen.   If this means is not successful, he will ultimately attempt blackmail, conveying to him in hidden words that he knows an anecdote, the publication of which would cause him displeasure and trouble.   At last the victim gives in and the *griot* goes away, singing the greatness of his benefactor. But flattery is not the only means of a *griot's* existence, for he has other strings to his bow.

"He is indispensable at feasts and ceremonies, because, besides the buffooneries he produces and the songs he knows, he can play music on instruments which he manufactures, a kind of xylophone, guitars, flutes and drums, with which he accompanies the dances which are highly appreciated in the black continent. He is found not only at all kinds of festivities, birth, baptism, circumcision, marriage, but he is equally indispensable at funerals where he tries to console the family by exalting the virtues of the deceased.

"He is also the chronicler who knows thoroughly all the deeds and happenings of the past and who sings of the exploits of heroes.   He is also a business man to whom all kinds of business is entrusted and who executes it with dexterity.   He both brings about marriages and executes the orders of lovers.   Finally, he is the magician, the charlatan who cures more or less empirically and sells drugs, be they efficacious or not. In war the *griot* encouraged the warriors and excited their bravery.   He never took part in battle, for he bore no arms.   If he was captured, he was not only sure of having his life spared, but also of not being reduced to slavery.   He then attached himself to his victors and, without any scruple, sang their bravery and glory.   He was also employed as a spy and messenger.

"Naturally the *griot* is rarely met with living by himself, for he nearly always depends on a house from which he draws his sustenance and for whose profit he exercises his manifold industries.   The wealthier it is the more *griots* it has, for it is a sign of opulence to be able to feed useless mouths for its mere pleasure.   The oldest *griot* always plays a considerable part in the household, for he is the recorder of the family, the trusty of the master, who makes of him a factotum and disburdens to him some of his privileges, by transferring to him some of his authority and power.   With the chief the *griot* becomes an intimate counselor, a minister; he is a more important personage than the greatest dignitary and, although always feared, enjoys everybody's respect and consideration.

"As to the *griot's* wife, whom he can choose only in his caste, she generally has very loose manners, to the great profit of her husband.   She lives on his insinuations, calumnies, and menaces, as well as on the sale of her good offices.   She is often the confidante of a free woman, but more especially she is a hair-dresser and dancer.

"One can see that the *griots* form the dregs of society. Indeed, the Blacks consider them to be abject and degraded beings, all the same having fear of them and, consequently, certain respect for them.   In fact, the right which they possess to overwhelm with injuries those of whom they have cause to complain is the cause of their being well treated during their life-time and being shown certain consideration, but revenge is taken upon them after their death by greater affronts. The *griot's* body being regarded impure, he cannot be allowed to rest in the earth, which he would defile; and so he is allowed to rot away in the hollow of a tree."[1]

"Each group on the shores of the Senegal has its *griots*, the Moors as well as the Peuls, the Mandingos as well as the Tukolors; but, as one proceeds southward, this institution is seen to change, the *griot* by degrees becoming fetishist, he who is in contact with the spirits and who recognizes and furnishes the sorcerers. His action on his compatriots has not by any means lost by this change; on the contrary, the fetishist has greater profit and kills off more easily those whom he dislikes among the idolatrous tribes than the *griot* in the Moslem conglomerates of Senegambia.

"The *griot* exists not only in the countries that the Senegal washes, but, to tell the truth, also in all Central Africa. He is found in the Gulf of Benin as at Futa-Dyalon, in the Sudan as at Bornu, in Wadai and Darfur, on the shores of the Atlantic as on the shores of Lake Chad and the shores of the Red Sea, at Zanzibar, etc., etc. What is more, some of them travel with the caravans over truly enormous distances, retailing on their marches legends, musical airs and songs which are the admiration of the natives whom they meet."[2]

So far as I know *griot* or, rather, *guiriot* was first used by Saint Lo.[3] Its etymology will be given in the

[1] G. Chéron, *La société noire de l'Afrique Occidentale Française*, Paris 1908, p. 31 ff.

[2] L. Bérenger-Féraud, *Les peuplades de la Sénégambie*, Paris 1879, p. 375 f.

[3] "Les *Guiriots* qui les font dancer sont en ignominie parmy le commun, & quand les François veulent fascher quelque Negre, il l'appellent *Guiriot*. Or ces *Guiriots* sont extrémement importuns, car n'ayans pas accoustumé de voir quelqu'vn, ils l'accostent, & en luy chantant toutes les louanges dont

next chapter. Here we are interested only in the name these *griots* assumed among the Mandingos. We have already seen that Ibn-Batutah called them *ǵālī*, that is, *jahlee* in English pronunciation. Jobson understood this as *juddy*. In Malinke it is *dyeli* or, more nearly, *djeli*, Bambara *dyeli*. This is Berber *dejjal* "pygmy, human caricature, Antichrist," *tjal* "pygmy, ill-built, used as an expression of contempt for a low fellow." This leads us at once to Arabic دجل *daǵala* "he lied," دحال *daǵǵāl* "a liar, great deceiver, Antichrist." The *daǵǵāl* is a very common personage in Arabic eschatology, being a kind of monster or false Messiah, whom the true Messiah overcomes. In some accounts he is supposed to live in an island of the Indian Ocean, where the Arabic sailors can hear music and dancing. It is clear that this Arabic appellation of the *griot*, and the latter, as we shall later see, is also an Arabic word, disposes of the Negro origin of the bard and buffoon. It is, in connotation, an exact parallel to Arabic خلوب *ḥalūb* "deceitful," خلا *ḥallā-bah* "enchanter," which led to the *Helebi* of Egypt, that is, we have here again a Gypsy. Indeed, among the Peuls this *griot* is called *haulube* or *kolibante*, which is derived from the same Arabic *ḥalūb*, etc.

Of course, at the present time and for centuries back, the *griots* have ceased to show any Gypsy characteristics in language or blood, but there can be no doubt that the caste draws its origin from a Gypsy ancestry, which, under Arabic rule, left the Egyptian home and migrated to the Niger. We have such persistent references

ils se peuuent aduiser, ne le quittent iamais qu'ils n'ayent receu quelque chose, & voyant que l'on ne leur veut rien donner ils crient si long temps aupres des personnes que à la fin on est contraint de leur donner. Quand ils sont morts l'on les estime indignes de sepulture, car on les met debout dans quelque arbre creux, i'en ay veu le corps d'vn en ceste sorte de sepulchre," A. de S. Lo, *Relation dv voyage dv Cap-Verd*, Paris 1637, p. 87 f.

among the Peuls and others to a migration from Egypt
or the east that there must be a measure of historical
truth connected with them.　The Niger River is in
Mandingo called *Dyeli-ba*, literally "the river of the
griots," which indicates that a migration of Gypsies
from Egypt to the Niger basin took place some time in
the past.　The caste of the *griots* is distinctly one of
"Touch-me-nots," and has remained immutable through
the centuries.　Individuals within the caste have not
been able to free themselves from the curse attached to
them in the *Cave of Treasures*, though Negroes from
without must have found it profitable to join the privi-
leged, though scorned, parasites of bards.　Once included in the caste, their exit from it was impossible,
and in the course of time its ethnological constituency
was completely changed, whereas the caste as such
remained immutable.

We are now in a position to trace the Gypsy migration
from Egypt to the Niger and to show the enormous
consequences it has had upon the social and religious
conditions of the Western Sudan and upon the Negroes
throughout Africa.

According to one native legend, the Peuls of the
Western Sudan, whose red skin has long ago roused the
suspicion that they originally belonged to the white
race and, according to Delafosse,[1] were Judaeo-Syrians,
were descended from Jacob, the son of Israel, the son
of Isaac, the son of Abraham, and from Suleiman, who
came from Syria and had settled in Egypt about the
time of Joseph.　After the death of Joseph, the
Egyptians tried to subjugate the Sons of Israel, and
burdened them with taxes.　It was then that the
Judaeo-Syrians escaped from Egypt.　Some of them
regained Canaan and Syria, under the guidance of
Moses.　The others crossed the Nile under the guid-

[1] *Op. cit.*, vol. I, p. 189 ff.

ance of Suleiman and marched westward. Pharaoh pursued them, but was drowned upon trying to cross the Nile. The Judaeo-Syrians, with their herds, came to Soritu (Cyrenaica) and since that time assumed the name of *Fudh* or *Fut*, in memory of their flight. Then they marched toward the Tuat, while a part travelled to Bornu, under the guidance of two chiefs, Gadya and Gaye. Kara or Karake, a son of Gadya, and Gama, a son and successor of Gaye, led their people from Bornu to Massina, where they were hospitably received by the Soninkes.[1]

This apocryphal story has a foundation of truth, as far as the migration from Egypt westward is concerned, for the old name of the Peuls, namely *Fudh* or *Fut*, is derived from Arabic فوت ‚*faut* "escape," which is also found in Coptic *pōt*, *fōt* "escape." But this is only an Arabic or Coptic transformation of a Syriac legend, for the Biblical *Put* was by the Syrians transferred to the Zott, because Syriac *fut* means "he expressed contempt," hence the nation so called belonged to the "Touch-me-nots," that is, was identified with the Gypsies. This Syriac meaning was changed to the Arabic or Coptic, where the word means "escape," even as the Greek translation of this word in *Nahum* gives τῆς φυγῆς "flight."

There is another persistent Peul legend of their migration which has an historical basis· "According to all the traditions collected at different periods among the Peuls in the different regions of the Sudan, the Peul tribes, scattered from the lower Senegal and the Futa-Dyalon in the west to the country between the Chad and the Nile in the east, declare unanimously to have come from the Senegalese Futa or from Malil, that is, from the countries situated between the Atlantic and

[1] *Ibid.*, p. 214 f.

the Upper Niger. But they all at the same time pretend that their western ancestors themselves were descended from others who originally arrived from the north or east, or, in general, the north-east The enormous majority of these traditions assigns to these primitive ancestors, as their original home, the country of Sam or Ham, that is, Syria, as considered in its largest aspect. From there, according to these indigenous traditions, they went to the country of Tōr (the Sinai Peninsula), then from Tōr to Misira (Egypt), and from Egypt to Soritu (no doubt, the Syrtes, Cyrenaica), whence they much later reached the country of Diaka, Diaga, Dia (western Massina), where we shall find them later.

"Those of the Peuls who have been strongly Islamized have amalgamated with their traditions recollections from Islamic history. Thus many of them pretend that their first ancestors were still at Sinai, after the death of Mohammed, when, in 639, the Khalif Omar-ben-el-Khattāb (634-644) sent from the Hejaz, by the Red Sea, an army commanded by Amru-ben-el-Assi, in order to convert the Jews and infidels of Sinai and of Egypt. Amru landed at Tōr a part of his troops, under the leadership of Okba-ben-Yāsser. He converted to Islamism the majority of the Jews of Sinai, while those who refused to abjure Judaism were massacred. When Amru returned from his expedition to Arabia, in order to get the news of Okba's successes, the king of Tōr asked the Arab general to leave in his country someone capable of finishing the religious instruction of the new converts, and thus Amru left Okba at Sinai and marched toward Medina, where Khalif Omar was residing. Okba, left in Sinai, there married Tadiuma, daughter of the king of Tōr, of whom he had four children."[1]

[1] *Ibid.*, p. 211 ff.

The historical substratum is this: "In 638 the Oswāris, a non-Persian contingent of the Persian army, concluded a treaty with the Moslem general, which was confirmed by Khalif Omar, promising to embrace Islam and enter the service of the conquerors on condition of receiving the highest pay given to soldiers, of remaining free, of being permitted to associate themselves with any Arab tribe they chose, and of having to serve only against non-Arabs. Their example was followed by the Zotts and Sayābidjas, who had established themselves in the ports of the Persian Gulf and in the Irāq, and they all associated themselves with the tribe of the Tamīm."[1]

Whoever the Oswāris and the Sayābidjas may have been, the Zotts were a Hindu race from among whom came the Gypsies, but de Goeje considers even the first as Hindus.[2] The Zotts were given to the rearing of buffaloes in swampy regions, and the Arabs had to contend with them bitterly before they were able to dislodge them from their lurking places in the Euphrates and Tiger valleys.[3] In 710 a mass of these Zotts were transported with their buffaloes to Antioch. No earlier transportations are recorded, but there cannot be the slightest doubt that in the Persian army of occupation in Egypt, in the beginning of the VII. century, there were not only Gypsies, but also Zotts, as, indeed, we hear of their entering the armies of the Arabs under very favorable conditions in 638.

Apparently the Zotts were not properly treated by the Arab authorities some time after 638, and they set out with their buffaloes and in company with the Gypsies in search of new places to rear their buffaloes. It is this migration that led to the establishment of the

[1] M. de Goeje, *Mémoire sur les migrations des Tsiganes à travers l'Asie*, Leide 1903, p. 86.
[2] *Ibid.*, p. 17 f.
[3] *Ibid.*, p. 20 ff.

red-skinned Peuls in the Niger valley, whither they brought their hump-backed buffaloes, where they are still to be found.   They adopted the language of their Tukolor surroundings and later became settled among the Mandingos.   It is they who carried the Mohammedan institutions and superstitions into the Western Sudan, where they have flourished more particularly among the Mandingos.   They remained free men, *horos*, but the castes of musicians and blacksmiths, although free in name, were, by Islamic prejudice, reduced to "slaves of slaves" and "Touch-me-nots," as which they have persisted up to the present time.

The blacksmith, although also a "Touch-me-not," stands higher among the Negroes than a *griot*.   Among the Bambaras, a blacksmith, called *numu*, is free from the death penalty, just as a member of the princely order, an exception being made only in case of adultery with a woman from another caste.   The chief of the *numus* crowns the kings and renders justice in cases between members of his caste.[1]   They tell fortunes, cure diseases, circumcise, act as go-betweens in marriages and intermediaries in divorces, and embalm the dead.[2]   The Mandingo name *numu* can be easily explained when we consider the Arabic name معلم *ma'lam* for "blacksmith" in Timbuktu and among the Sosos, which means "learned, skilful."

Similarly the Mandingo *numo*, Malinke, Bambara *numu* "blacksmith" is derived from Arabic تلميذ *ṭalmīdz* "a student," *talammūdz* "to study," through the Zenaga *edejmun*, *atejmuḍ* "pupil, student," *anmuḍ*, *enmuḍ* "blacksmith, potter," *almuḍ* "armorer."[3]   We have

---

[1] A. Raffenel, *Nouveau voyage dans le pays des Nègres*, Paris 1856, vol. I, p. 384.
[2] G. Deherme, *L'Afrique Occidentale Française*, Paris 1908, p. 298 f.
[3] R. Basset, *Mission au Sénégal*, vol. I, part I, in *Publications de l'École des Lettres d'Alger*, vol. XXXIX, pp. 240, 275.

also the Hausa *almajiri* "disciple, beggar." The Mande *numu* is obviously an abbreviated form for *numudz* or *numuḍ*. That such is the case follows from the fact that in Bambara *numu* also means "forge," while *numuliba* is recorded as "blacksmith." As the latter is a + *ba* derivative, expressing the agent, it follows that a form *numuli* must have preceded it, that is, one derived from the Zenaga word. The Zenaga *edejmun* "student" has produced a series of "griot" words in several African languages. In Songay we have *djam*, *zam*, *tam* "blacksmith, worker, artisan," *tamu* "slave." These two terms are in reality in opposition to each other because the artisans were not slaves but "slaves of slaves," yet free. The same confusion will be observed over a large territory. We get, from the Songay, Malinke, Bambara *dyõ*, Mandingo *jongo* "slave," yet Bambara *dyamuru* "corvée, forced labor," and yet *dyamuru bugu* "a free village." In Wolof we have *dyamburu* "free" and *dyãme* "slave." In Asante we have *džwumã* "business, occupation, employment, duty, office, trade, profession," *odžwumfo* "artist, artisan, workman, smith, saddler," etc., *otomfo* "smith, blacksmith;" in Akra, *tšũmo*, *tšũ* "labor, work, occupation," *tšũlo* "servant, slave." Thus we come to the extraordinary contradiction that "the wisest of men" is at the same time "the most contemptible" of all, which, as we have seen, is a direct result of the curse which rests upon the Egyptian diviner who manufactured the golden calf.

Although among the Berbers the blacksmiths are also looked down upon with contempt, and, as *Beni Niyāt*, form a kind of special group outside of society,[1] their status is not so well defined as in Egypt, Somaliland, Arabia, or the Western Sudan. The same is true of the *Beni 'Adēs*, who practise the art of tattooing, horsetrading, circumcision, while their wives tell for-

---

[1] E. Doutté, *Magie et religion dans l'Afrique du Nord*, Alger 1909, p. 42 ff.

tunes, whereas among the *Beni 'Amer* the women tattoo, while the men are horse doctors.[1]   Doutté himself proposed the question whether these tribes, although not considered accursed, were not identical with the Gypsies, and to these he added the mysterious *Zkāra*, an anti-Islamic tribe, who consider themselves to be fathers of 'Amer ben Slīmān, a disciple of Sīḍi Aḥmed ben Yūsef, whom the Beni 'Adēs consider to be their saint.   Doutté also propounds the question whether *Zkāra* is not a corruption of *Zingari* or some such form.[2]

Unfortunately the material is too scanty to admit of any verification, and this uncertainty is further accentuated by the *kar, kir* forms in the African languages, which refer to the blacksmith and his art, but are of various origins.   Thus Hausa *makeri, maikira* "blacksmith" is a *ma-* derivative of Hausa *kira* "to forge, metal," Berber *kir* "bellows," from Arabic *kīr* "bellows."   There are "among the Gwari, near Abuja and in other parts, communities of *Koro* who live apart and are at once feared and despised by the agricultural Gwari.   These *Koro* are light-colored and are blacksmiths."[3]   The Peul *haulube* "enchanter," that is, the Arabic ﺣﻼﺑﺔ *ḥallābah* "enchanter," seems to have survived in Soso *khabi*, Malinke *hrabi* "blacksmith."

It thus appears that among the Berbers the Gypsies never acquired the significance in the social order that they obtained in the Sudan, no doubt because their migration from Egypt, as indicated in the Peul legends, did not take place from the north, but from the northeast over Barka, approximately over the path taken nowadays by the Hausas who traffic between Tripoli

---

[1] *Ibid.*, p. 43 f.
[2] *Ibid.*, p. 48.
[3] H. R. Palmer, *Notes on the Kororofawa and Jukon*, in *Journal of the African Society*, vol. XI, p. 403.

and the Niger valley. But in the Western Sudan the whole historical development of Negro civilization, especially among the Mandingos, is intimately related to the legendary and religious separation of the divining and metal-working Gypsies as a race of "Touch-me-nots."

CHAPTER IV.

AFRICAN FETISHISM AND TOTEMISM.

Probably the oldest description of African fetishism is found in de Marees' *A Description of Guinea*,[1] which appeared in 1602. It runs in Purchas' translation[2] as follows: "Although they are altogether wild, rough, and uncivill, having neither Scripture nor Bookes, nor any notable Lawes that might be set downe, or declared to shew the manner of their policie and living, yet when they have past the six daies of the weeke in labour and paines taking, to get their livings, the seventh day they leave working, and reckon that to bee their day of ease, and abstinence from worke, or their Sunday, which they call *Dio Fetissos*, which in our speech should signifie Sunday, but they observe it not upon our Sunday, nor upon the Jewes Sabbath Day, but hold it upon Tuesday, the second working day in the weeke; what law or opinion they have to moove them thereunto, I know not, but they hold Tuesday for their Sunday, and that day the Fishermen goe not to the Sea for fish: The women and Countrie people that day bring no Wine to the Market, but all the Wine which that day they draw out of the trees, they deliver it unto the King, which in the evening hee giveth unto his Gentlemen, and they drinke it among them. That day they doe no kind of worke, nor traffique with other but such as dwell on the Sea-side, refraine not for all that to goe aboord the shippes, and to buy wares of the

[1] *Beschryvinghe ende historische verhael van het Gout Koninckrijck van Gunea*, 's-Gravenhage 1912.
[2] *Hakluytus Posthumus or Purchas His Pilgrimes*, Glasgow 1905, vol. VI.

Netherlanders.   In their Markets they have a square place foure foot every way, supported with foure Pillars, and about two cubits high from the ground, flat on the top and covered close with Reedes, and hanged round about Wispes or *Fetissos* of Straw, whereon they lay Millia with Palme-oile or water, and give their god that to eate and drinke to sustaine him withall, that he should not die for hunger or thirst, thinking that he eateth and drinketh it and lives by it, but the Birds of the Aire eate the graine, and drinkes the water, and when it is eaten they anoint the Altar with Oile, and set more meate and drinke upon it, thinking thereby to doe their god great sacrifice and service.

"They have also a Priest, who in their speech they call a *Fetissero*, hee upon their Sabbath day sits upon a stoole, in the middle of the Market before the Altar or place whereupon they sacrifice unto their *Fetisso*, then all the men, women and children come and sit round about him, and there he speaketh unto them, & they sit stil to heare him: but what it is, or what it meaneth that cannot I learne, nor perceive, neither can you get it from them, for I have oftentimes asked them about it, but they will not tell, but are ashamed to declare it. But I have seene this *Fetissero*, have a pot with a certaine drink, (wherein there was a Snake) standing by him, and a Wispe, and some women with their little children went to him, which children hee stroaked with colour, or with some of that drinke, and so they went away, which I ghesse to be a kind of Salve against their *Fetisso*, for they esteeme their *Fetissos* to be both good and evill.   And when their *Fetissero* hath made an Oration unto them, then he stands up and smeareth the Altar with his Wispe, and drinke out of his pot, and then the people using certaine words and making a great noise among them, clapping their hands together, cry I. ou, I. ou, and therewith their preaching is done, and so everie one goes home to his house.

"They hang many straw Wispes upon their heads, and thinke thereby to bee free and safe as long as they weare them, and that their *Fetissos* can doe them no harme.   In the morning betimes when they have washt their bodies cleane, they stroake their faces with white stripes, made of earth like chalke, which they do in honour of their *Fetisso*, and use it in stead of praiers in a morning; when they eat any thing they present their *Fetisso* (the straw Wispes which they weare about their legges) the first bit, and also the first draught that they drinke, giving him to drinke, which if they doe not, they thinke they shall have no good lucke that day, for they perswade themselves that their *Fetisso* would not otherwise suffer them to be quiet.   When the Fishermen take but small store of fish, then they thinke that their *Fetisso* is angrie, and therefore will give them no fish, then they make a great crie among them, and goe to their *Fetissero*, and give him Gold to conjure their *Fetisso*, to send them store of fish.   This Conjurer presently goes, and makes all his Wives (two, three or foure, or as many as he hath) put on their best apparell and ornaments, and with them goes howling and crying round about the Towne, striking themselves upon their brests, and clapping their hands flat together, and so making a great stirre and noise, goe to the Sea-side, and taking boughes from the trees, hang them about their neckes: those trees they esteeme to be their *Fetissos* Dusianam, who they thinke send them fish. Then, the Conjurer or he that should bewitch the *Fetissos*, comes with a Drumme, and plaies or sounds before the trees, which they esteeme to be good for that purpose, which done hee goes to his Wives upon the strand, and when they have spoken one unto the other a good while, he casteth Millia into the Sea for his meate, with other colours, thinking that thereby their god is appeased, and will let them take fish enough.

"When the King receiveth not custome enough, to maintaine himselfe withall, then he goeth to a tree which he esteemeth to be his *Fetisso*, and sacrificeth unto it, carrying it meat and drink; then the Conjurers come and conjures the tree, to tell them whether there will any Merchants come or not, which to doe they make a heape of ashes, in forme like a Sugar-loafe, and cutting a bough from the tree sticke that in it, then they take a Bason of water and drinke out of it, and therewith sprinkle the bough of the tree, which done they speake each to other, and then againe they sprinkle more upon it, after that they take some of the ashes, and be-dawbe their faces therewith, and in that manner use many foolish and vaine Ceremonies, and not long after they shall heare a voice which is the Devill, that saieth something unto them, and therewith they goe home againe, and bring word what their *Fetisso* hath said.   They hang many of those things about their children for diseases, as is said before, as also of their drinke of jealousie.

"When any man dieth, they also make a *Fetisso*, and desire it to bring the bodie into the other world, and not to trouble it in the way as it goeth, then the next our neerest kinsman killeth a Hen, and dresseth it ready to be sodden, which done, they goe and sit in a corner of their house: and with him take all his *Fetissos*, and place them in order, as their greatest god in the middle, and the rest of meaner sort by it, then he takes certaine beades, some made of shels, some of Beanes and great Pease, and others of feathers, mixed with Buttons made of barkes of trees, and hangs them upon the *Fetissos*. After that they take the bloud of the dead Hen, and therewith sprinkle their *Fetisso* (for a dead man must offer bloud unto his god) then hee fetcheth certaine

Herbs out of the fields, and hangs them about his necke
like a chaine. In the meane time, while the man is in
this sort made readie, the Hen is sodden, and being
sodden then he brings it, and putting it in a Platter,
sets it in the middle of the *Fetissos*, which done, hee be-
ginneth to conjure, using many words, and casteth
water or wine of Palme upon his *Fetisso*, then he takes
two or three of the greene leaves, which he hath about
his necke, and rolleth them betweene his hands, making
a little bowle or bale thereof, which he takes in the two
forefingers of both his hands, and thrusts it betweene his
legges, twice or thrice one after the other, saying, to his
Fetisso, Aucie, which is as much as if he should say,
All haile. After this he wringeth the sap out of that
ball, and lets it drop upon his *Fetisso;* which done he
laies the ball upon the ground, and takes two or three
leaves more of the Herbs he hath about his necke, and
rolles them in his hands, and having made them in a
Ball, thrusts them betweene his legges, speaking
certaine words as aforesaid, and then lets the sap drop
upon his *Fetisso*, and this he doth untill such time as he
hath rolled and wrung all the greene Herbs in that sort,
which he had about his neck; then he takes all the balls
or leaves together in his hand, and thereof maketh a
ball as bigge as a mans fist, wherewith he wipeth his
face, and that also is a *Fetisso*, which being done the
dead bodie shall rest in peace, and therewith he packeth
up all his trinkets, and laieth them aside untill another
time, that some other bodie setteth him a worke. This
kind of Superstition they esteeme for a great holinesse
for their bodies, for when they goe to warre they hang
such beades about their neckes, armes and legges, thinking that their *Fetisso* will defend them thereby, and
preserve them from killing, and thinke that they need
not feare any thing. They esteeme the Pittoir also for
a god, for when they goe from one Towne to another,

and heare it call, they are exceeding joyfull and glad, for they say that it is a *Fetisso*, which speaketh unto them, saying, that all those that then travell in the way, shall have no hurt, nor need feare any danger, for he will defend them from all men that seeke to molest them, and wheresoever they heare it crie, there they set Millia for him to eate, and pots full of water to drinke, and dare not passe that place without giving it something, whereby in some corners of streets, and in the Woods you shall see a number of pots, and other meates as Millia, Mais, &c. which they set there to honour the *Fetisso* the Petoir, whereby it appeareth that they make great account of Birds, and also of some fishes, as of the Tonny, which they by no meanes will take, but esteeme it to be their *Fetisso* or Sea-god. They take many Sword-fishes, and cutting of the Swords they drie them, which they also esteeme for a great *Fetisso*. Others put their trust in some trees, and when they desire to know any thing they goe to those trees, where the Devill oftentimes appeares in forme of a blacke Dogge, or of such like things, and many times invisibly, and maketh answere unto such things as they aske him. So that if you aske them any thing touching their beliefe, and they give you no answere, which maketh any shew of truth, then they say that their *Fetisso* said so, and willed them to doe it, for they esteeme him for their god, and use many foolish toyes and vaine shewes when they pray to him, and serve him, thinking that it doth them good, and that they merit much thereby, yet it helpeth them not. But they rather find themselves deceived, and as they deale with the Devill, and put their trust in him, so he rewardeth them, and yet they desire not to heare of him, but feare him much.

"There are some hils in those Countries, whereon oftentimes it thundereth and lighteneth, and thereby manie times some Fishermen, or other Moores, are cast away or receive some great hurt, which causeth them to thinke that their god is angry, and would have some meate and drinke, or wanteth some other thing, and by that meanes they hold manie hils to be their gods, and set meate and drinke upon them to pacifie them withall, and they dare not passe along by them, without going up and giving them something, fearing that if they did it not, they would doe them some hurt, and make each other beleeve such things, and whatsoever they beleeve, and once conceive in their heads, it will never be extirped, but have as firme an opinion of their *Fetissos* as possible may be.   But when the Netherlanders saw them use such vaine toyes, which were so foolish, and laught and jested at them, they were ashamed, and durst make no more *Fetissos* in our presence, but were ashamed of their owne apishnesse.

"We asked them of their Beliefe, and what opinion they had of divers things; as first, when they died what became of their bodies and soules.   They made us answere, that the bodie is dead, but they knew not what any resurrection at the latter day meant, as wee doe: but when they die they know that they goe into another World, but they know not whither, and that therein they differ from brute beasts, but they cannot tell you to what place they goe, whither under the Earth or up into Heaven, but when they die, they use to give the dead bodie something to carrie with him, whereby it is to be marked that they beleeve that there is another life after this, and that there they have need of such things as they have here on Earth, for when they lose any thing, or when any of their friends die, then they thinke that those that are dead came and fetcht it away, and that they had need of it, but they know not what the Soule nor the Resurrection is.

"Secondly, asking them of their god, they made answere, that he is blacke like themselves, and that he

was not good, but did them much hurt.   Whereunto
we said, that our god is white as we are, that he is good,
that he doth us much good, that he descended downe
upon Earth to save us, and how he was put to death
by the Jewes for our sakes, that when wee die wee goe
to dwell with him in Heaven, and that there we neither
need meat nor drink, whereat they wondred, and willingly heard us speake of those things, and said that we
were Gods children, and that he told us all things, but
yet they murmured, saying, why doth not your God
tell and give us all things (as well as he doth to you) and
why doth he not also give us Linnen, Cloth, Iron,
Basons, and other kinds of wares; whereunto we made
answere, that our God sent us all those things, and yet
that he forgot not them, (although they knew him not)
and sent them Gold, Palme-wine, Millia, Mais,
Hennes, Oxen, Goats, Bannanas, Juiamas, and other
fruits, to sustaine them withall, but that they denied,
or else they could not conceive that such things came
from God; but to the contrarie said that God gave them
no Gold, but that the Earth gave it them, wherein they
digge to find it: that hee gave them no Millia nor Corne,
but that they sowed it, and reapt it themselves, and that
the Earth gave it them; that the trees which they had
planted gave them their fruits, and were first brought
thither by the Portugals; that yong beasts came of the
old, that the Sea gave them fish, which they tooke
themselves, with many other such like things, which
they would not acknowledge came from God, but from
the Earth and the Sea, each according to their natures,
but they acknowledge that Raine came from our
Saviour Christ, and that by meanes of our God they
had much Gold, for that by meanes of the Raine they
found their Gold, and their Fruits and Plants grew,
and waxed ripe by meanes of the moysture, and for that
we brought them everie thing readie made to their

hands, therefore they thinke that wee find all such things, and need but goe into the fields to fetch them, as they doe their Fruits.

"And when it happened that some of our Hollanders being in their Houses, when it beganne to Raine, Blow, Thunder and Lighten (whereof they are in great feare) went forth through the streets, not once shunning the Thunder and Lightning, neither did it once hurt them, they wondred thereat, for they were afraid that if they should come out of their Houses at that time, that it would not be good for them, for that many times, (when it Thundreth and Lightneth there) it hapneth that some of them that are travelling abroad, are carried away by the Devill, and throwne dead upon the ground, whereby they are as much afraid thereof, as any man possible can be.   And for that they know that our God dwels above in Heaven, when it Thunders and Lightens they point upwards, and call him Juan Goemain.   And once wee had a Negro aboord our ship, whom we kept prisoner because he brought false Gold, and gave it out for good, which Negro everie morning tooke a Tub with water in it, and washt his face therein, which done, he tooke his hands full of water, and cast it over his head, speaking divers words unto himselfe, and after that spit in the water, and used many other Apish toyes, which wee seeing, asked him why hee did it, and hee made answere, that hee prayed his *Fetisso* that it might raine, that so his friends might find much Gold to release him, that hee might goe home againe.

"They circumcise their young children, therein following the Mahometicall Law, with divers other opinions which they hold thereof, as thinking it evill to spit upon the Earth, besides many other Superstitions which they use, but affirme, that they altogether use those toyes, and only trust in their *Fetissos*, were an untruth, for many of them that can speake Portugall (as having dealt with them and also daily traffique with us) beginne to leave those foolish toyes, and to have some understanding of Gods Word, which they doe by reason that wee mocke and jest at their foolish Ceremonies, and for that they say that wee are Gods Children, therefore they beleeve much of that which we say unto them, and begin to know God, but it is without any ground, for they grounded in their owne Superstitions, because they are not otherwise instructed.

"But the Negros which dwell among the Portugals, know much of God, and can speake of his Commandements, as I have found some among them, that could tell of the birth of Christ, of the Lords Supper, of his bitter Passion, and death of his Resurrection, and divers other such like points, concerning our Christian faith; specially, one whom I knew well, and that was my good friend: for he could write and read Portugall, and was indifferent well learned in the Scriptures. And which is more, when he spake unto him, and argued upon some points against the Romish faith, or against the Religion which the Portugals had taught him (for he had dwelt with a Monk in the Castle of Mina) he would dispute the contrary with us, and shew that it was otherwise set downe in such a Gospel, and in such an Epistle of the Apostles, & that it must so be understood: whereby we may perceive, that those among them that have any understanding of the Christian faith, are sharpe witted, and will soone comprehend any thing: but it seemeth, that it hath not pleased God to call them to the understanding of the Christian faith, and therefore we are much bound to prayse and thanke God, that it hath pleased him to vouchsafe us the knowledge of his holy Word, and to understand and know what belongeth unto our salvation."[1]

Ibid., p. 289 ff.

"The children being a moneth or two old, then they hang a Net about the bodie thereof, like a little shirt, which is made of the barke of a tree, which they hang full of their *Fetissos*, as golden Crosses, strings with Corall about their hands, feet, and neckes, and their haire is filled full of shels, whereof they make great account, for they say, that as long as the young childe has that Net about him, the Devill cannot take nor beare the child away, and leaving it off, the Devill would carrie it away, for they say, the childe being so little, it would not bee strong enough to resist the Devill, but having that Net upon the bodie, it is armed, and then the Devill hath no power over it; the Corals which they hang about the child, which they call a *Fetisso*, they esteeme much, for that hanging such a *Fetisso* about the childes necke, they say, it is good against vomiting; the second *Fetisso*, which they hang about his necke, they say, it is good against falling; the third, they say, is good against bleeding; the fourth is very good to procure sleepe, which they hang about the necke thereof, in the night-time, that it may sleepe well; the fift, is good against wild beasts, and the unwholsomenesse of the Aire, with divers other such like *Fetissos*, each having a name a-part, to shew what vertue it hath, and what they are good for, and they credibly beleeve them to be good against vomiting, falling, bleeding, (which they presently helpe) and for sleeping."[1]

"About their neckes they weare a string of Beades, of divers colours, which our Netherlanders bring them; but the Gentlemen weare Rings of gold about their necks, on their feet, they weare many strange wreathes, which they call *Fetissos*, (which name they derive from their Idolatry) for when they eate or drinke, then they power

[1] *Ibid.*, p. 260.

meat and drinke upon them: and first give them to eate and drinke."[1]

"After long disputation by them made, the *Fetissero* (which is the Priest that conjureth their *Fetissos* or gods) came thither with a certaine drinke in a pot, and set it downe before the Captaine, the woman tooke the pot and drunke thereof, to justifie that he had not contented her for the losse of her honour; and if hee would have drunke thereof before the woman drunke, to justifie that he had paid her, and owed her nothing, then he had beene quit from paying any thing; but knowing himselfe to be guiltie, he durst not drinke, but was found guiltie, and was judged to pay a Fine of three Bendaes, which is sixe ounces of gold.

"This Drinke among them is as much as an Oath, and is called Enchionkenou; which they make of the same greene herbs whereof they make their *Fetissos*; and as they say, it hath such a force, that if a man drinketh it falsely, their *Fetisso* causeth him presently to die; but if they drinke it innocently, then their *Fetisso* suffereth them to live."[2]

De Marees' *Dio Fetissos* for the African weekly holiday is obviously intended for the Portuguese *dia feitiço* "fetish day." The fact that the Guinea Negroes are mentioned as observing a seven-day week at once points to Arabic influence, whence alone this division of time could have reached them. Indeed, the name for Tuesday is in Mandingo, Wolof, Soninke, Hausa *talata*, Dahome *tlata-gbe*, from Arabic ثلاثاء *salāsā'u* "Tuesday." De Marees did not quite get the idea about the Negro holiday, when he identified it with the Christian Tuesday. It is not likely that the Negroes, who had borrowed the Arabic week, should have changed the day of rest from Friday to Tuesday. If

[1] *Ibid.*, p. 266 f.
[2] *Ibid.*, p. 315 f.

the fishermen did not go out to fish, the wine merchants did not bring wine to market on that day, it was so because Tuesday is an unlucky day with the Arabs, hence truly a "fetish" day with the Negroes.

De Marees' loose use of the word *fetisso*, which he inherited from the Portuguese, is responsible for the nondescript conception of fetishism as a peculiar aspect of African religion. De Marees understands by *fetisso* any charm which is intended to ward off diseases or protect against wild beasts, hence any trinkets worn on the legs. But he also transfers the meaning to the Negro gods, who are propitiated by meat and drink and wisps of straw. The *fetisso* is both a protecting spirit or object and a malign spirit or object, and also serves man as a totem. The priest or sorcerer, who mediates between the people and the fetishes, is a *fetissero*, but de Marees could not ascertain what views he held in regard to the after life and God, although he makes it clear that in his time Mohammedan and Christian ideas had already permeated the Negroes' primitive religion, if there ever had been such.

The origin of the Portuguese word *feitiço* "fetish" should be from the Arabic, since an overwhelming mass of Arabic "charm" words have found their way into the European and African languages. I have already shown that *Fée Morgain* arose from the Arabic, where it had the meaning of "amulet."[1] In the African languages I have already treated the "amulet" words that have arisen from the meaning "writing."[2] To these must be added Hausa *laya*, from Arabic الاية *al-'ayah* "token, sign," Hausa *hatumi*, *katumi*, from Arabic خاتم *hātim* "seal," Dahome *vodū* "good or bad spirit, fetish, idol," from Arabic عوذة *'ūdzah* "pro-

---

[1] See my *Contributions*, vol. IV, p. 141 f.
[2] See my *Africa and the Discovery of America*, vol. I, p. 108 f.

tection, phylactery." This produced the American *voodoo*.

The Latin grammarians used the Latin term *facticius* for anything made up, such as an onomatopoetic word, and similarly the early Christian writers and Pliny employed the word in the sense of "anything created" as opposed to "eternal," or of "artificial" as opposed to "natural." It never occurs with any other meaning in Latin literature. This Latin word produced Spanish *hechizo*, Portuguese *feitiço*, OFrench *faitis* "artificial," but in the Latin-Arabic vocabulary of the XI. century[1] we find not only "*factio* opus fallax," which is sporadically found in the older Latin, but also *faccio*, a back-formation from *facticius*, with the meaning "adolando inpedio decipio," which is identical with "*fascino* adolando inpedio laudando decipio " The latter occurs several times in Latin vocabularies, the first is found nowhere else, and *facticius* "amulet, charm" is nowhere recorded. Now, we have Arabic

فطسة *fatsah* "a certain bead used for fascinating and restraining men; one of the beads of the Arabs of the desert, with which women are asserted by the Arabs to fascinate and restrain men." This Arabic word is already recorded in the VIII. century, and is centuries older, since it is already found in early Egyptian texts as *petes* "globule, pill." Obviously this Arabic word entered into Portuguese at a time when Latin *facticius* had already changed to *feitiço*, and thus the latter, and with it Latin *facticius*, acquired the meaning of "amulet, charm."

Outside of *feitiço* there is another word which gained currency in Europe for the African "fetish," namely *grigri*. We find it for the first time in 1575 in Thevet,[2]

---

[1] Seybold, *op. cit.*

[2] "Ce peuple n'a point esté si estrangément tourmenté de ces fantosmes: lesquels vsent de pareil traitement sur les pauures Mores Idolastres de la

where it has the meaning of "a tormenting spirit."
This is, no doubt, from Mandingo *grigri, girigiri* "to
shake, tremble, thunder," which very soon was applied
to anything relating to primitive religion. Braun, in
1624, still applied the term to a spirit which caused
terror,[1] but Jobson speaks of *gregory* as a mere Arabic
talisman.[2] This produced French *griot* "sorcerer."

In all those cases where we have an Arabic word for
"fetish, medicine, amulet," it would be absurd to speak
of an aboriginal fetishism, dating back to prehistoric
times. All folk religions resemble one another, and
the gnosticism of the Arabs is not different from that of
the Greeks or Egyptians or Babylonians. In dealing
with a contemporaneous state of superstitions, it is
necessary first to reject the late borrowings, as evidenced
in specific practices, but more especially in the linguistic

Guinee, & sur tout par les boys, les effroyant auec des visions espouuentables,
& les battant souuent, qu'ils nôment en leur langue *Grigry*, le craignant, &
abhorrant sur toute chose," A. Thevet, *La cosmographie universelle*, Paris
1575, vol. II, fol. 921 b.

[1] "Die Konig daselbsten opfferen jhrem Abgott *Crycry* mehr alsz 2000.
Menschen," Samuel Brun, *Schiffarten*, Basel 1624, reprinted in *Werken
uitgegeven door de Linschoten-Vereeniging*, 's-Gravenhage 1913, vol. VI, p. 30.
Similarly p. 38 f.

[2] "The *Gregories* bee things of great esteeme amongst them, for the most
part they are made of leather of seuerall fashions, wounderous neatly, they
are hollow, and within them is placed, and sowed vp close, certaine writings,
or spels which they receiue from their Mary-buckes, whereof they conceiue
such a religious respect, that they do confidently beleeue no hurt can betide
them, whilst these *Gregories* are about them, and it seemes to encrease their
superstition; the Mary-buckes do deuide these blessings for euery seuerall
and particular part, for vppon their heads they weare them, in manner of a
crosse, aswell from the fore-head to the necke, as from one eare to another,
likewise about their neckes, and crosse both shoulders about their bodies,
round their middles, great store, as also vppon their armes, both aboue and
below the elbow, so that in a manner, they seeme as it were laden, and carri-
yng an outward burthen of religious blessings, whereof there is none so thr-
oughly laden as the Kings, although of all sorts they are furnished with some,
both men and weomen, and this more I haue taken notice of, that if any of
them be possest of any malady, or haue any swelling or sore vpon them, the
remedy they haue, is onely by placing one of these blessed *Gregories*, where the
griefe lies, which they conceite will helpe them: and for ought I can perceiue,
this is all the Physicke they haue amongst them, and they doe not onely
obserue this for themselues, but their horses doe vsually weare of these about
their neckes, and most of their bowes are hanged and furnished with them,"
op. cit., p. 50 f.

derivations, and then similar earlier borrowings must be carefully eliminated, before the original state of a belief may be even hypothetically put.   In eliminating such accretions, it must always be borne in mind that superstitions, amulets, fetish rites are very frequently the residuum of religious conceptions, medical practices and social customs of a superior civilization insidiously working its way into a lower civilization through the witch-doctor and quack.   Even thus have Arabic medicine and religion worked their way into the Western Sudan.   No doubt, before that, Christianity may have filtered into the Guinea Coast from the Atlantic border, but that influence must have been weak, since no powerful Christian state had developed in northern Africa.   But long before that, for whole millenniums, Egypt must have carried its religion and its medical science into the heart of Africa.   In the Sahara and the two Sudans it will be rather difficult to trace this earlier infiltration because of the later, more powerful Islamic interpenetration, but among the Bantus, away from the coast, we may, at least in the vocabulary, still observe the effect of Egyptian culture.

Sir Harry Johnston[1] has collected a large number of words among 276 Bantu and 24 Semi-Bantu languages, among which we shall study a few for the connotations "medicine, magic."   Only characteristic words of a group, without the classifier, will be given here, as the reference to a specific language or dialect would only burden the text unnecessarily.   A characteristic form *rōzi* for "magic" is found in the following groups: Nyanza *lōyi, rōgō, lōgō, rōji, rōzi, lōkō;* Wunyamwezi *lōzi;* Rufiji-Ruvuma *lōha;* Tanganyika-Bangweulu *lōzi, lōsi, dōci;* North-west Nyasa *dōzi, rōzi, dōsi;* South Nyasaland *lōzi;* Southern Rodesia *rōwa, royi, rōwi, loi;*

---

[1] *A Comparative Study of the Bantu and Semi-Bantu Languages,* Oxford 1919.

Sengwe-Ronga *loyi, roi;* Becuana *loi;* Zulu-Kafir *lōza, lōzi, loya, lōwi;* Zambezia *lōsi, lōzi, lōti;* Kongo *dōki;* Luba-Lunda *dōki, luwi;* South Kongo *lōji;* Central Kongo *nok', nōke;* Wele-Aruwimi *ōgō;* Kwa-Kasai *lō, logō, loñō;* Ogowe-Gaboon *loñgō, dōka, lok';* Duala *dōki;* Rumpi *dōwe.* As one reaches the Western Sudan this group entirely disappears. One at once recognizes in these words Coptic *lōž, lōži* "to cure," from Egyptian *àri utcha* "to heal," literally "to make healthy, strong, intact." As this is a compound word, it is evident that the Bantu words are all borrowings from the Egyptian, hence we have here an ancient infiltration of Egyptian medicine. Unfortunately the time of the borrowing by the Bantus cannot be ascertained, as it may have come through the Arabic *'ilaǵ* "doctor," which itself is derived from the Demotic *lek, leg,* and which produced the Germanic "medicine" words.[1]

Forms of *ganga* have in the Bantu languages the meaning "medicine," but also "magic," hence "gunpowder." Such are Sotho *ngaka,* Tlapi *ñaka,* Pedi *nak'a,* Zulu *nyanga,* Ronga *nanga,* Mochi *hanga,* Subiya *anga,* Nyika *ganga,* Kongo *nganga,* etc. All these are from Egyptian *ḥeka* "magic, the power of working magic, sorcery, spell, incantation, charm, word of power," from which we get Coptic *hik* "magician, demon." It would, therefore, appear that in the Bantu superstitions we have reminiscences of millenniums past, but the appearances are deceptive, since the words testify only to the uninterrupted existence of superstitions which may have been modified by later events. This is made a certainty by the presence of Arabic دوا *ḍawā'* "medicine" among the "medicine, charm" words in Bantu. We have Pokomo, Zangian *dawa,* that is, in the neighborhood of the Arabic colonies

---

[1] See my *Contributions,* vol. IV, p. 326 ff.

in East Africa the Arabic word has been preserved in its purity.

The most interesting "medicine" word in the Bantu languages is the one which in many cases coincides with "tree," because here we can study the overwhelming Arabic medical influence throughout Africa.   The Arabic شجر šaǵar "tree" is found in the Sahara oases,[1] where we get Soa ṣedar, Wadai ṣēdar, Adirar sadsārun, plural ladsāru, Beran sadṣar, plural sdār. We also find in Soa ṣidāri "doctor."   The word would be very puzzling, if we did not have constantly, in Ibn-al-Baitār, شجار šaǵǵār "botanist."   It is not surprising to find at Beran heṣāb "medicine," but this is not from Arabic خشب hušb "tree," but from اعشب 'ašāb "plants," since "botany" is in Arabic called "the science of plants." Now, we have the Arabic term شجاريه šaǵǵārīah "the plants or substances which enter into the composition of a medicament," hence we get the confusion of "tree" and "medicine" throughout Africa in those cases where these words are derived from the Arabic شجر šaǵar.

In the African languages, especially in Mandingo, Arabic š generally turns into t, and occasionally into s, hence Soa ṣedar should appear as tara or some such form in the native languages.   Sir Harry Johnston[2] records for "tree:" Nyanza ti, sali, sala (also "medicine"); Wunyamwezi ti; British East Africa ti, di, hi (taiga, di "medicine"); Kilimanjaro ti, di, ri, hi; Zangian ti, ci, iri, rrō; Usagara-Ugogo ti (also "medicine"); Rufiji-Ruvuma ti, tera, tela, nandi, landi (tera, tela, tende "medicine"); North Ruvuma tera, thende (also "medicine"); Ukinga thende (also "medicine");

[1] S. W. Koelle, Polyglotta africana, London 1854.
[2] Op. cit.

Tanganyika-Bangweulu *ti*, *sala* (*ti* "medicine"); North-west Nyasa *ti;* Yao-Ngindo and Moçambique *tera*, *tela*, *teñgō*, *toñgō*, *tali*, *ri*, *iri* (*tera*, *tela* "medicine"); South Nyasaland *ti*, *teñgō*, *ri*, *muti*, *buti;* Southern Rodesia *ti*, *ri;* Sengwe-Ronga *doñgō*, *ri;* Becuana-Transvaal *tl'are* (*tl'are*, *re*, *li* "medicine"); Zulu-Kafir *ti*, *tsi*, *hlahla*, *hlōhla* (*ti*, *tsi* "medicine"); West Central *samō* (also "medicine"); Western Zambezia *te*, *sakō*, *tondō* (*sambō*, *tondō* "medicine"); North-west Zambezia *ti*, *tondō*, *sakō* (*tumbu*, *emba* "medicine"); South-west Africa *ti* (also "medicine"); Angola *ji*, *ši* (*lañgō*, *loñgō*, *hemba* "medicine"); Kongo *ti*, *ci*, *tē* (*loñgō*, *nti* "medicine"); Luba-Lunda *ci* (also "medicine"); South Congoland *tondō*, *tondā*, *ji*, *ci* (*loñ*, *ōnō* "medicine"); Upper Kwango and Kwango-Kasai *ti* (also "medicine"); Central Congoland *tamba*, *suñgu;* Manyema *te;* Elila-Lowa *ti;* Ruwenzori *ri*, *ele*, *ti;* Upper Ituri *i*, *ě;* Wele-Aruwimi *le;* Aruwimi-Lomami *sandu*, *te* (*iso*, *ti*, *te*, *sisa* "medicine"); North Central Congoland *ite*, *ete*, *tele*, *tamba* (*le*, *te*, *ele*, *no*, *lō*, *ōlō* "medicine"); Kwa-Kasai *ti*, *te* (also "medicine"); Central Ogowe *ti*, *ri*, *eli*, *ere*, *rere*, *loñgu* (*loñgu*, *eli* "medicine"); Spanish Guinea *etse*, *eci*, *ele*, *li*, *lē*, *ē*, *ere*, *tu* (*le* "medicine"); Manenguba *el'*, *ed'*, *al* (*añ*, *e*, *el* "medicine"); Middle Sanaga *ete;* Pangwe *le*, *li* (*añ* "medicine"); Kadei-Sanga-Lobai *le*, *ti;* Fernandian *te*, *ti* (*wele*, *bele*, *beli* "medicine"); Cameroons-Cross River *ti*, *te*, *tsi*, *tya*, *txo*, *tij*, *tse*, *ji*, *šet*, *ale*, *ri*, *ni*, *nei*, *tǒ*, *tu* (*je* "medicine"); Northern Cross River Basin *ši*, *ji*, *ti*, *tete* (*ji*, *jik* "medicine"); Central Nigerian *ji*, *se;* Nalu *ti*, *ri;* Upper Gambia *ri*, *s*. To this must be added the words for "wood," which in Rufiji-Ruvuma is *sagala*, where the relation to the Arabic word for "tree" is obvious. The successive deteriorations from the Arabic word may be approximately arranged in the following scheme:

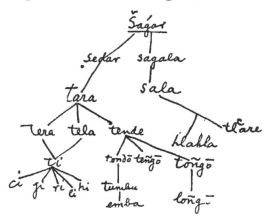

To the north of the Bantus the Arabic word is equally universal.   In the Mande languages we can study the word in Delafosse.[1] Here we have for "tree" Soninke *yite*, Muin, Mau *iri*, Gbin, Dyula *yiri*, Bambara *tige*, Foro *tīri*, Takponin *yire*, Gimini *kãgãrã*, to which must be added Malinke *djiri*, *iri*, and, in Koelle, Toronka *yiyi*, Kabungo *īro*, Tene *tewuri*, Gbandi *nguru*, Gbese *uru*, Toma *guru*, Gio *giri*, Soso *wuri*, *wudi*.   To understand the Mande forms, we must turn to the Berber dialects whence, no doubt, they were derived. In some of the dialects, as at Redames, we have *esejret*, which is pretty close to the Arabic word, but the Hassania-Arabic *sejar* becomes in Zenaga *šar*, in Chauya *tjert*, plural *tjur*, *tjari*, while in Kabyl we have *tejra*, plural *tjur*.   These at once explain Malinke *djiri*, Tene *tewuri*, of which the others are progressive deteriorations, but in Gimini *kãgãrã* we still recognize the original Arabic *šaǵar*.   In Peul *leggal*, *lekki* "tree, amulet, medicine," we have, no doubt, a reduction of a form *tige*, as in Bambara, just as in the Bantu languages

[1] M. Delafosse, *Vocabulaires comparatifs*, Paris 1904.

le, li are found for *te, ti.* In the Mossi languages we still observe the same forms as in Mande. We have Mossi *tēra*, Dselana *tĭv*, Legba *tāro*, *tān*, Kaure *tēro*, *tēn*, *tāro*, Kiamba *tēo*, Bagbalan *tĭa*, Kasm *tēnu*, Yula *tēo*. In Nupe *tšigbe* "medicine," etc. we have an original *sebe* "writing" word, but it led to *tšigbon*, *šigbon* "tree," hence Kupa *tsigmo*, Esitako *tsūgba*, Goali *dṣimo*, *sūva*, Basa *tsigwo*, Ebe *tugma*, as well as Gbari *shingwa* "tree," are similarly derived.

When the series is viewed in the inverse direction, from the Berber countries to the Bantus, it will be at once observed that the fuller forms are found in and near the Berber countries, hence the direction of the development must have proceeded from the Mediterranean southward, and then we observe that the "medicine" words are all contaminations with Arabic طِرة *tīrah* "a thing from which one augurs good or evil," hence Berber *tira* "destiny, evil omen, charm, amulet, writing," from which develops a verb *aru* "to fix one's destiny, to write, "hence Yoruba *tira* "a Mohammedan charm, anything written, a book."

A still greater number of "tree" words could be shown to be similarly related to the Arabic, but enough has been given to indicate that African fetishism, in so far as it deals with the curative powers of material objects, is above all else the residue of Arabic medical practice, just as the *grigri* and *sebe* are the residue of Islamism, as passed through the hands of the religious impostor. Hence the consideration of African fetishism independently of Arabic medicine and magic can only lead to disastrous results. This is well illustrated by the havoc produced in the conceptions of African totemism as though it were of native origin.[1] We shall

---

[1] For the status of the scientific aspect of totemism, see A. van Gennep, *L'état actuel du problème totémique*, Paris 1920, where (p. 341) not less than thirty-seven learned theories of totemism are classified.

approach the subject chronologically, from its Arabic source until the present time. Quatremère[1] has collected a number of passages from Arabic authors which show that the Persian *rang* "color, paint" produced Arabic كلوۍ, *rank* "coat of arms, banner, mark of distinction." The *rank* of the Abassides was a black garment. Melik-Dāher's *rank* was the figure of a lion, wherefore he had a stone lion placed on a bridge called "The Lion Bridge."[2] The *rank* of another prince "was composed of a white circle, cut by a green band on which there was a red dagger. This *rank* was very fine, and the women, even courtesans, were pleased to engrave it on their daggers." Sclar's *rank* was black and white. In their processions the participants were distinguished by their *ranks*, and the shop signs bore their distinctive *ranks* and *nišāns*.

Nišān, in Persian, hence in Arabic, means "sign, stamp, ensign, flag, standard, colors, armorial bearings," and *nišāndār* is "a standard-bearer, ensign." Both *rank* and *nišāndār* early entered into the European languages. In the XII. century OFrench *renc* means "the line of procession in a tournament," hence "rank (and file), distinction."[3] *Nišāndār* occurs as OFrench *estandart*, at first almost exclusively as the Saracen standard, with a golden apple on the pole or, more frequently, as the carriage which bore this ensign.

In the Moslem countries the *nišāns* representing animals, flowers, or any object were of common use in the armies,[4] and among the cattle-raising Bedouins the custom of marking the animals with a *wašm* was universal. "These *wašms* of the Arab tribes may often be seen on men and women, either tattooed or in deep

[1] *Op. cit.*, vol. II, part I, p. 14 f.
[2] *Ibid.*, vol. I, part II, p. 153.
[3] The correct etymology of OFrench *renc* was already observed by Yacoub Artin Pacha, *Contribution à l'étude du blason en Orient*, Londres 1902, p. 12.
[4] *Ibid.*, p. 83 ff.

cuts which leave on the skin marks of cicatrization.
This habit is particularly in use in the Egyptian Sudan,
because the tattooing does not show on the skin of the
Sudanese Negroes, while in the north of Egypt, either
in the valley or the desert, tattooing with indigo is of
frequent occurrence.   These tattooings are adornments imposed by custom, into which is introduced the
wašm of the tribe to which the individual belongs."[1]
The author proceeds to quote from C. W. Wilson, *On
the Tribes of the Nile Valley, North of Khartúm,*[2] to the
effect that the Semitic tribes of the Shagíah and Já'ali
"have adopted the African custom of gashing the cheeks
of their children; the Shagíah gashes are vertical, the
Já'ali horizontal, and the latter say they adopted the
custom from the former."

Tattooing and cicatrization are universal practices
and are recorded from antiquity, but we know them
chiefly as a manner of adornment or as a religious practice.   In Africa the custom is distinctly one of clan or
tribe distinction and, as such, cannot be separated from
the Arabic *wašm*.   Delafosse[3] says: "Tattooing of
the face by scarification is widely distributed over the
High-Senegal-Niger, but is not met with everywhere.
Certain peoples completely reject these mutilations:
the Moors, Tuaregs, Peuls, Tukolor, Bozo, Malinke,
Fulanke, Birifo, Lobi, Puguli.   Among others the
scarifications exist only in a part of the population or in
certain families.   Thus, though the Songay are in
general not tattooed, some have very long vertical
cicatrices on each temple, or upon the brow a long
vertical incision, surrounded by a dotted line, from
right to left; the Soninke are not tattooed, except the
Dyawara, who have three short incisions between the

[1] *Ibid.*, p. 191 f.
[2] In *The Journal of the Anthropological Institute of Great Britain and Ireland*, vol. XVII, p. 18.
[3] *Haut-Sénégal-Niger*, vol. I, p. 332 f.

two eyebrows; the Dyula of pure Mande origin are not tattooed, but those who are allied to the Senufu have generally on each cheek three large fan-like cicatrices issuing from the corners of the mouth; with the Kagoro the majority of individuals have no scarification whatsoever, but some of them have adopted the Bambara tattooing or have on each cheek a double fan of varied design; the Dyan and the Gan have adopted both the Bobo and Senufu tattoos.   The natives belonging to the other peoples of the High-Senegal-Niger have nearly all ethnic scarifications, of which the details follow, but I must observe that it is not at all rare, even among the latter, to meet with individuals who are not tattooed, and, moreover, the mark of one people or tribe has frequently been adopted by the members of another people or tribe or has been imposed upon slaves of foreign origin, so that the tattoo marks of an individual are not an absolutely certain indication of the ethnic group to which he belongs."

As the *wašm* was a mere sign of recognition and did not bear with it any honor or distinction, the practice of cicatrization has in Africa been neither universal nor imperative within the tribe, hence it is quite difficult to trace any progressive use of this type of recognition in Africa, whereas the Arabic *nišān* has left important results wherever it was introduced.   In the Berber country *nican*, from this Arabic word, means "target, distinction, decoration."   In the Mande languages the word has the specific meaning of "animal or other object serving as distinctive mark of the family."   Thus we have Bambara *n'tene*, *tene*, for Arabic *nišān*, since here *š* changes to *t*, Malinke *tana*, *tene*, *tne*.

Brun[1] summarizes the concept of the totem in the Western Sudan as follows:

[1] J. Brun, *Le totémisme chez quelques peuples du Soudan Occidental*, in *Anthropos*, vol. V, p. 863 f.

1.   Totemism does not appear as a precise stage of religious evolution exclusive of all other beliefs.   It is simply an element of beliefs.

"2.   It appears, indeed, as a universal fact in French West Africa.

"3.   Except for some details, the beliefs and practices have among these people a remarkable character of unity.

"4·   Although certain social institutions are placed under the protection of totemic beliefs, the whole of such institutions is not based on totemism.

"5·   It is a definite fact that at the present time there is no common totem for a whole people.

"6·   It is possible, but not demonstrated, that the names of several peoples are reminiscences of totemism.

"7.   Totemism is essentially familiar, in the sense of the *gens* of the Latins.

"8.   The totem is transmitted from the father to the children of both sexes.

"9·   Totemism does not present any exogamic character.

"10·   The native legends do not attach the origin of totemism to an animal descent, but to a benefit rendered by the animal to the family ancestor.

"11·   Finally, it seems that the sense of 'parentage,' when referring to the totem, should be explained by the belief in metempsychosis."

Brun says that he has never found any representation of the animal totem, either in painting or sculpture, or as a symbol.[1]   But Ibn-Batutah tells of a golden bird which surmounted the umbrella of the King of Malli,[2] and which apparently was of the nature of a totem. We shall later see that the Mexicans have preserved for us representations of Mandingo blazons on their

[1] *Ibid.*, p. 860.
[2] Defrémery and Sanguinetti, *op. cit.*, p. 406.

shields, which are of the nature of totems, in the sense of representing personal or clan dignity.   According to Artin,[1] in the XI. century "the Mamelucks of Syria and of Egypt, following in this the example which had been set them by the Oriental princes, also adopted these coats of arms, which they painted on their shields, their streamers, their standards, even on the garments of their slaves, and sometimes on their coins, and on monuments which they built."   In the XIV. century, when Ibn-Batutah visited the Mandingos, these were far more fully under Arabic influence than they are at present, and they imitated the custom of emblazoning their weapons and garments, which only in the XII. century became a universal custom in Egypt.   This is evident, as we shall see, from the Mexican records, which, therefore, cannot be of a date earlier than the XII. century of our era.   At a later time the Mandingos, with the loss of their empire, discontinued the method of representing their coats of arms, preserving only a vague reminiscence of animal antecedents, which, however, is neither universal nor definite, and which has wrongfully led to a conception of prehistoric totemism in the Western Sudan.

[1] *Op. cit.*, p. 11 ff.

CHAPTER V

The Bori.

Henry's work on the Bambaras[1] gives a complete account of the Mandingo *bori*, hence it will be summarized here to the extent to which it touches upon the religion of the Sudanese Negroes, and, ultimately, of the American Indians.

The benevolent spirits of the Bambaras are called *nyena*, better known under the Arabic name of *jine* (جن). These differ from the Islamic spirits in that they are conceived as intermediaries between angels and men, or between a vaguely conceived divinity and men. The *jine* sometimes assume a human form, when they are represented as white beings. The *nya* or *boli*, like the *jine*, may be male or female, but they are in constant opposition to God and the *jine*, and torment men with their mischievous acts. When they appear as human beings, they are represented as black and exceedingly ugly. While animals of a white color are sacrificed to the *jine*, the *boli* receive only black or red victims. There is, however, no strict line of delimitation between the two kinds of spirits, and women and children apply the term *nyena* to both. Men, too, are not always making a distinction between them. Some sorcerers invoke only the *jine*, others call upon both, but more frequently upon the *boli*, while others again travel from village to village dressed in the skin of a goat or wild cat, from whose paws hang little bells which announce their coming, and talk in the name of the *boli*, predicting

[1] J. Henry, *Les Bambara*, Münster 1910.

the future or reading the past. Such a sorcerer is known as *bolitigi*, literally "master of the *boli*."

The Bambaras have retrograded in religion, for the *jine* refer to a period when the Mandingos drew their religious concepts from the Koran. Since then they have almost entirely lost the idea of God or the positive injunctions of the Islamic faith. They have preserved the idea of sacrifice, the *saraka*, the Arabic صرقة *şaraqah* "alms," but it has deteriorated into a mere contribution to the sorcerer, to propitiate his good will. In every sacrifice there is a priest who is charged with the duty, but in the *saraka* there is, properly speaking, no priest. In the indirect *saraka*, by the request of a fetish, the person offering it addresses himself, out of respect, to the chief of the village or the family. In the direct *saraka* the sorcerer indicates the particular persons, provided they be circumcised or excised, who are to offer it. In a public *saraka* a woman is never chosen, but only a revered old man. After a public sacrifice the sacrificer generally receives a chosen morsel and the skin of the animal, and the assistants roast the meat and devour it on the spot, whereas in the *saraka*, except by special order of the sorcerer, the meat, the flour, the kola nuts, the cowries are abandoned at the place of the *saraka*, and only the poor may take it all and eat it. Generally the children of both sexes are called to partake of the food. What is left is taken up and is deposited at the cross-roads. In a *saraka* offered by the whole village it is nearly always a goat that is killed, and the hide folded into four or six parts is fastened with strings of the *Bauhinia reticulata* and is suspended on the end of a pole at the entrance to the village.

The *saraka* is never given to the fetishes *boli*, but only to the fetishes *jine* and to God, and it is either bloody or bloodless and is given directly or indirectly. The direct *saraka* is given by either men or women, provided,

according to sex, they are circumcised or excised.   In
an indirect *saraka*, whether at the instigation of a *jine*
or a *boli* (one given to God is never given through a
boli), one must have recourse to the owner or sacrificer
of such a *jine* or *boli*.   The animal of the *saraka* is killed
to the fetish taken as a mediator, and this fetish takes
the responsibility of averting evil from him who has
presented to him this tribute or impost.   In the *saraka*
two things are given, the material and the immaterial,
and when it is indirect, there is necessarily bloodshed-
ding in favor of the mediator, in order that he may
seize the life of the beast offered as tribute, and offer it
in turn to the proper person.   The *saraka* is the unique
religious act of the Bambara towards his creator and
sovereign master.   Although it is done at the fork or
crossing of paths, it may be given anywhere, and the
god of the Bambaras remains without priest, without
altar, without sacrifice, properly speaking.

Certain sorcerers of renown prescribe a *saraka* to a
whole village, and at times to a whole region.   The
entire wisdom of such a sorcerer, who can tell everything by rummaging in the entrails of chickens and
crushing them between his fingers, may be summarized
in these words: "The *jine* are dissatisfied, offer a
saraka to them, offer it quick, for, if you do not do so,
all the children under three years will die. . . .goats,
cows, horses, sheep will perish. . . .the springs will
dry up.   the *karite* butter will fail," etc.   Sometimes, after much persuasion, everybody offers a
saraka, even the Moslems taking part in it.   Sometimes a *saraka* is given in order to hurt a neighbor, in
which case a magical object is placed nearby.   The
Bambara is persuaded that if his enemy touches such a
magical object, his vengeance will be so much more
effective.   Certain merely superstitious practices,
which do not have a proper religious character, are also

called *saraka*. Rags and clusters of fruit suspended from trees are not so much an homage rendered by the Negro to his *jine*, as a tribute offered to his own personal, inarticulate fear.

The Bambaras use a number of Arabic terms for religious concepts, but this they do only for diplomatic reasons, for the adaptation of these forms has nothing in common with acceptation. The Bambaras have always struggled to maintain their religious independence and to save their faith and their fetishes. These religious struggles in themselves allow us to consider as an indisputable fact the statement that before the arrival of the Moslems they were animists and sacrificed to the genii.

In this résumé of a part of Henry's book the data are highly interesting, while the author's explanations are generally inadequate or wrong. The absence of an altar in the *saraka* does not point to a native origin of the *saraka*, since the altar is almost unknown to the Arabs.[1] The *saraka*, from Arabic صدقة *ṣaḍaqah* (not صرقة, which in Henry is a misprint), is unquestionably of the nature of an expiatory sacrifice, for in the Islamic orthodoxy the victim in such a case is generally distributed to the poor,[2] and in North Africa the *ṣaḍaqah* is the tithe on the capital for the current year, which is directly distributed to the poor in the form of alms.[3] Hence the Bambaras, by turning the sacrifice into a *saraka*, only imitate an Islamic custom. The killing of a goat at the sacrifice is based on the Koranic prescription that only a camel, an ox, or a goat may be sacrificed. As the pre-Islamic *ǧinns* have permeated the Islamic religion, it is only natural for the Bambaras, with their low intellectual develop-

[1] Doutté, *op. cit.*, p. 463.
[2] *Ibid.*, p. 474.
[3] *Ibid.*, p. 493.

ment, to give these *sarakas* to the *jine* rather than to
God.   Thus we have so far not a particle left of a non-
Islamic origin of the Bambara sacrifice.

According to Henry, the Bambaras believe in a great
variety of *nyena* or *jine*.   There is the *wokolo*, the
mischievous *jine* of the brush; the unnamed *jine* of the
village who must be propitiated, in order to keep the
children from diseases; the were-wolf, *suruku*; the
powerful *jine* who can do good; the *jine* of the springs,
the crops; *jine* protecting the children, the circumcised
and excised children, the women, the twins, etc.   All
such *jine* may be found among the Arabs, even as they
form the folk-lore of Europe, hence there is nothing
specifically Negro in them.

Far more interesting is the protecting *jine* of the village, the *dasiri*, who lives on a rock or, more generally,
in a baobab or cailcedra tree.   He is the property of a
family with which he shares the name, and his sacrificer
has the name of *dugu-tigi* "village chief," whereas the
civic head of the village is called *so-tigi* "house chief."
The great sacrifice to the *dasiri*, whose mount is generally a serpent, rat, lizard, ass, but more generally a
horrible billy-goat that has the freedom of the village,
takes place every year.   For at least three days the
village revels: men, women and children dance, gorge
themselves with food, drink, and get drunk.   Everybody takes part in the sacrifice, and the women, who
may not enter the sacred grove, at least go to its edge.
Everything is in abundance: honeyed flour, milk, millet
beer, and meats.   In the name of the village they
sacrifice at least a goat, and sometimes a bull, and the
chiefs of the families, according to their means, offer
goats and chickens.

Who does not see that we have here a close reminiscence of the Moslem '*īḍ-al-ṣagīr*, the "minor festival"
after the fast of the Ramadan?   In the Mohammedan

law only two holidays are specifically provided for,[1] the '*īḍ-al-ṣagīr* "the minor festival," on the first of Shawwāl after the Ramadan, hence also called '*īḍ-al-fiṭr* "feast of the breaking of the fast," and the '*īḍ-al-kabīr* "the great festival." For the latter it is prescribed for every free Moslem who may be considered as a father of a family to sacrifice an animal, provided his means permit. A goat is sufficient for one person, while seven persons may combine to sacrifice a camel or ox. It is recommended to distribute the meat of the sacrificial animal as a *ṣaḍaqah* among the poor and needy, the sacrificer retaining a part for the sake of the blessing it contains. As a matter of fact, the minor festival, which comes at the end of a long fast, has gained greater importance in all Moslem countries.

"On the first three days of *Showwal* (the tenth month, the next after Rumadan) is celebrated the minor of the two grand festivals which are ordained, by the religion of the Mooslims, to be observed with general rejoicing. It is commonly called *el-'Eed es-Soogheiyir;* but more properly, *el-'Eed es-Sagheer.* The expiration of the fast of Rumadan is the occasion of this festival. Soon after sunrise on the first day, the people having all dressed in new, or in their best, clothes, the men assemble in the mosques, and perform the prayers of two rek'ahs, a soonneh ordinance of the 'eed; after which, the Khateeb delivers an exhortation. Friends, meeting in the mosque, or in the street, or in each other's houses, congratulate and embrace and kiss each other. They generally visit each other for this purpose. Some, even of the lower classes, dress themselves entirely in a new suit of clothes; and almost everyone wears something new, if it be only a pair of shoes. The servant is presented with one or more new articles of clothing

---

[1] Th. W. Juynboll, *Handbuch des islamischen Gesetzes*, Leiden, Leipzig 1910, p. 126 ff.

by the master, and receives a few piasters from each of
his master's friends, if they visit the house; or even
goes to those friends, to congratulate them, and receives
his present: if he have served a former master, he also
visits him, and is in like manner rewarded for his trouble;
and sometimes he brings a present of a dish of *kahhk*
(or sweet cakes), and obtains, in return, money of twice
the value, or more.   On the days of this 'eed, most of
the people of Cairo eat *feseekh* (or salted fish), and
kahhks, *fateerehs* (or thin, folded pancakes), and *shooreyks* (a kind of bun).   Some families also prepare a dish
called *moomezzezeh*, consisting of stewed meat, with
onions, and a quantity of treacle, vinegar, and coarse
flour;   and the master usually procures dried fruits
(*noockl*), such as nuts, raisins, &c., for his family.
Most of the shops in the metropolis are closed, excepting
those at which eatables and sherbet are sold; but the
streets present a gay appearance, from the crowds of
passengers in their holiday clothes.

"On one or more days of this festival, some or all of
the members of most families, but chiefly the women,
visit the tombs of their relatives.   This they also do on
the occasion of the other grand festival, of which an
account will be given hereafter.   The visitors, or their
servants, carry palm-branches, and sometimes sweet
basil (*reehhan*) to lay upon the tomb which they go to
visit.   The palm-branch is broken into several pieces,
or its leaves are stripped off, and then placed on the
tomb.   Numerous groups of women are seen on these
occasions, bearing palm-branches, on their way to the
cemeteries in the neighbourhood of the metropolis. They
are also provided, according to their circumstances,
with kahhks, shooreyks, fateerehs, bread, dates, or some
other kind of food, to distribute to the poor who resort
to the burial-grounds on these days.   Sometimes,
tents are pitched for them: the tent surrounds the tomb

which is the object of the visit. The visitors recite the Fat'hhah; or, if they can afford it, employ a person to recite first the Soorat Ya-Seen, or a larger portion of the Ckoor-an. Often, a khutmeh (or recital of the whole of the Ckoor-an) is performed at the tomb, or in the house, by several fickees. The men generally return immediately after these rites have been performed and the fragments or leaves of the palm-branch laid on the tomb: the women usually go to the tomb early in the morning, and do not return until the afternoon: some of them (but these are not generally esteemed women of correct conduct), if they have a tent, pass the night in it, and remain until the end of the festival, or until the afternoon of the following Friday: so also do the women of a family possessed of a private, enclosed burial-ground, with a house within it (for there are many such enclosures, and not a few with houses for the accommodation of the females, in the midst of the public cemeteries of Cairo). Intrigues are said to be not uncommon with the females who spend the night in tents among the tombs. The great cemetery of Bab en-Nusr, in the desert tract immediately on the north of the metropolis, presents a remarkable scene on the two 'eeds. In a part next the city-gate from which the burial-ground takes its name, many swings and whirligigs are erected, and several large tents; in some of which, dancers, reciters of Aboo Zeyd, and other performers, amuse a dense crowd of spectators; and throughout the burial-ground are seen numerous tents for the reception of the visitors of the tombs."[1]

Among the Bambaras we have the same indulgence in sweetmeats, the same sacrifice of a goat by a chief of a family, the same procession of the women to the sacred grove, instead of the cemetery, the same revelry for

[1] E. W. Lane, *An Account of the Manners and Customs of the Modern Egyptians*, London 1837, vol. II, p. 240 ff.

three days. Mere accidents of resemblance are excluded. The only difference is, as usual, that the
Bambaras, whose Islamism is skin-deep, have recourse
to a specific *ĝinn*, even as the uneducated Christian or
Mohammedan masses favor a particular saint for some
holiday. But the very name of *dasiri* given to the
protecting village *ĝinn* is significant, for *dasiri*, in
Bambara, also means "to gag, to stuff," from Arabic
دسر *ḍasara* "to push, propel, stab." In Berber the
related Arabic دغر *ḍagara* produces *deger* "to push,
shake, drive away," which leads in Hausa to *dakara* "a
guard, soldier." Hence we have in Bambara *dasiri*
"the one who drives away disease, a protector."

Henry records another series of fetishes, which he
identifies as belonging to the cult of Satan, namely the
boli or *nya*, who prefer to take up their residence in an
inanimate object with which they become one and the
same, so that in the sacrifices one addresses oneself to
the object as a whole, whereas in sacrificing to a *jine*
one addresses the inherent spirit. The *boli* are in-
trinsically bad, in revolt against the Supreme Being,
the Creator and Master of all things. They reside in
the fire, in hell, and every black man will tell you that
the *boli* is a demon (setane).

There are the minor *boli*, bad fetishes that have
nothing terrifying in them, in so far as they rarely cause
anybody's death. A large number of these are above
all medicine, and everybody has some of them. Such
are tails of cows, goats, dogs, without any special name,
and called *fura* (medicine). To these may be added the
kana, ox-horns and hoofs, filled with an unguent of
which it is hard to give the composition, blood, grease,
and dried and powdered fire-flies, mixed with iron and
coal dust and other ingredients. These *kana* are
different from the *kana* which every major *boli* posses-

ses and are no longer *boli*, but a part of a *boli*. This word *kana* means "that which protects, preserves, keeps evil away from us." These small fetishes are not celebrated, every owner merely besprinkling them with blood and sacrificing to them. The most powerful of these *boli* are the *boli* of the house, to whom the *guatigi*, the chief of the family, sacrifices a goat and at least a chicken and a kola nut for every male child.

Henry calls the "major *boli*" all those *nya* whose cult is secret and in whose mysteries only the initiated participate, after having solemnly sworn not to betray them. These receive an endless number of victims, and some of them are constantly covered with blood. At the sacrifices five or six sacrificers may participate. This is the great and true Bambara cult, which gives rise to orgies lasting from four to eight days. These *boli* are very much feared. They render justice and preside at all disputes, they have the right of life and death over men, and through them the Bambaras wreak their vengeance against a real or imaginary enemy. No victims are too noble for these *boli*, and there was a time when human beings were sacrificed for them. These blood-slaked *boli* are made from tree-bark, roots, goat-horns, etc. Some look like roughly made dolls, or a hippopotamus, a cow, an elephant, etc.

The cult of these *boli* is complicated. We have the *boli-tigi*, the owner of the fetish, and the *murukala-tigi*, the sacrificer, and the two *wara da*, the intermediaries between the fetish and its possessor. Through them the *boli* makes known its wishes and gives its orders, and its mouth-piece is in this case always seized with fits of epilepsy, followed by catalepsy. When he has spoken, he is brought out of this state by sprinkling some holy water upon him, when he takes his place as though nothing had happened; although but a minute ago his body was covered with perspiration, his limbs were agitated with a nervous spasm, his haggard eyes seemed to roll from their orbits, a bloody spittle flowed from his mouth, and his respiration was wheezy and broken. The *boli* has his beadle, the *darotigi*, who rings the bell for the sacrifice and sings the praises of the fetish, wherefore he is also called *nyā dyeli* "*boli* griot."

Henry divides all the *boli* into three groups. In the first he places the kingly or governmental fetishes which formerly were propitiated with human sacrifices. In the second are the *Tyiwara* and the *Duga*. The first is represented by a well-made mask of a goat or fawn. The chief *boli* belong to the third group, among which are the *Komo* and the *Nama*. The sacrifice to the latter is described as follows: In an enclosure where there is a bee-hive which serves as a tabernacle, only the officiating sacrificers may enter. The crowd of the fraternity members stay outside and approach only to present to the sacrificer a chicken and kola nuts of the sacrifice While the *Nama* is sprinkled with blood, two men, naked up to their waists and facing the crowd, stand motionless on each side of the sacrificer, holding in their hands two pieces of wood on which three sheep-horns and two other horns are tied. It is a great honor to hold these pieces of wood, and these people are called *dyenfa tyeu*. Two sacrifices a year are offered to these *boli*, one before the rainy season, at a time when, as the Negroes say, the male and female idols copulate, and the other about three months later, just before the grain is ripe.

There are also talking *boli*, who are reputed to put to death those who show them contempt, but are chiefly known for causing sickness and misfortune. They are in the hands of self-appointed sorcerers, veritable blood-suckers who run from village to village during the dry season, always stretching out a hand and begging.

The talking *boli* is generally an ox-tail on which the sacrifice is made   The owner generally has his paraphernalia in a case of fawn leather, from which one end protrudes a little.   This is his ensign, his mark of identity, unless it be the bell suspended from the flap of his leather case, which he rings in order to announce his coming.   The Bambaras consult these men, in order to find out their future or have their fortunes told.

As before, Henry's data are valuable, while his explanations lack foundation.   It is clear that the Bambara *boli*, that is, a Satanic *ǵinn*, is no other than Arabic خبل *ḥabal* "a malicious *ǵinn*, Satan," which among the Bambaras is also evidently applied to an amulet, where *fura* "medicine" and *kana* "to protect" are exact translations of the various Arabic words for "amulet."   The bloody sacrifices to the *boli* are reminiscences of pre-Islamic practices not entirely done away with by Mohammed, for these are expressly sanctioned in the Koran.[1]   The Bambaras, however, have added a number of features in their sacrifices taken from the dervishes, whose frantic dances and madness are in no way different from the epileptic and cataleptic fits of the Bambara sorcerer.   "Who does not know the dervish, not the wild sectarian of Persia   . . but the dervish by derision of northern Africa, whom the sceptics riddle with sarcasms, and the common people, considering him sincere, adore and venerate."[2]   The intelligent people call him *maḥbūl*, that is, "crazy,"[3] but the uneducated take this term merely to mean "possessed by a *ḥabal*," that is, "a religious epileptic."   The identity of the term *maḥbūl*, for which we get Hausa *maiboli, maibori* "obsessed," with the one possessed by

[1] J. Wellhausen, *Skizzen und Vorarbeiten*, Berlin 1887, vol. III, p. 110 ff.
18[2] O. Depont et X. Coppolani, *Les confréries religieuses musulmanes*, Alger 97, p. 96.
[3] *Ibid.*, p. 97.

a *bori*, as in the Bambara practice, does not admit of
any other conclusion than this, that we have among the
Mandingos, chiefly the result of the activity of the
Moslem *marabut*, the fakir of the Sudan.   That *bori*
originally meant "obsessed, insane" is shown by the
fact that the Tuaregs understand by *būri* "a vertiginous
disease of the brain among the Negroes, which drives
them mad."[1]   We also have the fuller form in Berber
hebel "to have a disturbed mind, be insane," *hebbuel*
"to turn topsy-turvy," *hebbel* "to get mixed up, be off,"
by the side of *hebbala* "ingredient which enters into the
composition of a philter," that is, "something which
makes one lose one's mind."   Thus we are brought back
to the Bambara *boli* "amulet, medicine."   In Tama-
zirt we have *amehbul* "crazy."   Thus the relationship
of Bambara *boli* to the Arabic خبل *habala* is put beyond
any possible doubt.

As we shall later, in America, have to deal with the
talking *bori*, we shall here place an early account of him,
as given by Jobson: "And to make vp the number at
all these meetings, there is one sure card that neuer
failes, which is their roaring deuill, that before I spake
of, whose attendance may seeme to keepe the youth in
awe, and he is called by the name of *Ho-re*, whose
strange report I proceede vnto: There is at all these
meetings, some distance of from the place, heard the
noyse of a roaring voice, resembling the greatest base
of a mans voice; when we demand of them what it is,
they will answer, with a kinde of feare, it is *Ho-re*, and
then describe him to be a fearefull spirit, that none may
come neere, without danger of being destroyde, carryed
away, or torne in pieces: there is at all their meetings,
vpon the first notice of his voice, a preparation for him
of all manner of victuals, they haue amongst them, euery

---

[1] H. Duveyrier, *Les Touareg du Nord*, Paris 1864, p. 436.

one imparting somewhat, all which is carryed towards
the voyce, and there vnder a tree set downe, and within
small time, bee it of what quantitie soeuer; it will bee
found deuoured, and not so much as a bone to bee
seene, vneaten, or left behind, and if they be not ready
forthwith to carry him such prouisions, as shall content
him, some of their vncircumcised sons are instantly
taken away; females he meddles not with, and saide to
remaine in *Ho-reyes* belly, some of them nine or tenne
daies, from whence they must be redeemed with some
belly prouision: and it is strange to heare, how confidently they will report vnto you, that they haue beene
carryed away, and beene abiding there: wherein this is
obserued, that looke how many dayes he hath beene
kept away, or remaining, as they say in *Ho-reyes* belly,
so many dayes after they returne, it must be, before
they will, or dare open their mouths, to speake a word.
For confirmation of which, this I haue seene: as I walkt
one day into the countrey from our dwelling to *Feramb-
ras* house, distant some foure mile, in the way we were
to passe through a towne of the Fulbies, among the
people that lookt vpon vs, I was shewed a youth of
some eighteene yeares of age, who they said, came but
the night before out of *Ho-reyes* belly: I went towards
him, and vrged him to speake vnto me, but still he went
backe from mee, and kept his finger before his mouth,
and notwithstanding I made what meanes I could, by
pulling and pinching of him, and more to terrifie him,
making proffers with a false fyer to shute at him, beeing
naturally exceeding fearefull of our gunnes, I could not
preuaile, neither make him open his mouth: notwithstanding afterwards, the same fellow did often come,
and haue commerce amongst vs: nay our people, who
were lying, and dwelling in the countrey, had beene at
seuerall times frighted with the voyce of this *Ho-rey*, for
hauing staide in their fowling, or being abroade, vntill

night hath ouertaken them, in their comming home, as
they haue saide, they haue heard the voyce of *Ho-re*, as
they might conceiue, some mile from them, and before
they could passe tenne steppes, hee hath seemed to be
in their very backes, with fright whereof, maintained by
their imagination, of their report went of him, they
haue not, without a gastly dread, recouered home: vnto
which place of dwelling, he neuer was so bold to make
any attempt: and verily my opinion is, that it is onely
some illusion, either by the Marybuckes, or among the
elder sort, to forme and keepe in obedience those
younger sort: for better approbation of what I suppose,
I will craue the patience, to set downe what I obserued
at the circumcision of our blacke boy: The nights were
very light, the Moone being then about the full towards
midnight, comming from *Bo Iohns* house to the place at
Faye, *Ho-reyes* voyce was wondrous busie, as it seemed
to me, not farre of.   I spake vnto my consorts, we
would secretly take our armes, and steale downe, to see
what it was, one of our three was backeward and vn-
willing, whereby it came to passe, our Marybucke
vnderstood what we intended, who came earnestly vnto
mee, intreating, I would giue ouer that dangerous attempt, saying, I could not finde him, for one cry would
be hard by me, and another instantly beyond the riuer,
which was a mile of, and there was great danger, he
would carry me into the Riuer with him: when hee
perceiued, he could not alter my resolution, he held mee
by the arme, and pointing to a blacke, not farre from
mee, held downe his head.   I went to that man, being
a very lusty fellow, to speake vnto him, whose voyce
was growne so horse, by crying like *Ho-re*, he had no
vtterance, whereupon I returned to my Marybucke,
and saide, there is one of your Deuils; who with a smile
went his way from me."[1]

[1] *Op. cit.*, p. 115 ff.

Delafosse's account[1] of Mandingo fetishism on the whole coincides with that of Henry, but he gives more space to the Mandingo *subarha* "sorcerer:" "The *subarha* or fortune-tellers are initiated into the magic of possession, who voluntarily allow themselves to be possessed by the *nyama*, the life-spirit of a dead person, in order to increase their power and to execute the vengeance for which the *nyama* is thirsting. They are very much feared, and certain religious associations, such as the *Komo* and *Nama*, devote themselves to the discovery and execution of such *subarha*. The latter, whatever may be said of them, are not anthropophagous, properly speaking; when they say that they have eaten an individual, that is merely a simple way of saying that they have thrown upon him a *korte*, a mysterious and mortal poison, or one reputed to be such. Similarly a man afflicted by a bad sore thinks that a *subarha* has sucked his blood. If a child has been eaten up by a hyena, they say that the author of this exploit is a *subarha* for the time being transformed into a hyena. These beliefs are exploited by the *namatigi* or priests of the *Nama* and by the *gbassatigi* or owners of amulets against all kinds of evils, who, if they have a grudge against some person, accuse him of being a *subarha*, in order to put him to death. Diseases and death are generally ascribed to the anger of a *ǵinn* or the spirit of a dead person, or to the sorcery of a *subarha*."[2]

The Malinke dictionary gives *subaḥa* "a night-man, were-wolf, sorcerer who runs through the night in quest of some evil deed and is accused of eating the souls," while the Bambara dictionary has *suba* "night sorcerer, were-wolf." It would seem that this is a native word derived from *su* "night," even as Soso *kuera-mikhi* "sorcerer" seems to be compounded of *kue* "night" and

---

[1] *Haut-Sénégal-Niger*, vol. III, p. 161 ff.
[2] *Ibid.*, p. 182 f.

mikhi "man" Yet we certainly have here Hausa *subāhi* "the dawn," from Arabic ‎صبح‎ *ṣubḥ* "the dawn," which was dreaded because even then the pre-Islamic Arabs made their ‎صابح‎ *ṣābiḥ*, their terrible predatory raid.[1] No wonder that the sorcerer should be identified with the masked raiders of the night.[2]

Before passing to the investigation of the popularity of the Mandingo *boli*, which we have seen to be of Arabic origin, it must be pointed out that even *tigi* of *bolitigi* is an Arabic word. Mandingo *tigi* means "chief, master, possessor." The Portuguese called all the African chiefs *xeque*, from Arabic ‎شيخ‎ *šaiḥ* "elder, chief." This Arabic word produced Malinke, Bambara *tigi*, Mandingo *tio*. In Columbus' *cacique*, as I have already shown, we have a compound, in all probability, *kun-tigi* "village chief,"[3] where *cique* is still closer to Arabic *šaiḥ*. Thus the Mandingo *bolitigi* "possessor of a *bori*," which in other Mande languages assumes the meaning "sorcerer," bears at once a double reminiscence of Arabic influence.

The religion of the *bori*, if this gnostic Islamism may thus be called, is found scattered over a large territory. It reaches down into the Bantu countries of the Congo, where we have a detailed account of it.[4] The national fetish of the Fans is called *bieri* or *bieti*, among the Fiots *bwiti*. As these terms also denominate the members of the association who know the mystery of this fetish,

---

[1] For the history of this terror in Europe read my *Contributions*, vol. IV, p. 324 ff.

[2] In an article, *Sur les prétendus loups-garous et sorciers nocturnes au Soudan*, in *L'Anthropologie*, vol. XXXI, p. 489 ff., Delafosse withdraws his previous statement in regard to the Sudanese were-wolves and denies their existence in native belief. But the discussion of Hausa *amina* at the end of this chapter shows that Delafosse was more nearly correct before than he is now.

[3] See vol. I, p. 71 f.

[4] H. Trilles, *Le totémisme chez les Fan*, Münster 1912.

it follows that we have here confusions of Mandingo *boatio*, Bambara *bolitigi* "fetishist" with Bambara *boli*, Mandingo *boa* "fetish." The secret society of the *bieri* is also found among the tribes of the Ngunye and the High Ogowe, totally unrelated to the Fans. The Fan *bieri* is identical with the Abambu *m'biri*, *m'biti*, the Ba-Kalé *m'bwiri*, *m'bwiti*, the Galoa *om'biri*, the A-duma *m'bweri*, the Batéké *bwĕté*, the Pahuin *m'bieri*.[1] "The chief fetish of the Pahuins is the *bieri*, whom only the initiated may know or invoke. The *bieri* is merely the skull of an ancestor, religiously preserved by the new head of the family, after the decomposition has done its work in the tomb. It is religiously kept in a box carefully coated with palm-oil and redwood powder, which is deposited in a rudimentary temple in the neighborhood of the head of the family. The *bieri* represents the Lares of the ancients, the protecting genius of the house and family: it keeps away the sorcerers, destroys black magic, makes women fertile, and procures riches. It is invoked in all difficult circumstances, and, as they are persuaded that the soul of the ancestor ordinarily lives in it, they sacrifice to it food and different objects which the Pahuins consider as especially precious. Nothing of importance is done without consulting them, and they can always tell, by certain signs, whether the *bieri* approves or condemns a certain undertaking."[2] Except for the ancestor worship, which seems to be a specific belief of these Bantus, everything else is identical with the worship of the *dasiri* among the Bambaras. This is further shown by the connection with the totem of a snake or other animal, in this case among the Fans,[3] just as the *dasiri* is connected with a lizard, snake, goat, etc.

[1] R. Avelot, *Note sur les pratiques religieuses de Ba-Kalé*, in *Bulletins et mémoires de la Société d'Anthropologie de Paris*, series VI, vol. II, p. 213 f.
[2] V. Largeau, *Encyclopédie pahouine*, Paris 1901, p. 336 f.
[3] Trilles, *op. cit.*, p. 49 ff.

Among the Malinke, the *Nama* takes the place of the Bambara *dasiri*, although all the Mande people also have the *Nama*, which, they agree, comes from Misango, in the province of Beledugu, that is, it was originally a local fetish.[1] "The *Nama* is the great chief of the village, the beneficent genius, the anti-sorcerer, the occult force and supreme element in the service of goodness against evil."[2] The appearance of the *namatigi* "the chief sorcerer" in Mexico as *amanteca*[3] makes it necessary to assume *nama* is not the original word in Malinke for what, to judge from Bambara *dasiri*, should mean "protection, religion," or something like it. Now, we have Arabic امان *'amān* "protection, safeguard, freedom from fear," which is found in Berber *aman*, *laman* "religion, faith, security, safe conduct, aid," Hausa *lamuni* "security," *amana* "confidence, trust, security." In Malinke initial *l* and *n* are often interchangeable, as in *la*, *na* "in," *labo*, *nabo* "go out," *lŭntā*, *nŭntā* "stranger," *nu*, *lu* "habitation," *loho*, *noho* "need," hence Berber *laman* could appear as *naman*, and we really have *nama*.

In the Hausa country the *bori* worship has received its most elaborate development,[4] but without adding any substantial changes. From here the *bori* worship has spread to the west and north. The possessor of a *bori*, or, to be more correct, one possessed by a *bori*, is in Hausa called *maibori*, in the plural *masubori*, and these Hausa words may be observed far away from their native home. Thus the women initiated into the Mendi *poro* society are known as *mabori*[5] or *marbori*.[6]

[1] Henry, *op. cit.*, p. 150.
[2] F. de Kersaint-Gilly, *Le Nama*, in *Bulletin du Comité d'Études historiques et scientifiques*, Paris 1919, No. 4, p. 429.
[3] See p.
[4] A. J. N. Tremearne, *The Ban of the Bori*, London 1914.
[5] T. J. Alldridge, *A Transformed Colony*, London 1910, p. 209.
[6] C. B. Wallis, *The Advance of our West African Empire*, London 1903, p. 246.

This chapter was all finished when I discovered additional proof of the fact that the Mande *Nama* worship was, on the one hand, a degraded Islamic rite, and, on the other, was related to the "hyena" by a philological vicious circle. "The hyaena is the buffoon of the animal world, and is deceived by the goat, the jerboa, the ostrich, the jackal, the scorpion, the lizard, the dog, even the donkey, and, of course, man; but he sometimes manages to avenge himself on the two latter. The hyaena is a noted thief, and has a bad name, and she is very vain, being quite overcome by flattery. She is fond of dancing and of music, and she once returns a child to its mother because the latter has taught her a song. She has some magic power of appearing and disappearing (though this is not shown in the tales), and is sometimes called *amina*, the friend, though for what reason I could not discover. One man informed me that the name is given because she tries to come into a man's house at night, but it may be that the Hausa magician resembles his colleague in North-West Uganda in being able to make the hyaena take the place of a dog, and in that case *amina* would be better translated by 'familiar,' perhaps. Another man said that *Amina* was simply one of the names of the beast, she having taken several so that she may have an advantage in the division of food, as is shown in the following story. Some of the animals had found a carcase, and the hyaena, being the biggest present, said 'I will divide it up.' She took one quarter, and said 'This is for *Amina*'; she took another fourth part, and said 'This is for *Burungu*' (despoiler); she took a third quarter, and said 'This is for *Maibi derri*' (Traveller by night); and then she took the remainder and said 'Now the rest is yours.'"[1]

[1] A. J. N. Tremearne, *Hausa Superstitions and Customs*, London 1913, p. 35 f.

Tremearne's surprise at the Hausa name *amina* can fortunately be explained. One of the Arabic sobriquets of the hyena is ام عامر *'ummu 'āmir*, but we also have عامر *'āmir* "the hyena." But the latter also means "worshipper." In Hausa the more common Arabic امنة *'amīnah* "the faithful one, believer," which sounds very much like عامر *'āmir*, has assumed the additional meaning of "hyena" for the common Hausa *kura*. The Mandes have taken over the Hausa word for the Islamic faith and, side by side with it, the Hausa *kura* "hyena," which, however, in Mande, is near in pronunciation to *koro* "old," and thus the new fetish became *amankoro*, later changed to *namakoro* "the old hyena." The Hausa and Mande connections of the cult with the hyena is not entirely gratuitous. The عمرة *'umrah* was an ancient Arabic cult, consisting in the visiting of Mecca,[1] and, at the same time, عامر *'āmir* is "a *ǧinn*, inhabiting a house," which easily led to the idea of "prowling," hence "a worshipper" and "a hyena" suggested themselves alike from the same philological root.

[1] Wellhausen, *op. cit.*, p. 74 f.

CHAPTER VI.

FETISHISM AND SUFISM.

Arabic قرا *qara'* "to read, receive instruction recite from the Koran, teach, greet, present in the name of another," but more especially "to recite magic words, to recite prayers over the dead," قرّا *qurra'* "holy man, devotee" have in Asante produced an enormous number of words relating to fetishism. The original meaning is preserved in *krã, kãnã* "to pray, recite, repeat prayers, ask or inquire of God, prophesy, soothsay (said of Mohammedans)," hence *Krãmo, Krãmoni* "Mohammedan." The form *kãnã* leads to *kan* "to read, count, number, reckon," *kankye* "to pray, rehearse or speak a prayer, invoke or call upon a fetish," *kenkan* "to read, count, tell, wail for the dead," *kã* "to speak, say, emit a sound, and (in compounds) by spoken words to cause or incur debts, mischief, recommend, reprove, reprimand, censure, utter an oath, swear, foretell, predict," *nkã* "to perceive, learn, hear, scent, smell." In the Akra language we have similarly *kla* "to divine, especially used of the fortune-telling and divining of the Mohammedans," *klamo* "diviner, soothsayer, especially Mohammedan fortune-tellers." The same root is found in the Mande languages, where we have Mandingo *kãrang*, Soso *kharan*, Bambara *kalan*, *kran*, Malinke *karã* "to read, study, teach," Vei *kãra*, *karan* "to learn." The word has penetrated wherever Arabic influence has been exerted, hence we have Hausa *karatu* "reading, story, language, words, to learn," Peul *karamoko* "reader of the Koran," Gbari *karatu* "reading, education."

In the Asante language this root has received its fullest development. From "to read, to pray" we pass to "to give a message," hence *kăra, kra* "to tell a message, send word, advertise, inform, give notice, appoint, ordain beforehand, predestinate, take leave, bid farewell;" *ṅkra* "errand, mandate, order, commission, word, message, information, notice;" *krã, kanã, kenã* "mark, visible sign made upon a thing for some purpose, significant token, character made instead of signature by one who cannot write;" *akrasem* "secrecy, secret." Similarly we get Akra *kã* "to say, reprove," Bambara *kã* "word, voice, tone, accent, neck, responsibility," Malinke *kã* "word, voice, noise, throat, neck," Soso *khui* "word, voice, noise, language."

We have already passed into the meaning "predict, foretell," hence it will be seen at once how we get Asante *okra, okara* "destiny, fate, lot, luck;" *ṅkra-bea* "fate, destiny, appointed lot, allotted life, final lot, manner of death;" *akrade* "luck, good luck, fortune, godsend, a final present given by a trader or retail-dealer to the peddler employed by him, a beloved, favorite thing, a thing belonging to the soul." From this we at once pass to *okra, okara* "the soul of man. According to the notions of the natives the *kara* of a person exists before his birth and may be the soul or spirit of a relation or other person already dead that is in heaven or with God and obtains leave to come again into this world; when he is thus *dismissed* in heaven, he takes with him his *errand*, i. e. his *destination* or *future fate* is fixed beforehand; from this the name *okara* seems to be drawn, and the realization of his errand or destiny on earth is then called *obra* or *abra-bo*. The *kăra*, put by God or by the help of a fetish into a child, can be asked while it is yet in the mother's womb. In life the *kăra* is considered partly as *the soul* or *spirit* of a person, partly as a separate being, distinct from the person, who protects him, gives him good or bad advice, causes his undertakings to prosper or slights and neglects him, and, therefore, in the case of prosperity, receives thanks and thank-offerings like a fetish. When the person is about to die, the *kăra* leaves him gradually, before he breathes his last, but may be called or drawn back. When he has entirely left (whereby the person dies), he is no more called *kăra*, but *sĕsă* or *osămăn*." "*Pl. akrafo*, a male slave chosen by his master to be his constant companion and destined to be sacrificed on his death in order to accompany and serve him in the other world." "*Okra, okărawa, a female slave* destined to be sacrificed on the death of her master."[1] "*Akra-kwă, a slave*, considered as *the king's okăra; a soul-slave, body-slave, page, valet de chambre*."[2] Similarly we have *Akra* '*kla, okla* "ghost, spirit, soul, genius, demon, the slave chosen by his master to be his continual companion and—according to the notion of some tribes of western Africa—to be sacrificed over his grave that he may accompany him in the world to come. The word is one of the greatest difficulty to be defined. According to the notion of the natives the *kla* of a person exists before his birth and may be the soul or spirit of a relation or other person already dead; as soon as a woman is with child, she goes to a fetishpriest and asks the *kla* of her child which is called by the priest, sundry questions, which are answered by the priest who pretends to hear the *kla* etc. In life the *kla* is considered partly as the soul or spirit of a person, partly as a being apart of and without him, who protects him, gives him good or bad advices, etc.; receives thanks and thankofferings as a fetish. Every person is moreover supposed to have two *kla*, a male and a female, the former being of a bad, the latter of a good disposition. After death the *kla*

[1] J. G. Christaller, *A Dictionary of the Asante and Fante Language*, Basel 1881, p. 254 f.
[2] *Ibid.*, p. 256.

becomes *sisa.* In the language of Christianity the word *kla* has formerly been used= δαιμων, afterwards it was left unemployed."[1]

Asante *kra-befwye* "wonder, wonderful sight, worthy to be advertised to persons dwelling elsewhere to come and see" at once explains Bambara *kaba* "wonder, miracle," Malinke *kava* "to admire," Soso *kabe* "to admire," Bambara *kaba* "to admire, be astonished, cry from fear," hence *kabako* "wonder, miracle." The form of the word in the Mande languages is obviously borrowed from the Asante *kra-befwye* or *ṅkra-bea* "destiny," and this is of importance as indicating the direction from which many Arabic words may have come.

The conception that the spirit existed before birth and that it is merely accompanying life, to be freed after death, is taken from the Sufis, and we shall soon come across some Sufi terms in connection with African fetishism. According to the Asante idea the *okra* is the accompanying protecting spirit in life, hence we get the corresponding Mande terms to mean "protector." We have *kalfa* "protector, guardian, patron, to entrust into one's care" and *kana* "to protect," Malinke *karfa* "to confide," *kãnta* "to protect, guard," Soso *kãnta* "to watch, guard," hence we get Bambara *kana* "cure-all, fetish medicine,"[2] that is, "protecting amulet."

The close relationship of Asante fetishism with Sufism may be gleaned from the Asante root *kom*. We have *kom* "to dance wildly in a state of frenzy or ecstasy, ascribed by the Negroes to the agency of a fetish;" *akom* "in the state of being possessed by a fetish," that is, "a temporary madness or ecstasy, expressing itself in dancing and wild gestures;" *ṅkom* "oracle, communication, revelation or message delivered by God or

[1] J. Zimmermann, *A Grammatical Sketch of the Akra- or Gã-Language,* Stuttgart 1858, vol. II, p. 151.
[2] Henry, *op. cit.,* p. 45 ff.

a fetish to a prophet or fetish man, prophecy, predic
tion;" *okomfo* "a fetish man possessed with or proph-
esying by a fetish, soothsayer, diviner, charmer,
sorcerer; the *komfo* pretends to be the interpreter and
mouth-piece either of the guardian spirit of a nation,
town or family, or of a soothsaying spirit resorted to in
sickness or other calamities;" *ṅkommo* "talk, chat,
concern, care, sorrow, solicitude, complain, lament,
moan;" *ṅkongya, ṅkonyã* "miracle, wonder;" *kum*
"to tire, weary, wear out, cause to cease, defeat, overcome, destroy, kill, disfigure, defile, pollute, to hinder
from using, stop, prevent, render ineffective, finish,
accomplish, put out the fire, be effaced." Similarly
we have Akra *'komo, ṅkomo* "sadness, grief, to relate a
sad story, complain, commune with each other in
confidence," *'komoyeli* "sadness, grief, sad story, story,
discourse."

At first thought, it would seem impossible to derive all
these connotations from a common root, but the whole
matter becomes clear as soon as we have before us
the Arabic group from which they are derived. We
have Arabic غَمّ *gamm*, غَمّة *gammah, gummah* "grief,
mourning, lamentation, unhappiness," غَماء *gumma'*
"calamity, misfortune, a hard affair in relation to which
one knows not the right course to pursue," غَمَّى *gumma*
"he swooned, became senseless, and then recovered his
senses; an abstraction or absence of mind that over-
takes a man, with languor of the limbs by reason of a
malady." This is sometimes confused with غَمْره
gamrah "difficulty, trouble, distress, the rigors of death,"
غَمْر *gumr* "inexperienced in affairs, one in whom is no
good nor profit with respect to intelligence or judgment
or work," from غَمَر *gamara* "to become much in

quantity." In the circular dance of the Sufis, known as سما *sama'*, the dervishes worked themselves up into a state of senselessness caused by ecstasy, غمرة *gamrah*,[1] when they had communion with God and uttered mystical sayings, غمار *gimār*.

Thus we see how the Asante connotations have changed from "weakness" to "prophecy, fetish." The same root is found over a large territory. We have Berber *gami, gammi, gum, gumi* "to be at the end of one's rope, to be harassed or fatigued, to refuse to do, resist," Bambara *komo* "disagreeable, difficult, disgust, contempt," *kuma* "word, discourse," Malinke *kuma* "word, discourse." There can, therefore, be little doubt that Malinke *koma* "chief of sorcerers," Bambara *koma, komo* "fetish" are identical with the Asante *kom*. Indeed the worship of the *Komo* is accompanied by lascivious dances, howling, and ear-rending sounds. "At dawn the *warada* thanks the audience in the name of the god *Komo*, while talking through a horn tube, another repeats the phrases through a reed pipe, and a *griot* of the *Komo* renders the words of God more clearly to the audience. And the crowd expresses thanks, utters cries, puts forward its demands, and everybody retires crushed, contrite, with his throat aflame, the spittle on his lips, and with tottering limbs,—during these festivals one must become intoxicated, in order to please the god."[2]

We have here the same ecstasy which we observed in the case of the *dasiri* festival among the Bambaras, and it is clear that we have here again a reminiscence of the greater and lesser festivals of the Moslems. This is made a certainty by the two great festivals of the As-

---

[1] R. A. Nicholson, *The kitāb al-luma' fi 'l-taṣawwuf*, in "*E. J. W. Gibb Memorial*" *Series*, Leyden, London 1914, vol. XXII, p. 145.

[2] Henry, *op. cit.*, p. 190 f.

antes, known as the *Adae* festivals. "On the Great and
Little Adae festivals, it is customary to offer sacrifices
to the tribal and national deities, the chiefs and men of
rank offering human victims, and the poorer classes
sheep and poultry. The festivals last three days. In
Coomassie, the commencement of an Adae feast is announced by the beating of the large state drum at sunset; and, upon this signal being heard, shouts, songs,
and discharges of musketry break out from all quarters
of the town. The Ashanti Government has utilised
these festivals for the purpose of keeping up a species of
surveillance over all strangers in the capital. About
six days before the Adae the king holds a palm-wine
festival, at which every stranger in Coomassie is bound
to pay his respects in person to the king, receiving in
return a jar of palm-wine, or some other small present.
On the Adae itself the king visits the buildings within the
palace enclosure, where the stools of the former kings
are preserved, and sprinkles them with palm-wine, or
with the blood of sheep and fowls, which are killed and
cooked for the *asrahmanfo* of the deceased monarchs.
Blood is also poured upon the stool of the dynasty.
This duty accomplished, the king then proceeds with
his chiefs, preceded by bands of music, to a part of the
city called *Mogya-woh*, literally, 'The blood dries.'
Here he seats himself, surrounded by his chiefs, and
strangers again present themselves, and are treated
with palm-wine."[1]

Adae is "a festival day, returning every forty-third
day; one feast, called *adae kese, akwasidae* (*adwedae*)
is celebrated on Sunday; another, 24 days later, called
awukudae, falls on Wednesday. The king receives all
his elders and honoured guests in his residence and
gives them drink and presents."[2] This is from Arabic

[1] A. B. Ellis, *The Tshi-Speaking Peoples of the Gold Coast of West Africa*,
London 1887, p. 228 f.
[2] Christaller, *op. cit.*, p. 60.

عيد ‘īḍ "fair held every ninth day, festival in general."
The greater and lesser festivals by this name have
already been referred to.[1] Thus we see once more
that the fetishism of the Asantes is mere "denatured"
Islamism.

We have Asante *onyame* "heaven, sky, the Supreme
Being, God," *nyãmo* "lean, feeble, tender, small, faint,
drooping, languid," *onyankopon* "the visible expanse
of the sky, God, rain." In some of the connotations
this is confused with Asante *tšwãm* "to become dry,
lean, languish, pine away." *Tšwãm* is from Arabic
ظمى *ẓaman* "the withering, drying up of the lip from
thirst," ظمى *ẓami'* "thirsty, lean, fleshless," ظماء
zam'a "a hot, scorching wind," ظما *zama'* "long for
ardently, crave for;" ظم *ẓim'*, pl. اظماء *aẓma'*, is "the
time, interval, or period between two drinkings, keeping the camels from the water until the extreme limit of
the coming thereto," hence the idea of "long journey"
naturally evolves from it, and we also get "the period
from birth to death." On the other hand, the root
nyam is evolved from Arabic خمع *ġam'* "collection, assemblage, multitude, army," hence خامع *ġāmi'* "the
collector of the created beings for the day of reckoning,
God, the mosque, a great town," خماعه *ġamā'ah* "the
orthodox faith, the Moslem community, school, world."

The two roots have become equally confused in the
Mande languages. We have Bambara *dyama* "assembly, reunion, village," *dyamani* "country, province,"
but Songay *dyam* "artisan, smith," etc., which are ob
viously from Arabic خمع *ġam'*, and *dyama* "to go on a
long journey," *dyan* "long, high," *dyamandyan* "very

---

[1] See p. 147 f.

long," which are derived from Arabic ظيم‎ *zim'* "long journey." Just as the Arabic word خماعة‎ *ġamā'ah* also means "the Moslem community, school," so *dyama* has in Bambara and Malinke come to mean "church," hence we have Bambara *dyamaso* "church" and Wolof *dyāmu* "to pray to God, to render to God the worship due to him," hence *dyamōme* "the word used to greet the king with," hence there can be little doubt that in Malinke, Bambara *dyamu* "family name" we have a derivative from the same Arabic word.

The tendency of African languages to abbreviate words leads to a large number of contaminations, where it is not at all easy to unravel them. Thus it is hard to tell whether Hausa *dāmīna* "rainy season" is the original Arabic سما‎ *sama'*, or whether there is here a contamination with the Arabic words just discussed. Similarly Soso *nyamena* "rainy season," by the side of the *sama* words in the other Mande languages, makes it hard to determine whether *nyamena* is derived from there or from the same word as the Asante word for "heaven," which is certainly at least a confusion with the "dry" word in Arabic. But Soninke *kamme* "rain" is, no doubt, a mere transformation of *sama*, since here *s* and *k* constantly interchange, especially since we have also Soninke *kamu* "heaven." According to Henry,[1] the dynamic force is in Bambara called *nyāma* or *dya*. The latter word will be discussed later. *Nyāma* may merely be a corruption of *dya* under the influence of the "heaven" words, which is the more likely, since we have in Asante a conception of such a dynamic force, which is derived from a word "to create (said of God)," namely *obra* "the coming into the world, the state of existence or life in this world, manner of life, conversation, behavior, conduct;" *bra*, *băra* "to

[1] *Op. cit.*, p. 26 ff.

make, enact a law or laws, to order with authority, to lay an injunction, command, forbid, prohibit, settle, come, become habitual, deceive, withhold, keep back;" *obra* "moral law;" *abrabo* "life in this world;" Akra *bla* "to come again into the world, be born once more, to be or behave in the world, to attach oneself to, behavior, character of a person."

All these words are from Arabic بَرَا *bara'* "a writing conferring immunity or exemption, a manifestation of excuse and a warning from God and his apostle;" بَرَا *bara'* "(God) created mankind or the beings or things that are created after no similitude or model, but out of pre-existing matter;" بَرّ *birr, barr* "goodness in the service of God, in paying regard to relations, acting well to them, and in dealing with strangers." The group is represented in Malinke *bila* "to authorize, send a commission, leave alone, bring up an animal;" Bambara *bla* "to authorize, put on one's account, accuse, give guarantee, condemn, simulate, leave alone, permit." In neither language is the word applied to the rebirth into a new body. In Asante *bra*, Mandingo *nyāma* we have a philosophic speculation on the soul, which most likely belongs to the Sufis, for we have already seen that life was represented as a span of time between two drinkings, and Mandingo *nyāma* and *dya* go back to the same conception.

The conception of 'heaven' was by many African tribes directly derived from the Arabic. Arabic الجَنَّة *al-ğannah* "paradise," from جَنّ *ğan* "to hide, conceal," is responsible for an enormous number of words throughout the northern part of Africa. Among the Berbers we have *igenni, ijenni* "heaven, firmament, atmosphere." Koelle reports for "heaven" Biafada *harādṣenna*, Timne *arīanna*, Mandingo *arīdṣenne, arādṣenna, aid-*

şenye, aldşeṅne, Bambara ardşene, Vei aldşenna, Soso arīyanna, arīdsanna, Hwida dşinukuzu, Mahi ẽdsinik-usu, Nupe aldşenna, Puka aldşenna, Bornu. tsannā, dşanna, Pika alēdşanna, Bode aldşenna, şlina, Kanika dşinnawēş, Wolof hādşanna, Soninke aldşenna, Boko alezonda, Kandin āldşenna, lāna, Timbuktu aldşenne, Mandara aldşena, Bagrimi, Hausa, Peul aldşeṅna.

Many of these words can be rectified and expanded in the light of later authorities. Timne ariann "heaven, paradise" has also d-areṅ, r-areṅ "rainy season,"[1] which, as we shall later learn, is the usual second connotation of Arabic سما sama' Bambara ardyana, ardyine leads to a confusion with dyine "invisible spirit, ĝinn." The Ewe languages (Hwida dşinukuzu, Mahi ēdşinikusu) are most instructive. We have Dahome jinukūsū "heaven, firmament," which Delafosse[2] takes to be from ji-nukū-nusū "heaven-eye-cover," but this is mere popular etymology, the root being jinu, which, as usual in the African languages, is abbreviated and is found as ji "heaven, rain, top, above," hence jijohõ "rain and wind, storm," jijoõ, jijowõ "storm," jikpa "heaven," jikpame "garden." We get a far better account of the root in the Ewe language,[3] of which Dahome is a dialect. Here we get dziṅkusi, dziṅko, dziṅgo, dzivbo[4] "heaven, firmament" and the apocopated dzi "heaven, clouds, surface, above, at." Just as from "spirit" we got the concept "protector," so here "heaven" leads to "help," hence dzi "to be at one's side, to help." There is an enormous mass of compounds from this root, such as dziḍuḍu "to have the upper hand, to reign," dziḥose "faith, Christian religion," dzime "above," dzimeanyisi, literally "wife

[1] N. W. Thomas, Timne-English Dictionary, in Anthropological Report on Sierra Leone, London 1916, part II, p. 3.
[2] Manuel dahoméen, Paris 1894.
[3] D. Westermann, Wörterbuch der Ewe-Sprache, Berlin 1905.
[4] This vb is a bilabial f.

of heaven and earth," but meaning "a priest of heaven and earth, worshipped as a divinity," *dziʋadola* "angel." In Akra we have similarly *džeṅ, dže* "world, everything visible, atmosphere, weather, outward appearance, behavior, manner, circumstances, life, commonwealth," hence *dženbā* "behavior, character, coming into the world," *bo džeṅ* "to create the world, begin, exist, live, behave," hence there cannot be the slightest doubt that *dže* "to come out, appear, become, arise" is from the same root, and this brings us back to Ewe *dzi* "to bear, be born."

We have already seen that Arabic الجنّة *al-ǵannah* produced Soso *ariyanna*, Timne *arian* "heaven," *areṅ* "rain." This led to Yoruba *oruṅ* "the sky, heaven, bow, the invisible world, hades." In Asante no word begins with an *r*. Here Yoruba *oruṅ* has become *ahuṅ*, *ahuṅmu, ahunum* "the air, atmosphere, the apparently empty space above the earth," *ahum* "a strong wind, gale, storm," *honhom* "a spirit," *ahonhom* "a mild, gentle wind," but more commonly, as if from Timne *arian* or Soso *ariyanna*, we have *ewyim* "the air, atmosphere, firmament, heaven, weather, the course of things," *ewyi* "the apparently vacant space encompassing the earth, atmosphere, firmament, the revolving, lucid air, the apparent arch or vault of heaven, the course of things, the world," *ewyiase* "what is under the sky or heaven, the world," *wyiasefo* "inhabitants of this nether world, mankind."

The Arabic سما *sama'* "heaven, firmament, roof," plural *samiy, suman*, also means "a cloud, rain, heavy downpour." In the latter sense it has survived in a large number of languages. We have Bambara *samian, saminya, samia, samyen, somyen*, Malinke *sama, samanya* "rainy season." Koelle reports Kono *sama*, Vei *samaro*, Soso *nyamena*, Gbandi *samai*, Mende *hāma,* Gbese *sāma,* Bagrimi, Hausa *dāmīna* "rainy season." We have already seen that in Timne *d-areṅ,* Dahome *ji* "rain" we, by analogy, have similar derivations from Arabic الجنّة *al-ǧannah.* Koelle similarly gives for "rainy season" Dahome *dṣi, odṣi, ozi,* Mahi *edyi, esi,* Anfue *edṣinuali,* Adampe *esinole.* The latter two are dialectic forms of the fuller Dahome *juvenu* "the long rainy season from March until June." The shorter forms at once explain Yoruba *adžo, edži* "rain," although it also has the other Arabic word, namely *sañma* "cloud."

In Bambara we have not only the above-mentioned "rain" words, but also *suma* "fresh, cold, shade, odor, rest" and "to measure, weigh, appraise, adjust, compare, assimilate." We have also, from *samian* "rainy season," *sandyi* "rain," *sanfe* "in the air, above," *sangirigiri* "thunder." We find here a confusion with another Arabic root, namely شرى *šara* "to buy, sell," which produces Malinke, Bambara *sara* "to pay," Soso *sara* "to buy, sell, prepare." In Malinke and Bambara this has become contracted to *san* "to buy, exchange," *sã* "marketplace," *sani* "purchase, sale." Similarly we have Malinke *sama, samanya* "rainy season," *sã* "air, atmosphere, heaven, year, to buy, sell." In Asante the connotation "heaven" leads to a whole series of spiritual words. We have *sũma* "to hide, in secret," *sunsumma* "shadow," *nsunsuañ* "the water of a heavy shower of rain overflowing the ground, but quickly flowing away," *sũnsũmã* "shade, shadow," *esũm* "darkness." From these we pass to *sumãñ* "charm, amulet, talisman, worn as a remedy or preservative against evils or mischief, any protecting power including the *abosom,*" *osumãnni* "the owner of a charm, one who understands how to make amulets and sells them, sorcerer, magician." But we have

similarly the Arabic ‏سماء‏ *sama'* "heaven:" *asāmāṅ*
"the world of spirits, the nether world, the lower regions,
the place of the dead; by some it is conceived to be in
the upper regions, the milky way being the road leading
to it.　It is said: In the realm of the dead there are
kings as well as subjects (slaves).　If you were sick in
this world for a long time, you will be restored to health
there after three years; but one who died in battle or by
accident will be well again in a short time, perhaps in
a month or so.　It is said: the realm of the dead is
below (in the earth); some say: it is above (in heaven);
about this there is no surety.　Where one is taken to,
when he dies, there his spirit is; when you die and they
take you to the spirits' grove, then your spirit is in the
grove.　The town (or country) of the departed spirits
is not in the grove, but in the earth; it is a large town
(city), a long way off, and in going there a mountain
has to be ascended.　The way of one who died a common death, is dark in heaven; but if one who died in
battle or by accident takes that way, some of the white
clay, with which he is rubbed, drops down, therefore
his way (the milky way) appears white.—In the spirits'
grove the departed spirits do not stay always; only on
certain single days they come and assemble there for
drinking or eating or playing;"[1] *osāmāṅ* "departed
spirit, ghost, goblin, spectre, apparition, skeleton of a
man.　There are, according to the opinions of the
heathen Negroes, three different kinds of departed
spirits: a) those who fell in battle (or by an accident,
as by a falling tree); b) common spirits; c) lingering
spirits.　The last named are not admitted to the world of
spirits, where the others are, but hover about behind the
dwellings; the spirits of those who were killed do not
associate with the common spirits; they walk about,
rubbed with white clay and in white garments; they

[1] Christaller, *op. cit.*, p. 407.

are not afraid, whilst the common spirits flee when they see a man, and do not wish even to be seen "[1] Here we are once more brought back to a Moslem speculation, for according to some views there are three categories of spirits of the faithful: the prophets enter heaven at once, the martyrs after a while, while all others linger by the graves or with Adam in heaven.

The same confusion of the two Arabic roots is found in Akra, where we get *susuma* "shade, character, reflection, soul," and *susumo* "measuring, thinking, thought." In Yoruba, where we have already found the "heaven" word, we have the Arabic "measure" word best preserved, for we have *aśuwǫṅ, ośuwǫṅ,* and the apocopated *wǫṅ* "to measure, weigh." The abbreviated Akra *susu* "to shadow, measure, think," Asante *susu, susuw,* Fante *sūsũ* "to measure, think, imagine, suppose, meditate, guess, utter a suspicion" are also found in Ewe *susu* "to measure, length, mass, to consider, regard, think, believe."

In Akra we find *woṅ,* plural *wodśi,* "fetish, idol, demon, something holy or belonging to the fetish. The African theology is shortly the following: God (Nyonmo, Nanyonmo, Mawu, Nyonmo Mawu) is the highest Being, the only one, the creator of heaven and earth; the fetishes, heaven, earth, sea, rivers, trees etc. but considered as spiritual or personal Beings, are his sub-deities, whom he has given the government and care of the world, demons, good and bad, male and female; there are such common to all (f.i. earth, sea); or to a part of men (rivers etc.); to a tribe, a town, a family, a single person; a person may possess a fetish or demon or be possessed by one. Besides there are innumerable things holy to, or belonging to, or made effectual by, a fetish, as cords, to be tied about the

---

[1] *Ibid.*

body or the house; teeth, chains, rings, etc. worn and
the like; which gave rise to the absurd belief, that the
African makes any thing, even a bottle, a cork etc. his
God: and hasty travellers and other people not having
time to ask and to learn have sustained this saying,
whilst a comparison with religious things and superstitions in the very heart of christendom would have
fully explained the matter without casting the African
together no more with men, but with brutes."[1] From
this we get a vast number of derivatives, such as
wondžamo, wonsuomo, wontšumo "fetish service, idolatry, heathenish religion," *wontše, wontšemei* "possessor
of a fetish," *woyeli, wonyeli* "fetish-eating, "*wolomo*
"highest fetish priest." This is all derived from
Arabic عوذة *'ūdzah* "a kind of amulet, phylactery, or
charm, bearing an inscription, which is hung upon a
man, or woman, or child, or horse, to charm the wearer
against the evil eye and against fright and diabolical
possession." That this is the real origin of the Akra
word follows from Akra *wulo, wolo,* plural *wodži,* "skin,
hide, leather, parchment, paper, book, note." The
plural in both words has preserved the Arabic form,
while in the singular the word has been abbreviated to
wo and lengthened by new suffixes. In the Adanme
dialect we find *womi* "skin, parchment, paper, book,
letter" and *wo* "fetish, idol, demon."

In Yoruba the word appears as *onde* "fetish tied to
the body," in Dahome as *vodū* "good or bad spirit,
fetish," hence *vodūhwe* "temple," *vodūnõ* "priest,"
while Ewe has the abbreviated *dzo* "fetish, magic,"
with a very large number of derived words. Asante
has received its words from Akra, for we have *wõma,
ṅhõma,* Fante *ahõma, ṅwõwa* "skin, leather, paper,

---

[1] Zimmermann, *op. cit.*, p. 337.

letter, epistle, book," but Akra *woṅsuomo* "idolatry."
produced Asante *abonsam* "wizard, sorcerer, demon,
devil," *abosonsom* "fetish service, idolatry, heathenism,"
abosom "tutelar or guardian spirit of a town or family,
imaginary spirits subordinate to God worshipped or
consulted by the Negroes." In the latter case we have
a phonetic confusion with Asante words derived from
Arabic *sama'*, even as this process may be observed in
the case of Yoruba *woṅ*,[1] where a similar confusion of
Arabic *sama'* and *'ūdzah* has taken place. It is this
common phenomenon of phonetic confusions that makes
African philology so extremely difficult, as already observed by Steinthal.

[1] See p. 177.

CHAPTER VII.

The Caraibs.

Léry[1] gives the following account of the *Caraibs* in Brazil: "It must be known that they [the Brazilians] have among themselves certain false prophets whom they call *Caraibs*, who, going from village to village, like the carriers of indulgences in papacy, make them believe that by communicating with the spirits they may in this way not only give power to whom they please, in order to vanquish their enemies, when they go to war, but also that it is they who make grow the large roots and fruits, which I have said elsewhere this country of Brazil produces. Besides, as I have heard from the Norman *truchemens*, who have lived for a long time in this country, our Toüoupinambaoults have the custom of assembling every three or four years in a great festival, and I, finding myself there without thinking of it (as you shall hear), can tell you the following for a fact. So when another Frenchman, called Jaques Rousseau, and I with a *truchement* were traveling through the country, having one night slept in a village called Cotina, early the next morning, as we were thinking of passing on, we saw, to begin with, savages from neighboring places arriving from all sides; with whom those of the village, leaving their houses, joined and were soon gathered in a large space, numbering five or six hundred. So we stayed on, to find out for what purpose this assembly was collected, and when we returned we suddenly saw them separate into three groups, namely the

[1] J. de Léry, *Histoire d'un voyage faict en la terre du Brésil*, Paris 1880, vol. II, p. 67 ff.

men in a house apart, the women in another, and the children similarly. And seeing ten or twelve of these *Caraibs* among the men, and suspecting that they would do something extraordinary, I insisted on my companions staying there, in order to see the mystery, which request I was granted. Thus, after the *Caraibs* had told the women and children, before they separated, by no means to leave the houses in which they were stationed, but to listen to them attentively from there when they began to sing, and after we were similarly ordered to keep inside the house in which the women were, and soon after we had breakfasted, without knowing what they were going to do, we began to hear in the house where the men were (which was not more than thirty steps from where we were) a very low noise, as you would say the mumbling of those who recite their prayers.

"When the women, who were to the number of about two hundred, heard this, they arose and pressing close their ears gathered in a crowd. But when the men had little by little raised their voices, and we distinctly heard them sing together and frequently repeat the particle of encouragement *he, he, he, hé,* we were all so perplexed when the women on their part answering with a trembling voice and repeating the same interjection *he, he, he, hé,* began to cry in such a fashion for a period of more than a quarter of an hour, that we, looking at them, did not know what to think of it. And, indeed, not only because they wailed so, but because at the same time, jumping up with great violence, they caused their breasts to shake, and foamed at the mouth, and some (like those who with us suffer from the falling sickness) fell all in a swoon, I thought that nothing but the devil had entered their bodies and they suddenly became mad. When I similarly heard the children quake and torture themselves in the same way in the dwelling where they

were separated, which was close to us, I, in spite of the
fact that for more than half a year I had visited the
savages and had otherwise become accustomed to them,
cannot disguise the fact that I was somewhat frightened
and, not knowing the issue of the game, wished myself
back in our fort.   However, when these confused noises
and howlings were ended, the men making a short pause
(and the women and children keeping quiet), we heard
them once more singing and raising their voices in a
remarkable accord, and I, having reassured myself to
some extent, when I heard these sweet and more
pleasing sounds, it need not be asked if I wanted to see
them close by.   But when I wanted to go out in order
to approach them, not only the women held me back,
but our *truchement* said that in the six or seven years
that he had been in the country he had never dared to
be among the savages during such a feast, and he
thought that I should not be acting wisely if I went
there, and might put myself in danger.   I was somewhat in suspense, but considering the matter more
carefully it appeared to me that he had not given me
any good reason with his statement.   Add to this the
fact that I was sure of the friendship of some good old
men who lived in this village in which I had been four
or five times, partly by force and partly of my own will;
and so I hazarded to go out.

"When I approached the place where I heard the
singing, and since the houses of the savages are very
long and round-shaped (something like the trellises of
the gardens over there) and covered with grass to the
ground, I, in order to see better and at will, made with
my hands a little hole in the covering.   Making with
my finger a sign to the two Frenchmen, who were looking at me, they followed my example; having taken
courage and come near without let or hindrance, we
three entered the house.   Seeing that the savages (as

the *truchement* judged) were not disturbed by us, but, on the contrary, keeping their rank and file in an admirable manner, continued their songs, we nicely retired into a corner, and observed them to our hearts' content. But having promised above, when I spoke of their dances in their drinking bouts and *caouinages*, that I would also tell of their other manner of dancing, so, better to represent them, here are their looks, movements, and countenances as they showed them. Close to each other, without holding each other's hands nor budging from the spot, placed in a circle, bending forward, swaying the body a little, shaking only their legs and the right foot, each one at the same time holding the right hand on the hip, the left arm and hand merely hanging loosely, they sang and danced in this fashion. Besides, since on account of the large crowd they formed three circles, having within each three or four *Caraibs* richly attired with robes, hats and bracelets made of new and manicolored natural feathers, each one holding in his hand a *maraka*, that is, a rattle made of a fruit larger than an ostrich egg, of which I have spoken elsewhere. In order that the spirit should later talk through them and initiate them to this usage, they rattled them at every rest, and you could not do better, in the state in which they then were, than compare them with those bell-ringers or those cheats who over there in deceiving the poor people carry from place to place the relics of Saint Anthony, Saint Bernard, and other such instruments of idolatry. Outside of the above description I have tried to represent to you the following picture of a dancer and player of the *maraca*.

"Then these *Caraibs*, advancing and leaping forward, and falling back, did not always stay in one place, as did the others. I also observed that, taking frequently a wooden pipe, four or five feet long, at the end of which there was the herb *petun* dried and burning, turning round and blowing in all directions the smoke upon the savages, they said to them: 'In order that you may overcome your enemies, receive the spirit of power;' and thus did these master *Caraibs* several times. After these ceremonies had lasted about two hours, these five or six hundred savages never stopping their dancing and singing, there was such a melody that, considering the fact that they do not know music, those who have not heard them would never believe that they could sing so well together in time.   In fact, instead of being somewhat afraid, as in the beginning of this celebration (when, as I said, I was still in the women's house), I now had in turn such a joy that, in hearing the well-measured accords of such a multitude, and especially the cadences and refrains of the ballad, in which they drew out their voices and said, *'heu, heuaure, heura, heüraüre, heüra, heüra, oueh,'* I was quite enchanted.   Every time I think of it my heart quivers, and it seems to me I still hear them.   When they wanted to stop, they struck the ground with their right foot more strongly than before, and then, after each one had spit out before him, all in a raucous voice said together two or three times, *'hé, hua, hua, hua,'* and then stopped.

"And as I did not yet understand their language perfectly and they had said several things which I had not been able to understand, I asked the *truchement* to tell me, and he said that in the first place they had lamented their deceased forebears who had been so brave.   Finally they consoled themselves because after their death they would surely go to find them beyond the high mountains, where they would dance and rejoice with them.   Similarly they had sworn dire vengeance on the Ouëtacas (a hostile, savage tribe, who, as I have said elsewhere, are so brave that they have never been able to conquer them), and that they would soon be taken and eaten by them, as their *Caraibs* had promised them. Moreover, they had introduced into their songs the story that the waters had once swelled so much that they covered the whole earth and that all people except their ancestors, who had saved themselves upon high trees, had been drowned. This last point, which among them approaches most the account in Holy Writ, I have heard them reiterate several times. And, indeed, it is likely that they had heard something of the flood from father to son, who, from the time of Noah, in keeping with human custom, had always corrupted and turned the truth into a lie, and being, besides, as we have seen before, deprived of any manner of writing, they find it hard to keep things in their purity, and have invented this fable, just as poets do, that their ancestors saved themselves in the trees.''

I have already pointed out the fact that *Caraib* as the denomination of a tribe is a ghost word,[1] and is based on Columbus' attempt to identify the Indians with a people of the Great Khan, hence *Cambalu*, for which he was looking, appealed to him more especially. But there must have been some specific reason why he chose *Cariba, Caniba, Canima* as corruptions of such a local name. In Brazil the words *carai, caraiba, cary'ba* were not used in regard to an Indian tribe, but to strangers, more especially such as practised magic, hence Léry's story of the *Caraibs* is of great interest, in so far as it confirms our deduction. Columbus knew that some class of Indians, who were addicted to cannibalism, were thus called, and his unfortunate generalization of the name in time led to the application of this word to the tribes hostile to the Spaniards. In 1511 a number of island Indians revolted against the Spaniards and killed a number of white men. It does not appear that they ate any of their bodies, but the

[1] Vol. I, p. 42 f.

fact that they were hostile to the Spaniards at once caused them to be classed among the *Caraibs*, and they could be raided and sold into slavery, while those who had submitted to the government could not be seized.[1] In 1520, Judge Figueroa of Hispaniola gave a summarized statement as to what tribes he considered to be *guatiaos*, that is, pacific, and what tribes were *caribes*, and it is evident from his conclusion that as soon as a *caribe* tribe became pacific it was no longer *caribe*, but *guatiao:* "A las cuales dichas provincias é tierras de suso declaradas por de *caribes*, debo declarar é declaro que los cristianos que fueren en aquellas partes con las licencias é condiciones é instrucciones que les serán dadas, puedan ir é entrar, é los tomar é prender é cautivar é hacer guerra é tener, é traer, é poseer, é vender por esclavos los indios que de las dichas tierras é provincias é islas así por *caribes* declarados pudieren haber en cualquiera manera, con tanto que los cristianos que fueren á lo susodicho no vayan á lo hacer sin el veedor ó veedores que les fueren dados por las justicias ú oficiales de Su Majestad que para las dichas armadas diesen la licencia; é que lleven consigo de los *guatiaos* de las islas é partes comarcanas á los dichos *caribes*, para que vean é se satisfagan de ver cómo los cristianos no hacen mal á los *guatiaos*, sino á los *caribes*, pues los dichos *guatiaos* se van é quieren ir con ellos de buena gana."[2]

Guatiao is for the first time given by Herrera under the date of 1502. "The Indians of the province of Higuey, seeing themselves in extreme misery and in the hills, sent to ask for peace, and the Governor granted it to them, offering not to do them any ill if they agreed to give a part of their bread work to the King. Many caciques came to see Juan de Esquivel, as General of

[1] *Colección de documentos inéditos de Ultramar*, series II, vol. V, p. 258 ff.
[2] *Colección de documentos inéditos relativos al descubrimiento, conquista y colonizacion de las posesiones españolas en América y Occeanía*, vol. I, p. 383 f.

this emprise, and among them was Cotubanama, powerful and valiant, and of honored presence, who, from that time on was called Juan de Esquivel, because it was a league among the Indians to exchange names, and, when they did so, they became *guatiaos*, which meant as much as 'confederates,' and 'brothers in arms.' "[1] Las Casas similarly says: "This change of names in the common language of this island was called to be I and such a oné, who change names, *guatiaos*, and thus one called the other; they considered themselves closely allied and as establishing a league of perpetual friendship and confederation, and thus the Captain General and that lord became *guatiaos*."[2]

It does not take much to observe that we have here Arabic وديعة *wadīʿah* "subject, convention, protection," وديع *wadīʿ* "quiet, mild, gentle, peaceable," from ودع *wadaʿa* "to deposit, put in safety, make a treaty, enjoy in peace." The Arabic word is unquestionably from the LLatin *vadium*, Latin *vadimonium* "surety, pledge," but it has been confused with the Arabic وعد *waʿd* "promise," which has affected a large number of European words. Thus we have Gothic *wadi* "pledge" by the side of *gawadjon* "to promise in marriage."[3] In Africa the two produce an interesting series of words. We have Berber *uād* "to promise, make a vow, convoke," *uāda* "promise, vow, alms," Songay *wadu* "promise." In Hausa we get *wada* "treasure," *wadata*, *wodata* "riches." Asante records *aguade* "goods, merchandise," *aguadi* "trade," *aguadini* "trader," hence *egua* "public place, market, trade, council," hence *oguasoni* "member of a council,"

---

[1] A. de Herrera, *Historia de las Indias*, Madrid 1730, dec. I, lib. V, cap. 4. See also dec. I, lib. VII, cap. 4.

[2] B. de Las Casas, *Historia de las Indias*, Madrid 1875, vol. III, p. 47 f.

[3] Of the European development of the two Arabic words I shall treat in another work.

oguasonipa "gentleman." Asante *egua* explains Yor uba *owo* "trade." The series of words that interests us here is in the Mande languages. Here we have Malinke *wõndi, woli*, Bambara *wali, woli* "one's neighbor." In Wolof we have *ande* "friend." In all these there is a contamination with Arabic ولي *walī* "relative, neighbor, friend." Hence it is clear that in the Mande languages the Arabic وديعة *waḍīʿah* had assumed the meaning "a pledge, an exchange between two persons which constitutes friendship," which evolved from the idea of barter that led to the Asante "trade, market," etc., and the exchange of names among the American Indians is just such a barter. The *Caraib* soothsayer is more commonly called *paje* or *page*, and Stade tells of them as follows: "They believe in a thing which grows, like a pumpkin, about the size of a half-quart pot. It is hollow inside; they pass through it a stick, cut a hole in it like a mouth, and put therein small stones, so that it may rattle. Herewith they rattle when they sing and dance, and call it *Tammaraka*.

"Of these, each of the men has one of his own. Now, there are among them some who are called *Paygi;* these are esteemed among them as fortune-tellers are here. The same travel through the country once a year to all the huts, and assert that a spirit had been with them, who came from foreign places far off, and had given them the power to cause all the *Tammaraka* (rattles), which they selected, to speak and to become so powerful as to grant whatever was supplicated from them. Everyone then desires that this power might come to his own rattle. Upon this they make a great feast, with drinking, singing, and soothsaying, and they perform many curious ceremonies. The soothsayers thereupon appoint a day in a hut, which they cause to be vacated, no women or children being allowed to remain therein. Then the soothsayers command that each shall paint his *Tammaraka* red, ornament it with feathers, and proceed thither, and that the power of speech shall be conferred upon them. Hereupon they go to the hut, and the soothsayers place themselves at the head, and have their *Tammaraka* sticking close to them in the ground. The others then stick theirs also hard by: each one gives these jugglers presents, which are arrows, feathers, and ornaments, to hang to the ears; so that his *Tammaraka* may on no account be forgotten. Then, when they are all together, the soothsayer takes each man's *Tammaraka* singly, and fumigates it with a herb, which they call *Bitten*. Then he places the rattle close to his mouth, and rattles therewith, saying to it: 'Nee Kora, now speak, and make thyself heard, art thou therein?' Presently he speaks in a soft voice, and just a word or two, so that one cannot well perceive whether it is the rattle or he who speaks. And the other people believe that the rattle speaks; but the soothsayer does it himself. In such manner he proceeds with all the rattles, one after the other: each one then believes that his rattle contains great power. Thereupon, the soothsayers command them to go to war, and to capture enemies, for that the spirits in the *Tammaraka* desire to eat the flesh of slaves. Then they go forth to make war.

"Now, when the soothsaying *Paygi* has made gods out of all the rattles, each one takes his rattle, calling it his dear son, builds for it a separate hut, wherein he places it, puts food before it, and demands from it everything that he wants, just as we pray to the true God. These are now their gods. Of that very God who created heaven and earth, they know nothing, they consider the heavens and the earth to have existed from eternity; and they know nothing particular about the creation of the world.

"For they say, once there had been a great water, which had drowned their forefathers, some of whom had escaped in a canoe, and others on high trees. Which, I opine, must have been the Deluge.

"Now, when I first came among them, and they told me thereof, I thought there was such a thing as a devil-spectre (evil spirit); for they had often told me how the rattles spoke. But when I went into the huts wherein were the soothsayers, who were to make them speak, they were all obliged to sit down; and, seeing the imposture, I went from out of the huts, thinking what an un fortunate beguiled people it was."[1]

We have here the specific statement that the canni balism was of a religious character, "for that the spirits in the *Tammaraka* desire to eat the flesh of slaves," and we are also told that the Brazilians did not eat their enemies from hunger, but from great enmity.[2] Although pure cases of cannibalism for mere enjoyment may have occurred, it is significant that fallen enemies were not devoured, but those who were specifically kept for the occasion, after they had been given a wife to solace with. The cannibalism is clearly connected with the activity of the *Caraib*, the priest, and this brings us back to the African deteriorations of the Arabic *qara'*, the reader of the Koran, the learned priest who sacrificed to God. Even before Islam the Hebrew קָרָא *qārā* "the reader of the Bible" is found in Syriac *qarâitâ* not only as "invocation to God," but also as "invocation to spirits," and this led to LLatin *caragius* "soothsayer." This word is found in Caesar of Arelatum, in a church council of the end of the V. century, and in Pseudo-Augustine. The latter is certainly a late work, and the first, too, may have inter-

---

[1] A. Tootal and R. Burton, *The Captivity of Hans Stade of Hesse* (The Hakluyt Society), London 1874, p. 145 ff.
[2] *Ibid.*, p. 151.

polations. In that case the word got into the church through the Arabic. This *caragius* is found in Norman French as *carâs*, *quéras*, in OFrench as *caraut*. In America the word seems to be confined to the eastern part of South America, to the Tupi-Guarani and Caraib languages. The variant forms *cariba*, *caliba*, *canima*, *carai* are already found in the Mandingo languages, where we have the forms *kara*, *kana* side by side, and *ba* or *ma* are the usual suffixes denoting agent. Thus we have Mandingo *karamo*, Soso *kharamokho* "teacher," Bambara *kanfa*, *kalanfa* "professor," Mandingo *kantiba* "supervisor," and Bambara forms like *kariba*, *kaniba* are a matter of course,[1] though not recorded. Thus we are brought back to the Mandingo origin of the name of the American fetish man.

The calabash rattle is, according to our sources, the chief implement of the American fetish man, and in it resides the speaking divinity. Early in the XVI. century Cabeça de Vaca found the gourd rattle in universal use in North America: "At sunset we reached a hundred Indian habitations. Before we arrived, all the people who were in them came out to receive us, with such yells as were terrific, striking the palms of their hands violently against their thighs. They brought us gourds bored with holes and having pebbles in them, an instrument for the most important occasions, produced only at the dance or to effect cures, and which none dare touch but those who own them. They say there is virtue in them, and because they do not grow in that country, they come from heaven: nor do they know where they are to be found, only that the rivers bring them in their floods."[2] "When we came near the houses all the inhabitants ran out with delight and great festivity to receive us. Among other things, two

[1] H. Steinthal, *Die Mande-Neger-Sprachen*, Berlin 1867, p. 91.
[2] T. B. Smith, *Relation of Alvar Nuñez Cabeça de Vaca*, New York 1871, p. 142.

of their physicians gave us two gourds, and thenceforth we carried these with us, and added to our authority a token highly reverenced by Indians."[1] "For the protection of the messengers, and as a token to the others of our will, we gave them a gourd of those we were accustomed to bear in our hands, which had been our principal insignia and evidence of rank, and with this they went away."[2] Except for Alaska, the gourd rattle is universal in the two Americas, and among some tribes the sign for "rattle" also means "sacred."

The rattle, especially the gourd rattle, is the constant accompaniment of the African fetish man, as we have already seen. The shaman of all regions, in Asia as well, uses the rattle in order to scare away the evil spirits, but in Africa the use of the *gourd rattle* as a sacred instrument, in which the spirit resides, is due to a linguistic misunderstanding. The Arabs did not use bells to convoke the faithful, but merely called them to prayer. But in the Mohammedan countries the Christians for a long time preserved the use of the sounding board, the مطرقة *mitraqah*, which was also employed by magicians. In the Sudan this word is found, both with the original meaning of "hammer," and, much corrupted, of "bell, rattle." We have Berber *lemterqet*, Songay *ndarka*, Hausa *matalaka*, *muntalaka*, Malinke *mänterge*, Bambara *mantaraka* "hammer." Songay *ndarka* at once explains Bambara *n'tana*, *n'dana*, *dana*, *tana*, Malinke *talã*, Mandingo *talango*, Soso *tolonyi* "bell, rattle," which shows that at an early time the Arabic *mitraqah* had in the Western Sudan the meaning "rattle."

Arabic قرأ *qara'* "to read," etc. was by the Arabs confused with قرع *qur'a* "to tell fortunes," and the

[1] *Ibid.*, p. 149.
[2] *Ibid.*, p. 191.

divination called *qur‘a* was permitted by Moslem law.[1] This kind of divination, however, linguistically coincided with the word which means "gourd," for we have *qar‘*, *qar‘ah*, *qurai‘ah* "gourd," and the latter also means "rattle." We have, in Africa, Berber *qrāa* "divination," Hausa *gora*, *kworia* "calabash," *kuria* "dice, lots," Bambara *koro* "meaning, comprehension," *korofo* "to translate, interpret," *koroni* "small calabash," Malinke *koro* "meaning, sense, calabash." In Asante we have *kora* "gourd, a vessel made from one half of a dry gourd scooped out and used for various purposes," and also *apakyi*, from some other root, "a bread calabash," and *mpakyiwafo* "a man or woman possessing a soothsaying fetish in a calabash, which, when asked, he or she takes upon the head and, without holding, lets it slip forward or backward, to the right or left." The *Caraib* rattle is obviously a direct development of the Mandingo gourd rattle. The very name *maraca* is the Arabic مطرقة *mitraqah*. The Tupi dictionary records *maraca* "gourd rattle," *maracainbara* "wizard, witch." In Guarani we have similarly *mbaraca* "gourd rattle." In Arawak *marraka* means "gourd."

The imprecation of the *Caraibs* consists in a series of songs or chants, of which the refrain is *haüre*. Similarly the Mandingo Negroes call their talking devil *Hore*.[2] This is found in Malinke as *ḥera* "peace, tranquillity," in Bambara as *héra*, *hérè* "peace, luck, benediction." When one asks, "Kori *héra* bé How are you?" the answer is "*Héra* Peace!" The usual greeting is "Alla ma *héra* kényé" or similar words, which mean, "May God give you peace!" The same is found in Berber as *ḥir*, *hēr* "good," hence "Yaz-ik si-lḥir May God reward you!" In Asante we get *hyira*

---

[1] Doutté, *op. cit.*, p. 375.
[2] See p. 154 ff.

"to bless, wish happiness, invoke, bestow a blessing, esteem, curse, blaspheme, decide, give validity, renounce, resign." "*Ohyira n'ano*, 'he blesses his mouth,' is used for some religious or ceremonial observances of the heathenish negroes, viz. a) he washes at the watering-place;— b) he takes some water into his mouth and squirts it into the calabash again, uttering certain petitions to his soul (for money, length of life, honour, recovery of lost property &c.); or, he spurts the water to the ground and invokes a blessing or a curse on others;— c) he takes some consecrated fluid (water mixed with some 'medicine') into his mouth, spurts it and mentions something by which he brought a curse upon himself, asking for the removal of the same, and for new blessing."[1] We have also Yoruba *irè* "goodness, well-wishing" and *iré* "a curse," *rè* "to be good," *rère* "goodness," Ewe *yra* "to pray for a person, ask a blessing," *yre* "bad, malicious."

It will be observed that the *Caraibs* at the end of the ceremony spit out, obviously to invoke a blessing or a curse, just as in the Asante ritual. The whole thing is of Islamic origin. "There is in the collections of tradition a chapter, which is found in all the books of the ʿ*aḍab*, generally in regard to religious injunctions which have reference to commerce, and which is called '*istiḥārah*. The prophet there recommends a special prayer each time one finds oneself in indecision and when it is necessary to make up one's mind. This prayer is short: God is asked to indicate the part one is to take in such and such a circumstance, which is specifically mentioned: later one may make divinations by writing on pieces of paper the different solutions possible in the matter, unless one feels a decisive inspiration from above. Such is the orthodox '*istiḥārah*: it is, to sum up the case, a drawing of lots by invoking God, and

[1] Christaller, *op. cit.*, p. 208.

resembles the *qor'ah.*"[1] "Jābir says: 'The Prophet taught the *'istihārah*, as he also did a chapter of the Koran; and he said, "When anyone of you intends doing a thing, he must perform two *rak' ah* prayers expressly for *'istihārah*, and afterwards recite the following supplication: O God, I supplicate Thy help, in Thy great wisdom; and I pray for ability through Thy power. I ask a thing of Thy bounty. Thou knowest all, but I do not. Thou art powerful, and I am not. Thou knowest the secrets of men. O God! if the matter I am about to undertake is good for my faith, my life, and my futurity, then make it easy for me, and give me success in it. But if it is bad for my faith, my life, and my futurity, then put it away from me, and show me what is good, and satisfy me. And the person praying shall mention in his prayer the business which he has in hand.,'"'"[2]

Dozy[3] says: "What is called *'al-istihārah*, and at Medina *al-hīrah*, is a collection of religious practices by which one consults God on things one is about to undertake or on the issue of such an undertaking. One purifies oneself, says the prayers of obligation (*salāh*), or a prayer called *salāh ul-'istihārah*, recites a supererogatory prayer (*zikr*), after which one lies down to sleep and sees in a dream what one is to decide upon. Or one recites three times the first and the one hundred and twelfth chapter of the Koran and the fifty-ninth verse of the sixth chapter, after which one opens the Koran at random and draws an answer from the seventh line of the right-hand page." Lane, from whom this information is taken, mentions the fifty-eighth verse of the sixth chapter. As both are appropriate and bear on our subject, the whole is given here: "With him are the keys of the secret things; none

[1] Doutté, *op. cit.*, p. 412 f.
[2] T. P. Hughes, *A Dictionary of Islam*, London 1885, p. 221.
[3] *Supplément aux dictionnaires arabes*, Leyde 1881, vol. I, p. 415.

knoweth them besides himself: he knoweth that which
is on the dry land and in the sea: there falleth no leaf
but he knoweth it; neither is there a single grain in the
dark parts of the earth, neither a green thing, nor a dry
thing, but it is written in the perspicuous book.   It is
he who causeth you to sleep by night, and knoweth
what ye merit by day; he also awaketh you therein,
that the prefixed term of your lives may be fulfilled;
then unto him shall ye return, and he shall declare
unto you that which ye have wrought."

The divination of the '*istiḥārah* is in the Magreb
combined with the interpretation of dreams, wherefore
Doutté says: "The Magrebian '*istiḥārah* appears to be
nothing but an ancient incubation, not recognized by
Islam, and Islamized under the cover of the orthodox
'*istiḥārah*, which had nothing to do with it. . . .If one
could have good dreams and dream them aloud, it would
be a kind of oracle.   In the books on magic there are
prescriptions how to make the sleepers talk, but they
are not particularly adapted for divination.   Al-Bakrī
says that in the Rif there were individuals called *er
reqqāḍa*, that is, sleepers, who fell into a lethargy and remained in that stage for several days, making at their
awakening most astonishing prophecies.   The fumigations with incense, according to Ibn-Haldūn, put
certain individuals into a state of ecstasy, when they
foresaw the future."[1]   "The Egyptians place great
faith in dreams, which often direct them in some of the
most important actions of life.   They have two large
and celebrated works on the interpretation of dreams,
by Ibn Shaheen and Ibn Seereen; the latter of whom
was the pupil of the former.   These books are consulted, even by the learned, with implicit confidence.
When one person says to another, 'I have seen a dream,'
the latter usually answers, 'Good' (*ḥair*), or, 'Good,

[1] *Op. cit.*, p. 414 f.

please God.' When a person has had an evil dream, it is customary for him to say, 'O God favour our lord Mohhammad!' and to spit over his left shoulder three times, to prevent an evil result.''[1]

Just as in the Arabic practice, so in the African and in the American there is a use of incense, in America—the incense *par excellence*—tobacco, to produce or seem to produce a lethargic state, and then to prophesy. As in the Arabic, so in the Asante ritual, a curse or averting of the curse is accompanied by spitting, and the same is done by the *Caraibs* of the Brazilian ritual. And, to cap the climax, the *ḥair* of the Arabic prayer, which gives the very name to the whole ritual, becomes the name of the "speaking devil" of Jobson. In reality, however, it means exactly the same in Bambara as in Arabic, and in Tupi is the refrain of the ritual songs. As in the African festival of the tutelar deity, so in the American practice we have the separation of the women and children, the weird dancing, the shouting, the neurotic state of the communicants, the ensuing festivity, the offerings to the fetish priest. That dreams were the chief means of the *Caraibs* for predicting the future is distinctly mentioned by Stade: "When they desire to carry war into their enemies' country, their chiefs assemble, and deliberate how they will do it. This they then make known through all the huts, that they may arm themselves. And they name the fruit of some kind of tree, when it becomes ripe, (as the time) when they will set forth; for they have no denominations for year and day. They often determine a time for setting forth, when a kind of fish spawn, which are called Pratti in their language, and the spawning time they call Pirakaen. At such time they equip themselves with canoes and arrows, and with provisions of dry root-meal, which they call Vythan. Thereupon, they consult with the Pagy,

[1] Lane, *op. cit.*, vol. I, p. 358.

the soothsayers, whether the victory will be on their side.   These, then, probably say 'Yes'; but they also command them to pay attention to the dreams which they dream of their enemies.   If the greater number dream that they see the flesh of their enemies roasting, this means victory.   But when they see their own flesh roasting, it bodes no good; they must remain at home. Now, when the dreams please them well, they make ready, brew much drink in all huts, and drink and dance with the Tammaraka idols, each one begging of his, that he may help him to capture an enemy.   Then they sail away.   When they come close upon their enemies' country, their chiefs command them, on the eve of the day upon which they intend invading the enemies' country, to recollect the dreams which they may dream during the night."[1]   Thus we are brought to the positive proof that the Tupi ceremonial is identical in substance with the Mandingo ritual, which itself is based on the Moslem 'istiḥārah.

[1] *Op. cit.*, p. 151 ff.

CHAPTER VIII.

The Areyto.

Oviedo says: "The people [of the islands] had a good and gentile way of remembering past and ancient events; and this was in their songs and dances, which they call *areyto*, which is the same as we should say 'to dance singing.' This *areyto* they did in the following manner. When they wished to have some pleasure, celebrating among themselves a certain notable feast, or, without this, just for their pastime, many Indians (and sometimes the men and women separately) came together, and in the general feasts, such as in case of victory over an enemy, or when the cacique or king of the province married, or in any other event where the pleasure was in common, and men and women congregated. And, the further to extend their joy and pleasure, they sometimes took each other's hands, and at other times linked arms, walking in a close file (or even in a circle), and one of them took the office of leader (and it could be either a man or woman), and he made certain steps forward and back, in the manner of well-arranged countersteps, and immediately the rest did the same, and they walked around, singing in that high or low voice intoned by the leader, and did as he did and said, the steps being taken in perfect order and union, and in keeping with the verses and words which they sang. And as he says, the multitude responds with the same steps and words and order; and as they respond, the leader becomes silent, although he continues to take the counterstep. When they finish the response, that is, the repetition of what the leader has said, he immediately, without interval, passes to the next verse or words, which the circle again repeats; and thus, without stopping, he keeps them going for three or four hours or more, until the master or leader of the dance has finished his story, and sometimes he keeps them at it from one day to another.

"Sometimes they mingle with the song a drum which is made of a piece of round, hollow, concave wood, as large as a man, and more or less, as they wish to make it, and it makes a noise like the hollow drums of the Negroes, but they put no leather upon it, and there are only holes which pass to the hollow inside, whence it rattles badly. With this poor instrument or without it they in their singing (as was said) relate their past events and histories, and in these songs they relate the manner in which their caciques had died, and how many there had been of them, and other things which they do not wish to be forgotten. Sometimes these leaders or dance-masters make a change, and, in changing the tune and the counterstep, they proceed in the same story, or tell another (if the first is ended) in the same tune or in another. . . .

"While these songs and countersteps or dances last, other Indians come and give the dancers something to drink, without their stopping while drinking, but always shuffling their feet and swallowing what is given to them. What they drink is certain drinks used among them, and when the feast is finished most of them are intoxicated and without any consciousness, staying on the ground for several hours. And when one falls down drunk, he is removed from the dance, and the rest continue, until the very drunkenness makes an end of the *areyto*. This happens when the *areyto* is solemn and made at weddings and funerals or on account of a victory, or a victory and feast to be obtained; because they have other *areytos*, without becoming intoxicated.

Thus some from this vice, others from studying this kind of music, they all know this type of story-telling, and sometimes other similar songs and dances are invented by such among the Indians as are held to be discreet and possessed of a better genius and faculties."[1]

Although the word *areyto* is not used there, we are similarly informed by Oviedo that in Venezuela, at the death of a cacique or chief Indian, all the people of the village where he lived and his friends from nearby places gather and weep through the night in a loud voice and sing, relating in their song what the deceased man had accomplished in his life-time.[2] On other occasions Oviedo uses *areyto* for the native singing and dancing,[3] but this is a mere generalization from the case in the island.

The *areyto* is chiefly a eulogy on the dead and is in substance identical with the eulogy at an Arabic funeral, as described by Roger:[4] "If a man has died, all the women, slaves, relatives, and neighbors, who are present, begin to utter terrible cries, inviting all the other wives to come and lament their husband: who at once come running from all sides, and on the way pick up handfuls of dust, which they throw over their heads behind them, covering those who are running behind, and shouting loudly unknown, diabolical words, turning their hands as though they were winding a skein of thread, with howlings and strange cries, so that it would seem to be the confusion of Hell. When they are gathered, in order to execute the ceremonies and lamentations which they call *raqaz*, they go to the hall or yard, sometimes to a high and spacious place beyond the house, and take a position in a circle, as though they

---

[1] F. de Oviedo, *Historia general y natural de las Indias*, Madrid 1851, vol. I, p. 127 ff.
[2] *Ibid.*, vol. II, p. 297.
[3] *Ibid.*, vol. III, p. 142.
[4] F. E. Roger, *La Terre Saincte*, Paris 1646, p. 265 ff.

wished to dance without holding their hands. Then an old woman, who is hired for this sport, paints her face, chest, hands, and arms black with soot, and, imitating her, the same is done by the wives, sisters and daughters of the deceased, who similarly blacken their faces, all of them disheveled, in nothing but their shirts that are open to the navel. The blackened old woman stands in the middle of the dance, begins to tell all the prowesses and noteworthy deeds of the deceased man in the form of a litany, and at each she makes a pause, while the others repeat with a solemn and mournful voice, dancing all the time with equal step. The relatives, who are besmeared black, beat their breasts and cheeks with the palms of their hands so that the cheeks swell up, and continue this ceremony until the body is taken to the grave.

"As soon as the man has breathed his last, they wash the body and wrap it in a pall, which they do not sew up and do not tie at the head or feet. Then they place the body on a stretcher, and upon it his turban and arms which he has used, as also his scimitar, club, quiver, and bow. If it is a woman, they put there her silver miter, bracelets, and necklaces. After which, several monks and mosque servants come to see him, to take him to the tomb, without taking him first to the mosque. His relatives and friends accompany him with gravity, their arms hanging loosely like those of the monks, and all of them sing the psalms of David, which they have falsified by errors, and at intervals they stop and say with a sad voice these words: 'Merciful God, be merciful to him. There is no other God besides God!'

"The women follow the body from a distance as far as the cemetery, where they walk over to some convenient place, in order to begin once more their dance, not by the tune of a fiddle, but by the clicking sounds which they make by striking their hands against their

cheeks and breasts with such fury that they seem all
to be afire, their eyes glistening like candles and seeming
to drop out of their sockets. When the old woman tells
of something secret that has taken place during the
marriage, all the others stop, at the same time doubling
their shouts and howlings and pronouncing diabolical
words.

"While this frightful lamentation takes place, the
turban or miter and other belongings are removed from
the body; then they place a pillow under the head,
without covering the body with dirt, because they build
a small stone chapel over it. The monks and relatives
leave the body at the cemetery and go home, the women
continuing for some time either to dance or to pray.
Sometimes the widow takes the deceased man's scimitar
and sways it with both hands like one mad, without
hurting anyone. When they are tired of their exercises
they go together home to the house of the deceased man,
where they sit down to a feast which the servants have
prepared during the lamentation and sport. Thus the
lamentation passes, to begin again next day at dawn
and to last again two or three hours and to be continued
for six or seven days in succession. Sometimes they
repeat their dances two or three times a day, especially
when some relatives come from without to console them.
It is to be noticed that the women of the Schismatic
Christians observe the same ceremonies and take part
in the dances of the Mohammedan lamentations, the
Mohammedan women similarly dancing at the Christian
funerals."

Precisely the same ritual is observed in the Western
Sudan. Bosman describes a Gold Coast funeral as
follows: "As soon as the sick Person is expired, they
set up such a dismal Crying, Lamentation, and
Squeaking, that the whole Town is filled with it; by
which 'tis soon published that some Body is lately dead:

besides which, the Youth of the Deceased's Acquaintance generally pay their last Duty of Respect to him, by firing several Musquet-Shot.

"If the deceased be a Man, his Wives immediately shave their Heads very close, and smear their Bodies with white Earth, and put on an old worn-out Garment; thus adjusted they run about the Street like mad Women, or rather She-Furies, with their Hair hanging upon their Cloaths; withal making a very dismal and lamentable Noise, continually repeating the Name of the Dead, and reciting the great Actions of his past Life: And this confused tumultuary Noise of the Women lasts several Days successively, even till the Corps is buried.

"If a principal Man is killed in Battle, and his Companions have no opportunity, by reason of the continuance of the War, to secure, hide or bury his Body (for the Funeral Rites must be performed in their own Country) his Wives are then obliged in all that Interval, to be in Mourning, and a shorn Head, though they permit the Hair to grow again where Modesty does not allow me to speak more plainly.

"A long time after, perhaps ten or twelve Years, as Opportunity offers, the Funeral Ceremonies are renewed, with the same Pomp and Splendour as if they had died a few Days past: On which Occasion all his Wives again put on their Mourning, cleanse and adjust themselves as before.

"Whilst the Women are lamenting abroad, the nearest Relations sit by the Corps making a dismal Noise, washing and cleansing themselves, and farther performing the usual Ceremonies: The distant relations also assemble from all Places, to be present at these Mourning Rites; he that is negligent herein being sure to bleed very freely if he cannot urge lawful Reasons for his Absence.

"The Towns People and Acquaintance of the Deceased, come also to join their Lamentations, each bringing his Present of Gold, Brandy, fine Cloath, Sheets, or something else; which 'tis pretended is given to be carried to the Grave with the Corps; and the larger Present of this Nature any Person makes, the more it redounds to his Honour and Reputation.

"During this Ingress and Egress of all sorts of People; Brandy in the Morning and Palm-Wine in the Afternoon are very briskly filled about; so that a rich *Negroes* Funeral becomes very chargeable: For after all this, they are richly cloathed when put into the Coffin; besides which several fine Cloaths, Gold *Fetiches*, high-prized Corals, (of which I have several times spoken) *Conte di Terra*, and several other valuable Things are put into the Coffin to him, for his Use in the other Life, they not doubting but he may have Occasion for them.

"The Value and Quantity of his Coffin Furniture, is adjusted in proportion to what the Deceased left his Heir, or perhaps to the Heirs Conveniency. All this being over, and the Relations and Friends met to gether; after two or three Days the Corps are buried; before which a Parcel of young Soldiers go, or rather run, continually loading and discharging their Musquets, till the Deceased is laid in the Ground: A great Multitude of Men and Women follow without the least Order, some being silent, others Crying and Shrieking as loud as possible, whilst others are laughing as loud; so that all their Grief is only in Appearance.

"As soon as the Corps is in the Ground every one goes where they please, but most to the House of Mourning, to drink and be merry, which lasts for several Days successively; so that this part of the Mourning looks more like a Wedding than a Funeral."[1]

[1] W. Bosman, *A New and Accurate Description of the Coast of Guinea,* London 1721, p. 220 ff.

There are two points in this description which must be noted. In the first place, the Negresses naturally paint themselves white, where the Arab women put on soot. The Asantes similarly put on red paint.[1] In the second place, the wielding of the scimitar among the Arabs in Africa gives way to the use of the latest weapon, the firing of guns, which is universal throughout the Western Sudan.[2] Another good description of the funeral ceremony among the Mandingos is given by Jobson: "One ceremony more of their Religion, I will relate, if you please to remember, where and how I left the chiefe *Mary-bucke* sicke and full of danger, it did manifest no lesse, for in the euening, the day after I came from him, he died, the report whereof, was immediatly spread ouer the whole countrey, who from all parts came in, after that abundant manner, to solemnize his funerall, so many thousands of men and women gathered together, as in such a desart and scattered countrey might breed admiration, which I thinke was rather increased, in regard at that time he died, the moone was high, and gaue her light, and they in whole troupes trauelled, eyther the whole night, or most part of the same together; the place or port whereat my boat did ride, was a Passage or Ferry to the towne, from the whole countrey, on the further side, whereunto belonged a great Canoe, which I had hired, hauing likewise another of my owne, both which neuer stood still, but were vsed, night and day in passing the people, none of them came emptie, some brought beeues, others goates, and cockes and hennes, with rice, and all sort of graine the country yeelded, so as there came in a wonderfull deale of prouision, my Mary-bucke entreated mee, to send something of sweet sauour, to be cast vpon his body, which the people much esteeme of; I sent

[1] E. Perregaux, *Chez les Achanti*, in *Bulletin de la Société neuchâteloise de géographie*, vol. XVII, p. 126.
[2] Ellis, *op. cit.*, p. 238 f., was at a loss to explain this custom.

some *Spica Romana*, and some Orras, which by his
sonne was thankefully receiued: the manner of his
buriall, was after this sort, hee was layed in a house,
where a graue was digged, and a great pot of water set
in the roome, and iust after the same manner, as the
Irish doe vse, with a wonderfull noyse of cries and
lamentations, he was layed into the ground; the people,
especially the women, running about the house, and
from place to place, with their armes spread, after a
lunaticke fashion, seemd with great sorrow to bewaile
his departure. They also assembled themselues, in
the most conuenient place, to receiue the multitude,
and nearest vnto the graue, and sitting downe in a
round ring, in the middle came foorth a Mary-bucke,
who betwixt saying and singing, did rehearse as it were
certaine verses, in the praise and remembrance of him
departed, which it should seeme was done *extempore;*
or prouided for that assembly, because vpon diuers
words or sentences he spake, the people would make
such sodaine exultations, by clapping of their hands,
and euery one running in, to giue and present vnto him,
some one or other manner of thing, might be thought
acceptable, that one after another, euery seuerall
Mary-bucke would haue his speech, wherein they
onely went away with the gratifications, who had the
pleasingest stile, or as we terme it, the most eloquente
phrase, in setting forth the praises of him departed, in
which the people were so much delighted."[1]

The Arabic name of the funeral dance رقز *raqaz* is
preserved in Soninke *rege*, but the other Mande
languages have the same word for "dance" and "sing,"
which indicates the close relation between the two as
established by the ritual, namely words derived from
Arabic اذان *'ādzān* "the chanting for prayer." We

---

[1] *Op. cit.*, p. 70 ff.

have Berber 'aḍḍen "to call to prayer, sing," Bambara
don "dance, play, to know," and here the meaning "to
know," which is also found in Arabic اذن 'adzana,
shows unmistakably the Arabic origin of the "dance,
sing" word.   In Malinke we have dō "to dance," dōkili
"song," Asante edžwom "song, hymn, psalm," džwonto,
džwento "singing," hence adžwo "lament, wail."   In
Akra džō means "to dance."   In Koelle we get Adampe
dūo, Dahome, Anfue ndūwe, Aku dṣo "to dance."   All
these show that the Sudanese ideas of "singing" and
"dancing" are closely related to the Arabic religious
ritual.   At the same time it must be remembered that in
the XIV. century Ibn-Batutah records the dancing and
reciting of a laudatory poem before the King of Malli by
a griot in a masquerade attire consisting of a bird mask
and feather ornaments.   Whether of religious origin or a
development of the mime on Arabic soil, the dyala of Ibn-
Batutah represents the court fool in Europe, who, no
doubt, has a similar origin.   In Africa he, as a poet,
easily becomes merged with the fetish man.

The Arabic رثى rasa[1] "to sing the praises of one
deceased," ارثاء 'irsa' "elegy, in praise of a deceased
person," مرثاة marṯāh "funeral speech, elegy on a dead
person, solemnity in honor of or lamentation for the
dead."   These words are not recorded in the scanty
African dictionaries, that is, there are very few entries
under "lamentation" or similar words, hence but a few
linguistic derivatives from this group may be found.
But we have more than enough to prove their presence
at an early time.   Just as Bambara koroduga means
"griot, buffoon" as well as "dancer," so we have
Bambara malasa, from Arabic مرثاة marsāh "elegy,"

---

[1] It would be better to write ratha, which in pronunciation among non-
Arabs would lean towards rasa and rata.

FIG. 70. — Danseurs Tombo dans un village du cercle de Bandiaga

FIG. 71. — Danse Mossi, dans la région de Ouagadougou

AFRICAN DANCING, from Desplagnes' *Le plateau central nigérien*

p 144.

La danse sacrée en l'honneur du fétiche *Tji wara* ou génie du travail.

AFRICAN DANCING, from Henry's *Les Bambara*.

recorded as "to mystify, play," and *malasaba* as "juggler, mystifier," while Malinke *marsa* is "to play a trick." The funeral ritual, as well as the other festivities, proves through the vocabulary which expresses the enjoyment of the dances and songs that the origin of these is due to the activities of the *griots*, that is, originally of the Gypsies, as described by Ibn-Batutah. The Mande *dyala*, *dyeli* "griot, musician" lies at the foundation of words meaning "to amuse, laugh" in a large number of languages. We have Peul *dyelli*, *dyalli*, Hausa *dalia*, *daria*, Wolof *ree*, Yoruba *riṅ*, *reriṅ*, Aku *reri*, and in the Mande languages, Soso, Malinke *yele*, Mandingo *jelli* "to laugh, make fun of." In Bambara we have *dyelo*, *yele*, *yelema* "to laugh, make fun of," *yele ko*, *yele fen* "amusement, that which causes one to laugh." In the Akra and Asante languages we can see at once how this "laugh" word was applied to the funeral ceremony. In Akra we have *yara*, *yera*, *ya*, *yano* "funeral-custom, consisting of many ceremonies, as washing, dressing and providing for the corps, as well as the actual burial; weeping, lamentation, singing, dancing, rum- or palm-wine drinking, gun-firing etc., sometimes days and weeks together. In later periods all this is repeated. Formerly, and even now, when it can be done secretly, men, especially wives and slaves are slaughtered on the graves of people of importance to accompany and serve them in the world to come."[1] In Asante we have *ayi* "the funeral custom."

In America the funeral custom, as far as the singing and dancing are concerned, in no way differs from the *Caraib* festival, as, indeed, it is the same in Africa. Among the *Caraibs* the African "laugh, make fun of" word is used, as among the Akras and Asantes, in connection with solemn occasions. Here we find Galibi *eremi*, *ilemi*, Caraib *eremeri* "to sing," and we

---

[1] Zimmermann, *op. cit.*, p. 351.

get a good description of the ceremony by Breton:[1]
"*Eremericaba lao eroutou*, sing, dance, enjoy yourself,
for we are going to eat an Arawak. In the beginning,
when I was at Dominique, my host, Captain Baron,
having killed and brought from the continent an Arawak, made a great celebration for all those who wanted
to be present and gave to each woman a piece of the
Arawak, to cook in her pot and eat with her husband
and family, who were at the assembly, which they did
with great joy during the day, for, after having drunk
and entertained themselves with their prowesses in
their harangues, when night fell they with faltering
steps and rolling eyes began to sing, dance, and howl
with so much vehemence and fury that I was frightened.
Leremericayem boye loubara arali racautiu, the *boye*
sings to make the gods come down. When the *Caraibs*
go to war or when they have some sick people, they call
a *boye*, prepare an offering, which is placed at the further
end of the house, which is always round, and put there a
bed, while the people present seat themselves around
the wall. The *boye* having arrived (sometimes with
another person), he begins to sing, while one of the two
throws some tobacco smoke upwards in place of incense,
and in this way makes his pretended god come down
(I have heard them say that he falls down like a meal-
sack, but I have not heard the sound which they say
he makes with his fingers). The *boye* gives him the
bed to sit upon and the offering to eat and drink. This
spirit of darkness does not want any light, and makes
them put out the fire and close up all the avenues of
light, unless it takes place at night. I once wanted to
enter with a fire-brand, in order to prevent this abomination, but the women stopped me."

This Caraib *eremi*, *ilemi* is, no doubt, related to the
Bambara *yelema* "to make fun of," but we have also

---

[1] R. Breton, *Dictionaire caraibe-français*, Leipzig 1892, p. 216 ff.

Galibi *oalitago*, *aoualetago* "to sing," Arawak *aritin*
"to call, give a name," which show that a form *areyto*,
as mentioned by Peter Martyr and the other early writers, must have existed in the islands.   Indeed, we have
Caraib *eletouac* "a solemn festival, at which six or eight
of the feasters rub their bodies with elemy gum which is
still in a liquid form, over which down or small feathers
of the phaeton bird (festu en queuë) are sprinkled.
Their heads are crowned with large Arras feathers, then
they dance by twos around the council-house (Carbet),
one extending his right arm over the shoulders of the
other, and the other his left arm over his companion's
neck.   The others follow in the same posture, dancing
by twos, until they come to the place where they find
the large calabashes full of wine (oüicou), which has
to be swallowed to the last drop, even if they should
burst.   I have seen them almost choke, grow pale, and
unable to stand it any longer; to get relief a savage
would embrace another from behind and press his
stomach until he would vomit a part, to make room for
more."[1]

There seems to be little doubt that we have in these
Caraib and Arawak words the Arabic رسا *rasa* "to sing
the praises of the deceased," since in the Tupi languages
we have a corresponding word from Arabic مرساه *marsāh*,
namely Guarani *poraçei*, *mborasei*, *mborahei*, in the
other Tupi languages *morase*, *murasi*, *porasei* "to sing,
dance," while in some there is a confusion with *maraka*
"rattle," hence Kamayura *maraka* "to sing, dance."[2]
In the case of the Tupi word, there seems to have been an
attempt made to transform the word so as to bring it in
keeping with some popular etymology, for we have also

---

[1] *Ibid.*, p. 203 f.   See also *C.* de Rochefort, *Histoire naturelle et morale des
Isles Antilles de l'Amérique*, Roterdam 1658, p. 455 f.
[2] K. von den Steinen, *Unter den Naturvölkern Zentral-Brasiliens*, Berlin
1894, p. 315.

moçaray "to make fun of, triumph, play," *moçaray goera* "one made fun of, a fool," *moçaraytara* "dancer." A similar corruption of the original word is found in Bakairi *makanari* "mask dance, anything connected with the dance." However this may be, we have here the same semantic relation as in the African words. In the case of these "song" words an absolutely certain etymology cannot be established, not only because of the lacunae in the African dictionaries, but also because the "sing" words are easily confused with the *haüre* refrain of such songs, from which the Caraib *areyto* may equally well be derived. On the other hand, there may be in all of these a derivation from the African *yele* "song" words, since we have, by the side of Galibi *eremi, ilemi*, also Cumanagoto *huarage* and Bakairi *ali, ari, ori* "to dance, sing."

CHAPTER IX.

FEATHERS AND MASKS.

In 1189, on the eve of setting out to Jerusalem, Richard I promulgated a specific law for those who started out across the sea to Jerusalem, dealing with the punishments for various offences. A thief was to have his head shaven, and he was to be tarred and feathered, and landed at the first port, where people would at once know by his plight what his offence had been.[1] No such practice was in force in Europe, and it is evident that Richard here provided a form of punishment which was prevalent in the region to which they were going, that is, among the Moslems. According to Islamic law, a punishment called ta‘zīr is imposed in those cases in which there is no specific legislation. Thus ta‘zīr is applied in cases of forgery, deception, extortion, false witness, calumny, and petty thieving. The judge has in such cases discretionary powers. He may send the culprit to prison, have him whipped, give him a reprimand, put him in the pillory, have his face blackened,

---

[1] "Richardus Dei Gratia Rex Angliae & Dux Normanniae & Aquitaniae, & Comes Andegaviae, omnibus hominibus suis Jerosolymam per mare ituris, salutem. Sciatis nos de communi proborum virorum consilio, fecisse has justitias subscriptas. Qui hominem in navi interfecerit, cum mortuo ligatus projiciatur in mare. Si autem eum ad terram interfecerit, cum mortuo ligatus in terra infodiatur. Si quis autem per legitimos testes convictus fuerit quod cultellum ad alium percutiendum extraxerit: aut quod alium ad sanguinem percusserit, pugnum perdat. Si autem de palma percusserit sine effusione sanguinis: Tribus vicibus mergatur in mari. Si quis autem socio opprobrium aut convitia, aut odium Dei injecerit: Quot vicibus ei conviciatus fuerit, tot uncias argenti ei det. Latro autem de furto convictus tondeatur ad modum campionis, & pix bulliens super caput ejus effundatur, & pluma pulvinaris super caput ejus excutiatur ad cognoscendum eum, & in prima terra, qua naves applicuerint, projiciatur. Teste meipso apud Chinonem," T. Rymer, *Foedera*, London 1727, vol. I, p. 65.

etc.[1] The judge has also the right to impose similar punishments in cases not yet proven but indicating that the offender may be dangerous to the community.[2]

Richard's law shows conclusively that tarring and feathering was in use among the Moslems for petty crimes. We have already seen that the دَجَّال *daǧǧāl* was a low, contemptible fellow, and we have one distinct reference to him as a musician, hence there can be no doubt that the Gypsies, who later developed into the *griots*, were considered dangerous to society as cheats and offenders. Charlemagne's law of 789 shows that as early as the VIII. century means were sought to stop the nuisance. That the Arabs would cause the Gypsies to be tarred and feathered or, at least, to wear a special attire indicating this tarring and feathering is shown by the very word دَجَلَ *daǧala*. In all the Semitic languages except Arabic this root has no other meaning than "to lie, cheat," whereas in Arabic it has not only the meaning of "he lied, told a falsehood," but also "he smeared his whole body with tar." As دَجَّال *daǧǧāl* also means "having one eye and one eyebrow," it is likely that the pestering Gypsies were also punished in this more severe way.

From Ibn-Batutah we have learned that the *dyala* of Malli wore the distinctive costume of feathers, and a mask to accentuate the fact that he was "a bird." Thus it becomes clear that a bird mask was the original mask of the buffoon or *griot*, as he appears in the Western Sudan. Once the origin of the custom was forgotten, the bird mask gave way to any other kind of mask, but we are still able to see that the predominant mask is that of a bird. "Masquerades now take place,

[1] E. Sachau, *Muhammedanisches Recht*, in *Lehrbücher des Seminars für orientalische Sprachen zu Berlin*, vol. XVII, p. 849.
[2] *Ibid.*, p. 848.

though these are mainly performed by Arabs, the only one in which the Hausas have any part being the Bu Sadiya, in which a man dresses up in a mask ornamented with birds' feathers (to represent the head of an eagle), puts vulture wings upon his shoulders and wears a coat of pieces of various skins—*e.g.* jackal, fox, hyena, and, if possible, leopard and lion. But this is not confined to the Salla; it may take place at any time, the main care at present seeming to be a collection from the onlookers. Some of the Arab performances resemble the dance of Jato at the bori."[1]

In America the mask and the dance are intimately connected with "tarring and feathering." We have already seen this to be the case among the *Caraibs.* Precisely the same is told of the Tupis: "They all come painted in all kinds of colors, arrayed in feathers also of a certain color pressed out from the sap and juice of the fruit of a tree called *genipat* in their language, which they esteem greatly, not that the fruit of this tree is good to eat, but because of the quaintness of the hue. This tree is large and has leaves like those of a walnut tree, and the fruit like peaches over there, which grow at the end of the branches in a strange fashion. Having no other means for extracting this fruit, they chew it, then reject it from the mouth and squeeze it between their hands, as one would squeeze out a sponge, and the juice that comes out is as clear as the purest water: with this juice or sap they wash themselves when going to their feasts or massacres or to visit their friends. When this juice is dried up on their skin, it has a deep black color which does not become perfect unless it has had two days to soak into the skin. And thus painted they go to a feast without any garments, as contented as we are with our silk clothes, and the women paint thus more often than men, and seeing

[1] Tremearne, *The Ban of the Bori,* p. 241.

them from a distance you would think that they are dressed in black velvet. It must be observed that other savages who go to these feasts, in order to partake of caouin with their friends, before leaving the villages peel a certain tree, the inside of which is yellow or red, and chopping it very fine they mix it with the gum of a certain tree called *usup*. Then they spread these colors over the first made of *genipat*. As for the *usup* gum, it is very good for consolidating wounds, as I have found out from experience. Painted in this manner, they cover themselves with down, that is, with very small and fine bird feathers, which they apply to the said gum from their heads to their feet, when it becomes a pleasure to contemplate these gentile savage parrots, who seem all to be dressed in elegant red scarlet, and they have also large feathers, with which they surround their heads."[1] The same is told of the people of Cumana: "In war-time they put on mantles and feathers: for the festivals and dances they paint or blacken themselves or smear themselves with a certain gum and sticky unguent like birdlime, and then they put on feathers of various colors, and these feathered Indians do not at all look badly."[2] The custom is well-nigh universal. In the interior of Brazil, among the Bororo, feathering the body is of enormous importance.[3] Not only is it there used on festive occasions, but it is one of the most important "medicines." All feather ornamentations, except, perhaps, an occasional ear adornment among the Bakairi, are a part of festive occasions, including festive receptions. Feathers are of the same importance as the painting of the body.[4] The same

---

[1] Thevet, *op. cit.*, fol. 926 b.

[2] F. Lopez de Gómara, *La historia general delas Indias*, Anvers 1554, cap. LXXIX, fol. 102 a.

[3] Von den Steinen, *op. cit.*, p. 476.

[4] *Ibid.*, p. 328.

TARRING AND FEATHERING IN BRAZIL, from Von den Steinen's *Unter den Naturvoelkern Zentral-Brasiliens.*

FISCHNETZ-TANZ DER NAHUQUÁ.

TARRING AND FEATHERING IN BRAZIL, from Von den Steinen's *Unter den Naturvoelkern Zentral-Brasiliens*.

is true in North America, but the modern aspect of feathers and masks does not belong within the scope of our work. Sufficient has been shown to establish the fact that both have their origin in the forced adornment of the African *griot*, as a result of the Arabic "tarring and feathering," by which to distinguish the contemptible caste of the *griots*.

CHAPTER X.

The Caraib Social Order.

In *The Journal of the Second Voyage* we have a reference to the native *duho* "a low seat."[1] Oviedo described it for Nicaragua as "a small stool with four feet, made of fine, smooth wood."[2] This chair was a sign of nobility or royalty among the Indians and was also connected with their religion. It is not difficult to see that this is the Persian-Arabic ‎تخت‎ *taḫt*, plural *tuḫut*, "a royal throne, chair of state; sofa, bed; any place raised above the ground for sleeping, sitting, or reclining; a capitol, royal residence." The history of this word is fascinating.

Ibn-Batutah uses the term ‎منسا‎ *mansa* for the king of Malli, and this term is still in use, for we have Malinke *māsa*, Bambara *masa*, Soso *māge*, Vei *mandža* "king." This is from Arabic ‎منشا‎ *manša'* "place where one grows up, where anything originates, birthplace, one's country, origin, beginning, source," from ‎نشا‎ *naša'* "to grow up, originate," as the history of the word in Asante and Akra shows. We have Asante *omānsofwe* "reign, regency," *amān sāṅ* "all people," but more commonly the abbreviated *māṅ* in *omāṅ* "town, people, kingdom," *omaṅba* "citizen," etc., Akra *maṅtše* "king, first person of a town," *māṅ*, plural *mādži*, "town, people, nation, kingdom, country."

[1] *Raccolta di documenti dalla R. Commissione Colombiana*, Roma 1892, part I, vol. I, p. 192.
[2] *Op. cit.*, vol. IV, p. 109.

ASHANTI STOOL.

From Freeman's *Travels and Life in Ashanti and Jaman*

Similarly the word for "royal throne" is in the African languages derived from the Arabic خت‎ *taht, tuhut*. The royal chair is always carried wherever the king of Dahome goes.[1] It is generally made of one piece of wood and is highly ornamented.[2] "To succeed to the stool" is the expression in Asante for "to mount the throne."[3] "Of their woodwork the Ashanti stool is a fair specimen, which is cut from a solid block and variously ornamented."[4] In Asante we, therefore, have from Arabic *tuhut* the full form *dufŭá* "a rough kind of seat made of a block," hence *džwa, gua* "to carve," *adžwa, agua* "seat, chair, stool, throne," *egua* "public place, market," and this leads to Yoruba *aga* "chair, stool, table." In the Mande languages the meaning "chair" is not always preserved. Although we have Soninke *takhade*, that is, Arabic *taht* "chair," we get Wolof *dak, deuk* "village," and so in the Mande languages, Malinke *dugu* "land, country, village," Bambara *dugu*, Mandingo *duo, du* "earth, country, village, town."

We have no record as to the native name of the *Caraib* chief, except that of *cacique*, which is more likely a Spanish corruption of an African word than the name current among the *Caraibs*, although it will appear later that a similar word was in existence among the *Caraibs*. We have so far an unmistakable proof that his dignity was connected with that of the Mandingo stool, the *duho*, as amply recorded among the early writers on America. But we also know that there was a class of nobility, for, on December 23, 1492, the *Journal* recorded: "Up to this time the Admiral was unable to understand whether they use it [*caçique*] for

---

[1] L. Brunet et L. Giethlen, *Dahomey et dépendances*, Paris 1901, p. 304.
[2] E. Foà, *Le Dahomey*, Paris 1895, p. 173 f.
[3] W. Hutton, *A Voyage to Africa*, London 1821, p. 316.
[4] G. MacDonald, *The Gold Coast*, London, New York, Bombay 1898, p. 56.

'king' or 'governor,' but they have also another name
for a 'grandee,' whom they call *nitayno*.　He did not
know whether they meant it for 'hidalgo' or 'governor'
or 'judge.' "[1]　We have already seen that among the
Mandingos *n'tana, n'tene* represented the mark of
distinction, the same which in Europe led to heraldry,
hence in the *nitayno* we have the men who acquired
marks of distinction by colors and especial designs.
We shall later meet with them in Mexico, but here
may be pointed out the curious custom, recorded for
Venezuela, of acquiring degrees of nobility by colored
markings on the body: "I have heard of a manner of
military honor with which the natives of this land pre-
cede and are preferred and honored above the common
people and even above those of greater quality, and it
is a kind of nobility acquired by military discipline and
of this form.　For a deed of valor the right arm is
painted with a certain mark or device of black color,
by drawing blood and putting into the wound ground
coal.　Indeed, the painting is like the one put on for
show by the Moorish women of Berbery in Africa:
the which painting can never be taken off, except by
destroying the figure.　And from that time on such an
Indian is no longer a common man, but like an hidalgo
among the Spaniards, and marked as a military man,
and esteemed from that time on as a brave man.　And
when he gives another proof of his valor and has obtained victory, he is like an hidalgo whom the king
dubs a knight, and then his breast is painted with some
such device as the arm.　When he obtains his third
victory, they paint some lines which go from the ends
of the eyes to the ears, and those who are thus adorned
are highly esteemed, and there is no other honor to
aspire to, which is as though he were a Hector or a
Bernado del Carpio, or a Cid Ruy Diaz, or whomso-

[1] *Raccolta*, part I, vol. I, p. 76.

ever you may honor."[1] As we get in the same region the fullest and linguistically most correct form of the fetish man, there can be little doubt that we have here a description of the African *n'tene* which confers and records nobility as the result of deeds of valor.

We have already observed that in Africa the *griots* laid the foundation for a free corvéable population that was occasionally confused with slaves[2] We there met the Bambara word *dyama* "province, village," hence *dyama horo*, recorded in the compounded *dyam uru* "forced labor," *dyamuru bugu* "a free village," Wolof *dyambur* "free." This conception occurs in the encomienda of 1516 or 1517,[3] when the Indians were turned over as servants to the Spaniards. Here we frequently hear of "*naboria* de casa," that is, household servants. These *naborias* are mentioned by the side of *nitaynos*,[4] who, together with their *caciques*, were similarly placed in the encomienda of some Spaniard. Thus we get among the *Caraibs* the same social order as in the Western Sudan, except that the *naborias* "free workmen, not yet distinguished by a *n'tene*," were the mass of the Indian population, who were not slaves, whereas in Africa they were evolved from the originally foreign *griots*.

[1] Oviedo, *op. cit.*, vol. II, p. 322 f. In chap. XXII (p. 330) there is a fuller account of this custom.

[2] See p. 113.

[3] *Colección de documentos inéditos relativos al descubrimiento, conquista y colonizacion de las posesiones españolas en América y Occeanía*, vol. I, p. 50 ff.

[4] *Ibid.*, p. 82.

CHAPTER XI.

The Boratio.

According to Columbus[1] the *cemi, cimi,* or *cimini* were certain wooden images, which were worshipped by inducing intoxication. The *cimi* represented the *cacique's* ancestor, and was made to speak by trickery. Other fetishes were stones which were good to produce fertility, make women bear children, and preserve people against the sun and weather. Ramon Pane[2] adds the information that the *cimini* are immortal, as if in heaven, and have the bones of their ancestors, which are made of stone or wood. The *cimini* come to aid in the form of adders, just as the Fan fetish is connected with serpents. The resemblance is still further increased by the fact that the Fans use the skull of an ancestor for a fetish. But the Bambara *nama* and *dasiri,* too, represent the same qualities as the *cimi.*

Rochefort,[3] one hundred and fifty years later, says that the *Caraib* men call their good spirits *icheiri,* that is, *išēri,* while the women call them *chemijn,* that is, *šemīn,* which the missionaries translate by "God," while the evil spirits are by the *Caraibs* called *mapoya* or *maboya.* By the Galibis "spirit" is rendered by *issimei,* plural *issimeiri,* so that the masculine *išēri* may be a corruption of the latter. In Arawak *semetti* is a "witch-doctor." Hence there can be no doubt that we have here a real Caraib-Arawak word meaning

[1] See my *Africa,* vol. I, p. 67 ff.
[2] *Ibid.,* p. 88 ff.
[3] *Op. cit.,* p. 416.

"good spirit, fetish." There can equally be no doubt that in *maboya* we have the African *bori*, just as *cemi* is the Bambara *dyine, nyena*, from the Arabic *ǵinn*, but influenced by the Arabic *sama'* "heaven," even as we have observed such confusion in Asante and elsewhere.[1] This confusion may already be observed in the north, for in the Guanche of Teneriff we have *ašano* "heaven," from the Tuareg *aǵenna*, etc., by the side of *ašaman* "God," from the Arabic *sama'*,[2] even as the Tuaregs use *aǵenna*[3] for "rain" where the other languages have similarly derivatives from Arabic *sama'*.

We have already come across the fetish man under the name of *Caraib*. We shall now turn to the fetish man connected with the *maboya*, that is, the African *bori*. The "master of the *bori*" is mentioned by Ramon Pane[4] as *bohuti, buhuitihu*, for which Peter Martyr uses *boviti*.[5] Oviedo tells a great deal about the *boratios* of Venezuela: "They fear very much the devil, of whom the *boratios* affirm that they see him and talk with him frequently. They paint his face in their jewels and work it in relief upon wood and upon everything they esteem most. These *boratios* are, as it were, their priests, and in every chief city there is a *boratio* to whom all have recourse to ask for things to happen, and whether it will rain, or whether the year will be dry or abundant, or whether they are to go to war against their enemies or give it up, and whether the Christians are good people or will kill them, and the *boratio* says that he will give his answer after having consulted with the devil, and for this conversation and consultation they lock themselves up in a room alone, and here they make certain smokes (ahumadas) which

[1] See p. 174 ff.
[2] E. Laoust, *Mots et choses berbères*, Paris 1920, p. 187.
[3] *Ibid.*, p. 188.
[4] Vol. I, p. 80 ff.
[5] *Raccolta*, part III, vol. II, p. 52 ff.

they call *tabacos*, with such herbs as bereave them of their senses, and here the *boratio* remains a day, or two, or three, and sometimes longer, and, after coming out, he says that the devil has told him so and so, answering the questions put to him, according to the desires of those whom he wishes to satisfy; and for this they give the *boratio* some gold trinket or other things.   For less important matters the Indians have another way. There is in this country an herb called *tabaco*, which is a kind of plant as high as a man's breast, and more or less branching, which puts forth leaves a palm in length and four fingers in width, and of the shape of a lance iron, and they are hairy.   And they sow this herb, and the seed which it makes they keep for the next year's planting, and they watch it carefully for the following purpose: When they reap it, they put the leaves in bunches and dry it in the smoke in bunches, and they keep it, and it is a much appreciated article of commerce among the Indians.   In our Hispaniola there is much of it in the ranches, and the Negroes whom we employ value it highly for the effect which it produces by smoking it until they fall down like dead, and thus they are the greater part of the night, and they say that they do not feel the fatigue of the previous day

"To return to the Indians of Venezuela, to see whether they should travel or go fishing or sowing, or whether they would be successful in the chase, or whether a certain woman loves them, each one is a *boratio*, for, wrapping its leaves around an ear of corn, they light one end a little and put the burning part in their mouth and breathe it out, and when it is half burned, they crush what is wrapped around, and if the part of the tobacco burnt is in the form of a sickle, it is a sign that what they wish to know will succeed; and if it has burnt straight, it is a sign of the opposite, and that which was to be good is bad.   And they believe this so much that nobody and no reason can make them believe otherwise, nor that the *tabaco* is a joke or vanity: on the contrary they feel badly for being reprimanded by those who want to undeceive them.

"The *boratios*, besides doing as described above, act in the villages as doctors and cure in the following manner. When one is sick and cannot rise from the hammock, they call the *boratio* and ask him to cure the sick man and say that they will pay him, and he says that he will be glad to come. Arriving where the patient is, he asks what hurts him, and the sick man tells him. He also asks him whether he would like him to cure him, and he answers, 'Yes.' He again asks whether he knows that he can cure him since he is a very good *boratio*, and the patient says that he does. If to any of these questions the sick man says, 'No,' the *boratio* goes away and will not cure him. But if he answers in the affirmative, the first thing the *boratio* does is to order everybody in the house to fast and to eat nothing but their maize gruel, which they call *caça*, and not more than once a day. Then he turns to the patient and asks him what pains him most, and, when he says that the head or some other part of the body hurts him, the *boratio*, while opening and closing his hands and putting them over him, as one who wants to bring something in, says that he is taking in the soul, and then he closes his fist and blows upon it with his mouth, and says, 'Be gone, sickness!' And saying this the *boratio* utters such shouts and yells over the sick man that he grows hoarse and cannot cry or talk, and this lasts two hours or more. After having done so, he asks him whether it pains him as much as before, and if the patient says that it does, he sucks the member or spot with his mouth, spitting out from time to time. If at the end of five or six days of such operations, the patient tells the *boratio* that he is better, he puts a thorn or stone or whatever he wishes in his mouth, so as to make the sick man believe what he wishes, without anybody's noticing it, and, after having sucked where the pain was, spits into his hand the thorn or stone or stick which he has taken from his mouth, and shows it to the sick man, saying to him, 'See what has been killing you and caused your trouble!' Then he takes his leave and says that he wants to go, and they pay him. If, by chance, the patient does not say that he feels better from what the *boratio* has done, the *boratio*, instead of spitting out the stone or whatever he means to give as the cause of the sickness, as frequently happens from necessity, for what the *boratio* does is mere nonsense, he answers, 'I am going away, for you will not recover so soon from your sickness as you think, for the devil has told me so,' and he says good-bye and leaves."[1]

The resemblance to the Mandingo *boritigi, bolitigi,* etc. is so close, including the very name, that nothing needs to be added. We only need to pursue the variations of the name throughout the two Americas. There is recorded Tupi-Guarani *paje,* Caraib *boye, piudai,* Chayma *piache,* Bakairi *piaze,* Tamanaco *ptchiachi,* Aparais *puiacie,* Galibi *piaye* "doctor," Baniba *pinata,* Yabitero *epinatzi* "medicine." Herrera mentions in Cuba the doctor as *behique.* Las Casas calls him *bohique.* The most interesting forms to us are Nahuatl *pati* "doctor," *patli* "medicine," Kechua *'hampi* "medicine." The distribution of the African "medicine" word over an enormous territory bears witness to the tremendous cultural influence of the Mandingos in America. No wonder, then, that *mandinga* itself should in the Spanish of South America have received the meaning of "witchcraft."[2]

[1] Oviedo, *op. cit.,* vol. II, p. 298 f.

[2] D. Granada, *Vocabulario rioplatense razonado,* Montevideo 1890, p. 269.

Tobacco forms an integral part of the *boratio's* ritual, wherever it occurs, but nowhere is it referred to as being smoked. It is blown out of the pipe or roll, in order that the incense should reach the fetish. Tobacco, like cotton itself, was imported for ritualistic purposes, and smoking of tobacco, as we have seen, was of a slow growth, due chiefly to the habits of the Negroes after the discovery. There is no evidence whatsoever that it was used before the discovery for any other than ritualistic and, possibly, medicinal purposes.

CHAPTER XII.

THE MANDINGO ELEMENTS IN THE MEXICAN CIVILIZATION.

Oviedo says that in the province of Cueva, in Castilla del Oro, *tequina* was the equivalent of "master" in whatever art.[1] This word is, of course, Mande *tigi* "master." Its most important development is found in Mexico. Here we have *tecutli* "chief, knight," hence *tecutilia* "to ennoble," *tecuuia* "to act as a chief, drill the soldiers," *tecutocaitl* "name of nobility," *tecuti* "to become a nobleman," *tecunenenque* "chief merchants who traveled far and whom the monarchs of Tenochtitlan considered as lords," *tecuacan* "chief city, court, residence of sovereigns," *teca* "of somebody," *tecpan* "lord's, king's palace."

The last word has entered into the Maya languages, where we have Kiche *tecpan* "communal house, palace," hence *tecpanir* "to increase the tribute," hence *tec* "to increase, heap one thing upon another," *tequeba* "to put in layers." These at once explain another series of Nahuatl words: *tecpanir* explains *tequitl* "tribute, impost, labor, functions, duty," *tequiotl, tequiutl* "exercise, labor, fatigue, servitude, contribution," *tequio* "hard, difficult," *tequiti* "to work, pay tribute," *tequitlato* "agent, distributer of tribute or work;"

---

[1] "Deste nombre *tequina* se haçe mucha diferençia; porque á cualquiera ques mas hábil y experto en algun arte, assi como en ser mejor montero ó pescador, ó haçer mejor una red ó una canoa ú otra cosa, le llaman *tequina*, que quiere deçir lo mesmo que maestro: por manera que al ques maestro de las responsiones é inteligençias con el diablo, llámanle *tequina* en aquel arte, porque aqueste tal es el que administra sus ydolatrías é çerimonias é sacrifiçios, y el que habla con el diablo, segund ellos diçen, é á él dá sus respuestas," Oviedo, *op. cit.*, vol. III, p. 127.

similarly Kiche *tec* explains Nahuatl *te, tequi* "much," *teca* "to put layers of stone or wood, to lie down in bed," hence *moteca* "they unite," *nic-teca* "to plant." This is still better brought out in the compound *tecpana* "to put in order, arrange in layers," *tecpanti* "to distribute."

Tec, as we see, represents a word designating "the master, master mechanic." There is hardly a language in the neighborhood of Mexico that does not bear witness to the enormous influence wielded by those who introduced the word together with the arts. We have Zoque *tec* "house, room," *tectzecpa* "to build," Pokonchi *tzakal* "builder, maker," hence *tzakal aj* "maker of mats," etc., *tzakol* "mason," *tzak* "worth," and Tarascan *tecari* "carpenter."

Sahagun[1] devotes the whole of Book IX to the Mexican merchants and workers in gold, precious stones, and rich feathers. The merchants, *pochteca*, according to a tradition, at first appeared at Tlatelulco in the reign of Quaquapitzauac. There were only two of them, and they trafficked in green, blue, and red feathers of the *quetzalli*. Later turquoises and green stones and garments of cotton were added, for, heretofore, only *nequen* cloth was used. This puts the origin of the merchants and of cotton cloth in the first quarter of the XV. century Still later, rings, gold nuggets, ·cut stones, skins, and other articles were added to the trade. The word *pochteca* is obviously a compound, but *poch* cannot be explained from any Nahuatl word. In Maya a merchant was known as *p'olom*, which apparently is related to a Maya root *p'ol* "to swell," not recorded in the other Maya languages. *P'olomkay* is given as a forbidden song and dance, no doubt of the kind described by Sahagun and connected with human sacrifices. The

---

[1] B. de Sahagun, *Histoire générale des choses de la Nouvelle-Espagne*, Paris 1880, p. 547 ff.

other Maya languages do not seem to record any
"merchant" word from this root except Tzotzil *polman*
"to buy." The Maya *p'ol* and Nahuatl *poch* are unquestionably related and point to a form *bor* or *for* as
their root.

The Arabic المال في *fī-al-māl* "rich" has undergone
some violent changes in Africa. While it is found in the
Arabic Wadai as *fī-al-māl*, it has deteriorated to *alman*
"wealth" in Songay, while in the Berber languages it
has become *bu-el-māl* "possessor of wealth, rich,"
which has reëntered the Arabic Soa as *abuhumām*
"rich." This Berber *bu-el-māl* became, in its turn,
Wolof *borom alale* "rich," and has broken into *borome*
"chief, lord," *mbor* "rich," and *alale* "wealth."
In Soninke we have the forms *fogome* and *naburugume*
"rich," which lead to Malinke *nafulu*, Bambara
nafolo "wealth," Soninke *nabure* "merchandise,"
Soso *nafuli* "money." We have also the simpler
Bambara *fuale*, *fale*, Malinke *faliñ*, Mandingo *făling*,
Wolof *wakhale*, Songay *bora* "to exchange, traffic,
barter," Malinke *firi* "to sell," *firila* "merchant,"
Hausa *falāla* "a rich man." The Soa Arabic
abuhumām has not only produced Soninke *fogome*, but
is found all along the western coast in much reduced
forms. We have Malinke, Bambara *fama* "rich man,
king," Duala *mbuan*, Bayon *mfōn*, *ebōn*, Mimboma
mfūmu, Musentandu *mpfuāma*, Kongo *vwama*, Kiriman
ufuma, etc. "rich." Thus we arrive at an ancient form
folom, *forom*, represented in Soninke *fogome*, *naburugume*, which is responsible for Maya *p'olom* "merchant"
and Aztec *poch* in *pochteca*. If Sahagun's chronology
is at all trustworthy, the Mandingo merchants first
appeared in Mexico in the beginning of the XV. century.

In Sahagun's account of the Mexican merchants we
are constantly reminded that they sold mantles (*tilma*,
chimalli), waistcloths (*maxtli*), and chemises (*uipilli*).

It can be shown that all these characteristically Mexican garments are of African origin. Unfortunately the scanty African vocabularies do not give us any account of the ancient garments,[1] and we have to draw our conclusions chiefly from the Arabic names, which fortunately give us all the data we need. In Molina's dictionary *tilmatli* is translated by "manta," and *chimalli* is explained as "shield, buckler," while "manta para combatir" is translated by *vapalchimalli* or *quauhchimalli*. "Manta para combatir" would be a "battle cloak" rather than a "buckler," and a study of other Indian languages proves conclusively that there is a direct relation between "buckler" and "mantle." In Maya we have *chim, chimil* "bag, pouch, bird-crop," *chimal* "shield," but in Huasteca we have the Nahuatl *quauhchimalli* as *cuachim, cuachimal* "any kind of garment," hence *cuachimzal* "to dress." That the Huasteca has preserved the original meaning follows from the Arabic, whence the word and the thing were taken, through the Mandingo. The Arabic شمل *šamlah, šimlah*, plural *šimal*, is "a garment in which one wraps himself" and شمال *šimāl* is "a sort of bag put to the raceme of a palm tree, in order that the fruit may not be shaken off, or to the udder of the ewe or goat, when the udder is heavy with milk."

In Africa it has generally preserved the meaning of "wrapper, girdle," as in Berber *cemla* "girdle, turban." In Biblical Hebrew we have שִׂמְלָה *śimělāh* "cloak, in

---

[1] "Il règne une grande confusion dans la terminologie berbère relative aux vêtements. A côté de représentants, que l'ancien berbère appliquait à des parties du vêtement dont l'usage a disparu depuis longtemps, existent des appellations locales, fort nombreuses, et ces expressions étrangères, arabes le plus souvent, désignant, parfois même, des vêtements d'origine africaine. Le problème du vêtement se complique en conséquence; la linguistique, en tout cas, ne peut fournir sur la question que des données insuffisantes," Laoust, *op. cit.*, p. 123 f.

which one wrapped himself at night," and also שַׂלְמָה *śalĕmāh* "garment." This latter transposed form is recorded in Songay *tilbi*, *derbe* "garment," which presupposes a form *tilme*, and this is still further proved by Soso *domma* "shirt, blouse, cloak, large wrapping-cloth. The Soninke *irame* "shoulder-cloth" is derived from the same, through a form *tirme*, as in Songay *tilbi*, *derbe*. We find similar forms to the Soso in various Mande languages, Kono *dumā*, Tene *rimo*, Gbandi *ndomai*, Mende *ndōma*, Vei *doma*, *duma* "an upper garment of males, of the form of a shirt, without sleeves and collar, but generally provided with a breast pocket." Outside of the Mande languages it is found in Landoma *dūma*, plural *sedūma*, Baga *duma*, plural *suma*, Temne *ruma*, plural *suma*, Bulom *lumo*, plural *ṣilumo*, and this form shows how all the others are derived from the Arabic *śilmah* or *śimlah* by apocopation. The latter is also preserved in the Arabic of Adirar as *taṣmīr*. In a series of languages Songay *derbe* has become further corrupted to *derge*, as in Mandingo *durūkī*, Bambara *doloki*, *dloki*, Mandingo *dondiko*, Soninke *dorōke*, Gura *delegoa*, Peul *dolokie*, dialectically *togore*, Dsarawa *lugod*, Koro *loga*, Hausa *riga* "shirt," and this has become still more corrupted in Bornu *kalugu*, *kaluru*.

Equally interesting is Nahuatl *maxtli* "waistcloth to hide the nudity." The early writers on America, Columbus and Cortes included, have used the Arabico-Spanish word *almaizares* with which to designate this piece of adornment, frequently the only one observed on women. But this Arabic word got to Mexico through the Mandingos before Columbus. Herodotus tells of the Arabs as wearing ζειραί.[1] This is the Arabic ازار *'īzār* "a garment which covers the lower part of the body,

[1] VII. 69.

AFRICAN ALMAIZAR, from Freeman's *Travels and Life in Ashanti and Jaman.*

from the waist to the thigh, also a woman's veil,"
hence مِئْزَر mī'zar, mai'zar "a loincloth for girls,
mantle, wrapping-cloth," etc.   Both forms are found
in the Mande languages.   We have Mandingo *sitti*
"to tie," Malinke *siri, sitti* "to tie, attach," Bambara
siri "a bundle, to tie, make a knot," and Malinke *mas-
iti* "adornment, jewel, to tie," Bambara *masiri* "adornment, to make one's toilet," *masirili* "ornamentation,
toilet."   The derivation of Nahuatl *maxtli* from this
is obvious.

Still more interesting is the history of Nahuatl *vipilli*.
Arabic غَفَر *gafr* means "to cover, conceal, hide, to cover
one's crime, forgive, pardon," hence غَافِر *gāfir* "covering
and forgiving the sins," غِفَارَه *gifārah* "skullcap, mantle,"
غُفَيْرَه *gufīrah* "small mantle"   This is found in the
African languages as the denomination of the waistcloth or drawers generally worn by the uncircumcised
boys, to cover the nudity.   We have Fulup *gabil*, plural
obil, Guresa *galpali*, Bagbalan *garpal*, Soso *kufura*
"waistcloth," and in the latter case the meaning "to
forgive" is preserved in the form *khabari*, while in
Zenaga we have *r'afar* "to pardon," *r'ufara* "a cap."
Similarly we have Arabic (in Adirar) *ofāra*, plural
gofāfer, (in Beran) *r'ofāra, gofāra*, Soninke *kufune*,
Peul *hufune*, Mandingo *fūla*, Asante *fīla*, Aku *ēfila*,
Yoruba *fila*, Mossi *fōwila*, Gurma *fōalera*, Nupe *fula*,
Timbuktu *fūla* "cap."   In the other Mande languages
gabil, obviously through a form *wabil*, has still further
been reduced, and we have Malinke *bila*, Bambara
bila, bla "waistcloth for uncircumcised children, to
permit, leave alone, put to one's account, put away,"
while in Vei we have *bere* "a strip of cloth about two
inches broad worn by girls from about their eighth year
up to their marriage, to cover their shame, and hanging

down before and behind to about half a foot from the ground." It is, therefore, identical with a mark of virginity, and *beremo* means "a virgin." Thus we get to Nahuatl *vipilli* "the nether garment of an Indian woman" and "protective garment used in war." In the Maya language we have this Mexican *vipilli* in the form *cuyub*, no doubt from *cuyubil*, just as *chim* has developed from *chimil, chimal*.

The early writers, Encizo, Las Casas, Oviedo, Bernal Diaz[1] use *naguas* as a native name for a woman's loin-cloth, which fell from the waist to the middle of the thigh. This word is from Arabic لجام *laĝām* "bridle, strap by which a horse is led, menstrual cloth." This we find in Berber, Hassania *lejām* "bridle," Wolof *lakhabe* "leather strap by which a horse is led," Malinke, Dyula *lagba* "vêtement intimè de femme," and this produced Spanish *naguas*. The change of *lagba* to *nagba* must have already taken place in Mande, for we have side by side Malinke *lamaḥa, namaḥa* "to shake," *latege, natege* "to cut," etc., and, as *la, na* are common prefixes, they have a tendency to drop off even from words that are not compounded. Indeed, we have already in Zenaga and Tuareg *ar'ba* "bridle," which presupposes a form *agba*, and Malinke *karafe*, Bambara *karbe, karabe, karfe* "a bit, bridle" show that *agbe* led to *karbe*, because this guttural Arabic *g* introduced the letter *r* after the *k*. Thus there arose in Mexico the form *cueitl* for the island *nagua*, meaning "a woman's nether garment." Thus we have identified all the garments handled by the early Mexican merchants as of Mandingo origin.

In Nahuatl we have both *tilmatli* and *chimalli*, but the latter is recorded only with the meaning "shield." It would, therefore, appear that the round object with

---

[1] A. Zayas y Alfonso, *Lexicografía antillana*, Habana 1914, p. 396 f.

Wattepanzerreiter aus Kano.
(Nach Aquarell von Carl Arriens.)

SUDANIC ARMOR, from Frobenius' *The Voice of Africa*.

a cloth fringe at the bottom, so often represented in
Mexican manuscripts, is and has always been a shield.
But there are a number of disconcerting facts in such an
assumption.   In the first place, in the vast majority of
representations of warriors and tributes in Mexican
manuscripts, the garments are the *vipilli*, and *maxtli*,
and the *chimalli* shield, whereas in the vast majority of
cases of the representations of men wearing the *tilmatli*,
the shield is absent, but the "devisa" is woven or
painted on the mantle itself.   It, therefore, appears
that the mantle is, indeed, a *quauhchimalli*, a "large"
chimalli, whatever the *chimalli* may have been.   In
any case, the mantle and the shield were known in
Nahuatl as *tlauiztli*, which means "arms, insignia,"
and this shows at once that we are dealing here with
defensive armor, which at the same time had the dis
tinctive mark, the *n'tene* of the Mandingos.

We have Arabic لبس *labisu* "to dress, accoutre,"
لبوس *lubūs* "cuirass, a kind of linen covering filled with
cotton, which in battle covers the back, flanks, neck
and chest of the horse, and which, they say, is impene-
trable to the lance or sword," لابس *lābis* "one covered
with a cuirass," لبوس *labūs* "coat of mail," تلبيس *talbīs*
"dressing, investiture."

In the Mande languages we have traces of this ancient
Arabic defensive armor. We have Malinke *labiti*,
mabiti "to cover oneself," and, as usual, assuming *la*,
ma to be a prefix, we get *biti* "to cover," hence *bitīnkā*
"a cover."   Similarly we have Bambara *biri*, *bri*,
Mandingo *bitta* "to cover."   In Hausa we get *lufudi*
"coat of mail put on horses and men, made of cloth
stuffed with cotton, wool, etc., not of iron."   In the
Berber language we naturally have the Arabic word
well preserved. Here we have *lebsa* "garment."

This gets into Songay as *dabiri* "a cover," *dabu* "to dress." All these prove that the Arabic *lābis* "one covered with a cuirass," etc. had an enormous effect upon the development of protective armor in the Western Sudan. Hence it follows that the African *n'tene*, from Arabic *nišān*, "the mark of distinction," passed among the Mandingos, no doubt together with the formation of the Malli state under Arabic influence.

According to Yacoub Artin Pacha,[1] blazonry among the Arabs had its origin in the activity of the Persian poet, Firdūsi, in his *Shah-Nameh*, in the beginning of the XI. century, since he roused with it the historic sense and a love for heraldry. "In a multitude of verses he, indeed, makes mention of personal marks of distinction and of colors, which form true coats of arms, blazoning the warriors, heroes, kings and nations, whose great deeds he sings. These coats of arms make them known at feasts, tourneys, military reviews, and even on the battlefield. The sovereigns and their mamelucks, reading the *Shah-Nameh*, naturally felt the desire to imitate in everything the costumes and usages of the kings and heroes, whose valiant deeds were sung and glorified in this epic. Therefore, they adopted for themselves, for their great dignitaries and knights, and even for their armies, symbolical colors and graphic symbols, like those of the heroes and kings of the *Shah-Nameh*. Thus, from the XI. century on, the mamelucks of Syria and of Egypt, following in this the example set them by the oriental princes, also adopted the coats of arms, which they designed on their bucklers, their pennants, their standards, even on the garments of their slaves, and sometimes on coins, and monuments which they constructed."[2] As there is no evidence of the development of heraldry in western Europe before

[1] *Op. cit.*, p. 8 ff.
[2] *Ibid.*, p. 11 f.

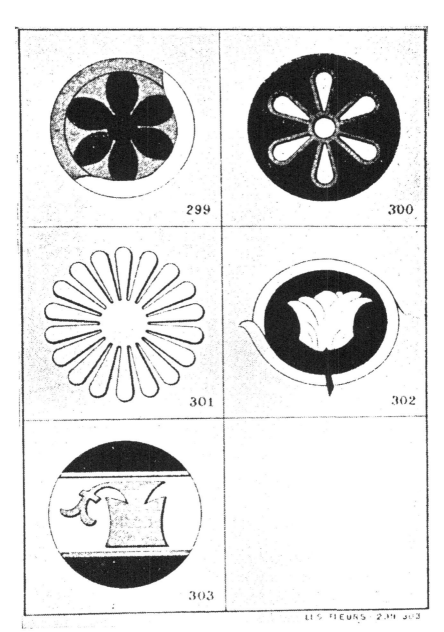

299

300

301

302

303

LES FLEURS 299 303

ARABIC BLAZONRY, from Artın Pacha's *Contribution à l'étude du blason en Orient.*

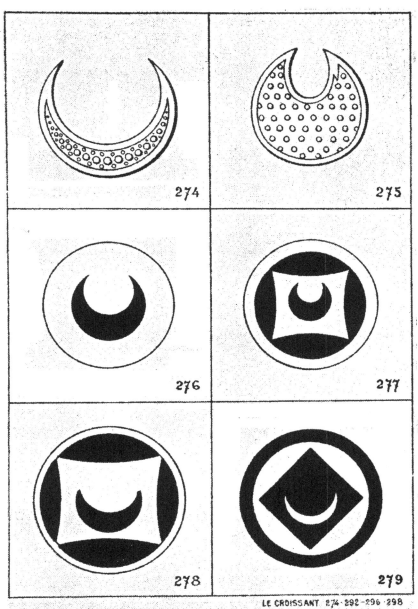

274   275   276   277   278   279

LE CROISSANT 274-292-296-298

ARABIC BLAZONRY, from Artın Pacha's *Contribution à l'étude du blason en Orient*

Abb. 57. valiente *tlacatecoatl*.
Codex Mendoza 68, 20

Abb. 58. valiente *tlacochcalcatl*.
Codex Mendoza 68, 21.

Abb. 59. valiente *uitznauatl*.
Codex Mendoza 68, 22.

Abb. 60. valiente *ticocyauacatl*.
Codex Mendoza 68, 23.

MEXICAN BLAZONRY, from Seler's *Gesammelte Abhandlungen*.

the XII. century,[1] it follows that the European heraldry had its origin in the same Persian source.   Of course, banners and special insignia had been in use in the armies of Rome, Greece, Egypt, etc., but the perpetuation of personal "devices" on bucklers and garments, so as to form a heraldic science, is something of which we have no earlier record.

"In the Orient, the whole heraldic science seems to have consisted in the emblazoning of knights with coats of arms which, so to speak, spoke.   The design, in fact indicated in the greatest number of cases the functions of the knights at the court or in the camps of the sultans whom they served and whose mamelucks they were. The coats of arms were generally personal and attached to the very functions of the knight.   When the knight changed his functions, his coat of arms changed also or was surcharged with some new design which indicated his new functions.   They were nearly always designed on the banners and round bucklers which the oriental knights carried, bucklers that resembled the Roman clipeus.   Also, if they wished to reproduce the coat of arms of a knight upon monuments, furniture, household utensils, cloth, arms, etc., which belonged to him, they represented it as inscribed in a round shield, representing the round buckler then in use."[2]

The description given above fits the Mexican method down to the minutest details.   Artin goes on to describe the coats of arms representing the lion, the eagle, the fish, and a variety of other geometric designs, but the most interesting to us is the representation of the crescent, because it is by far the most characteristic Moslem emblem.   It is generally represented by one upward sign, but frequently it has three stars connected with it, or the crescent is repeated two or three times.[3]   In the

[1] *Ibid.*, p. 15 f.
[2] *Ibid.*, p. 43.
[3] *Ibid.*, p. 165.

great majority of Mexican shields we have the crescent accompanied at the bottom by three more crescents. Unfortunately we have no representation of the Malli coats of arms preserved, except the *n'tene*, which pictures animals or some objects and vaguely stands for a clan or brotherhood, but these are no longer represented on standards or shields. But the name *n'tene*, as I have shown, represents a sign of nobility, and we have found the word preserved in the same sense in the Carribean Islands. Thus there cannot be the slightest doubt that the Mexican coats of arms are evolutions of the Mandingo *n'tene* in its original signification.

The Mexicans represented certain dignities or functions on the banners called *panitl*, *pantli*, or *pamitl*. We have also Maya *pan* "banner," while in Kiche *pan* means "leather or cloth cover." This latter sense shows that the original meaning of *panitl* was "a square piece of cloth" Encizo in his *Suma de geografía* says that the women put on a *pampaniya*, a leaf tied with a cotton string, if they did not have *naguas*, and Oviedo says that a *pampaniya* is a piece of cloth of the size of a hand.[1] These meanings are nearer to the Kiche than to the Nahuatl meaning. We find this word in Soninke *fendeli*, Wolof *mpendel* "a woman's loincloth, petticoat." We have it in Songay *bankarey* "cloth," Hausa, Nupa *bante* "towel, apron, cloth," Mandingo *fano*, Malinke *fanu*, Bambara *fini* "square piece of cloth," the French "pagne," which is not, as generally supposed, from Spanish "paño" but from Persian-Arabic بند *banḍ* "a knot, tie, ribbon, wrapper," بنداريه *banḍārīyah* "drapery, curtain." But the Arabic *banḍ* very nearly acquired the meaning "banner," from the Greek βάνδον, from the same Persian word, hence it unquestionably had the same meaning in the African

---

[1] Zayas y Alfonso, *op. cit.*, p. 412.

languages, where the word "banner" is not mentioned in the scanty vocabularies.   The Mexican *pantli* is of the same Arabic origin.   In Molina only the compound is recorded, *quachpantli*, where *quachtli* means "a large mantle, cloth," so that the relation of the two is in Mexico the same as in the Arabic.

This Nahuatl *quachtli* is the Malinke, Bambara, Songay *kasa*, Hassania Arabic *kasi* "coverlet."   It is the Arabic ·لكس *kisa*,[1] which is also found in Spanish *alquicel, alquicer* "Moorish garment in the form of a mantle, table-cloth."   Covarrubias says that "it is a covering for a bench or table, and is woven without a seam, like a bed-cover."   Leo Africanus, speaking of the Berber dress, says that "their ordinary garment is an *alquicel*.   It resembles a linen bed-cover in which one wraps oneself, but it is finer and it is used to wrap around the body."   Cadamosto says that the Zenaga wear white cloaks which they call *alchezeli*. That this is identical with the Nahuatl *quachtli* is seen from the fact that the word is used in compounds, where it means "bed-cover, veil."   Thus we get *quachicpalli* "pillow," *quachpepechtli* "mattress, pillow, coverlet," *quachpanyo* "that which has sails."   There was also a small mantle called *patolli coachtli*, which the Spaniards called *patoles coacheles*,[2] and here the Spanish form *alquizeles* is even more prominent.

While *pochtecatl* is the usual word for "merchant," a more important designation is *tiamictli, tianquiztli*, for which there is no Nahuatl etymology.   Fray Toribio de Motolinia calls the Mexican market *tiantiztli* or *tianquizco*.[3]   It is not likely that *tiantiztli* is a blunder for *tianquiztli*, since it is once more repeated as

[1] Dozy, *Dictionnaire détaillé des noms des vêtements*, p. 383 ff.
[2] J. García Icazbalceta, *Memoriales de Fray Toribio de Motolinia*, Méjico 1903, p. 330.
[3] *Ibid.*, p. 321 ff.

tiantiztli,[1] and since we find it in Aymara as *tinta*. But all the words of this group are derived from *tangoman*, *tangosmãos* "the white Negroized trader on the west coast of Africa."[2] Indeed, one of the chief places of sacrifice was at *Tianquizmanalco*, and that this originally meant "marketplace" follows from *tianquizmanaloyan* "marketplace, fair." *Tianquizman* or some such form for "merchant" preceded the shorter *tianquiztli*, which is obviously not a Nahuatl word. In Central America *tianguiz*, *tiangue* is still used colloquially for "marketplace, fair."

Molina[3] records *toltecatl*, plural *tolteca*, "master mechanic," hence *toltecauia* "to produce a work of mechanical perfection." Since *teca* is "master," it follows that *tol* must mean "mechanic, artisan." The historical myth which makes of the Toltecs an ancient race from whom the Aztecs received their culture is not worth considering seriously, as has already been pointed out by Brinton.   It can easily be shown that the name arose only after the Mandingos had influenced the Mexican civilization.   I have already pointed out the development of Arabic ‫دبر‬ *ḍabr* in Africa.[4] I shall now trace its more important developments.   In the Koran we frequently find the verb *ḍabbar* in the sense of "he devised, planned, or plotted a thing, he managed, conducted, ordered, or regulated an affair, he acted with consideration of the issues or results of affairs." Hence we get Berber *debber* "to conduct, manage, influence" and *amdebber* "counselor, guide, director," Hausa *dabara* "contrivance, skill, counsel," Songay *dabari* "counsel, means."   In Wolof we get *defără* "to make, establish, restore," and the abbreviated

[1] *Ibid.*, p. 326.
[2] See vol. II, p. 112 ff.
[3] A. de Molina, *Vocabulario de la lengua mexicana*, Leipzig 1880.
[4] Vol. I, p. 109 f.

defă "to make, place, construct, create, form, produce, manufacture, compose." In the Mande languages we get Soso *rafalla* "to arrange, make," Bambara *dabali* "means, expedient, industry," and the frightfully apocopated Bambara *dala, dla* "to arrange, put in order, build," *da* "to do, manufacture, put, lay down, add," *Daba* "God," Malinke *dala* "manufacture, maker," *da* "to make, manufacture, compose, arrange." In Bambara or Malinke "master mechanic" would be *daltigi*, and this is unquestionably the origin of Nahuatl *tolteca* "master mechanic." In the Mande languages this would refer to the Arabic conquerors who brought the arts to the Malli kingdom, and in the Mexican myth we have some kind of recollection of this historic fact.

In Nahuatl we have a parallel to *toltecatl*, the term *patecatl*, for "the god of the pulque," which was considered a medicine, from *pai* "to drink a medicine," *paitia* "to take a purgative," *patli* "medicine, plaster, unguent," which are all related to the *bori* words already discussed, hence *patecatl* is the Mandingo *boritigi*. We have another "fetish man" word, which is far more interesting. In Caraib there is recorded *amaoti* "retired, sedentary man," while in Bakairi, in the interior of Brazil, we have *omeoto* "fetish man." In Aymara *amaotta* means "very wise," while among the Peruvians the *amauta* was the teacher of the youth, who instructed them in the wisdom of government and of religion and was in charge of the *quipu* records. In Mexico Molina's dictionary gives for *amantecatl* the meaning "master mechanic," as in the case of *toltecatl*.

Sahagun has the following account of the *amanteca*: "According to the accounts of the ancients, in regard to the name of the *amanteca*, the first inhabitants of the country brought with them from the regions whence they came a god called *Coyotlinauatl*, whom they never stopped worshipping. These immigrants were called

icnonitlacapixoani mexiti, which means 'the first colonists who are called *Mexiti,*' whence came the name of
Mexico. The people who settled in this region
multiplied, and their descendants put up a sculptured
wooden statue and erected a temple in a quarter to
which they gave the name of *Amantlan.* Here they
worshipped the god whom they called *Coyotlinauatl,*
and made offerings to him, and, on account of the
name of the quarter, which is *Amantlan,* these inhabitants assumed the name of *Amanteca.* On holidays they clothed this god in a dressed coyote skin.
The privilege of preparing this skin was left to the inhabitants of this quarter of *Amantlan.* He kept the
coyote head, but was covered by a human mask. His
canine teeth were of gold and all his other teeth were
very long and pointed. In his hand he carried a stick
which was adorned with black *itztli* stones and on which
he leaned, and he had a buckler made of reeds, on the
border of which was painted a light blue circle. On
his back he carried a pot from which a large number of
quetzalli feathers issued. On his ankles he had a kind
of gaiters with a large number of small white shells
like rattles. He wore *cotaras* of the leaves of a tree
called *yecotl,* because this was the footgear that the
immigrants wore when they came to this country
They always put them on his legs, in order to let it be
known that they were the first Chichimec colonists who
established themselves in this country of Mexico.

"In this quarter of *Amantlan* they worshipped not
only this god, but also seven other idols, of whom five
were dressed as men and two as women. But *Coyotlinauatl* was none the less the chief god of all. The
second who came after him was *Tiçaua,* the third—
Macuilocelotl, the fourth—*Macuiltochtli;* the two women
came in the fifth rank. One of them was called

Xiuhtlati, the other *Xilo*.   The seventh who was called *Tepuztecatl* was placed opposite them all.

"This was the way of adorning all these gods: the male gods wore the costume of *Coyotlinauatl*, except the god called *Tiçaua*, who was not dressed in a coyote skin.   But he did have on his back the pot with the *quetzalli* feathers, and he carried the stick and buckler, and wore the white *cotaras*.   The god called *Macuilocelotl* was dressed in a coyote skin.   His head was covered with it, and he looked out from the jaws of an animal.   He, too, carried on his back the pot with his *quetzalli*, and he had the stick, the buckler, and the white *cotaras*.   The god *Macuiltochtli* was dressed up in the same manner.   As to the women, the one who was called *Xiuhtlati* was dressed in a blue *vipilli;* the other, called *Xilo*, who was the second, was dressed in a red *vipilli* dyed with cochineal.   Both had their garments profusely adorned with rich feathers from all kinds of birds of beautiful plumage; the borders were formed by beautiful feathers, as we have already said.   The goddesses carried in one hand green ears of maize in the form of a stick, in the other a fan of rich plumes and a gold jewel in the shape of a *comal*.   They had well-polished and brilliant gold earrings; they carried nothing on their backs, and paper bands took the place of their hair-dress.   Their wrists were adorned with all kinds of rich feathers, and their legs were similarly garbed from the knees to the ankles.   They, too, wore *cotaras* of *yecotl* leaves, in order to show that they belonged to the Chichimecs, who had settled this country.

"Twice a year they celebrated these divinities with a festival, one in the month *panquetzaliztli*, and the other in the month called *tlaxochimaco*.   In the month *panquetzaliztli* they killed the image of *Coyotlinauatl*. If no one came forward to offer a slave, called *tlaaltiltin*, these *amanteca* united and bought one, in order to kill him in honor of the God, in exchange for mantles called *quachtli*, which were used to pay the tribute with. But if some *amantecatl* celebrated for himself a feast and killed some slaves, one of these was sacrificed in honor of the god *Coyotlinauatl*.   He was covered with all the ornaments of the god, as was told before.   If the one who celebrated the feast was a rich man, he killed one, two, or three slaves, and even more, always in honor of these divinities.   If he was not well-to-do, he was satisfied with one single victim, in order to honor *Coyotlinauatl*.   When they celebrated the holiday, all the old men, men, and women, gathered in the quarter called *Amantlan*.   There they sang, and compelled all those who were to be sacrificed to keep awake.   They generally made them take a draught called *itzpachtli*, so that they would not fear death.   This drink intoxicated them and made them lose consciousness.   For that reason they made use of it, so that they would not be conscious when their breasts were opened.   There were some slaves who were mad enough to start running toward the top of the temple, driven by the desire to be killed forthwith, in order to make an end of life.

"When the holiday of these divinities was celebrated a second time, in the month of *tlaxochimaco*, no slaves were sacrificed.   The solemnity was then celebrated in the name of the above mentioned goddesses, without, however, forgetting the five other gods.   All *Amanteca* women then gathered in the *Amantlan* quarter and dressed up like the goddesses, in the manner explained, whereas the men were satisfied to cover their legs with red feathers.   Then the *amanteca* offered up their boys and girls to these divinities, promising to put the boys in the *calmecac*, where they would learn the art of a *toltecayotl*, while for the girls they invoked the goddesses to help them become good workers and dyers of *tochomitl* of every color, either with feathers or rabbit wool.

"The quarters of the *amanteca* and *pochteca* were confused, and the same happened to their gods, of whom one was called *Yacatecutli*, god of the merchants, and the other *Coyotlinauatl*, who is the god of the *amanteca*.   For that reason the merchants and feather-workers honored each other, and when they seated themselves at a banquet, the merchants placed themselves at one side, and the feather-workers at the other. They were about equal in their wealth and in the manner of celebrating their holidays and banquets.   This was so because the merchants brought feathers from distant countries, and the *amanteca* worked them and manufactured from them coats of arms, such as the bucklers of which the kings and high personages made use, which were very numerous in form and bore various denominations, as had been explained in the text.   Before they became acquainted with the rich plumes, from which they manufactured their coats of arms, these *tolteca* made the dancing-gear from the white and black feathers of chickens, herons, and ducks.   They did not then as yet know the finer points of their profession.   They limited themselves to fixing the feathers in a coarse way with *itztli* knives on *aueuetl* boards. The rich feathers were known in the time of King *Auitzotl*.   They were brought by the *tecunenenque* merchants, when they conquered the provinces of *Anahuac*, as we have said.   It was at that time that the *amanteca* began to make fine and delicate pieces of work."[1]

In this account we have the same confusion of the mythical *Amanteca* with the *amanteca* artisans that we had in the case of the *Tolteca* people and *tolteca* artisans. The god of the *amanteca* is *Coyotlinauatl*, which Seler

[1] Sahagun, *op. cit.*, p. 587 ff. (book I, chaps. XVIII, XIX).

writes *coyotl inaual*, and says that the god was in the form of a coyote.[1] But as the latter word is derived from *naualli* "magician," I shall show that this refers to an African origin. Brinton very long ago recognized it as not of native origin: "To illustrate this I shall subjoin several series of words derived from the same radical which is at the basis of the word *nagual*, the series, three in number, being taken from the three radically diverse, though geographically contiguous, linguistic stocks, the Maya, the Zapotec and the Nahuatl.

From the Maya, of Yucatan.

Naual, or *nautal*, a native dance, forbidden by the missionaries.

Naatil, talent, skill, ability.

Naat, intelligence, wisdom.

Naatah, to understand, to divine.

Nanaol, to consider, to contemplate, to meditate, to commune with oneself, to enter into oneself.

Noh, great, skillful; as *noh ahceh*, a skillful hunter.

From Maya Dialects.

Quiche-Cakchiquel.

Naual, a witch or sorcerer.

Naualin, to tell fortunes, to predict the future.

Qui naualin, to sacrifice, to offer sacrifices.

Na, to feel, to suspect, to divine, to think in one's heart.

Nao, to know, to be alert or expert in something.

Naol, a skillful person, a rhetorician.

Naotizan, to make another intelligent or astute.

Natal, the memory.

Natub, the soul or shadow of a man.

Noh, the god of reason.

Noh, to fecundate, to impregnate (*Popol Vuh*).

[1] E. Seler, *Gesammelte Abhandlungen zur amerikanischen Sprach- und Alterthumskunde*, Berlin 1904, vol. II, p. 970.

Tzental.

X-qna, to know.
X-qnaulai, to know often or thoroughly (frequentative).
Naom, wise, astute (*naom vinic*, hombre sabio).
Naoghi, art, science.
Naoghibal, memory.
Ghnaoghel, a wise man.
Alaghom naom, the Goddess of Wisdom.

From the Zapotec, of Oaxaca.

Nana, gana, gona, to know.
Nona, to know thoroughly, to retain in the memory.
Nana ticha, or *nona lii*, a wise man.
Guela nana, or *guela nona*, wisdom, knowledge.
Hue gona, or *ro gona*, a teacher, a master.
Na lii, truth; *ni na lii*, that which is true.
Naciña, or *naciina*, skill, dexterity.
Hui naa, a medicine man, a 'nagualist.'
Nahaa, to speak pleasantly or agreeably.
Nayaa, or *nayapi*, to speak easily or fluently.
Rigoo gona, to sacrifice, to offer sacrifice.
Ni nana, the understanding, the intelligence, generally.
Nayanii, the superior reason of man.
Nayaa, ⎫ superiority, a superior man (gentileza, gentil
Naguii, ⎭ hombre).

From the Nahuatl, of Mexico.

Naua, to dance, holding each other by the hands.
Naualli, a sorcerer, magician, enchanter.
Nauallotl, magic, enchantment, witchcraft.
Nauatl, or *nahuatl*, skillful, astute, smart; hence, superior; applied to language, clear, well-sounding, whence (perhaps) the name of the tongue.
Nauati, to speak clearly and distinctly.
Nauatlato, an interpreter.

"I believe that no one can carefully examine these lists of words, all taken from authorities well acquainted with the several tongues, and writing when they still retained their original purity, without acknowledging that the same radical or syllable underlies them all; and further, that from the primitive form and rich development of this radical in the Zapotec, it looks as if we must turn to it to recognize the origin of all these expressions, both in the Nahuatl and the Maya linguistic stocks.

"The root *na*, to know, is the primitive monosyllabic stem to which we trace all of them. *Nahual* means knowledge, especially mystic knowledge, the Gnosis, the knowledge of the hidden and secret things of nature; easily enough confounded in uncultivated minds with sorcery and magic.

"It is very significant that neither the radical *na* nor any of its derivatives are found in the Huasteca dialect of the Mayan tongue, which was spoken about Tampico, far removed from other members of the stock. The inference is that in the southern dialects it was a borrowed stem.

"Nor in the Nahuatl language—although its very name is derived from it—does the radical *na* appear in its simplicity and true significance. To the Nahuas, also, it must have been a loan.

"It is true that de la Serna derives the Mexican *naualli*, a sorcerer, from the verb *nahualtia*, to mask or disguise oneself, 'because a *naualli* is one who masks or disguises himself under the form of some lower animal, which is his *nagual;*' but it is altogether likely that *nahualtia* derived its meaning from the custom of the medicine men to wear masks during their ceremonies.

"Therefore, if the term *nagual*, and many of its associates and derivatives, were at first borrowed from the Zapotec language, a necessary corrollary of this conelusion is, that along with these terms came most of the superstitions, rites, and beliefs to which they allude; which thus became grafted on the general tendency to such superstitions existing everywhere and at all times in the human mind.

"Along with the names of the days and the hieroglyphs which mark them, and the complicated arithmetical methods by means of which they were employed, were carried most of the doctrines of the Nagualists, and the name by which they in time became known from central Mexico quite to Nicaragua and beyond.

"The mysterious words have now, indeed, lost much of their ancient significance. In a recent dictionary of the Spanish of Mexico *nagual* is defined as 'a witch; a word used to frighten children and make them behave,' while in Nicaragua, where the former Nahuatl population has left so many traces of its presence in the language of to-day, the word *nagual* no longer means an actor in the black art, or a knowledge of it, but his or her armamentarium, or the box, jar or case in which are kept the professional apparatus, the talismans and charms, which constitute the stock in trade or outfit of the necromancer.

"Among the Lacandons, of Mayan stock, who inhabit the forests on the upper waters of the Usumacinta river, at the present day the term *naguate* or *nagutlat* is said to be applied to any one 'who is entitled to respect and obedience by age and merit;' but in all probability he is also believed to possess superior and occult knowledge."[1]

All these words are from the Arabic, of course, through the Mandingo. We have Arabic نبأ *naba'* "to proclaim, prophesy," نبي *nabī* "prophet," نبه *nabah* "intelligent, penetrating, vigilant," and these two roots

---

[1] D. G. Brinton, *Nagualism*, Philadelphia 1894, p. 56 ff.

have become in Africa welded into one, and have to a great extent disappeared from the native vocabularies because of the confusion with *nama*.   And yet, we have Peul *nabīu*, Dyula *nabiu*, Soso *annabi* "prophet," Wolof *nabīna* "prophet, the legislator of a sect." Among the Mossi *nāba* means "chief, master," and among the Habbes-Gara the masked young men, who among the Malinke are known as *nama*, are called *naba*.   Here we have a confusion of two Arabic terms, but the remarkable thing is that the men wearing the masks among the Malinke are called *namakoro*, literally "the hyena wise men,"[1]   that is, an exact translation of Nahuatl *coyotlinauatl*, where the American coyote is substituted for the African hyena.   The *Nama* in Africa protects the people against the *suba*, or *subaga*, the were-wolf, the hyena,[2] and there is a male and a female *Nama*, and sacrifices are made twice a year to them.   The resemblance of the *Nama* worship and that of the *Coyotlinauatl* is striking.   Even the word is preserved, for *naualli* and *naba*, *nama* are identical.

The resemblance does not rest here.   Let us look at the celebration of the *Nama* among the Bambaras: "The two heads of the male and female *Nama* seem to represent two fantastic birds, and when they are preceded by the *darotigi*, who shakes the rattle and carries a burning fagot, and the *dyenfa mussu*, who run through the village and around the walls in search of the *siri*, the illusion is complete.   It is still more so when they put them on their brows and mix with the dancers, who shake their bodies which are naked as far as the waist, and howl at the sound of drums and fifes their sacred songs: 'He is our host, the *nyā*, great killer of men, he is our host.   It has blossomed in order to bear its fruits, this *boli* has blossomed, it has its fruit.   *Suba*, *yo*, this

---

[1] See p. 193 for *koro* "sense, wisdom."
[2] Henry, *op. cit.*, p. 40.

p. 150.

Fétiche *Nama.*

From Henry's *Les Bambara.*

was done for shame's sake.   If one has been addicted to the practice of the *suba*, we have a means of getting away from it.'   The sacrifice of the *Nama* is not less imposing.   In the enclosure where is the beehive that serves as a tabernacle, only the members of the staff enter.   The mass of the brethren stay outside and nobody approaches the palisade except when his turn has come to present to the sacrificer the chicken and the kola nuts of the sacrifice.   While the idol is being smeared with blood, two men, naked to the waist and facing the crowd, stand motionless on either side of the sacrificer, holding in their hands two sticks a meter in length, upon which three sheep-horns and two other horns are tied.   It is an honor to be allowed to hold these horned sticks, it is even a dignity, and these people are called the *dyenfa tyeu*. . . .During these nights the women stay inside the village, and the streets that abut against the place where they meet are cut off with *kara* or rough mats.   They hear from time to time near them the loud sounds of trumpets and horns, and they see over the mats the outline of a hideous mask which they cannot distinguish and even are unable to say to have seen.   When the *Nama* comes out, the women are called at day-break, just as the god is put back in the beehive, and they, at the foot of the tree where our devotees have been howling and dancing all night, are shown the *siri* found by the *dyenfa tyeu* and the *darotigi* or *darotala*.   While these *siri* are burned, the women dance and sing praises to the idol.   Our *boli* have two days of rest during the week, Monday and Thursday.''[1]

I have already shown the relation of the *Nama* worship to the Islamic practices.   It now can be shown that here we have, indeed, the *aman* ''the faith,'' for the singing of the prayer at day-break, to keep off the

[1] *Ibid.*, p. 149 ff.

suba, is, of course, the Arabic prayer at day-break, the
صبح *ṣubh*. The *Nama* is connected with the Arabic
seven-day week, two of which are used as rest days, that
is, unlucky days. The *Namatigi*, the priest of the
Nama, that is, here the *naba* "the prophet," is among
the Malinkes and Bambaras also called *fura tigiba* "the
great master of medicine," *fura* meaning originally
"leaf of a tree," hence "medicine which comes from the
trees." This is brought out in the prayer where the
boli has blossomed its fruit, with which the *suba* "the
hyena, were-wolf" can be warded off. As the *boli* of
the *Nama* is the chief medicine, he is connected with
the bees, and so resides in a beehive. This is based on
the Koran, XVI. 70, 71: "Thy Lord spake by inspiration unto the bee, saying, Provide thee houses in the
mountains and in the trees, and of those materials
wherewith men build hives for thee: then eat of every
kind of fruit, and walk in the beaten paths of thy Lord.
There proceedeth from their bellies a liquor of various
colour, wherein is a medicine for men. Verily herein is a
sign unto people who consider." To this Sale says:
"The same being not only good food, but a useful
remedy in several distempers, particularly those oc-
casioned by phlegm. There is a story that a man
came once to Mohammad, and told him that his
brother was afflicted with a violent pain in his belly:
upon which the Prophet bade him give him some honey.
The fellow took his advice; but soon after coming again,
told him that the medicine had done his brother no
manner of service: Mohammad answered, 'Go and
give him more honey, for God speaks truth, and thy
brother's belly lies.' And the dose being repeated,
the man, by God's mercy was immediately cured."

Among the Mexicans the "medicine" god has split off
from the "hyena" god, and we find him as *Ixtlilton*

"the one with the black face." "They built for this god an oratory from painted boards, a kind of tabernacle in which his image was placed.   In this oratory or temple there were a large number of bowls and jars filled with water and covered with boards or *comalli*.   This water was called *tlilatl*, which means 'black water.'   When a child fell ill, they took it to the temple of this god *Ixtlilton*, opened a jar, made him drink this water, and he was cured.   If one wanted to celebrate the feast of this god with personal devotion, its image was taken to the house.   It was then neither painted nor sculptured, for a satrap just put on the ornaments of this divinity. During the transportation they burned copal before it, until the image came to the house where it was to be celebrated with dances and songs, as was their custom, for their manner of dancing is very different from ours. I shall describe here the one which we call *areyto*, and which they denominate in their language as *maceualiztli*. They came together in large numbers, by twos or by threes, and formed a more or less large circle, according to their numbers.   They carried flowers in their hands and were adorned with all kinds of feathers.   They produced all together a uniform motion with their bodies and with their feet and hands, a thing well done and well worth seeing.   All the movements were in harmony with the music of the drum and *teponaztli*. They accompanied the instruments with their voices, singing in unison the praises of the god whose feast they were celebrating.   Even nowadays they give themselves over to the same exercises, although for a different purpose.   They regulate their movements and adornments according to the nature of their songs, for their dances and their intonations vary considerably, without ever ceasing to be very charming and even full of devotion.   The forest of their idolatry has not yet been rooted up.

"The image of the god having arrived at the house of him who was celebrating the occasion, they at first set out to eat and drink, after which began the dances and songs with which they honored the divinity. The god himself having danced for a long time, descended to the cave where the *pulque* had been kept in various jars covered for four days with varnished boards and *comalli*. He opened one or more, an operation which was called *tlayacaxapotla*, which means 'the wine is new.' Then he and those who accompanied him drank this wine; then they went out and repaired to the yard of the house where were the jars full of black water which was dedicated to him and which had been covered for four days. The one who played the part of the god opened them, and if, having opened them, he found in any of them any impurity, such as a piece of straw or hairs or coal, they at once said that the man who gave the feast was a bad man, an adulterer, a thief, or a libertine, and everybody insulted him, imputing to him some of these vices, and pretending that he was only a sower of discord and trouble, and these offenses were addressed to him publicly in the presence of all. When the man who was the image of the god left the house, they gave him stuffs, called for that reason *izquen*, which means 'face cover,' to allude to the shame of the celebrator of the feast, when the waters were altered."[1]

From this description we see that *Ixtlilton* was a dance god, just like a "medicine" *griot*. That he split off from the *Nama* worship follows from his use of the "black water," which, as we shall later see, refers to a honeyed drink, used as medicine. Just as in the *Nama* prayer the words are, "This was done for shame's sake," so the *Ixtlilton* priest receives a face cloth, apparently to be used as a veil. But in the *Nama* ritual the women were not allowed to see the

[1] Sahagun, *op. cit.*, p. 34 f. (book I, chap. XVI).

Nama, and, obviously, "for shame's sake," the streets were cut off by mats to serve the same purpose. Seler has pointed out that *Ixtlilton*, as a dance god, paints his face black and is related to the *Ueuecoyotl* "the old coyote."[1] The painting of the face black, just as the feather adornment and dance, is obviously of *griot* origin, that is, points to the "tarring and feathering." *Ueuecoyotl* is a translation of Malinke, Bambara *namakoro* "the old hyena," which is a synonym of *nama* "hyena, fetish." This *Ueuecoyotl* is represented as the regent of the fourth *Tonalamatl* division, and is clearly represented as a dance god,[2] and is identical with the *Coyotlinauatl* of the *amanteca*.[3]

Among the Mayas the African *Nama* is represented by the long-nosed black god *Ekchuah*: "God L's features are those of an old man with sunken, toothless mouth. His hieroglyph is Fig. 44, which is characterized by the black face.

"God L, who is also black, must not be confounded with M whose description follows. L is represented and designated by his hieroglyph in the accompanying text, in Dr. 14b and 14c and Dr. 46b; the figure has the characteristic black face. He appears entirely black in Dr. 7a. The hieroglyph alone occurs in Dr. 21b and 24 (third vertical line in the first passage) with a variation, namely without the Ymix-sign before the head. This deity does not occur in the Madrid and Paris manuscripts.

"The significance of god L does not appear from the few pictures, which are given of him. In Dr. 46b the god is pictured armed and in warlike attitude. Both in Dr. 14b and 14c he wears a bird on his head and has a Kan in his hand.

---

[1] *Op. cit.*, p. 462.
[2] E. Seler, *Codex Borgia*, Berlin 1904, vol. I, p. 98.
[3] *Ibid.*, p. 99.

"According to Förstemann, his day is Akbal, darkness, night.

"Cyrus Thomas (Aids to the Study of the Maya Codices, in the 6th Annual Report of the Bureau of Ethnology, Washington, 1888, p. 358) thinks he is the god *Ekchuah*, who has come down to us as a black deity. God M seems, however, to correspond to *Ekchuah* (see the description of M).

"God M's hieroglyph is Figs. 45,46; it seems to represent an eye rimmed with black, though the figure of the god himself displays an entirely different drawing of the eye (see Fig. 47).

"The god is found in the Dresden manuscript only three times, namely in Dr. 16b (with a bone in his hand) in picture and sign, in Dr. 13c grouped with an animal, without the hieroglyph, and in Dr. 43a (with his sign) while finally his hieroglyph alone appears in Dr. 56 (top, left) in a group and of a somewhat different form.

"On the other hand, god M appears with special frequency in the Madrid manuscript, which treats of this deity with great fullness of detail. While he is represented in the Dresden manuscript (16b) with his body striped black and white, and on p. 43a entirely white, he is always entirely black in the Codex Troano. His other distinguishing marks are the following:

"1· The mouth encircled by a red-brown border.

"2· The large, drooping under lip. By this he can be recognized with certainty also in Dr. 43a.

"3· The two curved lines at the right of the eye.

"His significance can be conjectured. He seems to be of a warlike nature, for he is almost always represented armed with the lance and also as engaged in combat, and in some instances, pierced by the lance of his opponent, god F, for example in Tro. 3c, 7a, 29*a. The peculiar object with parallel stripes, which he wears on his head is a rope from which a package frequently hangs.   By means of a rope placed around his head the god frequently carries a bale of merchandise, as is the custom today among the aborigines in different parts of America.   On 4b and 5a in the Cod. Tro. this can plainly be seen.   All these pictures lead us to conclude, that we have here to do with a god of *travelling merchants*.   A deity of this character called *Ekchuah* has been handed down to us, who is designated explicitly as a *black* god.   In favor of this is also the fact, that he is represented fighting with F and pierced by the latter.   For the travelling merchant must, of course, be armed to ward off hostile attacks and these are admirably symbolized by god F, for he is the god of death in war and of the killing of the captured enemy. The god is found in the Codex Troano in the following places and on many pages two or three times: pp. 2, 3, 4,5, always with the hieroglyph, then without it on pp. 6, 7, 19, 4*c, 14*b, 17*a, 18*b and again with the hieroglyph on pp. 22*a, 23*a, 25*a; finally it is found again without the hieroglyph on pp. 29*a, 30*a, 31*, 32*, 33*, 34*.   In the Codex Cortesianus god M occurs in the following places: p. 15, where he strikes the sky with the axe and thus causes rain, p. 19 (bottom), 28 (bottom, second figure), 34 (bottom) and 36 (top).   M is always to be recognized by the encircled mouth and the drooping under-lip; figures without these marks are not identical with M, thus for example in Tro. 23, 24, 25, 21*.   Tro. 34*a shows what is apparently a variant of M with the face of an old man, the scorpion's tail and the vertebrae of the death-god, a figure which in its turn bears on its breast the plainly recognizable head of M. God M is also represented elsewhere many times with the scorpion's tail, thus for example on Tro. 30*a, 31*a.

"Besides his hieroglyph mentioned above, Figs. 45 and 46, another sign seems to refer to god M, namely

Fig. 48 (compare for example Tro. 5a and Cort. 28, bottom). The head in this sign has the same curved lines at the corner of the eye as appear on the deity himself. Förstemann mentions this sign in his Commentary on the Paris Manuscript, p. 15, and in his Commentary on the Dresden Manuscript, p. 56. He thinks the hieroglyph has relation to the revolution of Venus, which is performed in 584 days. A relation of this kind is, I think, very possible, if we bear in mind that all the god-figures of the manuscripts have more or less of a calendric and chronologic significance in their chief or in their secondary function.

"It should be mentioned that god M is represented as a rule as an old man with toothless jaw or the characteristic solitary tooth. That he is also related to bee-culture is shown by his presence on p. 4*c of the Codex Troano, in the section on bees.

"Besides gods L and M, a few quite isolated black figures occur in the Codex Troano, who, apparently, are identical with neither of these two deities, but are evidently of slight importance and perhaps are only variants of other deities. Similar figures of black deities are found in the Codex Tro. 23, 24 and 25 (perhaps this is a black variant of B as god of the storm?) and on 21*c we twice see a black form with the aged face and the solitary tooth in the under jaw (perhaps only a variant of M). In the Codex Cortesianus and in the Dresden manuscript no other black deities occur, but in the Paris manuscript a black deity seems to be pictured once (p. 21, bottom)."[1]

That this *Ekchuah* is identical with *Nama* follows from his being represented as old and as connected with bee-culture. That he is identical with the "old coyote" follows from his being represented as the god of the

---

[1] P. Schellhas, *Representation of Deities of the Maya Manuscripts*, in *Papers of the Peabody Museum of American Archaeology and Ethnology, Harvard University*, vol. IV, No. I, p. 34 ff.

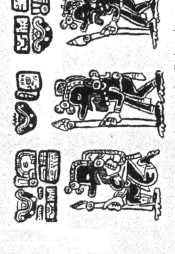

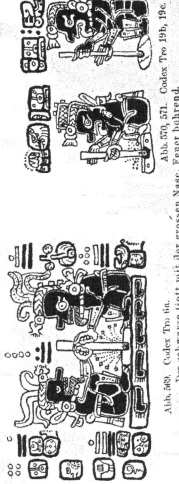

Abb. 569. Codex Tro 6a.
Der schwarze Gott mit der grossen Nase, Feuer bohrend.

Abb. 570, 571. Codex Tro 19b, 19c.

Abb. 572—576. Der schwarze Gott mit der grossen Nase, der Gott der Reisenden.
Codex Tro 5a, 4a, 3b, 2b.

THE LONG-NOSED GOD, from Seler's *Codex Borgia*.

traveling merchants, with whom, as we are informed by Sahagun, the god of the *amanteca* was generally confused. The Mayas celebrated his holiday together with *Hobnil*, the god of the bee-keepers,[1] and during the feast they drank only three bowls of honey wine.[2]   The long nose of the *Ekchuah* is due to the fact that the idol of the *Nama*, called the *Kungolo Nama* "head of the *Nama*," is represented by a fantastic bird, that is, with a beak. The *Ekchuah* becomes among the Mexicans the *Yacatecutli* "the lord of the nose," the god of the merchants, with whom the *Ixtlilton* of the *Amanteca* is confused.

It is not more difficult to identify the Mexican god *Quetzalcouatl*, even though we observe here the same tendency to split the original god into a number of subsidiary forms, each accentuating a special attribute, and though the Mexicans often confused the god with the priest.   The Mexican *Quetzalcouatl*, literally "the Fine Feather Snake," "originally, no doubt, was the symbol of water or the moisture produced by rain, which, after a long drouth, awakens vegetation to new life.   Even thus the Chiapanec priests explain *Cuchulchan* as 'the feather snake which goes into the water.' It is the regent of the seventh sign, that is, as we shall soon see, these priests identified this feather snake with the rain god *Tlaloc*.   Similarly *K'ucumatz* of the Guatemalan myth appears entirely as the principle that lives in the water.   *U c'ux cho u c'ux palo* 'heart of the sea, heart of the water' he is called in the Popol Vuh: *xa pa ya xu col vi ri* 'in the water is his realm of activity' say of him the Cakchiquel annals.   And when Sahagun tells us that the sacrifices brought by the Mexicans in the beginning of their year, according to the statement of some are dedicated to *Tlaloquê*, the rain gods,

[1] Seler, *Codex Borgia,* vol. I, p. 321.
[2] *Ibid.,* p. 322.

according to others to *Chalchiuhtlicuē*, the water goddess, and according to others again to the chief priest and
wind-god *Quetzalcouatl*, and when in the Codex Borbonicus the sixth annual holiday *Etzalqualiztli*, which was a
great rain ceremonial and was dedicated to the rain
gods, was represented by the image of *Quetzalcouatl* and
his twin brother *Xolotl*, the same basic conception seems
to be represented even here. And yet it must be somewhat baffling to find the god everywhere in Mexican
tradition represented as the *Eēcatl*, the wind god."[1]

"A peculiarity of *Quetzalcouatl* is the priestly character attached to him, and that to him are ascribed the
invention and conscientious execution of penance and
chastisements, of blood-letting and offering of one's own
blood, which was one of the most common ritual performances of the old tribes of Mexico and Central
America. This is related to his rôle as master and king
of the Toltecs, since the Toltecs were supposed to have
been the inventors of all civilization and with it of the
ritual and priesthood. . . . The most plausible and
simplest assumption is this, that in the remarkable
figure of this god, the rain god was combined with the
rain magician, who, with his prayer and his practices,
insured to his people the rain needed for their crops.
No doubt it was a later interpretation which added to
him the nature of a wind god, since the wind god was
explained as the forerunner and road-cleaner of the
rain god. Before the rains begin there are great winds
and dust storms, and so they said that *Quetzalcouatl*,
the wind god, swept the roads for the rain gods, so that
they could rain."[2]

From all the accounts of *Quetzalcouatl* it appears that
he was a tutelar deity, from whom prosperity could be
received through his grant of rain necessary for the

[1] *Ibid.*, p. 83.
[2] *Ibid.*, p. 85.

crops. We have in him obviously the Bambara beneficent *dasiri*, the protector of the village, the favorable
ǵinn, whose sacred animal is a snake, a rat, a lizard,
etc., who is addressed with the words· "Preserve us
from evil-doers, from discord, quarrels, and brawls,
from the fury of women who easily succumb to the
power of the devil, from disease; *above all, give us rain,
without which the harvest is impossible.*"[1] The feast of
the *dasiri* takes place once a year,[2] just as that of
Quetzalcouatl. But the worship of the *dasiri* is closely
connected with the activity of the Mandingo *kuare*,
kore, or *kote*, a semi-secret society, with which we must
now become acquainted. "The fundamental basis of
power and authority, the cult of the *dasiri*, may, with
good right, be considered as the first and oldest of all.
That of the *kote* or *kore* seems to me equally respectable
from this standpoint and equally old. As the first of
all, it is held in a small grove near the village, and the
baobab, the khay, the nettletree are the three trees he
likes to live in. The cult of the *kore* is especially honored in the Bani. Although not all the villages now
possess the fetish, all at least have adepts who belong to
the sect. This semi-occult sect, which counts women
in its midst, is divided into eight groups, each ruled by
the oldest under the authority of the *koretigi*, highest
chief of the association. In the yearly sacrifices and
especially in those which take place every seven years
on the initiation days (and one has to be a *kore de*, in
order to participate in the inner circle of the mysteries
which take place in the sacred grove), these groups
present to us the most burlesque assemblage of the
circle of Segu. The *kara mau* carry a perforated board,
painted red and white, and about two meters long;
the *suruku* (hyenas) put on a mask resembling that of

[1] Henry, *op. cit.*, p. 120.
[2] *Ibid.*, p. 101.

the hyena and walk leaning on two canes; and the *koroduga* (buffoons) are dressed up in an indescribable manner. The *ta tugula* (fire-burners) dance with a burning torch in each hand; the *n'goni sama* (thorn-attractors) wrap themselves in thorns or lacerate their breasts and armpits, and the *bisatyila* (flagellants) strike themselves with long, flexible scourges. There are also the *dyara* (lions), who wear masks resembling those of the hyena, but of a larger shape, and the *sula* (monkeys), who walk about in a hideous, grimacing mask and wear in the back tails made of plaited grasses.

"The sect of the *kore* is semi-occult, for if the adepts alone are admitted to the sacrifices and to penetrate the sacred grove, the dances take place in the village, and everybody, men, women, and children, take part in them. The wives of the *koroduga* belong to the brotherhood by right, but they do not know the pass-word *dyantema* (men of the *dyante*), and so are refused admission to the sacred grove. It is their great privilege to wear the livery of their husbands, a long necklace of red beans, to be able to sit down with the men to the beer calabashes, and, finally, to dance the indecent, disgusting dance of the *koroduga* without blushing. The fetish *kore* guards the crops and gives its adepts the only pleasure which they know and long for, eating and drinking, and the enjoyment of women, and all this, as one may convince himself, follows from their dances and orgies. The initiation or affiliation with the sect of the *kore* takes place once every seven years. It is long and painful; for two weeks our young initiates live in the sacred grove and may not enter the village. As they need a little training for their future dances, the old people come every day at noon-time, during the greatest heat, to torture them, and every adept, according to the group to which he belongs, suffers a few moments of torture by fire, thorns, and the rod. .

Independently of the yearly sacrifice, they sacrifice to the *ĝinn* every time an adept passes away. They also sacrifice at the anniversary of his death and *during the dry season*, and our *kore de* run from one feast to another, passing their nights in drinking bouts and inexpressible orgies."[1] "After the initiation, the *koretigi* (priest of the *kore*) proceeds to the sacrifices. Everything is as with the *dasiri*; after the libations of flour and beer, the trunk of the sacred tree is smeared with blood, and all about it are tufts of hair and feathers stuck to the bark by bits of chewed kola nuts. They smear with blood a hyena mask called *kore kungolo* (head of the *kore*), then the *kārā*, emblem of the *ĝinn*, which serves as an altar for the deceased adepts. A part of the viands is taken to the village, and the remainder, roasted on the spot, is eaten without any condiments. In these sacrifices they ask the *kore* and those who form his court to watch over the crops, so that they should be abundant, to watch over the flocks, so that they should prosper, to have all their lives enough to eat and drink, to have a lusty old age, etc., and all this is asked with the only purpose in view 'of being able to enjoy women and giving themselves over to carnal pleasures.'"[2]

The very name of the society, *kuare, kore, kote*, shows that we are dealing here with an aberration of an Islamic brotherhood, no doubt of Sufi origin, known by the Arabic name of خونية *hauniyah*, اخوة *ahuwwat*, and preserved in Berber *hauni*, plural *huan*, "member of the pious brotherhood of the *Khuan*." As the *kore* is the society of the *koroduga*, the buffoon, it is not unlikely that the obscene practices in these societies and the masquerading are of Asiatic origin. In any case, it is clear that the practices of the *kore* are subsidiary to

[1] *Ibid.*, p. 102 ff.
[2] *Ibid.*, p. 124.

those of the tutelar divinity, the *dasiri*.   But in the
Quetzalcouatl myth we have the same reference to the
chastisement and use of the thorn-pricking that we have
in the case of the *kore*.   Finally, *Quetzalcouatl* is represented with a beard,[1] and so is the sun god *Tonacotecutli*.
But the beard appears again in the case of an unnamed
old god, whose mask resembles that of the feathered
snake and of the water goddess *Chalchiuhtlicue*.[2]   There
can be no doubt that the beard is to represent an old
man, and this is precisely what we find in Africa in
connection with the *dasiri* worship, in which all the
house chiefs, the *sotigi*,[3] are old men, and the religious
priest, who presides over them, the *nyenansonaba*, is
an old man[4] and, as Henry says, a *barbe blanche*.

As the *dasiri* and *kore* festivals take place annually,
the god, or spirit, becomes the measurer of time.
Similarly, *Quetzalcouatl* is considered to be the inventor
of the *tonalamatl*, the calendar, and it is significant that
in this case he is represented in connection with a tree,
even as the *dasiri* and *kore* are inseparable from a tree.
The *dasiri* is supposed to live on a specific tree, which
is sacred;[5] even thus *Quetzalcouatl* is represented as a
humming-bird kneeling on the top of a tree.[6]   The
dasiri is also worshipped on an altar of a conical or
truncated form, which supports a clay bowl.   If this
altar is not near a cross-road, or in a public place, but in
the house, it will be of any simple shape, a stake with
three-cornered prongs on which to place the bowl.[7]
Otherwise the bowl which receives the libations is placed
under the tree or on the first branches of the tree.[8]   We

[1] Seler, *Codex Borgia*, vol. I, p. 87 *et passim*.
[2] *Ibid.*, p. 243.
[3] Henry, *op. cit.*, p. 100.
[4] *Ibid.*, p. 116.
[5] Delafosse, *Haut-Sénégal-Niger*, vol. III, p. 168.
[6] Seler, *Codex Borgia*, vol. II, p. 66.
[7] Delafosse, *Haut-Sénégal-Niger*, vol. III, p. 169.
[8] *Ibid.*, p. 168.

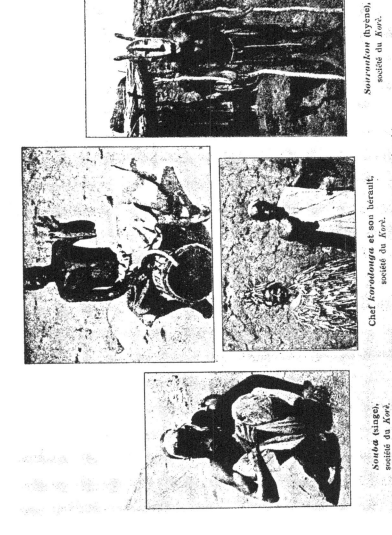

Souroukou (hyène),
société du Koré.

Chef korolonga et son héraut,
société du Koré.

En haut: Denoubu (grand tambour) et kinge (triangle),
société du Koré, se joue au Bani à la mort.

Souba (singe),
société du Koré.

KUARE CEREMONIES, from Henry's *Les Bambara*.

P. 111

Fête du *N'tomo*,
Flagellation des enfants

En haut: Fête du *N'tomo*,
Avant la flagellation

AFRICAN CHASTISEMENT from Henry's *Les Bambara*

Arbre fétiche *dasiri* (de Songobougou)

From Henry's *Les Bambara*.

have the representation of this tree in America: "One of these is the central design in the Chilan Balam, or Sacred Book, of Mani. It was copied by Father Cogolludo in 1640, and inserted in his History of Yucatan, with a totally false interpretation which the natives designedly gave him.

"The lettering in the above figure is by the late Dr. C. H. Berendt, and was obtained by him from other books of Chilan Balam, and native sources. In Cogolludo's work, this design is surrounded by thirteen heads which signify the thirteen *ahau katuns*, or greater cycles of years, as I have explained elsewhere. The number thirteen in American mythology symbolizes the thirteen possible directions of space. The border, therefore, expresses the totality of Space and Time; and the design itself symbolizes Life within Space and Time. This is shown as follows: At the bottom of the field lies a cubical block, which represents the earth, always conceived of this shape in Mayan mythology. It bears, however, not the lettering, *lum*, the Earth, as we might expect, but, significantly, *tem*, the Altar. The Earth is the great altar of the Gods, and the offering upon it is Life.

"Above the earth-cube, supported on four legs which rest upon the four quarters of the mundane plane, is the celestial vase, *cum*, which contains the heavenly waters, the rains and showers, on which depends the life of vegetation, and therefore that of the animal world as well. Above it hang the heavy rain clouds, *muyal*, ready to fill it; within it grows the *yax che*, the Tree of Life, spreading its branches far upward, on their extremities the flowers or fruit of life, the soul or immortal principle of man, called *ol* or *yol*."[1]

[1] D. G. Brinton, *A Primer of Mayan Hieroglyphics*, [Philadelphia] 1895, p. 47 f.

Here Brinton equally missed the explanation, for the picture exactly represents the Bambara altar, the bowl on the lower branches, the rain which comes from the clouds. We shall return to the thirteen heads later. The *Codex Cortesianus* has the representation of *Quetzalcouatl* under a tree: "Turning now to the central design of what has been called the 'Tableau of the Bacabs,' in the Codex Cortesianus, Fig. 10, we can readily see in the light of the above explanation that its lesson is the same. The design is surrounded by the signs of the twenty days, beyond which the field (not shown in this cut) is apportioned to the four cardinal points and the deities and time-cycles connected with them.

"Again it is Life within Space and Time which the artist presents. The earth is not represented; but we readily recognize in conventionalized form the great Tree of Life, across it the celestial Vase, and above it the cloud-masses. On the right sits Cuculcan, on the left Xmucane, the divine pair called in the *Popol Vuh* 'the Creator and the Former, Grandfather and Grandmother of the race, who give Life, who give Reproduction.' In his right hand Cuculcan holds three glyphs, each containing the sign of Life, *ik*. Xmucane has before her one with the sign of union (sexual); above it, one containing the life-sign (product of union); and these are surmounted by the head of a fish, symbolizing the fructifying and motherly waters.

"The total extension of the field in these designs resembles the glyph *a* in Fig. 6. It is found in both Mayan and Mexican MSS., and expresses the conception these peoples had of the Universe. Hence I give it the name of the 'cosmic sign.'"[1]

Here again we have the *dasiri* tree, bowl, rain, and god, although a second, a female divinity, is added.

[1] *Ibid.*, p. 48 ff.

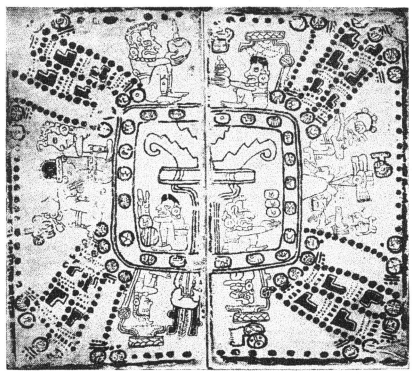

Codex Cortes 41, 42

Die vier Viertel des Tonalamatl's und die vier Himmelsrichtungen

PLATE OF THE BACABS, from Seler's *Gesammelte Abhandlungen*.

This is only natural, since the *dasiri* is equally used as the tutelary god of women: "If the women will give birth to a baby, they vow to call it *dyiriba* (great tree), *nyenamake* (male *ǵinn*); they even take pleasure in adding the name of the village where the beneficent *dasiri* is found: '*Kolotomo nyena ma*, boy, girl of the *ǵinn Dasiri* of Kolotomo.' The name *nyenama* is, indeed, given only to girls, and for the boys they add the appellation *ke* 'male.'"[1] But this drawing, generally known as the "Plate of the Bacabs," has a far greater significance. Its full form is described by Cyrus Thomas as follows: "This page consists of three divisions: *First*, an inner quadrilateral space, in which there are a kind of cross or sacred tree; two sitting figures, one of which is a female, and six characters. *Second*, a narrow space or belt forming a border to the inner area, from which it is separated by a single line; it is separated from the outer space by a double line. This space contains the characters for the twenty days of the Maya month, but not arranged in consecutive order. *Third*, an outer and larger space containing several figures and numerous characters, the latter chiefly those representing the Maya days. This area consists of two distinct parts, one part containing day characters, grouped together at the four corners, and connected by rows of dots running from one group to the other along the outer border; the other part consisting of four groups of figures, one group opposite each of the four sides. In each of the four compartments containing these last-mentioned groups, there is one of the four characters shown in Fig. 1 (*a b c d*), which, in my 'Study of the Manuscript Troano,' I have concluded represent the four cardinal points, a conclusion

[1] Henry, *op. cit.*, p. 101 f.

also reached by Rosny and Schultz Sellack."[1]   We shall now begin *ab ovo* and will show the evolution of certain aspects of astrology and magic from the Arabs through the Mandingos to the American Indians, especially of Mexico and Central America.

Among the Arabic talismans the most highly prized are those which are written on paper and are called جدول *ĝaḍwal*: "*Djadwal* (Pl. *djadāwil*) means firstly, 'brook,' 'watercourse'; it further means 'table, plan' (in this meaning derived from *schedula?*).   It thus becomes a special technical term in sorcery, synonymous with *khātim*; here it means quadrangular or polygonal, sometimes also circular figures, into which names and signs possessing secret magic powers are inserted in the most varied fashion.   These are usually certain mysterious characters, Arabic letters and numerals, magic words, the names of God, the angels and demons, as well as of the planets, the days of the week, and the elements, and lastly pieces from the Ko'rān, like the *Fātiḥa*, the *Sūrat Yasīn*, the so-called 'throne-verse' etc.   The application of these figures is manifold; frequently the paper on which one has been drawn is burnt to smoke some one with its smoke; or the writing may be washed off in water and drunk; along with the *da'wa* (conjuration) and often also the *ḳasam* (oath) the *djadwal* forms the contents of a *ḥirz* (amulet).   The very popular *da'wat al-Shams* is, for example, prepared as follows: it is quadrangular, is divided into 49 sections by six lines drawn lengthwise and six drawn across its breadth and contains: 1. The *sab'a khawātim*, i. e. Solomon's seal and other peculiar figures.   2. The seven *sawāḳiṭ* or consonants which are not found in Sūra I.   3. The names of God, *Fard, Djabbār, Shakūr,*

---

[1] *Notes on Certain Maya and Mexican Manuscripts*, in *Third Annual Report of the Bureau of Ethnology to the Secretary of the Smithsonian Institution, 1881-'82*, Washington 1884, p. 7.

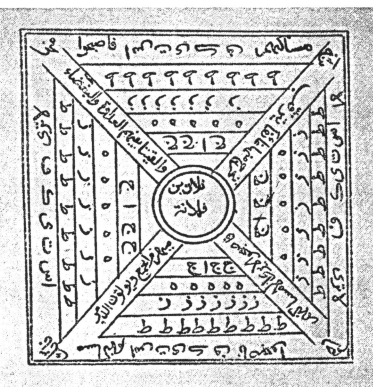

Il serait facile de multiplier indéfiniment ces exemples. Nous nous bornerons à donner ici encore deux amulettes. La première est destinée à procurer à son bénéficiaire la bienveillance, l'affection, l'amour de telle ou telle personne et aussi un bon accueil de la part des personnages puissants :

ARABIC ĠADWAL, from Doutté's *Magie et religion dans l'Afrique du Nord.*

MEXICAN GADWAL, from *Codex Fejervary-Mayer*.

Thābit, Zahīr, Khabīr and *Zakī.*   4. The names of the seven 'spirits': *Rūkiyā'il, Djabriyā'il, Samsamā'il, Mīkā'il, Ṣarfiyā'il, 'Aniyā'il* and *Kasfiyā'il.*   5. The names of the seven kings of the djinns: *Mudhhib, Marra, Aḥmar, Burkān, Shamhūrash, Abyaḍ* and *Mīmūn.*   6. The names of the days of the week.   7. Those of the planets.   The underlying notion is that secret relationships exist between those various components and the *djadwal* is therefore made to obtain definite results from the correlations of the heterogeneous elements composing it.   In this way new *djadwals* for particular purposes come to be made: these are also made by using the above mentioned seven seals.   The extremely complicated system of mystic letters, which is based on the numeral values of Arabic letters, is very frequently used for the *djadwal.*   A special class is formed by the squares called *wifḳ*, in the fields of which certain figures are so arranged that the addition of the horizontal and perpendicular lines, as well as that of the diagonals gives the same total (e. g. 34 or 15).   The quadrilateral containing the celebrated magic name *budūh* is derived from such an arrangement."[1]

To us the most interesting *ǧaḍwal* is the one which is the basis of the "Plate of the Bacabs" in Central America.   Like that one, it consists of a central circle with four radiating demi-diagonals of a square surrounding it.   In the center are the words, "Such a one, son of such a woman."   The diagonals bear as inscriptions four verses or parts of verses from the Koran, and parts of these verses are given in the corners, while the rest of the square is filled with Arabic letters making no sense whatsoever.   The form is identical in a general way with the American "Plate," but the American "Plate" belongs to one of the more complicated *ǧaḍwals*, as de-

[1] M. Th. Houtsma, etc., *The Encyclopaedia of Islam*, Leyden, London 1913, p. 992.

scribed above. We have no means of ascertaining whether the Mandingos possessed the *ǵaḍwal* from which the American "Plate" and its like were produced, since nothing of documentary antiquity has come down to us, but we have still ample documentary evidence to prove that the American "Plate" has gone through a Mandingo redaction.

In the first place, the central square contains the Mandingo tutelary god with his attributes and appurtenances. The numerical calculation based on 20 and 13, which is the essence of the American calendars, is surely built on African models. Here again we possess but the scantiest material for verification, but just enough to be startling and unique. Travelers have taken no trouble to ascertain African calendars and chronologies. The following few facts are about all we know. The Habbes have a lunar month of five weeks of six days each.[1] The Tchi tribes have a seven-day week of varying length,[2] while the Yorubas have a week of five days, six of them making a lunar month.[3] The Islamic week has everywhere else taken the place of the native time reckoning, but as the numeration of the Mandes, like that of most Sudanese people, is based on "five,"[4] the original week was unquestionably the same as that of the Yorubas. For astrological purposes there was in use a division of the zodiac in thirteen parts, such as has been found on three calabashes in western Africa,[5] and it is a curious fact that a similar division into thirteen is recorded only among the Kirghizes and in America. The division of the year into thirteen parts would demand a twenty-eight day month, but, in

[1] Desplagnes, *op. cit.* p. 377.
[2] A. B. Ellis, *The Yoruba-Speaking Peoples of the Slave Coast of West Africa*, London 1894, p. 142 f.
[3] *Ibid.*, p. 143.
[4] Delafosse, *Haut-Sénégal-Niger*, vol. I, p. 404.
[5] F. Bork, *Tierkreise auf westafrikanischen Kalebassen, in Mitteilungen der vorderasiatischen Gesellschaft*, vol. XXI, p. 266 ff.

Fig. 85 — Types d'indigènes Habbe-Kas-Amba, devant les dessins rupestres de Songo.

Fig. 84. — Dessins rupestres de Songo.

Fig. 83. — Le rocher de Songo, qui porte sur sa partie verticale blanche
de nombreux dessins.

SUDANIC ROCK INSCRIPTIONS, from Desplagnes'
Le plateau central nigérien.

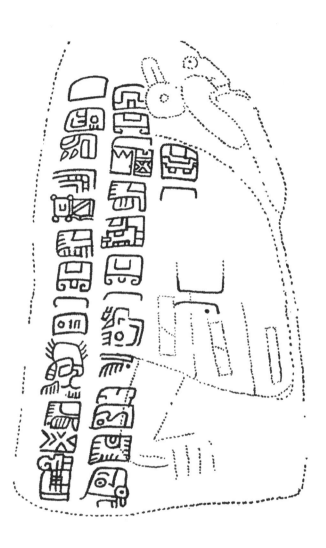

NEPHRITE STATUETTE FROM SAN ANDRES TUXTLA, VERA CRUZ
SIDE VIEW

From *American Anthropologist*, Vol IX.

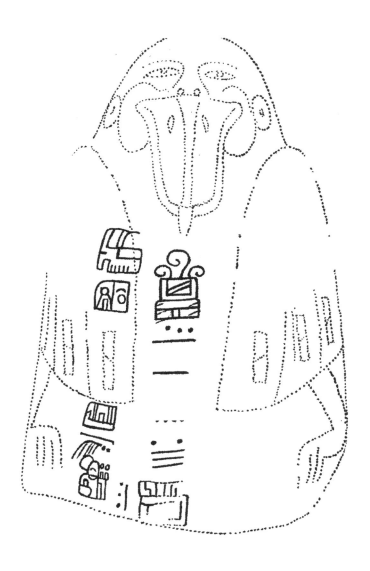

NEPHRITE STATUETTE FROM SAN ANDRES TUXTLA, VERA CRUZ
FRONT VIEW

From *American Anthropologist*, Vol. **IX**.

reality, the order is reversed, for we still have among the Berbers a division of the year into twenty-eight parts, of thirteen days each,[1] which is based on the astronomical or astrological calculations of the Arabs, whose twenty-eight lunar mansions of thirteen days each were, in the IX. century or later, adopted from the Hindus,[2] who had by that time arranged the twenty-eight *nakshatras*, or constellations, into equally spaced divisions of the zodiac, which naturally led to the thirteen days unit of time.

The Arabic *ǧadwal* has also the meaning of "vertical column, table of the zodiac, talismanic signs written in columns." Precisely such *ǧadwals* have been found in the region of the Mandingos,[3] and these have glyphs that bear an amazing resemblance to the Central American glyphs, especially those of the Tuxtla statuette, where we find similar signs encysted in squares and parallelograms.[4] Unfortunately we possess only the three photographs of the African inscriptions which Desplagnes has reproduced. Most of the columns in two of these begin with the forms of animals, the spider and lizard, which are also scattered throughout the columns. The spider is identical in form with the one given on Mound-builders' gorgets,[5] where the cross in the center indicates that it is related to the *tonalamatl* of the Mexicans and the Maya calendar. In Africa the

---

[1] "The solar year is divided into twenty-eight *mänazil* (sing. *ménzla*), each containing thirteen days, with the exception of the *žebha* (18th–31st July), which contains fourteen," Westermarck, *Ceremonies and Beliefs*, p. 73.

[2] C. A. Nallino, in *History of Arabic Astronomy* (in Arabic), in *Mitteilungen zur Geschichte der Medizin*, vol. X, p. 552.

[3] Desplagnes, *op. cit.*, p. 78 ff.

[4] S. G. Morley, *The Inscriptions at Copan*, Washington 1920, p. 403. See also W. H. Holmes, *On a Nephrite Statuette from San Andrés Tuxtla, Mexico*, in *American Anthropologist*, N. S., vol. IX, p. 691 ff.

[5] W. H. Holmes, *Art in Shell of the Ancient Americans*, in *Second Annual Report of the Bureau of Ethnology to the Secretary of the Smithsonian Institution, 1880–'81*, Washington 1883, p. 286 ff.

spider is connected with an enormous number of tales,[1] and among the Hausas the rainbow is called *bakan gizzo*, literally "the spider's bow," which indicates the relation which the divinities that came down from heaven bear to the spider. Indeed, "since the spider is the king of cunning and craftiness, all fables are told in his name."[2] Among the Hausas "*Gajjimare* is the god of rain and storms, which has the shape of a snake, and is double-gendered, the male part being red, the female blue. It lives in the storm-clouds (same name), but is supposed to come out at night, and it is also said to inhabit walls, and in fact all watering-places, so a pot is kept full in every house. *Gajjimare* (rainbow) may be represented by the water-serpent killed in the legend of Daura before referred to, but sometimes it is said to be the husband of *Uwardowa*, and the father of *Kuri*. Other names of the rainbow are *Masharua*, 'water drinker,' and *Bakkan gizzo*, 'spider's bow.'"[3] In Tchi "legend" is called *anansesem*, which means "story of the spider."[4] That the Mandes similarly connected their stories with the spider follows from Bambara *n'tale*, which means both "proverb, parable," and "spider." The African connection of the two concepts is, however, not of native origin, but is due to Arabic homonyms. Bambara *n'tale*, Malinke *tali* "fable, story," *talīn* "spider" are all derived from Arabic رتلة *ratlah*, رتيلة *rutailah*, Hassania رتلة *retla* "spider." But among the Arabs there are a number of words from the same root which mean "to recite in a leisurely manner, and distinctly, to chant the Koran,"

[1] C. Spiess, *Fabeln über die Spinne bei den Ewe am Unterlauf des Volta in Westafrika*, in *Mitteilungen des Seminars für orientalische Sprachen*, Berlin 1918, vol. XXI, part III, p. 101 ff., and *Fortsetzung der Fabeln über die Spinne bei den Ewe am Unterlauf des Volta in Westafrika*, ibid., vol. XXII, part III, p. 1 ff.
[2] Tremearne, *Hausa Superstitions and Customs*, p. 10.
[3] *Ibid.*, p. 112.
[4] Perregaux, *op. cit.*, p. 186.

THE SPIDER IN MOUND-BUILDER GORGETS, from Holmes' *Art in Shell of the Ancient Americans.*

FIG. 26.—Pattern on boot similar to fig. 25.

GADWAL DESIGN IN AFRICA, from Tremearne's *Hausa Superstitions and Customs*

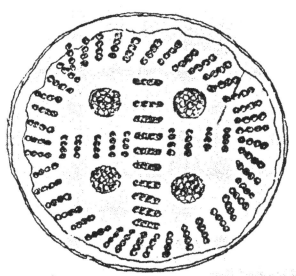

FIG. 38.—Pattern on knob of fig. 35.

GADWAL DESIGN IN AFRICA, from Tremearne's
Hausa Superstitions and Customs.

GADWAL DESIGN IN MOUND-BUILDER GORGETS,
from Holmes' *Art in Shell of the Ancient Americans.*

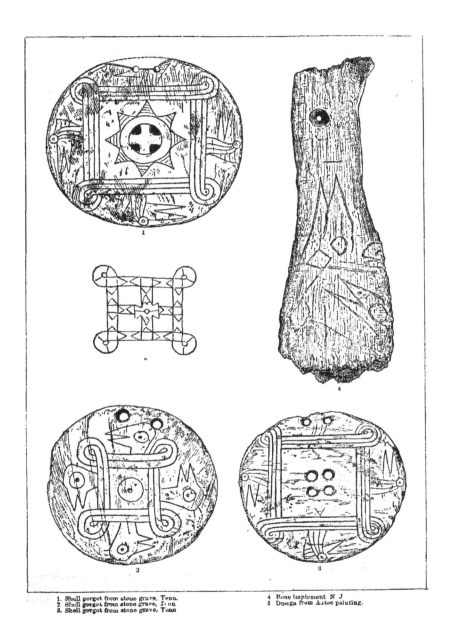

1. Shell gorget from stone grave, Tenn.
2. Shell gorget from stone grave, Tenn
3. Shell gorget from stone grave, Tenn

4 Bone implement N J
5 Design from Aztec painting.

THE BIRD.

GADWAL DESIGN IN MOUND-BUILDER GORGETS,
from Holmes' *Art in Shell of the Ancient Americans.*

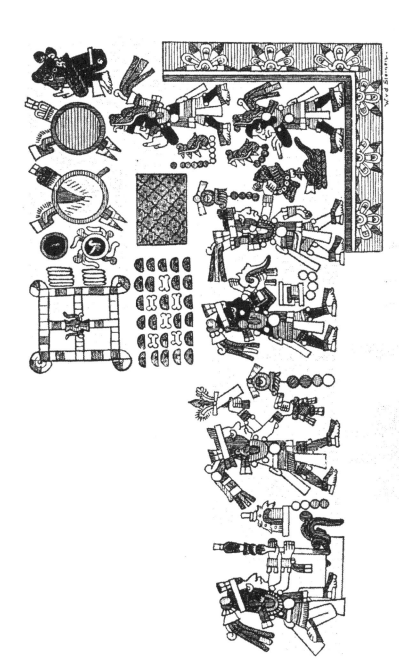

bb. 288. Die Götter *Naui cipactli* „Vier Krokodil" und *Matlactliace cipactli* „Eilf Krokodil".
Wiener Handschrift. Blatt 12, 13 (Kingsborough'scher Zählung).

GADWAL DESIGN IN MEXICO from Seler's *Codex Borgia*.

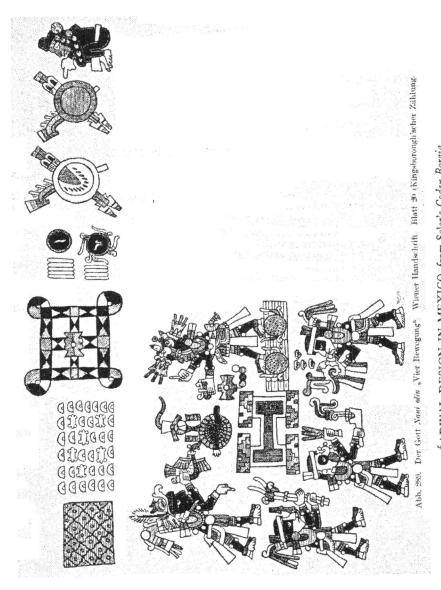

Abb. 280. Der Gott *Naui olin* „Vier Bewegung" Wiener Handschrift. Blatt 3⅛ (Kingsborough'schen Zählung.

GADWAL DESIGN IN MEXICO, from Seler's *Codex Borgia.*

and this became contaminated by Arabic ﻻ‍ *ṭalā* "to recite the Koran," hence the spider has become closely related to a well-told story.

In some places in Africa the scorpion has taken the place of the spider, for in Songay *don* "to sing" also means "scorpion," which can only be the result of a translation of Arabic ﻟﺔ‍ *raṭlah*. As the spider is connected with the rainbow, it connects heaven with earth, and the spirits of heaven, the stars, the constellations, are thus brought in contact with the spider; whence it is only natural that the *ġaḍwal*, which deals with astrology or astronomy, should be connected with the spider. For this reason the spider of the Mound-builders has in its middle the cross, which is the simplest representation of the fourfold division of the *ġaḍwal*. This ornamentation is in constant use in the Western Sudan. It forms the central design of circular objects,[1] is done in square patterns with looped ends, exactly as in bird *ġaḍwals* in Mound-builders' gorgets,[2] and is worked in dotted line form upon knobs.[3] The cross so often found in these designs has nothing whatsoever to do with the Christian cross.

In the Mound-builders' gorgets we not only have the spider with its *ġaḍwal*, but the looped-end *ġaḍwal*, with a cross in the middle, all placed within a circle, is the most striking object found in the mounds. That we have in these cases a development and simplification of the *ġaḍwal* with the Mandingo *dasiri*, the tutelar god and rain giver, who lives upon a tree, is brought out in a number of cases, where each side of the square has the representation of a bird's head.[4] Thus the Mound-builders' gorgets are mere modifications of the "Plate

---

[1] Tremearne, *Hausa Superstitions and Customs*, p. 29.
[2] *Ibid.*, p. 97.
[3] *Ibid.*, p. 145.
[4] Holmes, *Art in Shell of the Ancient Americans*, p. 282 ff.

of the Bacabs," where the bird god is represented as the long-nosed god. In the Codex Cortesianus (plates XLI-II) we have an interesting evolution of the *tonalamatl*. The four squares are filled respectively with figures of *Tlaloc, Macuilxochitl, Quetzalcouatl, Tlaçolteotl*, while the middle of the *ġaḍwal* is occupied by a convention-alized spider, representing the setting sun. Before dealing with this new aspect of the *ġaḍwal*, which in-troduces the sun as the central figure, it is necessary to investigate the close relationship which exists between certain games of chance and the astrological *ġaḍwal* in Africa and in America.

Ferrand[1] has given an exhaustive treatment of the Malagassy divination called *sikidy*, which is nothing but the Arabic geomancy, found, with certain varia-tions, wherever Islamic influence has been exerted. Burton has described the geomantic board of the Yorubas· "The Buko-no ignored the Yoruban triad, Shango, Oro, and Obatala; but he agreed with the Egbas about Afa. Seeing that I had some knowledge of the craft, he produced from a calico bag his 'book,' a board, like that used by Moslem writing-masters, but two feet long by eight inches, and provided with a dove-tail handle. One side of this *abacus* contained what are called the sixteen 'mothers,' or primary, the other showed as many children, or secondary, figures. Each was in an oblong of cut and blackened lines, whilst at the top were arbitrary marks—circles, squares, and others, to connect the sign with the day. It began with the Bwe-Megi, the figure, assigned to Vodun-be—fetish day, or Sunday,—whose mnemonic symbol was six dots in a circle; whilst Monday had a sphere within a sphere. It was a palpable derivation from the geom-ancy of the Greeks, much cultivated by the Arabs under the name of El Raml الرمل , 'The sand,' because the

---

[1] G. Ferrand, *Les Musulmans à Madagascar*, Paris 1891, vol. I, p. 73 ff.

figures were cast upon the desert floor. 'Napoleon's Book of Fate' is a notable specimen of European and modern vulgarisation. The African Afa is not, as in Asia, complicated with astrology; and no regard being paid to the relative position of figures, it is comparatively unartful. Two details proved to me its Moslem origin: the reading of the figures is from right to left, and there are seven days, whereas the hebdomadal week is beyond the negro's organisation." "The following note will explain the use of the palm-nuts, and the names of the figures:—

"In throwing Afa, the reverend man, or the scholar, if sufficiently advanced, takes 16 of the fleshy nuts of a palm, resembling the cocoa-trees; these are cleared of sarcocarp, and are marked with certain Afa-du, or Afa strokes.

"When Fate is consulted, the 16 nuts are thrown from the right hand to the left; if one is left behind, the priest marks two; if two, one (the contrary may be the case, as in European and Asiatic geomancy); and thus the 16 parents are formed.

"The 16 are thus named and made:—

1. | | Called Bwé Megi: it is the Mother of
    | | all.
    | |
     | |
2. | | Yeku Megi.
    | |
    | |
    | |
3. | | | | Wudde, or Odé-Megi.
    | |
    | |
  | | | |

4.   Dí-Megi.

5.   Losu Megi.

6.   Urán Megi: an inversion of No. 5.

7.   Called Abla Megi.

8.   Akla Megi; or Abla inverted.

9.   Sá Megi.

10.   Guda Megi: an inversion of No. 9.

11.   Turupwen Megi.

12.   Tula Megi.

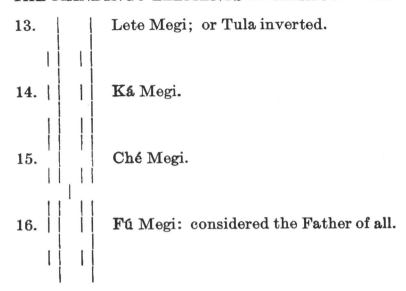

13.   Lete Megi; or Tula inverted.

14.   Ká Megi.

15.   Ché Megi.

16.   Fú Megi: considered the Father of all.

"These 16 parents may have many children. Nos. 13 and 2, for instance, make

—and so on, showing an infinite power of combination."[1] Becker has shown the fallacy of Frobenius' work on the Yorubas, because of his neglect to connect their Ifa worship with the Arabic geomancy, and has explained some of the terms of Yoruba divination and fetishism as translations from the Arabic.[2]

Some of the terms of the chief geomantic figures are found in Hausa in the sense of "story," while one of these, from its association with the zodiac, also means

[1] R. Burton, *A Mission to Gelele, King of Dahome*, London 1864, p. 332 ff.

[2] C H. Becker, *Der Islam*, Strassburg 1913, vol. IV, p. 303 ff.

"star." Thus the first sign,[1] ∴ ·.ˈ حماعه ǧamāʻah "con-
gregation" produces Hausa *aljama, aljima*; the eleventh,

حمره ḥumrah "red" leads to Hausa *almara*; the

third, ∴ ·.ˈ احتماه iǧtimāh "gathering" leads to Hausa
gatana; another Hausa term, *tatsuniyu, tasunia, tasinia*
"story, star," I am unable to identify as to origin, but
the two connotations show that they similarly arise
from the astrological *ǧaḍwal*.

An Englishman, upon reading an account of the
Malagassy geomantic table, devised a game of Skiddy,
"played with boards of 8 squares, markers, counters,
and dice."[2]   In this he simply duplicated what had
long been observed by the users of the geomantic *ǧaḍwal*,
for forms of pachisi, as found over an enormous territory, are nothing but *ǧaḍwals* used for games of chance.

In Arabic قمار *qimār* refers to any game of chance.   The
Spanish-Arabic dictionary in the beginning of the XVI.
century translates Spanish "dados" and "naypes" by
quimar, which shows that even at that late date "dice"
and "cards" were not yet fully distinguished.   But
"cards" were called *naipes* in Spanish from Arabic نائب
naib "lieutenant," and the first fundamental row of the
geomantic *ǧaḍwal* is called *alanaua*,[3] unquestionably
from *naib* "lieutenant, regent," for we find this word as
laïbe "story" in Wolof, which indicates that in the
Western Sudan the game was closely related to the
ǧaḍwal.   Cards seem not to have been known before
the end of the XIV. century, and it is significant that,

---

[1] M. Steinschneider, *Die „ Skidy " oder geomantischen Figuren*, in *Zeitschrift der deutschen morgenländischen Gesellschaft*, vol. XXXI, p. 762.
[2] J. Sibree and R. Baron, *The Antananarivo Annual and Madagascar Magazine*, Antananarivo 1885, vol. IX, p. 324.
[3] Steinschneider, *op. cit.*, p. 763.

Abb. 41. *Macuil xochitl* Gott des Spiels. Sahagun Ms. Bibl. del Palacio (Madrid)

Abb. 42. Der Gott *Macuil tochtli* „Fünf Kaninchen". Sahagun Ms. Bibl. del Palacio (Madrid.)

Abb. 43. Der Gott *Macuil cuetzpalin* „Fünf Eidechse", Bannor- und Fackelträger vor dem Sakrarium des Gottes *Uitzilopochtli*, des Gottes von México. Sahagun-Ms. Bibl. del Palacio (Madrid.)

Abb. 44. *Macuil xochitl*, Gott des *patolli*-Spieles. Codex Magliabechiano XIII, 3 fol. 60.

MEXICAN GAME OF PATOLLI, from Seler's *Codex Borgia*

although the original deck of cards had 4X18 and more cards, it soon developed into a deck of 4X13 cards, in which 13 is identical with the calabash zodiacs of western Africa. It, therefore, follows from this that in western Africa there was, for reasons which we do not at present know, in vogue the 4X13 astrological cycle, which forms the basis of the same cycle in Mexico and Central America.

It is significant that in Mexico the game of *patolli* is under the supervision of the god *Macuilxochitl*, who represents one form of the sun god, and this god, in his turn, is related to and confused with *Xolotl*. Here we are once more on safe ground, and the Mandingo origin of the sun myth becomes clear. The Mexicans placed their terrestrial paradise in the west, but also thought of it as connected with the heavens, where the gods were born. Its name, for which the Nahuatl furnishes no explanation,[1] is *Tamoanchan*. This, of course, is Malinke *duna do arjana* "paradise." The heaven divinities of the Mexicans are nothing but the zodiacal signs of the nocturnal sky, "the descenders from heaven." *Xolotl* is distinctly the gemini of the zodiac. The word means "twin,"[2] in various connotations. It is used for "twin, house-slave, dog," that is, "companion." This at once identifies it as Arabic عَشَرَة *'ušārah* "to accompany one," عَشَراً *'ušara'*, plural of عَشِير *'ašīr*, "associate, friend, relation." This word is found throughout the Sudan. We have Songay *tjero* "friend," *tjere, djere* "half, comrade," Malinke *teri*, Bambara *teri, terike, terke, nterge* "comrade, friend," etc. The twin god was the god of twins among the Bambaras: "This fetish protects the mother of twins

---

[1] Sahagun's derivation from *tictemoa tochan* "we seek our *home*" is useless. *Op. cit.*, p. 9.

[2] Seler, *Codex Borgia*, vol. II, p. 37.

and unites them in so close an affection that one never receives a present without sharing it with the twin. If one of the twins dies young, and this is generally the case, the surviving child receives a small statue which he always keeps with jealous care, and to which he gives the name of the deceased child. He dresses it in the best manner possible, often covers it with beads, pearls, bits of amber, rings, etc., and refined people never give him a present without adding at least five cowries for the statue. The *sinsin* gratifies the twins with a peculiar privilege. Not only can no scorpion sting them, but it is always at their service, and at their command will sting a companion with whom they are dissatisfied."[1]

Xolotl is the accompanying god in the *tonalamatl*, where otherwise *Quetzalcouatl* or *Ueuecoyotl* are represented. The center of the *tonalamatl* thus frequently represents the sun, which is only natural, since the Arabic *qimār*, the game of chance, is also applied to the sun and moon, as the chief representatives of the *ǵaḍwal* zodiac. In Arabic we have القمر *al-qamaru* "the moon," القمراني *al-qamarāni* "the sun and moon," but *Xolotl* is for some reason connected with a cooking-pot. This is due to an Arabic philological calculation, because اعشار *a'šār* means "a cooking-pot that boils the ten portions of a camel slaughtered for sacrifice."

Xolotl is generally confused with or turned into *Nanauatzin*, whose glyph is the same cooking-pot with human bodies boiling in it.[2] *Nanauatzin* is supposed to be the god of syphilis, his name being derived from *nanauatl* "syphilis." But this is a mistake: *nanauatl* is translated by the early writers as "bubas," and this means "pustules, itch," which shows that we are dealing

---

[1] Henry, *op. cit.*, p. 98.
[2] Seler, *Codex Borgia*, vol. I, p. 287.

in the early Mexican accounts of *nanauatl* with the same disease, which in Hispaniola was given as *caracaracol*,[1] although there can be no doubt that during the Spanish occupation *nanauatl* was also the name of syphilis. It must be observed that Bambara *manyā* means not only "the itch," but also "syphilis,"[2] hence it may be that syphilis was actually introduced into America by the Negroes before the landing of Columbus. Sahagun tells the following story of *Nanauatzin*: "This is the way the moon began to shed light upon the world. It is said that before day existed the gods united in the place called *Teotiuacan*, and said to each other, 'Who will undertake to enlighten the world?' To which a god called *Tecuciztecatl* replied, 'I will do so.' The gods spoke a second time and said, 'And who will be the second?' They looked at each other, trying to find out who it would be, and no one wanted to offer himself for the undertaking; they were all afraid and excused themselves. On of them, whom they did not consider and who had the *bubas*, did not speak and listened to what the others were saying. They finally turned to him and said, 'You be it, *bubosito*.' He listened gladly to what they ordered him to do and answered, 'I receive your order as an act of grace,—be it so.' The two chosen ones immediately began a four days' penance. Then they lit a fire in the hearth made in a rock, which even now has the name of *Teotexcalli*, rock of the gods. The god called *Tecuciztecatl* offered up only precious things, for in place of bouquets he made offerings of rich feathers called *quetzalli*; instead of straw wisps he offered gold balls; thorns made from precious stones in place of maguey thorns, and thorns of red coral in place of bloody thorns. Besides, the copal used in the offering was of the best.

---

[1] See my *Africa*, vol. I, pp. 76, 78, 160.
[2] Henry, *op. cit.*, p. 47.

The *buboso*, called *Nanauatzin*, offered nine green reeds tied in threes, in place of the usual branches.   He offered straw wisps and maguey thorns reddened with his own blood, and in place of copal he offered scabs of his own *bubas*.

"They built a tower in the form of a hill for each of the two gods.   There they did penance for four days and four nights.   These hills are at present called *Tzaqualli*,—they are found near the village of San-Juan, called *Teotiuacan*.   After the four nights of penance were passed, they threw all about the place the branches, bouquets, and all other objects which they had used.   The next night, a little after midnight, when the service was to begin, they brought the ornaments to *Tecuciztecatl*; they consisted of the feathers called *aztacomitl* and a jacket of light cloth, while the head of *Nanauatzin*, the *buboso*, was covered with a paper cap called *amatzontli*, and he was dressed in a vestment and girdle also of paper.   When midnight had come, all the gods placed themselves around the hearth called *teotexcalli*, where the fire had been burning for four days.   They divided themselves in two rows and placed themselves on both sides of the fire.   The two chosen ones seated themselves in front of the hearth, with their faces turned to the fire, between the two rows of the gods, who stood up and, addressing themselves to *Tecuciztecatl*, said to him, 'Come now, *Tecuciztecatl*, jump into the fire.'   He tried, indeed, to do so, but, as the hearth was very large and hot, he became frightened, as soon as he felt the heat, and withdrew.   For a second time he took courage and was about to leap into the hearth, but as he approached it, he stopped and did not dare to do so.   In vain did he make four separate attempts, but it was ordered that no one could try more than four times.   When these four attempts had been made, the gods turned to

Nanauatzin and said to him, 'Come now, *Nanauatzin*, it is your turn to try.' Scarcely had they said this to him, when he collected his strength, closed his eyes, leaped forward, and jumped into the fire. He began at once to crackle, like a thing roasting. *Tecuciztecatl*, seeing that he jumped into the fire and was burning, also dashed forward and threw himself upon the coals. It is said that an eagle that entered the fire at the same time burned himself, and so this bird now has blackish wings. A tiger followed him, but he did not burn himself; he only singed himself, and so he remained speckled white and black. From this legend arose the custom of calling men expert in the use of arms *quauhtli*, *ocelotl*. They say *quauhtli*, because the eagle was the first to enter, then *ocelotl*, because the tiger was the second to rush into it after the eagle.

"After the two divinities had thrown themselves into the fire, and were consumed in it, the other gods sat down, thinking that *Nanauatzin* would not fail to arise. They had waited for a long time, when the sun began to glow, and the dawn was seen to arise. The gods, they say, fell upon their knees to wait for *Nanauatzin* to turn into the sun, without knowing where it would arise. They turned their glances in all directions, but they could not tell where its rising would take place. Some thought that it would be to the north, and they turned their eyes there. Others thought that it would be to the south. In fact, their suspicions were directed everywhere, because the dawn glowed in all directions. Some fixed their attention upon the east, and insisted that the sun would rise there. This was the correct view. Those who waited for that region, they say, were *Quetzalcouatl*, also called *Ecatl*; *Totec*, who also bears the names of *Anaoatlytecu* and *Tlatlauic Tezcatlipoca*; others, who are called *Mimizcoa*, who are innumerable, and four women, of whom the first is called *Tiacapan*, the second *Teicu*, the third *Tlacoeua*, and the fourth *Xocoyotl*. When the sun was about to rise, it looked very red, tottering from side to side, and nobody could fix his gaze upon it, because it blinded him, so bright was it with its rays that escaped from it and spread in all directions. The moon arose at the same time, and also in the east, that is, at first the sun and then the moon, in the same order as before at the hearth. Those who tell these stories say that the sun and moon had then the same light, and that the gods, perceiving this equality of splendor, conversed with each other once more and said, 'O gods, how can this be? Will it be all right if they are both equal and enlighten the world in the same manner?' And then they uttered words and said, 'Let it be as it may.' . And immediately one of them began to run and struck with a rabbit the face of *Tecuciztecatl*, who at once became brown, lost his splendor, and assumed the form which we all know to-day. When the sun and moon had risen upon the earth, they both remained motionless. Then the gods spoke once more to each other and said, 'How can we live this way? The sun does not move. Are we to pass all our lives among unworthy mortals? Let us all die and let our death give life to the luminaries.' The wind then undertook to cause the death of the gods and killed them. The one called *Xolotl* refused, they say, to die, and he said to the gods, 'Gods, I do not want to die!' And he cried so that his eyes were swollen. When the one who caused the massacre came to him, he fled and hid in a field of maize, where he was changed into a stalk of this plant with two ears, which the farmers call *xolotl*. But, as he was recognized among the maize, he fled a second time and hid in the magueys, where he was changed into a double maguey, which is called *mexolotl*. When he was once more discovered, he fled again and threw

Abb. 67 *Nanauatzin*, der Syphilitiker, die andere Form *Xolotl's*, des Gottes der Zwillinge und der Missgeburten. Codex Borgia 10 (= Kingsborough 29).

NANAUATZIN, THE MEXICAN GOD OF SYPHILIS,
from Seler's *Codex Borgia*

himself into the water, where he was changed into a fish called *axolotl*.

"There they seized him and killed him. But, although all the gods were killed, the sun did not get into motion.   Then the wind began to blow and to rush violently, which caused the luminary to move and start upon its journey; but the moon stayed still where it was.   It began to move only after the sun had done so. Then only they separated from each other and acquired the habit of rising at different hours.   The sun lasts a whole day, and the moon shines and works during the night.   They said justly that *Tecuciztecatl* would have been the sun, if he had been the first to throw himself into the fire, because he was the first to be shaped and because his offering had consisted of precious things."[1]

I have given the whole cosmogonic story in order to show the conflate manner of a Mexican myth.   The constituent parts can be easily reconstructed with the aid of the Mandingo myths, even though in this case the information is unusually scanty.   The Malinkes call the itch *ñaña*, and a person suffering from the itch is called *ñañãto*.   This *ñaña*, that is, *nganya*, is unquestionably derived from Arabic نَقَل *nagal* "corrupted, irritated," نَقِلَ *nagila* "the itch," which is very likely also the origin of French *gale* "the itch."   In Bambara this has become *manya*.   But we have also Malinke *manã*, Bambara *manyan* "black, stinging ant, whose stings are painful,"   Mandingo *menango, merango, melango* "ant."   These "ant" words are most likely related to the "itch" words, since the Arabic word also means "creeping worms."   In any case, in the Bambara the two concepts are connected, as meaning "something that itches, stings."   But Bambara *manyan* also means "fetish whose pyramidal altar may be seen near the

---

[1] Sahagun, *op. cit.*, p. 478 ff.

villages."[1] Unfortunately we have but the scantiest reference to this fetish by Henry,[2] where he speaks of a round tower used as an altar and surmounted by a bowl to receive the victims' blood, which is dedicated to *Manya* and is always placed under a *ceiba* tree. Among the Mayas the *ceiba*, called *yaxche*, was the tree which represented heaven and was the abode of the blessed.[3] The philological and semantic identity of Malinke *ñañāto* with Nahuatl *Nanauatzin* "the *buboso*" is obvious. Both have a pyramidal altar, called in Nahuatl *tzaqualli*, in the Western Sudan, in Hausa *dakali* "pagan altar, raised clay bed, seat," from Arabic دَكْل *dakl* "to knead clay." Not only do we have *Nanauatzin* as jumping into the fire, but in the Codex Borgia *Xolotl* is represented as *Nanauatzin* sitting in the cooking-pot.[4] This makes it necessary to connect *Nanauatzin*, on the one hand with ants, and on the other with twins. Here again the fragmentary Sudanic tradition solves the question completely.

In southern Nigeria twins are in many localities killed. "Although the destruction of twins is not, in the strict sense of the word, a sacrifice, it is all the same a sacrificial offering, very much in the same light as the purification ceremonies which have been just described. For the custom, based on the identical spiritual principle of an evil react, is treated as one of offence against the ancestral gods that must of necessity be removed, along with the offending cause—the woman.

" As I have already pointed out with regard to human sacrifice, this too is a purely religious custom, the origin of which is lost in antiquity, and due apparently to the conception that one birth at a time is the distinguishing

[1] P. Sauvant, *Grammaire bambara*, Maison-Carrée (Alger) 1913, p. 134.
[2] *Op. cit.*, p. 148.
[3] Seler, *Codex Borgia*, vol. I, p. 316.
[4] *Ibid.*, vol. II, p. 53.

feature between man and all other creation, and therefore the birth of twins was regarded as an unnatural event, to be ascribed solely to the influence of malign spirits, acting in conjunction with the power of evil. And the custom has been tenaciously adhered to, in spite of the fact that every child born into a family, apart from all other human considerations, has a monetary and a practical value attached to it.

"Indeed, according to their ancient faith, although two energies are requisite to produce a unit, the production of two such units is out of the common groove, therefore unnatural, because it implies at once a spirit duality, or enforced possession by some intruding and malignant demon, in the yielding and offending person of a member of the household, consequently an outrage committed upon the domestic sanctity. For in their opinion, the natural product of two human energies, as a single unit, is only endowed, or provided with, one soul-spirit. The custom that prevails among the Ibo and Brassmen of allowing one—always the first-born of the twins—to live, is a practical admission of this conception.

" The custom is universal throughout the Delta, and is only dying out in those few localities in which the people are actually in touch with civilisation. The advent of twins is looked on in every home of the Delta not only with horror and detestation, but as an evil and a curse that is bound to provoke the domestic gods to anger and retribution. In order, therefore, to avert the expected vengeance, it is the standing law of the priests that no time is to be lost in at once removing the unfortunate infants. This is generally done by throwing them into the bush, to be devoured by wild animals, or the equally ferocious driver ants, or sometimes, as is done by the Ibibio, Ijo, and other coast tribes, by setting them adrift in the rivers and creeks in roughly made baskets of reeds and bulrushes, when they are soon drowned, or swallowed by sharks or crocodiles.

"In most cases the mothers, who are looked on as unclean, are driven out of the town and into the bush, and unless given protection by the people of another community, or surreptitiously fed by some old crony, they often fare as badly as their offspring, whom they look upon as the work of evil spirits.

"In some cases, however, humaner treatment is accorded to them. In Ibani, for instance, it was customary, as it now is among the other middlemen, to quarantine the unclean mothers in an out-of-the-way hut for a period of sixteen days. Here neither man, woman, nor child dare visit them, with the exception of certain old women who were specially set apart to tend and provide them with food, water, and other necessary requirements. At the end of this time they were brought out and obliged to undergo the ceremony of purification, at the hands of the priests, which, in addition to washing off the chalk that had previously been smeared all over their bodies, consisted of the sacrifice of a chicken, or a new-born pup. Besides this, the father, or in the case of a slave or poor member of a family, the head of the house, was also obliged to avert the wrath of the enraged deity and the consequences that were to be expected, by offering special sacrifices and presenting gifts to the priests—an undertaking which, as a rule, implied a minimum outlay of at least 1600 manillas, equal in those days to about £6: 13s., or less or more, according to existing rates. Purified and once more clean and free from evil, the women were received back into the family circle, and the threatened evils were considered to be averted.

"In the Ibibio country, and formerly among the Efik, the regulations with regard to the women are much more elaborate, and in a certain sense humane.

" Here, as invariably in all similar cases, the ancestral gods are propitiated by gifts and sacrifices, but the women, looked on as unclean for the rest of their lives, are obliged to reside in villages, which are known as *Twin Towns*, or the habitations of defiled women, appointed for that particular purpose.   From this time forth the husband, whether he be head of the house or not, is obliged to maintain a wife who has been so defiled; although at the same time he is strictly forbidden to cohabit or to have any dealings with her, being, as he is in every religious and personal sense, human and spiritual, divorced from her.   But in spite of the fact that to him, as well as to all the members of his or her community, the woman is unclean and therefore tabu, the penalty of death being inflicted on both in the event of their breaking the law in this direction, she is allowed to form connections, but on no account to marry with strangers, or men belonging to outside communities, and the offspring resulting from such intercourse becomes, as a matter of course, the property of her husband, or the head of the house.

" In order to remove the child from the defiled locality, which cannot, however, be done until it is weaned, *i.e.* when from two to three years old, a special sacrifice of chickens and fowls must first be made.   Sacrifice, in fact, is imperative and inevitable in all cases in which intercommunication is necessary, and an interchange of visits is made between all members of the households in question and the defiled women.   Thus, for example, when it is obligatory on certain occasions for any near relatives or others of either sex to visit one of these women, the visitors are compelled to sacrifice fowls or goats to the domestic deities, so that the act of contact may not be productive of the evil effect of twins, in any subsequent issues of children, on the part of female visitors; and on exactly the same conditions defiled women are permitted to visit relatives, also to work for their husbands.

"But in the event of the defiled woman herself bearing twins again, these must be destroyed unknown to any one. For, if known, the probabilities are that the death of the mother would be demanded by the household and the community as well. Or if not killed, she would be driven into the bush and left to die, although, if discovered by a stranger, he is at liberty to claim her as his own property, that is, at least, if he feels inclined to run the risk of a venture so truly provocative of offence.

"Among the various clans of the Ibo, when the birth of twins takes place, the people belonging to the quarter in which the mother resides are obliged to throw away all the half-burnt firewood, the food cooked, and the water brought in the previous night—everything, in a word, in the shape of nourishment, solid or liquid, because the advent of the unholy twins defiles the house and practically all its contents. To purify the place from this unwelcome pollution, the inevitable sacrifice, consisting in this case of fowls and goats, is there and then performed, and the unclean mother is at once removed from the house and town. Indeed, as soon as a pregnant woman is delivered of a child, and it is known that another is to follow, she is instantly carried into the bush, and when the second is born it is immediately thrown away, while the first-born is retained, and named M'meabo, which means two people.

"If it happens also that during childbirth the infant comes out of the womb feet foremost—the event which is referred to as Mkporo-oko, i.e. bad or evil feet—it is regarded in the same light as twin-birth, and the unfortunate mother is accorded exactly the same treatment, her eventual destination in either case being a Twin Town.

"The Ibo customs are, however, practically identical with those of the Ibibio, Ijo, and other tribes, except for one or two trifling differences.   For example, in the event of the defiled woman bearing issue by a stranger, the children, although the property of the husband, must be maintained by the natural father, who is obliged to pay over the legitimate expenses to the former.   The women and the children are, however, placed under certain laws or restrictions, the use of certain trade markets and roads being prohibited to them, but they are permitted to have a market of their own."[1]

"All deformed children are not human; they are devils, and their influence is evil.   They must be killed. These devils' usual dwelling-place is in the bush and they annoy travellers by night by 'throwing stones at them.'   Some men assert that often a woman who gathers herself a new dress, i.e., leaves, from a bush which is inhabited by a devil seizes the devil together with the leaves, and in this way he has intercourse with her, with the result that a devil-child is born, i.e., a deformed baby.   Apparently the women do not believe this—they say that some men are devils themselves.

"As to whether one's child is a devil or a human being only the sorcerer can say.   I will explain later how the information is imparted.   Almost invariably a deformed child is a devil; twins sometimes are, and now and then a quite healthy child is so proclaimed. Once the father is certain that his wife has brought forth a devil, he proceeds to the devil-killer, who returns with him to the house where the child is.   There he receives a red-and-black hen and a goat, and gives in return the devil-killing medicine to the child and ties round its neck a ram's horn filled with a powder of

[1] A. G. Leonard, *The Lower Niger and its Tribes*, London 1906, p. 458 ff.

earth, shea-butter and ashes. The child soon after dies and the killer is called back to bury the corpse. This he places in a large water-pot, and the father carries it into the bush, where, finding an ant-heap, he buries the pot and its contents."[1]

"A former resident of Onitsha on the Lower Niger, informs me 'Twins are objected to and both are killed in the Ibo country. The killing is brought about by placing the children in a large earthen pot which is then carried into a part of the bush which is tabued and called *tonton*. The children are soon killed by the ants and other flesh devouring insects. Passing Europeans hearing the wailing of the children have carried them off, but in most cases the exposure had already been too much and they succumbed. A child so rescued and surviving would, if a girl, experience difficulty in getting married for fear she have twins. Bishop Hill in traversing a piece of bush which the natives had made over to him for missionary purposes, found a tonton with over 200 pots which had contained babies. The natives would not assist to clear the spot.' "[2]

"Infanticide of a peculiar nature likewise prevails among them: twins are never allowed to live. As soon as they are born, they are put into two earthen pots, and exposed to the beasts of the forest; and the unfortunate mother ever afterward endures great trouble and hardships. A small tent is built for her in the forest, in which she is obliged to dwell, and to undergo many ceremonies for her purification. She is separated from all society for a considerable time; her conjugal alliance with her husband is for ever dissolved; and she is never again permitted to sit down with other women in the same market or in the same house. To give birth to twins is, therefore, considered to be the greatest

[1] A. W. Cardinall, *The Natives of the Northern Territories of the Gold Coast.*, London, New York, p. 27 f.

[2] H. L. Roth, *Great Benin, its Customs*, etc., Halifax 1903, p. 36.

misfortune that can befall a woman of the Ibo nation. If any person wishes to annoy an Ibo woman, he lifts up two fingers, and says, 'You gave birth to twins;' which is sure to make her almost mad.'"[1]

The specific exposure of twins in a cooking-pot can only be due to the same philological connection which brought about the representation of *Xolotl* with a cooking-pot, namely the Arabic homonyms which mean both "comrade" and "cooking-pot," and this led in Mexico to the burning of *Nanauatzin* and *Tecuciztecatl* in the fire, while otherwise *Nanauatzin* is represented in a cooking-pot. The Mande homonyms for "ant" and "itch" led to the correlation of *Xolotl* with the *buboso*. The Arabic conception of *qamarān* as "sun and moon" led to the Mexican correlation of *Xolotl* with *Tecuciztecatl*, and the usual connection of the "ant-god" with the pyramidal altar among the Mandes led to the same pyramidal altar to *Nanauatzin* and *Tecuciztecatl* in Mexico.

We are unfortunately badly informed as to the invisible triune gods of the Mandingos. Delafosse says: "The spirits often form a veritable mythological family, at the base of which one generally meets Heaven, male spirit and fecundating principle, and Earth, female spirit and fecundated, generating principle. The Heaven, at times identified with the Sun, has married the Earth, at times identified with the Moon, and from their union or from the union of their children have arisen all the chief spirits which direct the world and there dispense life and death, happiness and unhappiness in all their forms.

"Heaven and Earth, parents of the spirits, are often called upon as witnesses in oaths or invoked in wishes;

---

[1] J. F. Schön and S. Crowther, *Journals of the Expedition up the Niger*, London 1842, p. 49 f. See also W. Allen and T. R. H. Thomson, *A Narrative of the Expedition to the River Niger*, London 1848, vol. I, p. 243, and J. R. Harris, *The Cult of the Heavenly Twins*, Cambridge 1906, chaps. I and II.

but the cult directly rendered them is much less widespread than the one rendered to their eldest child, who, endowed both with the male and female virtues of its progenitors, is the true intermediary between the mysterious power of God and the timid weakness of man.

"Generally Heaven and Earth remain entities, if not abstract, at least without any palpable representation; sometimes, however, the first is invoked under the form of a man provided with an enormous phallus, or even under the form of an isolated phallus, while Earth, or the female spirit, is represented by a woman with large breasts or simply by a pair of breasts.

"As to the eldest son of Earth, he is represented under various aspects, sometimes as a hermaphrodite, more often as an animal figure, as the head of an ox, crocodile, fish, or serpent. The cult of this spirit, under the various aspects of his external representation, is, I believe, common to all the non-Islamized populations of West Africa, and it exists, in a reduced form, even among several Islamized peoples. It is found among all the Mande tribes, under the name of *Koma* or *Komo*, and, under the name of *Do*, among the Senufu, the Agni-Asante, etc.; elsewhere he is known under different names, but, whatever may be the name given to this spirit, his cult is found everywhere, from the Senegal to the Congo and, no doubt, beyond, with quite analogous external ceremonies. Everywhere, too, these ceremonies are forbidden to women, and certain of their rites are hidden also from non-initiated men; the initiation to the cult demands a whole series of tests which are surrounded with mystery and which they do not like to reveal to strangers; the religious association which has for its principal aim the cult of this spirit is one of the most widely spread and most firmly constituted in western Africa."[1]

[1] Delafosse, *Haut-Sénégal-Niger*, vol. III, p. 173 ff.

It seems that Delafosse has confused two separate worships, that of the *Komo* with that of the invisible triune divinities. We are better informed on the latter in the Mossi country: "The Mossi have the idea of the One God. One finds among them two beliefs: according to one God is the Sun; according to the other, he is a material being which they cannot represent. They have borrowed from the Moslems the idea that God has created everything, even the Sun, which is only fire. This fire, if it were left by God constantly at liberty, would consume everything, so he built a house where nine of his children (*malekdamba*,—this is the Arabic word for 'angel'—*malakum*) keep it shut up at night, thus producing night. This god is well materialized, since he has a wife (*tinga*, which also means earth) and a child, and eats and drinks (but not *dolo*, which is reserved for his followers). This infinite being, all-powerful *Naba*, is obviously surrounded by a considerable number of pages or good spirits, but there are also others, bad ones, who run away from him (*djidamba*, in Arabic *djinun*) and are the cause of all bad acts. We find in all this exposition a reduced and naïve Moslem theology."[1]

Among the Habbes the highest triune divinity is called *Ammo* or *Amma*: "To this triune divinity they raise three-pointed altars from cut stone, upon which the religious chiefs, called Hogon, offer their sacrifices."[2] "The Divine Force which they invoke is called, as at Timbuktu, *Harkoy* or *Herkoy*, 'Chief of the Males,' and the altars raised to this celestial fecundating power are built of clay, in the form of cones and painted red. These are sometimes nothing but conical stones or monolithic pieces put up vertically in the yard of every

[1] E. Ruelle, *Notes anthropologiques, ethnographiques et sociologiques sur quelques populations noires du 2e territoire militaire de l'Afrique Occidentale Française*, in *L'Anthropologie*, vol. XV, p. 689 f.

[2] Desplagnes, *op. cit.*, p. 269.

family house. In all these families the decoration of the pillars supporting the verandas of public places and of beams sustaining the ceilings of the chambers, and the ornamentation of the front walls of houses agree with the conventionalized designs of the *tana* animals of the confederacy, of conical pilasters and innumerable phallic emblems like the decorative motifs which crown the door-fronts in the Djenne houses."[1]

The coincidence of the corresponding Mexican belief with the African triune divinity is most striking. "The god of fire, called *Xiuhtecutli* (master of the stars), has also two other names, one of which is *Ixcoçauhqui*, which means 'the one with the yellow face,' and the other *Cueçaltzin*, which signifies 'flame.' He was also called *Ueueteotl* 'the old god,' and everybody considered Fire to be his father, in consideration of the effects produced by him, because he burns, and because his flame shines and burns."[2] He is also identified with *Tonacatecutli*, "the lord of our flesh,"[3] "God, lord, creator, governor of everything,—all these names were referred to him, since he was the god of whom it was said that he had created the world, and so he was represented with a royal crown upon his head."[4] No sacrifices were made to this god, because he did not want them.[5] "The same interpreter says in the notes to *Codex Vaticanus A* (No. 3738): '*Tonacatlecotle*, which means lord of our bodies, while others say that he was called the first man, and possibly it is intended that the first man be so called. . . . This is the image of the first lord that the world has had and who, when it pleased him, blew and separated the waters from the heavens and earth, which formerly had been mixed up, and it is he who put them

[1] *Ibid.*, p. 270 f.
[2] Sahagun, *op. cit.*, p. 27 f.
[3] Seler, *Codex Borgia*, vol. I, p. 116 f.
[4] *Codex Telleriano Remensis*, vol. VIII, in E. K. Kingsborough, *Antiquities of Mexico*, London 1830, vol. II, p. 1.
[5] *Ibid.*

Fig. 146. — Autel à trois pointes élevé à la Triade Céleste au village d'Engem-Guimini.

AFRICAN THREE-POINTED ALTAR, from Desplagnes'
Le plateau central nigérien.

Fig 145. — Autel à trois pointes sur lequel le Hogon de Dourou
offre des sacrifices à la Triade Divine.

AFRICAN THREE-POINTED ALTAR, from Desplagnes'
Le plateau central nigérien.

in order, as they are now, and so they called him the lord of our bodies and lord of abundance, who gave them all things, and so they represented him alone with the royal crown.   He was also called Seven Flowers (*Chicome xochitl*), because they said that he divided the principalities of the world.   He had no temple whatsoever, nor were any sacrifices made to him, because they say that he did not want them, as it were for his greater glory. .   He was called *Tonacatecotle* and otherwise *Citallatonali*, and they say that he is the sign that appears at night upon the sky, which by the people is called *Via San Giacomo* or *The Milky Way*.'"[1]   *Tonacatecutli* is frequently represented with his wife *Tonacaciuatl*,[2] and the two are frequently called *Ometecutli*, *Omeciuatl*, who live in the thirteenth heaven and are the gods of generation.[3]   *Ometecutli* means "the lord of two," but this is mere popular etymology, since we have the same life-giving principle in Africa as *Ammo*, and in the Mandingo language similar words refer to the life-giving principle.   We have Malinke *lamo, namo* "to ripen, bring up, raise, educate," *mo* "to be ripe, brought up, raised, educated," Bambara *mô* "ripe, to grow up," *lamo* "to ripen, raise, nourish, educate, take care of," Soso *mô* "to grow, to grow old," *môkhi* "ripe."   No doubt, all these are derived from Arabic نمٮ *namu* "to produce, procreate, give birth," and we have also النامية (*al-nafs*) *al-nāmiyah* "the vegetative soul, which makes the plants grow."

While Ruelle may be right that the idea of the One God, creator of all things, was by the Mossi, hence by the other Sudanese people, derived from the Arabs, the triune divinity, to whom no temples are raised and for whom there is no visible worship, is unquestionably of

---

[1] Seler, *Codex Borgia*, vol. I, p. 78 f.
[2] *Ibid.*, vol. II, p. 41.
[3] *Ibid.*, vol. I, pp. 32, 55 *et passim*.

Christian origin that has percolated through an Arabic source into the Sudan. This is again made clear from the worship of the god of fire, that is, the triune divinity, by three hearth-stones,[1] just as in Africa we have the three-pronged stone altar. Among the Mayas the relation of the divinity to the Christian religion was obvious to the priest, Hernandez, who tells of the one god in heaven, who was father, son, and holy ghost. The father was called *Içona* (*Itzamna*), and he created men and all things; the son was called *Bacab*, who was born of a virgin called *Chibirias* (*Ix chebel yax*), who lived in heaven; the holy ghost they called *Echuac* (*Ekchuuah*).[2]

If the Mexicans and Mayas received their triune divinity and the sun god from the Mandingos, they also received from them such notions as are perpetuated in their calendars. We find in Mexico and Central America, as among the Mossi in Africa, the *Nine Lords of the Night*, that is, the regents of the hours of the night mentioned upon their calendars, and the presiding divinities, of which the first is *Xiuhtecutli*, the fire god, are identical with nine of the day divinities, and the night hieroglyphs are the same as those of the day.[3] This puts the whole Mexican calendar, in so far as the hours are concerned, into a very recent period, and there is no reason for assuming that the calculation of the days and the divisions into years are any older.

It has sometimes been supposed that Mexican *teotl* may have something to do with the Latin or Spanish word for "god," but such is not the case. To begin with, Seler has shown that *teotl*, in the narrower sense, is equal to *Tezcatlipoca*, the evening sun god: "In Mexico, according to Duran, there was a confraternity consisting exclusively of people of noble or royal origin, who consecrated a special cult to the sun. But among the

[1] *Ibid.*, pp. 30, 116, 124, 322.
[2] *Ibid.*, p. 322.
[3] *Ibid.*, p. 218 ff.

historical tribes there is, in fact, no mention of any that worshipped the sun as a tribal or national god. Only of the old *Teotiuacan*, the cultural locality long deserted in historical times, do we hear that the old tribes there had built a pyramid each for the sun and moon. And the name *Teotiuacan*—which, it is true, in the text is explained differently from 'place where the dead kings were turned into gods'—may, perhaps, be translated as 'place of the sun-worshippers,' for under *teotl*, 'god' *par excellence*, is to be understood the sun. *Teotl āc* 'god has entered the earth,' the Mexicans said for 'sundown.' And wherever in city glyphs the syllable *teo-* was to be brought out, the Mexicans represented a whole or a half of a sun disc. Of late there have been those who went so far as to express the belief that originally the sun played no part in the Mexican cult, and that only the custom of sacrificing a demon of growth at an important place of the solar course, 'in order that he may provoke the heat necessary for the year's crops,' has led to the development of the vegetation demon into a sun god, and that the latter ultimately gained the upper hand over the terrestrial and vegetation demons, the types of primitive culture.

"Against such an explanation is the circumstance that, as I have already indicated, among the Mexicans the concepts of *teotl* 'god' and 'sun' are interchangeable, and that correspondingly the dead kings and warriors, who went to the sun, themselves became suns (*in aquin oonmic oteut*). And the remarks, such as that of the interpreter of the *Codex Telleriano Remensis*,— 'they said that it was the sun which produced all things, and, therefore, the maize was called *tonacayotl*, that is, it was produced by the sun (todas las cosas dizen que la produce el sol y ansi dizen al *tlaule tonacayotl* que quiere dezir, ya se criava del sol)'—in spite of the mistake which is obviously contained in the etymological in-

terpretation, point to a definite conception of dependence on this celestial luminary, and in this dependence
and fear does the essence of religion consist.   Then the
other remark of the interpreter of *Codex Vaticanus A*
in another place, where the picture writing represents
the sun god opposite the death god, that this juxtaposi-
tion meant, 'winter is so disagreeable on account of the
absence of the sun, and summer so agreeable on account
of the presence of the sun, and the return of the sun to
the zenith means that this their god comes to show them
a favor,' and referred to a definite annual festival, the
feast of *Toxcatl* as a sun festival."[1]   Sahagun says:
"The god called *Tezcatlipoca* (smoking mirror) was
considered a true and invisible god who penetrated all
places, heaven, earth, and hell."[2]   There can, therefore,
be no doubt that we are here dealing with a triune god,
but he represents more nearly the setting sun or the
rising moon.[3]

Before identifying him with a Mandingo conception,
we shall begin *ab ovo*, with the Arabic conception, from
which the Mexican religious ideas and the very name
ultimately are derived.   We have Arabic ظل *ẓil* "shade,
i.e., the light of the sun without the rays; anything
that shades one; an apparition, phantom, or a thing
that one sees like a shadow, the jinn; God's means
of protection; a state of life ample in its means or
circumstances, unstraightened; or plentiful and easy,
pleasant, soft, delicate; paradise."   But we have also
ظلّة *ẓullah* "a thing that shades one from the sun, a
cloud," and ظليل *ẓalīl* "a collection of trees tangled,
or luxuriant, or abundant and dense."   This root has
entered into the Berber languages, where we have Beni,

[1] *Ibid.*, p. 205.
[2] *Op. cit.*, p. 14.
[3] Seler, *Codex Borgia*, vol. II, pp. 12, 23, 32, 35, 57, 63, 298.

Menacer, Bougie *thili*, Bot'iua *thiri*, Zenaga *tiji*
"shade, image." This has led to Bambara *dya* "spirit,
sense, image, tangled woods, obstruction, trap, net,
dryness," *diya*, *dia* "pleasant, good, agreeable, fortunate, successful, hospitable," and Malinke *dya*
"spirit, faculty, memory, image, hospitality, to become
warm or dry," *dia* "ease, contentment, joy."

"*Dya* is a difficult word to translate. We translate
by *dya* the words 'phantoms, images, photographs,
shades, reflections in the water, mirror.' But it has
also other acceptations, and in the phrases *a dya tikera*,
a dya ulila, *misiu dya ulila* it is not a question of the
shade or image, for they mean: 'He is afraid, he is mad,
the cows are mad.' In the eyes of a Bambara, the
dya is not only the shade, image, contour of an object,
it is also that which produces it. It is a force, a power
common to beings from all kingdoms, and although it
cannot be compared to a *jinn*, the soul, there is none
the less in his mind a kind of being which he cannot define, but which exists and can act by itself. The
Bambaras are convinced that a man can take away his
dya, and then it will not cast a shadow. If the people,
out of fear of the European, and several, because they
have been for a long time in contact with him, readily
pose before the camera, we may none the less say
they in general do not like to be photographed.
Especially the old people make difficulties and are recal-
citrant the moment they see a lens. They are obsessed
by the idea that their *dya* will escape from them, in
order to impress itself upon the plate and leave there
its form, the portrait, and that thus a part of their being
will be in the hands of the photographer, and that they
will be at his mercy. They are afraid that in the
photographer's retaining them they will lose their

shadow and will henceforth be unable to cast it, hence
will become idiots.''[1]

If we now turn to *Tezcatlipoca*, we see that he is ''the
smoking mirror,'' that is, the mirror that gives shade,
but *tezcatl* ''mirror'' is unquestionably the Arabic
زجاج *zǵāǵ*, زجنجل *zaǵanǵal* ''glass, mirror,'' which we
find in Hausa as *tsokachi* ''to look, gaze,'' *matsokachi*,
Songay *didji, digi* ''glass, mirror,'' and we have Malinke
dūngari, Bambara *dugare, dungare* ''glass, mirror.''
Whether the Nahuatl *tezcatl* is the Arabic word or not,
there cannot be the slightest doubt that in *Tezcatlipoca*
we have the setting sun, *teotl*, which is our Mandingo
dya, hence the relation that *Tezcatlipoca* bears to the
underworld, the realm of the dead. Hence *teotl* is
etymologically derived from Mande *dya*.

The investigation of the Mandingo influence among
the Mayas and other non-Aztec tribes becomes in-
creasingly more difficult because of the unsatisfactory
information we have of the religious development outside the direct Aztec influence. In Peru the Mandingo
influence is as obvious as elsewhere, but here the
documentary evidence we have upon religious practices
is negligible, while the absence of written records of a
type contained in the Mexican and Mayan manuscripts
makes it impossible ever to reconstruct in full the
Peruvian antiquity.

Like the Mexicans and Mandingos, the Peruvians
worshipped the invisible Trinity. The monks who in
1550 began the investigation of the Peruvian idolatry
wrote as follows: ''We asked the priests what they
thought of God, whom they worshipped, and they
said, *Ataguju*, creator of all things, whom they considered to be the principal end, according to their religion. And they said that he was in heaven and did

---

[1] Henry, *op. cit.*, p. 41 f.

not move away from there, but that he governed all the things from there and created them, and they say that he created heaven and earth, and rules them from there, and, seeing himself alone, he created two others (they say 'cross' or 'to do' for this verb, *ruram*, which means 'to do') so that there should be three, and all should have one will and power, and they had no wives and were equal in all things.   The devil, who is like the *xamua* of God, told them this and this most false Trinity."[1]   From other sources we learn that they called this invisible chief god *Illa Tecce*.   For a long time no temple was built to him, and later only one temple was erected to him.   The eldest son of this first cause was *Inti*, the sun god, and his sister and wife was *Quilla*, the moon goddess.   There were a number of secondary gods attached to these, and many of them bear the name of *illa*, such as *Illjapa* or *Catoylla*, the god of lightning and thunder, also called *Chucuylla*; then there was *Auki-ylla*, the prince of glory, *Llari Ylla* and others.

We shall try to ascertain the exact meaning of *Illa*. This was also the name of an idol or fetish: "When they capture some wild animal, they look into its stomach and if they find in it a stone or hardened excrement, they keep it in a pouch and worship it and sacrifice to it the blood of the *coy*.   Only lately the devil has taught them, since the arrival of the Spaniards in Peru and since they have goats, to look into their stomachs, when they kill them, for a small ball of dry herbs, and this they keep in their houses and worship it, so that their goats should multiply.   This they call *Illa-cabra*, and offer to it the blood of the *coy*, and celebrate its holidays like other holidays."[2]

[1] *Colección de documentos inéditos relativos al descubrimiento, conquista y colonización de las posesiones españolas en América y Occeanía*, Madrid 1865, vol. III, p. 13 f.
[2] *Ibid.*, p. 50.

Here we see that the bezoar-stone of the Arabic medicine has become a fetish. The bezoar-goat is called كلْ 'ail, and Al-Damīrī says: "When it is bitten by a snake it eats the crab (as an antidote). It associates with fish on terms of friendship, and walks to the sea-coast to see them upon which they also approach the shore to see it. Fishermen know this and with that view put on its skin for the purpose of meeting fish which they then catch. It is addicted to eating snakes which it seeks in places where it can find them; if it is bitten by any of them, tears flow down from its eyes to the hollows which are under the sockets of the eyes, and which are deep enough to admit a finger. The tears get congealed and become (lustrous) like the sun, in which state they are used as an antidote for the snake-poison, and are known as the animal bezoar-stone. The best kind of it (bezoar-stone) is yellow, and the places in which it is found are India, Sind, and Persia. If it is placed on a snake-bite or the sting of a scorpion it is beneficial; and if a person who has drunk a poison holds it in his mouth, he too will be benefited by it. It has a wonderful property in warding off the effects of poisons."[1] In reality, the bezoar-stone is a globular concretion in the large gut of certain ruminants, chiefly goats.[2] The Peruvians wore the *illa* as a talisman to ensure good luck, hence *illa* also means "that which attracts good luck, good luck." In Aymara, *illa* means "bezoar-stone, anything kept for a future day, provisions, clothes, jewels," etc. The Kechua has similarly *illa* "kept for a long time," *illa kollke* "old piece of silver, generally with a hole through it and worn on a string around the neck as an amulet and supposed to attract silver." In spite of the close re-

[1] A. S. G. Jayakar, *Ad-Damīrī's Hayât Al-Hayawân*, London 1906, vol. I, p. 222.
[2] H. Fuhner, *Bezoarsteine*, in *Janus*, vol. VI, p. 318 ff.

semblance of Kechua *illa* and Arabic *'aīl*, we cannot connect the two, because we have no proof of the survival of the latter word, in the sense of "bezoar," in Africa. But this much is certain, *illa* has reference to something that is old and precious as an amulet. It is precisely what *il* means in Nahuatl and the Maya languages.

We have Nahuatl *Ilamatecutli* "the old goddess," that is, the goddess of the Trinity, the mother of the later gods, wife of the fire god *Ueueteotl*, the old god. *Ilama* has in Nahuatl assumed the meaning "old woman," but *Ilamatecutli* shows that the reference is to the "old goddess," that is, that *ilama* must mean "the old god." Indeed, we have Bambara *alla*, *ngala* "god" and *allama* "divine," while in Mandingo both *alla* and *allama* mean "god." This *allama* is from Arabic علَامُ *'alāmu*, علّامُ *'allāmu* "the omniscient; he who knows what has been and what will be, from whom nothing is concealed in earth nor in the heaven, whose knowledge comprehends all things, the covert thereof and the overt, the small thereof and the great, in the most complete manner." The confusion of this with Arabic الله اللّٰه *Illah, Allah* "god," and of both, in Africa, with the "old god," has produced Nahuatl *ilama* "the old (goddess)" and *il*, in compounds, with reference to heaven or knowledge. This Arabic علَامُ *'alāmu* has been understood as *al-āmu, al-nāmiyah* "the vegetative soul," and from the confusion with "the old god," that is, the Moslem god, has been superimposed upon the Habbes' *Ammo*, and has led in America to *Omeciuatl*, by the side of *Ilamatecutli*. In Kiche we have *il* "to obtain, see, preserve; much, great; guilt, misfortune, evil." It would seem impossible to connect all these meanings, but if one keeps in mind that the original meaning is "noteworthy and remarkable," as shown in the Peruvian, one sees how it means "to preserve, obtain," and "great," and "a noteworthy, but unfortunate, event," that is, "misfortune." We shall meet with this in the other languages. Pokonchi has *il*, *ilvuic* "to see," Kekchi has *il* "to see," *ilbal* "to take care of, watch," Maya has *ilah* "to see, watch, observe," *ilil* "vicious thing." The Nahuatl *ilhuia* means "to imagine, invent, do a thing with the use of all one's powers," hence "to increase." Here we not only see what seems to be a borrowing from a Maya language, but we get the fundamental meaning "to do something noteworthy or remarkable," and pass over to the meaning "much," hence *ilhuice*, *ilhuiz* "much more, above all." Hence we get *ilhuitli* "merit, recompense" and *ilhuitl* "celebration day," that is, "a noteworthy day," and then "day in general." We have also the compound *ilnamiqui* "to remember, imagine, think, reflect," from *namiqui* "to meet, grasp," that is, in *ilnamiqui* we have the connotation "to grasp a noteworthy thing." In Nahuatl *ilhuicatl* "heaven" we have, no doubt, *il-uica* "god government, the reign of the old gods."

Among the Peruvians *illa* is similarly applied to the celestial divinities, hence *illay* "to shine," *illaj* "light," *illapa* "lightning and thunder, misfortune." In the latter case we have the identical meaning as in Kekchi and Maya. "After Viracocha and the Sun, the third *huaca*, and the one most venerated, was the thunder, which they called by three names, *Chuqui-illa*, *Catu-illa*, *Intu-illapa*, imagining that it was a man in heaven with a sling and club in his hand, in whose power is rain, hail, thunder, and everything which belongs to the region of the air where the clouds are created. This is the general *huaca* of all the Indians, and different sacrifices are offered to him, and in Cuzco they also used to sacrifice children, as to the Sun."[1] We have too scanty infor-

[1] *Colección de libros y documentos referentes á la historia del Perú*, Lima 1916, vol. III, p. 6 f.

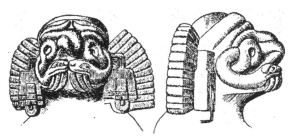

Abb. 299. *Tlaloc, Der Regengott.* Steinfigur der Uhde'schen Sammlung im Königl. Museum für Völkerkunde zu Berlin

Abb. 300. Thonfigur in Form eines Kruges, mit dem Gesichte des Regengottes *Tlaloc* ½ natürlicher Grösse Uhde'sche Sammlung Königl. Museum für Völkerkunde, Berlin

Abb. 301. Thongefäss mit dem Gesichte des Regengottes *Tlaloc* ½ natürlicher Grösse Königl. Museum für Völkerkunde, Berlin

Abb. 302. *Tlaloc* — Figürchen aus grünlichem Silikatgestein. ½ natürlicher Grösse. Königl. Museum für Völkerkunde, Berlin

THE RAINGOD TLALOC, from Seler's *Codex Borgia*.

mation here, but the use of the club and the sacrifice of children at once identify the Peruvian thunder god with the Mexican rain god, *Tlaloc*. The Mexican *Tlaloc* is hard to define etymologically, but we can locate his prototype in Africa.

"The god which bears this name of *Tlaloc* was one of the most popular figures of ancient Mexico, and representations of this god belong to the most common finds from pagan times   The crest of mountains over which the road goes from Tetzcoco to Uexotzinco and Tlaxcallan was the region to which the name of *Tlaloc* or *Tlalocan* was more particularly applied and which was considered to be the seat of the rain god and where there was an ancient idol of this god, made from lava, with its face turned to the east, and carrying upon its head a dish, into which every year was placed every kind of reaped edible seeds. . . . The god, who was considered by the inhabitants of the Mexican plateau to dwell on these heights, and was at the same time worshipped throughout the land, is everywhere represented in a fairly uniform and very remarkable way. His face, as may very well be seen in a stone figure of the Uhle collection in the Royal Museum for Ethnology at Berlin, consists entirely of the windings of two serpents, which, spirally winding about each other in the middle of the countenance, form a kind of nose, then on each side twisting into a circular knot encircle the eyes, and, finally, meeting each other with their muzzles, represent the upper lip and the long, descending fangs of the god. This fundamental form has in a continuous simplification of the design assumed the usual shape of the stone figures and manuscripts."[1]

Thus we arrive at the identification of *Tlaloc* with serpents. At the same time the syncretized forms of *Tlaloc* represent him as a fire god or as *Xolotl*, hence we

[1] Seler, *Codex Borgia*, vol. I, p. 108 f.

have the constant equation of "serpent-heaven-rain." In the Maya documents *Tlaloc* is called *Chac*. He is painted red, is represented with a skeleton body, and carries on his head a bowl with kernels or ears.[1] In Maya *chac* means "red," but we have *chacal* "cooking," *chacah* "to boil in water," and *chaac* "rain, downpour," so that here we have the "rain" word connected with "red, ripe," as in the case of the Mexican rain god. Similarly we have Kiche *chag* "ripe," Pokonchi *chak* "cooked," *chakij* "dry, hot," *chaklaj* "ripe," and similarly in the other Maya languages, so that "rain" is brought in contact with the sun and fire.

Here, similarly, "sky" and "serpent" are correlated. In all the Maya languages a root *can* means "serpent," but in Maya we have *caan* "sky," *caanal, canal* "high," where "sky" has arisen from the meaning "serpent." In Nahuatl *couatl* means not only "serpent," but also "twin," so that we are once more brought back to the twin god *Xolotl*, with whom *Tlaloc* is confounded. In Maya we have also *Ah bolon tz'acab* taking the place of *Chac*,[2] but the sentence means "he of the nine genealogies," so that we are once more brought back to "the nine guardians of the night," with which the sun god and the fire god are connected.

It would seem maddening and impossible to connect heaven, serpent, and rain, if we did not possess a complete solution of the matter among the Bambaras. "I have always been surprised by the facility with which the black man designates a divine favor by the name of its author, and when in the rainy season he receives the chief favor, the rain, which makes everything germinate and the crops grow, this is the way he expresses himself: '*Alla bi fign, Alla bi na, Alla bi kulu-kulu, Alla bi yege yege, Allo do*, etc. God is growing dark,

[1] *Ibid.*, p. 335.
[2] *Ibid.*, p. 217 and vol. II, p. 154.

God comes, God rumbles, God makes lightning, it is God,' etc. These are all purely metaphorical expressions, to say 'the clouds are gathering, it is going to rain, thunder is rumbling, it is lightning, it is raining,' etc.

"These same metaphors I find, in an absolutely identical sense, but this time in Bambara terms, '*Sa bi fign, sa bi na, sa bi kulukulu, sa bi yege yege, sa do,*' which also mean 'the clouds are gathering, it is going to rain, thunder is rumbling, it is lightning, it is raining.' The word *sa* being exclusively Bambara, it cannot reasonably be considered as posterior to the Arabic word, hence the Negro possessed it before knowing the word *Alla*. This word did not mean 'cloud, thunder, lightning, rain,' and there is reason to believe that there was a time when, as to-day, it awakened in his mind an identical idea as does now the word *Alla*, and by this word *Alla* he expresses merely a concept long possessed by him.

"What does this word *sa* mean? Could it be the primitive name of the divinity? Since certain Bantu tribes had much respect for serpents and worshipped them, the Europeans wanted to see in it a translation of the word 'serpent.' But that is a gross error. The word *sa* 'serpent' and the word *sa* in the phrases *sa bi fign, sa bi na,* etc. may have the same orthography, but the pronunciation is different. The hard *s* of *sa* 'serpent' is pronounced by slightly opening the teeth and puckering the lips, while the word *sa* in *sa bi fign,* etc. is pronounced by compressing the teeth and opening the lips. Therefore these are two different words. It seems to me a bit of stupidity to consider the serpent as being or having been a Bambara divinity. If even with his tabu taken from among the animals he does not look for any physical and real tie of relationship, one must *a fortiori* assume that he cannot consider as creator and sovereign master an animal, even if it were a serpent.

Certain Bambaras have it for a family tabu, and a branch of the Mande race has so great a respect for the python *Minia* that it can be recognized only under the name *Minianka*, the people of the serpent *Minia*. But have the Minianka ever worshipped the serpent as their god, their supreme divinity? They are less stupid. The serpent is a common tabu, the residence of a jinn, an infernal spirit, a demon, and nothing more.

"The word *sa* in the phrases *sa bi fign, sa do,* etc. 'the clouds are gathering, it is raining,' etc. has a broad meaning. It signifies everything that is upon high, everything which is above us. Has the word itself ever been the name of a divinity, as the word *Alla* actually still is? I think not. The word *sa* was a veiled expression for divinity,—it expressed essentially everything that the word *Alla* did as a principle, an idea, and not 'a being.'

"God being according to those concepts a spirit residing above us with his court and angels, these expressions *sa bi na, sa bi fign, sa bi kulukulu, sa dyi,* etc. should be translated, to have any meaning, by *Min be sa-n-fe bi na, Min be sa-n-fe bi fign, Min be sa-n-fe bi kulukulu, Sa-n-fe ta dyi,* He who (the spirit that) is above comes (will do us the favor of giving us rain), He who is above gets black (gathers the clouds), He who is above rumbles (makes his voice heard), The water of him who is on high.

"The favor *par excellence* granted to human beings by the divinity, the supreme being, is rain, and the Bambara, as I shall show presently, not being allowed to pronounce the name of this god, has in his gratitude used a metaphor. This metaphor, *Alla bi na, Alla bi fign,* identical with the one into which the word *sa* enters, namely *sa bi na, sa bi fign,* etc., leads me to believe, nay, compels me to believe that this word *Alla* originally expressed less an individual, a being, than an idea, a concept."[1]

One must be grateful to Henry for the very explicit account of this matter, though his explanation is obviously wrong. I have already shown that in the Sudanic languages God and heaven and rain, that is, *Allah* and *sama'*, are interchangeable,[2] and that the latter has led to Mande *sama* and *sã* "heaven, rain," hence the Bambaras are logical when for *Allah* they substitute the more common *sã*, which means so much the more to them, since the chief benefaction of the invisible divinity is rain. Just as in Hausa "rain" is interchangeably *ruan sama* or *ruan allah*, literally "sky water" or "god water," so in Malinke and Bambara *sã* takes the place of *Allah*. But this *sã*, which also means "year, age," was naturally confused with Malinke, Bambara *sa* "time, moment, end, cessation, death," from Arabic ساعة *sā'ah* "hour, instant, resurrection, death, distress." But this Malinke, Bambara *sa* also means "serpent." The origin of the word is not certain, but Soninke *samaqhe, samake,* Soso *sanyina* indicate that we have here a frightfully reduced Arabic *samak* "fish, eel," but the verb سمك *samaka* also means "to elevate, raise" and refers to heaven, so that the confusion may already have occurred in Arabic, especially since the serpent was considered to be a jinn and messenger of God. "The true form of the jinn is a serpent, with which, however, other reptiles and vermin are connected under the common name of *ḥanaš*. The serpent is *ǵānn* and *gūl*; in every serpent there is a jinn. Nöldeke has collected several examples. During the war of ditches, in the fifth year of the flight, a man from Medina ran his lance through the body of a serpent which he found lying

---

[1] Henry, *op. cit.*, p. 76 ff.
[2] See p. 174 ff.

upon his bed, and planted the lance in the yard, with the trembling serpent on its point, but the moment the serpent died he himself fell dead. Mohammed was asked to invoke God, to bring him back to life, but he said: 'Ask forgiveness for him, for it is a devil.' When the prophet was on his way to Tahuk, a large, fat, male serpent crawled up to him and remained long in one place, while he stopped with his camel, then he moved aside and stood up straight. 'Do you know,' said Mohammed, 'what this is? It is one of the eight jinn who wants to hear the Koran. He must be greeted since he is visiting the messenger of God in his country. He himself is greeting you, so you must return the greeting!' And the people did so, but the prophet said, 'Love God's servants, whoever they be!'"[1]

The confusion of "serpent," "rain," and "God" was inevitable in Mande, and has similarly passed over to America. But the parallelism does not stop here. The modern Malinke, Bambara *sa* "serpent" is not the original form, because we have in the other Mande languages a form *ka, kan, kali*, such as Kono, Vei *kā*, Gbondi, Landoro, Mende, Gbese, Toma *kāli* "serpent," and this appears in the neighboring Bornu as *kādi, gadi*, and here Wolof *dyan* shows that these words are most likely derived from Arabic خان *ǧān* "snake." In Bambara and Malinke *kã, ka, kan* means "above," and just as Mandingo *santo*, Malinke *sãfe*, Bambara *sanfe* "above, upon high" are derived from Arabic *samā'* "heaven," so this may have arisen from Mande *ar-dyan* "heaven." But whether this etymology is correct or not, there can be no doubt as to the homophony with the "snake" word. Again, Malinke *ka*, Bambara *ka, kan, kana* mean "to cut with a sickle," and in the other Mande languages we have Vei *kali*, Soso *kēri*, Gbandi *kalī*

[1] Wellhausen, *op. cit.*, p. 137 f.

"hoe." This latter word is of very wide distribution in Africa. In the Arabic oases we have Wadai *dṣarai*, Adirar *dṣālo*, Beram *kēri*, and both occur in Peul, Filham *ēbara*, plural *ṭibara*, Baga *dāba*, plural *sāba*, and *kāra*, plural *tsāra*, Timne *ketsala*, plural *tsetsala*, Bulom *kara*, plural *ṣikara*, all show that we have in all these various corruptions of Arabic سوقر *sauqar* "a pickaxe," and Malinke, Bambara *daba* "native hoe" is apparently borrowed from a language like Baga, where *dāba* occurs as the singular of *sāba*, and this for *kāra*, *tsara* side by side with it, from *sikara* in Bulom.

However this may be, we have the remarkable fact that in Malinke and Bambara we have the homonyms *ka*, *kan* "to cut with a sickle" and "above, upon high," while the other Mande languages have *kā* "serpent." It is, therefore, hardly a coincidence that we have Maya *can* "serpent," *caan* "heaven," but also Nahuatl *coatl* "serpent, hoe," the latter sense being also recorded by Las Casas as *coa* for the Caraibs. *Coa* in Nahuatl also means "to buy," and in *coaca* "to invite to a repast," *tecoani* "merchant who invites to a banquet" it obviously has something to do with merchants. Now Malinke *s* and *k* are interchangeable in many cases, and the *ka*, *kā*, *kan* words are thus brought into intimate relation with the *sa*, *sā*, *san* words, but here we have *sã* "to buy, sell," *sāni* "purchase, sale," *sānila* "buyer, seller," Bambara *sã* "market," *san* "to buy, exchange," *samba* "buyer, peddler," *sani* "purchase, sale," *sanikela* "buyer." Just as Nahuatl *coa* "to buy" is related to *coatl* "snake," so we have Maya *con* "to sell" related to *can* "serpent," and in both the merchant is brought in contact with the serpent, that is, with *Quetzalcouatl*, the feathered snake, with whom *Yacatecutli*, the merchant god, is syncretically connected. Before giving the precise meaning of the bird snake, as which *Quetzalcouatl* is to be understood, we must analyze the *uactli* of the Mexican religion, to which *Quetzalcouatl* is related.[1]

Among the Aztecs the *uactli*, identified as the *Falco cachinnans*, was considered as a bird of omen, more generally of good than of bad omen, and sometimes connected with *Quetzalcouatl*. Among the Mayas, another bird, the *moan*, apparently an eagle or vulture, is a mythical bird connected with *Quetzalcouatl* and represented as a bird with a snake body and often a snake tail. There can be little doubt that we have in these birds a graphic representation of the god, the feathered snake. The relation to the god becomes clear only when we consider the African bird of omen, described by de Marees.[2] One need only compare this description with Sahagun's description of the *uactli*. "Its augury was indifferent, since it as frequently announced good as evil. It was considered good when its laughter simulated the ordinary laughing, because it then seemed to say *yeccan, yeccan*, which means 'good weather, good weather.' When the bird uttered such a sound they had no suspicion of any evil. On the contrary, they were glad to hear it, because they expected good luck. But when this bird in singing seemed to imitate laughter in a high voice that seemed to come from the very depth of the chest, as happens upon the occasion of a great joy, those who heard it lost their voice and strength. They stopped talking among themselves."[3] Then Sahagun gives a lengthy account of the merchants' plight when they heard the *uactli's* unfavorable laugh. The *pitoir* of de Marees is the Spanish "buitre," the vulture, who is in Malinke and Bambara called *duga*, but this word also means "imprecation, benediction, curse," and is the Arabic دعاء *du'a'* "a prayer, supplication, in-

---

[1] Seler, *Codex Borgia*, vol. I, p. 215.
[2] See p. 120 f.
[3] *Op. cit.*, p. 295 f.

vocation of good, a blessing, benediction, a calling or crying for aid or succor." Here we have a purely linguistic reason for selecting the vulture as the bird of omen, and *Allah*, the giver of a blessing, who is invoked with a prayer, has thus changed into a vulture, even as through the *sa* and *ka* words he became identified as a serpent. Thus God became the bird and snake *par excellence*, the *Quetzalcouatl* of the Mexicans, the *Kukulcan* of the Mayas. Indeed, we hear that *Quetzalcouatl* was the god of the *Tolteca*, that is, the race that civilized Mexico, but since in Africa *dala* refers to the "makers, manufacturers," that is, to Arabs, we have in *Quetzalcouatl* the god of the Arabs, that is, *Allah*, as has already appeared from previous considerations. No wonder, then, that the *uactli*, the bird of omen, should also appear as *Toluactli*, the bird of the *Tolteca*. But the linguistic homonyms of *coatl* also lead to the identification of *Quetzalcouatl* with the hoe, which he is represented as holding in his hand.[1]

It is more likely, however, that *Toluactli* is a mere popular etymology of a word which should be *touactli*, since the Malinke *duga* stands for Arabic ضوع *duwaʿ* "a certain night bird, a species of owl," from the verb which means "it frightened him," that is, the bird of omen *par excellence*. The confusion of the bird of omen with "divine interference, blessing, curse" was perfectly natural. The Maya *moan* bird looks much more like an owl than an eagle, and has thus been identified by Seler.[2] The owl, *tecolotl*, is among the Aztecs a symbol of death,[3] and among the Bambaras death is frequently applied to the fetish *Duga*.[4] There can be little doubt that *tecolotl* stands for *tocolotl*, and, in the first part,

[1] Seler, *Codex Borgia*, vol. II, p. 187.
[2] *Ibid.*, vol. I, pp. 13, 180, etc.
[3] *Ibid.*, p. 68.
[4] Henry, *op. cit.*, p. 48 ff.

represents the Malinke *duga*, for we also have Maya *tunculuchu* "owl," apparently borrowed from the Aztec, or both from a third source. In its turn *tecolotli* is but a different form of *toluactli*. The apparent discrepancy, in applying one to the owl, the other to the falcon, while *duga* itself in Malinke refers to the vulture, is due to the fact that the Arabic name *duwaʿ* is "shared in common with it by other birds, that is to say, is applied to all nocturnal birds, which come forth from their nests at night."[1] "Al Masʿūdi has copied from Al-Jaḥid, that the owl does not show itself in the day out of fear of the influence of the evil eye affecting it, on account of its beauty and handsomeness; and because it considers itself the handsomest of all animals, it does not show itself excepting at night."[2]

This leads us at once to the Mexican *quetzalli*, the beautiful feathers found in *Tecolotlan*, literally "the country of the owl," "a province situated near Honduras, where formerly the feathers of the *Quetzaltototl* were found." Thus once more *Quetzalcouatl* is the bird snake, the bird represented by feathers from Owl-Land. But the Nahuatl *quetzalli* is an African name. For *Quetzalcouatl* the Mayas say *Kukulcan*, in which, as we have seen, *can* means "serpent," hence *kukul* should mean something like "owl-feather." Indeed, Maya *kukum, kukumel* means "feather." But both Nahuatl *quetzal* and Maya *kukum* are represented in Wolof *khergej*, Hassania Arabic *kujil*, Soninke *gugute*, Serere *lukukuk*, Malinke *kïkïn*, Bambara *gingi, guelu* "owl," while in Songay *gaga* is vulture." The handsome *quetzal* bird took the place of the African owl, which, according to Arabic tradition, was the handsomest bird, and was applied to the chief divinity, the *Quetzalcouatl* the god of the Toltecs.

[1] Jayakar, *op. cit.*, p. 346.
[2] *Ibid.*, p. 347.

We have already seen that the social and religious orders are of African origin. It now remains to show that the political order of the Mexican state is nothing but Mandingo in every detail. Nahuatl *tepetl* means "country, locality, mountain," while *altepetl* means "town, state, king, sovereign." This Nahuatl word has entered many American languages. We have Maya *tepal* "king, majesty, highness," Kiche *tepeu* "greatness, glory," Huasteca *altê* "woods, monte," Tarascan *tepacuaro* "city," *tepani* "to be large," *tepamani* "to rise." I have already pointed out that the mounds of the Mound-builders were town sites, with the hill for the cacique's residence and temple, just as in the Sudan, and that the North American stockade is identical with the one in West Africa. The close relationship between the art of the Mound-builders and that of Mexico has been shown by Holmes. It now can be shown that all that is a development of the Bedouin encampment in the Mandingo country.

Arabic دار *ḍār*, plural *aḍwār*, *aḍwirah*, etc., "habitation, house, residence," دائرة *ḍā'irah*, plural *dawā'ir*, "suite of apartments, convent" have had peculiar developments in western Africa. We not only have at Timbuktu the *duaria* "houses with one wall open and supported by columns," but Ibn-Batutah and Idrīsī report there دوار *ḍawwār* "encampment of the Bedouins with the tents in a circle and the cattle within the circle," which is obviously the simplest form of a stockade. In the Hassania Arabic we have both *diar* "house" and the much corrupted *dašera* "village," from Arabic *ḍā' irah*, though *dašera* is supposed to be of a different origin. We have similarly, in Africa, Biafada *dare*, Padsade *yār*, Bulom *ter*, Gura *dṣawa*. To us the most interesting development of this Arabic word is in the Mande languages. We have Malinke, Bambara *dugu* "village, earth," which has been shown to be derived from Arabic ـحت *ṭuḥuṭ*, and which crowded out the Arabic دوار *ḍawwār*, preserved in Soninke. We have Soninke *debe*, which is the older form, and is obviously derived from the Arabic. This is independently proved by Malinke *debe* "to curl or braid the hair," which is also from Arabic دائرة *da'irah* "the circular or spiral curl of hair upon the crown of a man's head," which is also preserved in Hausa *dauri* "twisted locks of hair arranged on either side of woman's face." By the side of دار *ḍār* the Arabs use الدار *al-ḍār* "the City of the Prophet," and similar expressions are found in Africa. Thus, by the side of Hausa *gari*, *kauye*, Timbuktu *koyra* "town," from Hassania Arabic *garīatun*, Arabic قرية *qaryah* "village," we have also Hausa *alkaria* "large city, capital of a chief, town placed on the commercial highways."

Even thus Mande *debe* produces Nahuatl *tepetl* "town with its hill" and *altepetl* "large city, royal power."

It can now be shown that the very crown of the Mexican kings was derived from the Mandingos. I have already given a part of the vast number of "enclosure, cover" words derived from a root *karpar*,[1] which led to the "cotton, garment" words. I will now treat with that development of the group which led to the perpetuation of the conical hat with a neck-flap as a distinctive head-gear of kings and priests. We have in Assyrian *karballatu* "name of a garment, cap." We can tell what kind of cap was meant from the occurrence of the word in the other Semitic languages, for we have Syriac *karbâltâ* "cockscomb," and while Hebrew כַּרְבֵּל

---

[1] See vol. II, p. 11 f.

kirbēl means "to be dressed in a cloak," Talmudic בַּרְבַּלְתָּא *karbalṭā* means "covering of the head, helmet; cockscomb." By the side of *karballatu* the Assyrian has also *kubšu* "head-gear, cover," so that both represent an original *karpar*, the latter having passed through a form *kurpaš*, that is, the Sanskrit *kurpaša* "coat of mail." That this Assyrian *kubšu* was originally *kurbšu* follows from the Greek κυρβασία, recorded by Dionysius and Herodotus as meaning "high, conical hat," by Aristophanes as "cockscomb" and "hat of the great Persian king." But Pollux also writes κυβαρσία, which is not a mere blunder, since similar forms, including Assyrian *kubšu*, occur. A form *kurbaš* is responsible for *kalpak*, the name of the pointed hat over an enormous territory among the Tatar tribes, while in Tibetan we have *kebs* "cap, hood."

The phonetic form of the original word deteriorated very early. A garment *kubbū* is already mentioned in Assyrian, but the exact meaning is not ascertainable. However, we have Talmudic כּוֹבַע *kōbaʿ* "high cap, turban, priestly hat, Adam's apple," כּוּבְעָה *kūbʿāh* "sheaves tied together over the ear of corn," קוֹבְעָא *qōbʿā* "cap, turban," Hebrew מִגְבָּעָה *migbāʿāh* "cap or fillet of the priest," Syriac ܩܘܒܥܐ *qūbʿâ*, Ethiopic *qobue* "cap." The development of this from a longer form is seen in Persian *kulbak* "a covering for a stack of grain," *kulbe*, *kurbe* "hut." It is this shorter form which entered Europe in the form of *cappa* "hood," but I must forego here the extremely interesting development of this word, and confine myself exclusively to the conical hat.

The Assyrian conical hat, which was also the royal hat of Persia, played an important part among the Magi and entered into the Mithra worship. It generally was the representation of the visible heaven, and so was painted to represent stars,[1] and St. Augustine called Mithra "*deus pileatus.*" It is this starred hat of the Magi that we find in the Middle Ages upon the head of a magician, and the Arabic magic unquestionably perpetuated this hat together with the eastern magic. Indeed, we find the same Semitic word in Arabic, namely قبع *qub'* "cap, conical hat," but more commonly the form اقروف *'ūqrūf* "conical hat," غفاره *gifārah* "cap."

I have already summarily treated the hat in Africa,[2] and now we can study it in greater detail. The latter word is recorded in the Arabic oases as *ofāra, ṛofāra, gofāra* "hat." But we have also Arabic مغفر *migfar* "what is wore beneath the helmet, a piece of mail,—a man throws it upon his head, and it reaches to the coat of mail,—sometimes they make above it a tapering top of silver; the term is also applied to the helmet itself." This leads to Hausa *malafa* "a large hat made of plaited straw," hence Peul *malafāre*, Afudu *mfoar*, Kamuku *malāfa*, Esitako *marāfa*, Musu *marafūa*, Bornu *malāwa*, Pika *malufa* "hat." Arabic *'ūqrūf* is found in Soninke *kurūfe*, Bornu *gurumbā*, Karekare *gurumpa*, while Arabic *gifārah* is found in Boritsu *gībur*, Gurma *kapīra*, Legba *gboro*, Yula *yīpura*, Timne *alapra*, Bulom *lapora*, and in the Mande languages in Gio *gbira*, Mano *gbola*, Gbese, Toma *gbara*, Mende *gbawere*, Gbandi *gbaralei*, Tene *lavāra*, Vei *gbāra*, Bambara *libīri*, Malinke *libīdi, libri, sibri*, Soninke *kufune*. Malinke *gabā*, Peul *hufune*, plural *kufune*, bear witness to the fact that the Mande forms *gbara, gbira* go back to Arabic *gifārah*, and the Mande form *fula* "cap,"

---

[1] F. Cumont, *Textes et monuments figurés relatifs aux mystères de Mithra*, Bruxelles 1899, vol. I, p. 115 f.

[2] See p. 233.

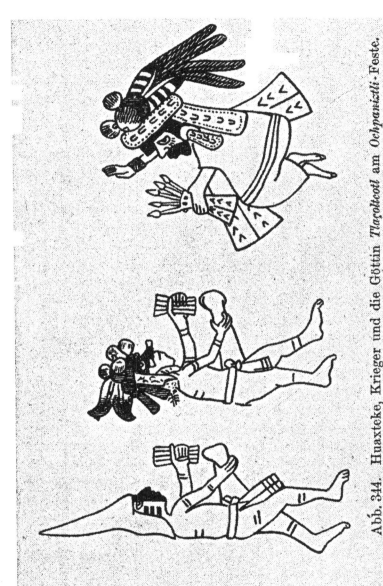

Abb. 344. Huaxteke, Krieger und die Göttin *Tlaҫolteotl* am *Ochpaniztli*-Feste.
Codex Borbonicus 30.

Abb. 284. *Quetzalcouatl*, der Büsser von *Tollan*.
Codex Vaticanus A (Nr. 3738) fol. 7 verso
(= Kingsborough 11).

CONICAL HAT, from Seler's *Codex Borgia*

found over an enormous territory, is an abbreviated *gufula*. We have Gio *gbilēn*, Dewoi *fule*, Gbe *file*, Hwida *fila*, Aku *ēfila*, Wossi *fōwila*, Gurma *foalerah*, Kupa *efula*, Dsarawa *fōla* "cap," and all these point to an older form *gofila*, *kofila*, by the side of Arabic *gifārah*, and this is actually preserved in Swahili *kofīa* "cap." We also have Arabic قَبِيلَة *qabīlah*, قَبِيلر *qabīlar* "hood," which is a contamination with Spanish *capilla*, itself of Asiatic origin, like the Arabic قَبِّع *qubʻ*.

Clavigero says that "the crown which was called by the Mexicans *copilli*, was a sort of small mitre, the fore-part of which was raised up, and terminated in a point, and the part behind was lowered down, and hung over the neck. . . It was composed of different materials, according to the pleasure of the kings; sometimes made of thin plates of gold, sometimes wove with golden thread, and figured with beautiful feathers."[1] The *copilli* was a specifically Huastecan head-dress,[2] and was frequently made of an ocelotl skin, so as to represent a lot of dots, that is, the stars of the magician's cap. That the kingly and priestly cap of the Magi should have been preserved in America in the identical form, with the identical decoration, and should, besides, have kept the name current for it among the Mandingo people, makes it impossible to admit any other solution than the one that the Mandingos established the royal and sacerdotal offices in Mexico. Ultimately this external representation of the royal power goes back to Persia, even as a vast amount of the Arabic magic has its origin there, and many of the religious motifs in the Mexican religion, through the Mandingo prototype, go back to Persian conceptions, but only as they seeped into Africa through Arabic magic. The universal

[1] D. F. S. Clavigero, *The History of Mexico*, trans. by C. Cullen, London 1787, book VII, sect. VIII.
[2] Seler, *Codex Borgia*, vol. III. See under *copilli* in the vocabulary.

Arabic vocabulary and the popular Arabic etymologies on which the religious speculations are often based make this conclusion positive and final.

Further analogies in America and Africa must be left for a future time. Here I wish only to do homage to the man who long ago had suspected the African influence in Mexican civilization, though he could give no analyses of special cases or define the time at which the transference of African fetishism had taken place. It is no mere accident that in 1862 a colossal granite head, representing a Negro, was found in the canton of Tuxtla, that is, near the place where the most ancient statuette was discovered, and that at Teotihuacan, that is, the oldest Mexican city of temples, a number of Negro heads in stone have been discovered. Orozco y Berra was forced to the conclusion from these finds that in the past a relation had existed between the Mexicans and the Negroes.[1] It has been my good fortune to establish this relation on positive and irrefutable evidence.

[1] M. Orozco y Berra, *Historia antigua y de la conquista de México*, México 1880, vol. I, p. 109 ff.

CHAPTER XIII.

THE MEXICAN NEW YEAR.[1]

The 62. canon of the Council at Trullo prohibited the celebration of the calends of January and the "vota brumalia," which took place on March 1; at least, men were not permitted to dress in women's clothes, and women in men's clothes, nor to put on any masks. This legislation against the pagan celebrations is only natural, and no specific importance is to be attached to the demand that men abstain from donning women's clothes, and women men's clothes, for these acts represent forms of the pagan mummery scorned by the church. But, at even an earlier date we find a frequently repeated prohibition against acting as an old woman, which cannot be explained from any classical source, to which it may refer.

In the first canon of Auxerre we read that no one is allowed on the first of January to act the old woman.[2] Nothing definite is known about the date of this council, which is variously dated from 573-603. That the passage in question is, to say the least, an interpolation follows from the bad Latinity "vetolo," "cervolo," which is out of keeping with the rest of the text. The canon itself is based on the 23. canon of the Council of Tours (A.D. 567), which objected to the celebration of the calends of January, but where there is no reference to acting as an old woman. In the

---

[1] After the book was finished the startling discovery here discussed was made. It is given without the pregnant consequences to which it leads.

[2] "Non licet kalendis Ianuarii *vetolo* aut cervolo facere vel streneas diabolicas observare, sed in ipsa die sic omnia beneficia tribuantur, sicut et reliquis diebus," *Monumenta Germaniae historica, Concilia*, vol. I, p. 179.

second book of the *Vita Eligii*, which is of late origin, that is, belongs to the VIII. century, we have the same reference to the calends of January,[1] which, with the interpolation in the Auxerre canon, is taken out of some late source.

The earliest reference historically to this word, from the VIII. century, is found in *Dicta abbatis Priminii, de singulis libris canonicis scarapsus*,[2] namely: "ceruulos et *uetulas* in Kalendas uel aliud tempus nolite anbulare." This prohibition is also found in Cummianus, Theodor of Canterbury, Halitgarius, Burchard of Worms,[3] all of which are of later origin, and need not detain us. More interesting and more important is the treatment of the matter in two pseudo-Augustinian sermons: "Who can be considered to be wise or of sound mind who 'making the stag' (cervulum facientes) wish to transform themselves by donning the vestments of beasts? Some put on animal skins; others put on the heads of beasts, and rejoice when they have thus transformed themselves into wild animals and no longer appear as men. By this they show and prove that they have, not so much the vestments, as the intellect, of beasts. For while they wish to express in themselves the similitude of animals, it is certain that there is in them more the heart of beasts than their forms. Again, how stupid it is for those who are born men to put on women's garments, and by an indecent transformation to effeminate their virile strength with a woman's form, without a blush putting their soldierly arms through women's tunics: they show their bearded faces and want to appear as women. Indeed, they no longer have their virile valor who have assumed the garments of women, and so it is to be considered a just judgment of God that

[1] "Nullus in Kalendas Ianuarii nefanda et ridiculosa, *vetulas* aut cervulos vel iotticos faciat," *Scriptores rerum merovingicarum*, vol. IV, p. 705.
[2] C. P. Caspari, *Kirchenhistorische Anecdota*, Christiania 1883, vol. I, p. 175.
[3] *Ibid.*

those who appear in the form of women have lost their military valor."[1] "Some commit that vile turpitude of 'making the stag' (de hinnicula vel cervula exercere)."[2]

It is clear that these sermons distinctly refer to two separate mummeries, that of an animal, and that of an old woman. In the latter case we read *annicula, anula, agricula* in some manuscripts, and this is for *anicula* "old woman," that is, an equivalent of "vetula." This is taken out of some Graeco-Latin gloss, for we have in Placidus "grauescella. grauesidus anni," "grauascela graues id est anni,"[3] which obviously should be "γραῦς id est anicula," and all the interpolations and forgeries read the first as "cervus" and produced the "cervula aut anicula," "cervula aut vetula" of the texts. Indeed, "anicula γραῦς" is a very common gloss. The "anni" of the Placidus gloss is due to "anui anicule" found there elsewhere.[4]

It is now possible to show that the whole prohibition is directed toward the mummeries of the Arabs, introduced by them into Europe from the practices among the Christians in Egypt. The Egyptian solar year consisted of twelve months of thirty days and a thirteenth, five-day month, called the "little" month. The Christian Copts did not disturb the Egyptian calendar, and called the thirteenth month *pi-abot n-kuži* "the little month," which was considered worthless, and during which time no important work was undertaken. This month fell in the end of February, and the old Greek and Roman custom of celebrating the calends of January was also applied to this period of the year. The Arabs transformed the Coptic word *kuži* "little" into Arabic عجوز *'agūz* "old woman," and

---

[1] *Sermo* CXXIX.
[2] *Sermo* CCLXV.
[3] Goetz, *op. cit.*, vol. V, pp. 24, 72, 107.
[4] *Ibid.*, p. 167.

let loose a mass of folklore with this philological blunder, which has swept over Europe, Africa, and America.

The Arabic عجوز *aǧūz* is recorded in the Spanish-Arabic vocabulary for *vetula*, the word which we have already found in a mass of forgeries. The idea that there were seven last days is already found in the Koran: "Thamúd was destroyed by a terrible noise, and Ád was destroyed by a roaring and furious wind, which God caused to assail them for seven nights and eight days successively." It does not appear that these referred to the intercalary days, which is the case with "the days of the old woman."

Among the Berbers[1] the old Roman calendar was not entirely superseded by the Arabic nomenclature. Among them the New Year is called *yennair, inneir, nnáir*, etc., from "Januarius," and *byenni, byánnu*, apparently from "bonus annus." At Fez the New Year's day and the following day are together named *haǧūza*, elsewhere *l-haǧūza, haidūza*, which is represented as a female spirit of an old and hideous appearance, which is obviously derived from the Arabic, by a misinterpretation of the Coptic *kuži* "little." At Tlemcen they say that Ennayer once came in the form of an old woman to ask for alms. At Tangier, Rabat, and Fez "parents press their children to eat much of the New Year's food, telling them that otherwise *Haǧūza* will come and fill their stomachs with straw. A small portion of it is sometimes left for *Haǧūza* in a covered plate, and if any hair is found there the next morning it is said that she has been there and partaken of the food."[2] "In the Garb *haǧūza* is an unlucky day, when

---

[1] E. Westermarck, *Ceremonies and Beliefs Connected with Agriculture, Certain Dates of the Solar Year, and the Weather, in Morocco*, Helsingfors 1913, p. 56 ff.

[2] *Ibid.*, p. 63 f.

no ploughing is done but the people hunt and play at ball."[1]

'From 25th February to 4th March (Old Style) there is a period, lasting for eight days and seven nights, which is called *la-ḥsūm* (Fez) or more commonly *ḥáyyan*. The Braber of the Ait Waráin call it *támgart*, 'the old woman,' probably because the winter is then coming to an end. I was told that Támgart was an old woman living at the foot of Búiblan, the highest mountain in the district of Ait Waráin. Once when it was raining during the three first days of the said period the calves in her yard took refuge in her tent, but she drove them away telling them not to be afraid of a little rain. Then Ḥáyyan said to Márssu (March):—'O March, lend me an evil day, I shall kill by it the bad old woman.' March, who then had thirty-two days, lent one of them to Bráyer (February) so that only thirty-one remained. Now there came much rain and cold and snow. Támgart with her tent and all her animals were transformed into stone, and are still to be seen at the foot of Búiblan where there is a large stone which from a distance looks like a woman at a churn, another having the shape of a tent, a third looking like a shepherd leaning on his staff, and a collection of smaller stones resembling sheep. In the Ḥiáina, where the second day of *ḥáyyan* is called *nhār la-'gūz*, 'the day of the old woman,' the following story is told. There was an old woman who went out on the pasture with the sheep and goats. As the ground was very dry and the crops were suffering from drought, she asked Ḥáyyan to send rain. Ḥáyyan in his turn asked March to lend him one day; this he did, and rain fell so heavily that the old woman was killed, whereas the animals escaped to the village.

"*Ḥáyyan* is represented as a bitterly cold time of the year, known for its rain, wind, and snow, which are

[1] *Ibid.*, p. 67.

considered very dangerous for people, animals, and crops. It is called *bu-tlūž*, 'the master of snow,' in the saying, *Ḥáyyan bu-tlūž, lūlu báida u ahēru 'aslūž* (Hiáina), which means that on its first day the partridges begin to lay eggs and on its last day the young sprouts of various wild herbs are big enough to be used for food. Nobody likes to travel during this period, hence all necessaries have to be provided in advance (Garb, Ḥiáina, At Ubáhti). A Berber from the At Ubáhti told me that when he and some relatives once during *ḥáyyan* went to fetch dates from a neighbouring Arab tribe, two of their donkeys died on the road in consequence of the rain; but he said that people, also, may die if they expose themselves to the rain by travelling in *ḥáyyan*. In the same tribe it is the custom to keep the sheep inside the tents during a rainy *ḥáyyan*, but even then they are supposed to be in danger owing to the cold. There is a saying, 'Don't separate your kids from the flock till the nights of *ḥáyyan* have passed,' or, 'till *ḥáyyan* has passed;' they, as also the lambs, are then only too liable to be killed by the rough weather. Especially the second day, *nhār, la-'gúz* or, as it is called in Andjra, *nhār l-mā'za u r-rā'i*, 'the day of the she-goat and shepherd,' is considered to be full of danger; the shepherd must then be thickly clad and eat well, and, at least if he is a young boy, somebody must accompany him to look after him and the flock (Hiáina, Andjra). But rain in *ḥáyyan* is considered equally injurious to the grass, crops, vegetables, and fruit-trees, its water being salt (Hiáina). Among the Ait Waráin and Ait Sádden nobody must go in the fields during the three first days of this period; should anybody go, the crops would get dry or be beaten down by a thunderstorm, and even the owner of the field might be personally affected by it. Nothing can be worse than a thunderstorm in *ḥáyyan*: it hurts the little children, animals, and bees, and makes milk and honey scarce. The Arabs of the Ḥiáina therefore say:—'May God save us from the thunder of *ḥáyyan.*' On the other hand, 'if an east-wind blows in *ḥáyyan* the durra will have a bath in the *nīsan*, and the year will turn out good without scarcity'. For there is no rain while an east-wind is blowing."[1]

That this is all an Arabic, and not a Berber, conception, follows from the Arabic word, which is due to a Coptic homonym, and because the legend is equally familiar among the Arabs in the east: "عجوز also called ايام العجز, because they come in the latter part (عجز) of winter; but the former is the correct appellation; accord. to the usage of the Arabs, Five days, the names of which are صن and صنبر and و بر and مطفى· الجمر and مكفى· الظعن; said by Ibn-Kunáseh to be of the نو· of الصرفة [by which is meant the auroral setting of the Twelfth Mansion of the Moon, which, in Central Arabia, about the commencement of the era of the Flight, happened on the 9th of March O.S.: in the modern Egyptian Almanacs, the ايام العجوز are said to commence now on the 9th of March N. S., which is now the 26th of February O. S.]: or, accord. to Abu-l-Ghowth, they are seven days, named صن and صنبَّر and مطفى· الجمر and المعلِّل and المو·تمر and الامر and و بر or مكفى· الظعن · and some reckon مكفى· الظعن an eighth: but most authors hold these names to be post-classical: accord. to Esh-Shereeshee, they are seven days; four of the last [days] of February, and three of the first [days] of March: during these days blew the wind by which the tribe of 'Ád was destroyed: and

[1] *Ibid.*, p. 70 ff.

they are thus called because they are [in] the latter part
(عجز) of winter; or because an old woman (عجوز) of
'Ád concealed herself in a subterranean excavation,
from which the wind dragged her forth on the eighth
day, and destroyed her: or امر and مو٬تسر are the names
of the last two days; the former being the sixth, and
the latter the seventh. Ibn-Aḥmar says, The winter is
driven away, or is closed, by seven dusty (days), our
old woman's days of the month; and when her days
come to an end, and Ṣinn and Ṣinnabr, with El-Webr,
and with Ámir and his little brother Mu-temír, and
Mo'allil, and with Muṭfi-el-Jemr, pass, the winter goes
away, retiring quickly, and a burning wind comes to
thee from the first day of the ensuing month."[1]

At a later time other Arabic names were used for the
February intercalation,[2] which itself is known under
the name of سابٴة sāb'aṭ, and begins on February 24
and lasts to March 4. The Arabs brought the superstition to Spain, where the witches' night is consequently still known as "la noche del sabado," perpetuated in English as the witches' sabbath, and by Goethe
as the Hexen-sabbat. But the German Hexe is itself
the Arabic عجوز 'agūz, Berber ḥagūza. The early Anglo-
Saxon vocabularies translate haegtis, haegtes, haehtis,
hegitisse by "Eumenides, Erenis, furia," and similarly
we have the OHGerman hāzus, hāzes, hāzis with similar
meanings. Unfortunately no earlier text contains any
explanation as to the nature of such a hag, but in the
Ancren Riwle the seven capital sins are called the
seven hags (seouen heggen),[3] which agrees with the
conception of seven hags among the Arabs.

---

[1] E. W. Lane, An Arabic-English Lexicon, p. 1961.
[2] E. Destaing, Fêtes et coutumes saisonnières chez les Beni Snoùs, in Revue Africaine, vol. L, p. 244 ff.
[3] J. Morton, The Ancren Riwle, London 1853, p. 216.

While the intercalary days were considered to be useless, they were celebrated with good cheer, and a simple porridge, having some religious significance, is considered indispensable.[1] In some places they eat barley porridge with oil poured over it, or gruel made with milk, to which salt butter or oil has been added, or pounded wheat boiled in water. The Arabs of the Ḥiáina eat on New Year's Eve *tšiša* made of wheaten meal boiled in water to which, while still boiling, are added salt, milk, and salt butter. This *tšiša* had originally medicinal properties. Ibn-al-Baitār mentions it as جشِيش *ĝašiš*, coarse flour made of wheat or spelt, and refers to Galan and Dioscorides as to his authority that it is very nourishing and easily digested.[2] It is also known as *dšiš*, and the جشِيش *hašiš* mentioned by me before[3] are other forms of the same word. They are all from Coptic *oouš* "porridge," which is frequently referred to by the Greeks under the name of ἄδαρα or ἄδηρα, and mentioned by Pliny as of Egyptian origin, but it is really a Semitic root, found also in Arabic as عصر *'aṣara* "to crush (grain)." This very ancient custom of eating porridge on a religious festival is universal in the Western Sudan; among the Bambaras it is known as *dege*. But the non-Islamic Bambaras have also the fermented grain, *dlo*, the maize beer, which, as has already been pointed out,[4] is frequently produced by mastication.

In America where this religious custom has led to the use of the phonetically identical *chicha*, masticated and fermented mash, and to the use of pulque in Mexico, we have thus a direct reminiscence of the African habit,

[1] Westermarck, *Ceremonies and Beliefs*, p. 57 ff.
[2] L. Leclerc, *Traité dessimples par Ibn El-Beithar*, in *Notices et extraits des manuscrits de la Bibliothèque Nationale*, vol. XXIII, No. 485.
[3] Vol. II, p. 114 f.
[4] *Ibid.*, p. 115.

which itself, through the Berbers and Arabs, goes back to Egypt. The purpose of eating the porridge and generally gorging oneself with food during the intercalary days is due to the desire to produce a *baraka* "a blessing," a return of fortune for the ensuing year. Thus "the Arabs of the Ḥiáina on the day in question take some barley to the field, put it into the *késkas*, or steamer used for the making of *ṭʻam* (*séksu*), leave it there for a while over the fire, then dry it in the sun, roast it in an earthenware pan, grind and sift it, and at last mix it with fresh milk or buttermilk together with the root of a plant called *buzeffūr*. This is eaten to destroy the *bas* (evil), it makes the people strong as there is much *baraka* in it—but only on the condition that the rainbow is seen on that day; otherwise, the *baraka* in it is slight, and if it thunders then there is none."[1] As there is *baraka* in New Year's Day, all observances at that time have a religious significance. Among the Mandes, as elsewhere, *barika*, *barka* means "force, vigor, energy, benediction, gratitude." But more usually another Arabic word has taken its place through the Sudan, as it has among the Berbers and in Europe.[2] The Arabic نعم *naʻam* "to live in ease and affluence, enjoy life, grant, rejoice, overwhelm with riches," *nuʻm* "luxurious life," *naʻima* "well, excellent," *niʻam* "benefit, bounty, favor, mercy, kindness" have left a long trail behind them in western Africa. We have the Berber *nām* "to approve, accede to the desires, obey," *nāma* "grace, favor, benefit, prosperity, abundance." These lead to Peul *nammude* "to be abundant, much," *nammaḍuru* "great abundance," hence *Nammaḍīri* "the Futa, the country of abundance;" Hausa *naima*, *nema* "kindness," *nima* "pleas-

---

[1] Westermarck, *Ceremonies and Beliefs*, p. 77.

[2] The European development of this word and idea I shall treat at another time.

ure," *niam* "prosperous;" Timne *namfa* "to thrive," *namra* "to satiate, be satisfied," *namsarne* "overeat;" Dahome *neme* "good;" Asante *nĕm* "to be diligent, assiduous, sedulous, careful;" Bambara *nema* "God's gift, fortune, ease, satisfaction, luck;" Bambara, Malinke *nyuma* "good, benefaction, generous," hence a Bambara says "*barka da mā yé a ka nyuman na*, to thank one for favors bestowed" and "*Alla m'i nyuman ségira*, may God grant you a safe return." We know nothing of the Mande calendar, but there can be no doubt that many of the holidays or religious festivities have their origin in the solar or lunar events, and that the celebration with bountiful food and *dege*, and with masquerades is identical with the similar religious observances among the Berbers, that is, that the intercalary days, though "useless" for the counting, were a source of *baraka* and led to "abundance, increase of flocks," etc., if properly celebrated. Ultimately, no doubt, the origin of these festivities was forgotten in the Sudan as much as among the Berbers and Arabs, and the celebration was transferred to other occasions as well.

In the Mexican calendar the eighteen months of twenty days were followed by five intercalary days,[1] called *nemontemi* "superfluous," which were considered useless and to which no divinities were attached. On these days people did not quarrel, for fear of laying a foundation for a year of dissent, and, in general, kept from doing that which they did not want repeated during the year. We have here exactly the same days as in Africa, during which that had to be done which would bring *nāma* "grace, favor, prosperity, abundance." There can be no doubt as to the derivation of Aztec *nemontemi* from a word which also led to *nen*

---

[1] Seler, *Gesammelte Abhandlungen zur amerikanischen Sprach- und Alterthumskunde*, vol. I, p. 510 ff.

"superfluous, vain." The precise meaning can be ascertained from a study of the root in the languages bordering on the Nahuatl. In the Maya languages, Huasteca does not record any word from this root, and Tzendal and Chol have no such word for "large," while all the other languages have some derivatives from it. Maya has *num* as an ending of cardinal numbers meaning "times;" in composition it means "very, too much, greatly;" it does not exist as an individual word. In the other Maya languages *nim* means "much," hence Pokonchi *nim* "large," *nimaj* "to obey," *nim kij* "holiday," Kekchi *niman* "to grow, become large," *nink* "large, to provide with things, be rich," but here we also have *nume* "to surpass, overtake," *numta* "to surpass, too much, be overripe," Kiche *nim* "impulse, large, fat," *nimah* "to obey, revere, extol," *nimar* "to grow." Similarly we have Tarascan *nimani* "to pass (the time)," *nimaqua* "later," *namucheni* "to be numerous," *nimatehpei* "to be a grandfather," *ninini* "to mature." In all of these cases we proceed from the meaning "abundant," as in the African words from the Arabic *nāma*. In Nahuatl we have *nemi* "to live," that is, "to grow, feed," as may be seen from *nemitia* "to live, nourish oneself," *nemilia* "to live from one's labor, to think, consider;" but it also has the connotation "too much," as in the Maya languages, hence *nen* "superfluous, gratuitous, useless." The root in these languages is distinctly an intrusive one, and is unquestionably due to the *baraka* of the intercalary days.

The most extraordinary object for a *baraka* among the Berbers consists in the game of ball, which is connected with the intercalary days and with other religious observances. We have already seen that ball is played during the *ḥaǵūza* days. Similarly "games of ball are frequently played with a view to obtaining rain.

Among the Ait Waráin two or four naked women for this purpose play a kind of hockey, not, like the women of the Tsūl, with ladles but with sticks. Among the Ulād Bu-'Asīz some good old women play at ball when rain is wanted, whilst in the Ḥiáina under similar circumstances the men of two neighbouring villages have a football match in the afternoon, after which they drape a ewe with a woman's shawl, as has been said above. Among the At Ubáhti men and youths in spring play at ball with sticks, as a means of producing rain. It may be asked why games of ball are supposed to have a rain-producing effect. An explanation given me by an old Arab was that the ball is dark like a rain-cloud, but the accuracy of this statement is doubtful. Among the Tsūl the men play at ball to put a stop to a long-continued rain, the scribes and students playing with the feet and other men with sticks, and I was told that in Andjra one game of ball is played to obtain rain and another to obtain dry weather. From these facts we may conclude that the essential function of playing at ball as a weather-charm is to bring about a change in the weather through the movements and changing fortune of the game."[1] "It should be added, however, that both the tug-of-war and games of ball are believed to have a strengthening or purifying effect and are also practised on that account. So far as the former is concerned, I have given instances of this in my article on the popular ritual of the Great Feast in Morocco and above, whilst games of ball are reported to be played both at the Great and Little Feast (Ait Waráin) or on the last day of the year (Garb), and are in certain cases expressly said to remove evil influences. The ball—in Arabic called *l-kōra*, in Berber *tašurt* (Ait Waráin) or *tašurt̤* (At Ubáhti)—is considered haunted;

---

[1] Westermarck, *Ceremonies and Beliefs*, p. 121 f.

in the Ḥiáina it must not be taken into a house, nor must a game of ball be played in the yard or close to the domestic animals, but it should be played on the waste land so that all the *bas*, or evil, goes there."[1]

Doutté has given an elaborate account of the games of ball in northern Africa: "A very popular sport among the Reḥāmna, as elsewhere in the whole of northern Africa, is the game of ball or *kūrah*. It is played there in three different ways, as we shall describe one after the other. In the first, the players are divided in two camps and each camp attempts to throw the ball into the adversary's camp. This ball, which is made of wool and is covered with leather, is thrown between the two camps, and is kicked off by him who can reach it with his foot. When the ball has reached the camp, in spite of the camp's efforts to push it back, the camp loses the game. One recognizes in this the game of *soule au pied* of our old France, which is in vogue especially in Normandy and Brittany. The English are said to have borrowed it from us during the Hundred Years' War, and we have received it back from them as a novelty under the name of *football*.

"At other times the *kūrah* is played, not by kicking it with the foot, but by striking it with a stick, '*aqfah*, which is bent at the end. No one has a right to touch it and only the stick must be used. The attempt is made to ward off with the stick the adversary's blow about to be given to the *kūrah*, in order to send it to his own camp, for in the *kūrah* played with the stick each camp tries to get the ball to its own side, and whoever succeeds in doing so wins the game. This game is no other than our old *soule à la crosse*, which, carried by our Norman and Breton colonists to Canada, has there become the national game; up to the XIX. century our game of billiards was played with lacrosse bats.

[1] *Ibid.*, p. 122 f.

Fig. 85. — Le jeu de la koûra en Algérie, à El Milia

(*Cliché de M. Ménétret*)

From Doutté's *Merrākech*

"The third way of playing is much more brutal: the ball is thrown up, and he who catches it must throw himself upon the ground, turn a somersault with his hands (*itšeqleb*), hit his nearest neighbor, and then in his turn throw up the ball. He is not allowed to throw it before making the somersault and giving a blow. One must marvel at the dexterity with which the natives execute this complicated rule. The blows, which are generally given with the feet, are very violent and make the game very brutal. The people are not divided into camps, and the most resistant fellow is the victor. This form of the game has naturally a more popular character than the other games. In some regions of Morocco they play this kind of game with a *belṛa*, or slipper, in the form of a *kūrah*. This is the case among the Šiaḍma. Here the players place themselves in a circle; one of them holds the *belṛa* and throws it to another player at his will. This one catches the *belṛa*, turns a somersault on his hands, at the same time trying to hit another, who tries to evade the blow, and he throws the *belra* to a third person, who proceeds with the game. If the person to whom the *belṛa* is thrown is unable to catch it in its flight, he picks it up and has to pass it to his neighbor without turning a somersault, whereas he who gets it in the regular course may throw it to whomsoever he pleases.

"As we have said, the game of the *kūrah* is played in the whole of northern Africa; it is especially popular in all of Algeria, where it is generally played with a stick. The players form two camps, and each of them is provided with a bat. A level piece of ground is usually chosen; when everybody is gathered, one of the players throws the *kūrah* up into the air; around him the players are waiting, with bat in hand, trying to strike the ball in such a way as to bring it into their camp. The *mêlée* never ceases, all the players throwing themselves upon the ball, some to drive it to one side, others to the other side. Often they make use of their bats to keep off the adversaries; veritable hand-to-hand fights take place; the players strike with all their force, and many a shank gets the blow intended for the *kūrah*, and fractures are not rare. The ball is generally made of wood, more frequently of rags, or of wool or cow-hair. The game is generally without stakes, but cases are known when there is a stake, a goat, a lamb, and sometimes even an ox, which is eaten together at the expense of the camp losing the game. In certain regions, at Miliāna, for example, the rule of the game is more difficult; the ball has to be returned not only to one of the camps but also to a hole dug out in the ground. The game of the *kūrah* is at Algeria also played without a bat; in this case it bears in the Little Kabylia of Collo and Jijeli the name of *dūkha*; the ball is thrown by hand.

"It is most remarkable that in Morocco the *kūrah* is generally played by the *tolba*, the priests, which is not so common in Algeria. In Morocco itself, the game of the *kūrah*, without bat and with the feet, is the monopoly of the *tolba*, and only they play it, at least in this fashion. Thus, for example, in the Ḥāḥa, where we have made a special study of it, only the *tolba* play at the *kūrah*, and in the following manner: they are, to begin with, divided into two camps, and they kick alternatingly the ball with their feet; by degrees the camps approach each other, and a veritable fight takes place. Everybody tries to throw him who comes near to the ball, in order to send it ahead with his foot, but they are not allowed to use their hands; they may push only with their chests, or shoulders, or legs, or feet; they may even kick in the shin, but they must keep their arms down. At Mogador, everybody plays at the *kūrah* with the feet, but without kicking it: only the *tolba*, who play separately, follow the method used in the Hāḥa, so that this game is at the same time almost a battle.   This way of playing seems for the rest to be the most popular among the *tolba* of Morocco.

"This curious specialization of the ball game as being in some way an attribute of the *tolba*, the clerics, occurs also in other places; without going any further than our own country, we know that in the Middle Ages they played ball in France in the churches; up to the revolution the Bishop of Avranches and his canons played on Shrove Tuesday a game of lacrosse in the cemetery, and the signal for it was given by ringing all the cathedral bells. It is precisely at the same time that in northern Africa they play at the *kūrah*.   Indeed, in a very large number of countries, it is played only in springtime, and in every country in which it is played spring remains the classic period; especially for the *tolba* at Aurès, and perhaps elsewhere, it is an integral part of the ceremonies which take place in springtime.   But often they organize in a drouth at any time a game of *kūrah* in order 'to bring about rain.'   Hence the *kūrah* cannot be identified with a simple sport, because they do not generally play it during the native feasts: it is not, like the 'fantasia,' the usual accompaniment of any celebration.   If one stops to consider all these different circumstances, one cannot fail to see that the *kūrah*, which takes place during certain solar dates, or to bring about a change in weather, and which often is the privilege of a class of people of a religious character, has entirely the appearance of a survival of agrarian ceremonies celebrated by a special caste.   I do not doubt that a more extended investigation and one more precise than mine will some day establish this in a definite manner."[1]

[1] Doutté, *Merrākech*, Paris 1905, p. 318 ff.; see also his *Magie et religion dans l'Afrique du Nord*, p. 554.

We shall now investigate the ball game discussed by Doutté from its beginning and in its ramifications which concern us here. In Firdūsi's *Shah-Nameh* there are frequent references to the game of *chaugān-goy*. "*Chaugān* means a bat as well as the ground on which the game is played, *goy* means a ball."[1] These two words are not of Persian origin. Although there is a word *chaul*, *chūl* "crooked," *gān* means nothing, and no native etymology for *goy* is possible. We have unquestionably here three Chinese words, *ts'uh* "to kick (a ball)," *kan* "a bat," *k'iu* "a ball," hence the game is most likely of Chinese origin. It cannot now be decided whether the Arabs first brought it out of China or borrowed it from the Persians, but the fact that it was already popular as a royal game in Byzantium in the X. century would indicate its importation by the Arabs. The Greeks called the game τζυκάνιον, while τζυκανίζω was "to play golf or polo" and τζυκανιστήριον was "the place where the game was played." We have a good description of the game by Cinnamus: "At the end of winter, when the weather had cleared, Nicephorus devoted himself to the game which since ancient times had been a special privilege of kings and their children. The youths divide themselves into two equal parts and drive a leather ball of the size of an apple to a previously designated spot. Then they ride to it at full speed as to a prize placed in the middle, having in the right hand a stick of fair size, which suddenly ends in a circular breadth, the middle of which is made of dried guts woven in the form of a net. Each party strives to drive the ball beyond the other to a previously designated spot, for whoever with his racket first reaches the goal with the ball is considered to be a victor. Such is the game, which is dangerous and leads to falls. It is necessary

[1] J. J. Modi, *The Game of Ball-Bat among the Ancient Persians, as Described in the Epic of Firdousi*, in *The Journal of the Bombay Branch of the Royal Asiatic Society*, vol. XVIII, p. 39.

159   160

161   162

163   164

HOCKEY STICKS, from Artın Pacha's *Contribution à l'étude du blason en Orient*

for those who take part in it constantly to lean to one side, and to turn to the other side, so as to guide the horse to the ball, and they have to undergo all kinds of motions, in order to reach the ball."[1]

In Persia the game became very popular at court under the name of *chaugān*, which led to Arabic حوكان *ǵaukān* and صولجان *ṣaulǵān*, while the ball itself was known among the Arabs as كرة *kurah* or اكرة *'ukrah*. According to Mas'ūdi, Harūn al-Rašīd was the first khalif to play the game in a polo ground.[2] Neither Persian *goy* nor Arabic *kurah* has become the usual word for "ball" in those African countries outside of the Berber regions, but another Persian word. We have from a universal Indo-European root for "hot," Persian *tābah* "tile, brick." It is assumed that Persian *tāb* "curling" is from another root, but it is more likely that it evolved from the first. In any case the two meanings have become united in all the languages in which these Persian words have been borrowed. We have Arabic طاب *tāb* "ball, game at balls," طوب *tūb* "brick," طوف *tauf* "go around." The Tatar languages have the latter root *top* "around," but it is hard to ascertain whether this is borrowed from the Persian; in any case the Arabic root is not found in the other Semitic languages and, although already used in the Koran, is unquestionably a borrowing from the Persian.

In the Negro countries this root is very popular. We have Swahili *tufali* "a brick dried in the sun" and *tuffe* "ball (to play at tennis or cricket); the natives put a stone or sand into rags and sew them up or tie them as a ball." Here the relation of "brick" to

---

[1] *Corpus scriptorum historiae Byzantinae*, vol. XXV, p. 263 f.
[2] Quatremère, *op. cit.*, vol. I, part I, p. 121 ff.

"ball" is clear, since pieces of brick or round pieces of sunburnt clay were used in many of the games where a ball is generally employed. Similarly we have Hausa *tubali* "a ball or brick made of mùd." Hassania *tob* "brick" is found in Soninke and Bambara as *tufa*, but in Bambara we also have *kura* "round, anything round," and we are thus still under Arabic influence. Although we have no information as regards the Negro ball games, the vocabulary shows that the same rough games were known there as among the Berbers.

Polo, as recorded for Byzantium, was a seasonal game, coinciding with the beginning of spring and an exclusive prerogative of the emperors. Among the Arabs it was equally a royal pastime, though we have no reference to a seasonal celebration. Among the Berbers, where the spring festival, beginning in March, was generally confused with the Christian New Year, on the first of January, many of the celebrations refer equally to one season as to another. Among the Berbers the prerogative was transferred to the clergy, a prerogative which unquestionably also existed in Spain, purely from philological considerations. In Arabic we have, from the root *kūr*, مكوّر *mukawwir* "theologian, magistrate, man of law," because they alone in Spain and elsewhere were allowed to wear a *mikwar* "turban," but as this is from the root *kūr*, it may also mean "one who plays ball." As the beginning of the year was transferred from the first of March to the first of January, the playing of the ball was identified with the *ḥaǧūza* days, that is, with the time when *vetula* "the old woman" was part of the celebration.

The ball games were brought by the Arabs into Europe, where they became very popular and led to their introduction among the clergy and, in a rougher and simpler form, among all classes of people. In 1165

John Beleth, referring to the Church at Poitiers, told of "a certain December license which at this time is observed in certain places. There are certain churches in which it is customary that even bishops and archbishops in their monasteries play with their inferiors and give themselves up to the ball game, and this license is called the December license, because it was formerly a custom among the pagans for servants and shepherds to enjoy in that month the privilege of being equal to their masters and of celebrating common feasts after the harvest time. Although some large churches, such as that at Rheims, observe this custom of playing, it seems more worthy not to play."[1] The game is recorded in France as *choula* as early as 1152,[2] and later we find for it the names *soule, sole, choule, chaule, solce, cheole, soulette*, etc., and *ceoler, choler, soler* means "to play, kick the ball." At Berry it was generally played by the clergy and in the diocese of Bourges it took place on the holidays of Saint Ursula and St. John the Evangelist, that is, on December 27 and 29.[3]

The Arabic صولجان *şaulĝān* is also found in the abbreviated form صولج *şauliĝ, şūliĝ*, and from this is formed the root صلج *şalaĝa* "to beat, cudgel." This has led to the French forms *soule*, etc. But the Arabic جوكان *ĝokān* produced Portuguese *choca*, Spanish *chueca* "football, golf," which in its turn has led to French *choquer*, originally "to kick," then "to shock." But we have in French the fuller form for the game, namely *chicane*, which has similarly led to *chicane* "chicanery," from the rough and brutal way in which the game was played by the populace. We have also derivatives from the Arabic طاب *tāb*, namely French *taper* "to tap," etc.

[1] W. Mannhardt, *Wald- und Feldkulte*, Berlin 1904, vol. I, p. 477.
[2] Ducange, sub *houla*.
[3] H. F. Jaubert, *Glossaire du centre de la France*, Paris 1864, p. 623.

That the Romance words of this class are really derived from the polo game follows from Arabic طبطاب
tabtāb, طبطب tabtab "bat for tennis or polo," obviously
from طاب tābah "ball," hence Arabic طبطاب tabtāb also
means "to tap, knock lightly." In the Germanic
languages we have the earliest and most striking derivative from the "polo" words, for here Arabic صلح
ṣalaġa "to beat" produces Gothic and OHGerman
slahan "to beat." OHGerman slaga "hammer" shows
how "to beat" developed from "the polo bat." In
Anglo-Saxon, the word is not recorded in the Leyden
Glossary and but sparingly in the Corpus Glossary
with one meaning "collisio, bellicum," exactly as in
the French souler.

In Africa and in Europe the ball game became associated with the intercalary days and gained a semi-
religious significance. Precisely the same has taken
place in Mexico, where the names connected with the
game, derived from the Arabic, bear conclusive proof
of the African origin of Mexican culture. Torquemada
described the Mexican ball game as follows: "These
Indian tribes know the game of ball as we play it,
though they play it differently from us. The place
where it was played is called tlachco, which is like our
cricket ground. They used to make the ball from the
gum of a tree which grows in the hot lands and which,
when tapped, distills thick, white drops that very soon
congeal and being pressed and kneaded become blacker
than pitch. From this ulli they made their balls,
which, although heavy and hard to the touch, were
well adapted for the manner of their playing. They
were as resilient as air-filled balls, and better, too, since
they did not have to be blown, nor did they play to
stop it, but to win it, just as at the chueca, which is to

Abb 12   Historia Tolteca-Chichimeca, Sammlung Aubin-Goupil (Manuscrits mexicains
Nr 51—53 Text im Ms Nr 51—56)

MEXICAN BALLGROUND, from Seler's *Codex Borgia.*

kick it to the wall held by the adversary or to pass it overhead. They kicked the ball with the haunches or the buttocks, and not with any other part of the body, for every other stroke was foul. It was agreed by them that the game was lost by him who touched the ball with any other part of the body than the haunch, buttock, or shoulder, and this was done very gracefully by them, and, that the ball might more easily rebound, they bared themselves and wore only the *maxtlatl*, which was their loincloth, and put on a stiff piece of leather over their buttocks. They could make it rebound as they pleased, and it did rebound in rapid succession so as to appear like a living thing. They used to play two against two or three against three, and sometimes two against three; and in the chief *tlachcos* there played lords, princes, and great players, and, to celebrate their market days, especially the days of the fair, they went there to play, and they played for stakes, such as a bundle of mantles, more or less, according to the players' wealth, whether they were kings, cities, or municipalities. They also played for gold and feathers, and sometimes they put themselves up for stakes. This *tlachco* was in the very market square, but there were also others in other parts or wards. The playgrounds were built in such a way as to form a street of two heavy walls, narrower at the bottom than at the top, so that although the players were in the narrower part, the game widened out overhead. The greatest width of the space was twenty fathoms, and even less, and in some places these *tlachcos* were topped by very curious battlements. The walls were higher at the sides than at the ends. To play the more easily, they had them whitewashed and smooth, even as they fixed the floor. At the sides of the walls they placed certain stones, resembling millstones with their holes, in the middle of the grounds, whither the ball rarely reached; and he who put the ball through it won the game, and, as this was a rare victory, which only few attained, the mantles of all the onlookers belonged to him by an ancient custom, and it was considered a bit of fun, when the ball went through the hole in the stone, for the people to laugh and run off with their capes, while others deprived them of their mantles for the benefit of the victor; but he was obliged to make certain sacrifices to the idol of the playgrounds and the stone, through the hole of which he put the ball.

"Upon seeing this trick of putting the ball through, which to the spectators appeared a miracle, which it was perchance, they said and asserted that the winner must be a thief and adulterer, or that he would die soon, since he had had such a piece of luck; and the memory of this victory lasted for many days, until the next victory made them forget the first. Each playground was a temple, because they placed in it two images, one of the god of the game, the other of the god of the ball, above the two walls which were lower toward midnight (north?), on a day of good omen, with certain ceremonies and sorceries, and in the middle of the ground they made other similar ones, singing songs; then there came a priest from the chief temple, with certain ministers, to bless it (if this detestable superstition may be called blessing), and he spoke certain words; he threw the ball four times to begin the game, and with this they said that it was consecrated and they could play with it, and not before. This was done with much authority and attention, because they said that with it came the ease and peace of the heart. The master of the playground, who was always a lord, did not begin to play ball until he had carried out certain ceremonies and offered sacrifices to the idol of the game, from which it may be seen how superstitious they were, since even in matters of pastime they held such communion with their idols. Montezuma sometimes took the Spaniards to this game, because he considered it good. Lords and chiefs went from one town to another, and brought with them good players, to play against others, and they gave this game more attention than we do, and those who played better or won made fun of the others and said: 'Tell your women to hurry up the spinning, because you will need other mantles.' Others said: 'Go to such and such a fair to buy clothes,' and with this the spectators laughed. They served the ball, and if it was not good they would not accept it. Later, when it began to pass, those who threw it over the front wall or struck the wall, got a score against them; or if they struck with the ball against the adversary's body or played badly, that is, not with the haunches, they got a mark also, and the whole game consisted in these scores; and they did not drive the ball back. People made bets for one side or the other, and thus there were more stakes than in the principal of the game. Those who played either loudly or mentally called upon a demon who, they said, was of prominence in this game to help them. Of the good player who was successful in the game they said that his good fate or luck or sign under which he was born had helped him, while the loser's misfortune they ascribed to his bad sign."[1]

Seler has shown that the Mexican ballgrounds were generally placed strictly from north to south, which pointed to their relation with the vernal equinox, especially since the god *Tecatlipoca* is shown playing the game about the beginning of the New Year, which coincided with the vernal equinox.[2] On the other hand the twin god *Xolotl* is the regent of the seventeenth day sign, *olin*, which means "rubber, from which the

[1] J. de Torquemada, *De la monarquia indiana*, Madrid 1723, vol. II, lib. XIV, cap. 12.
[2] Seler, *Codex Borgia*, vol. I, p. 290.

ball is made." *Xolotl* is distinctly mentioned as the god of the ballgame.[1] It has already been shown that the god *Xolotl* is derived from the Arabic عشر *'ašara* in its various connotations. But the Arabic عشورى *'ašūra*, that is, the tenth day of the month of Muḥaram, which approximately coincides with the vernal equinox, is also used for the New Year, on which games are played, as already discussed at great length. We thus see that as *'ašūra* in northern Africa became identified with the carnival time during which the ballgame took place, so in America this *'ašūra* of necessity led to the identification of the god *Xolotl* with the ballgame, since *Xolotl* is philologically derived from the same root.[2]

Thus it is made clear that the ballgame in vogue throughout the regions visited by the early voyagers is of African origin. This can be further proven by the very vocabulary connected with this game. In Caraib, according to Breton, the gummy substance from which the ball was made and the ball itself are called *tibueli*. The same name is found in the Aztecan *tapayolli, tapa-yulli* "ball;" both are ultimately from Arabic طابه علك *tābah 'alek* "rubber ball." This *'alek* is found in the Mande languages as Mende *ḥole* "gum," Mandingo *folio*, Malinke *fole* "rubber, landolphia owayensis." In the West Indian islands the ball and the place where it is played is by the early writers given as *batey*, but this is not a native word, for Durand informs us that *batel* was the Spanish term for "rubber."[3] That the first part of the Nahuatl word is from Arabic *tābah*

---

[1] *Ibid.*, p. 193.

[2] See p. 279.

[3] "Llámase la materia de esta pelota *olin* lo cual en nuestro castellano he oido nombrar por este nombre *batel* lo cual es una resina de un árbol particular que cocida se hace como unos nierbos," D. Duran, *Historia de las Indias de Nueva España*, México 1880, vol. II, p. 244.

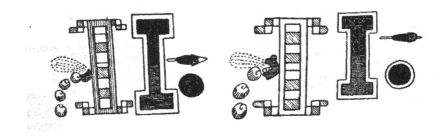

Abb. 3a. Die gekopfte Göttin, der Pulquegott.
Kautschukkugel, Spindel und Ballspielplatz.
Wiener Handschrift 22, 20, 13.

MEXICAN BALLGROUND from Seler's *Codex Borgia.*

follows from the fact that the same root in the compound *tapalcatl* means "brick, tile, potsherd," exactly as in Arabic. The name of the ball-ground and of the game itself is in Nahuatl *tlachtli*, where *tlach* represents the Germanic *slag*, for Arabic صلغ *şalaġa* "to beat, kick the ball." Coptic *čloi* "ball" indicates that the Arabic had not only a form صولج *şūlġ*, but also صلوج *şlūġ* or صلج *şlaġ* for the game. From this is derived Nahuatl *tlachtli* for "the ballgame." The ball grounds are represented in the picture writing by a long H-shaped space, in which the two stones containing the holes through which the ball has to pass are represented in the middle of the structure, but more frequently a spindle crossing the picture represents the millstone. This is due to the fact that the hole in the millstone is, like the spindle, called in Nahuatl *malacatl*, generally *temalacatl*, in which *te* means "stone." The strange relation between "spindle" and "hole" is at once made clear from the Arabic words from which the two are derived. Arabic مسلك *maslak* means "a breach, a place of passage," from سلك *salaka* "he inserted (a thread in the eye of a needle)," while مسلكة *mislakah is* "a reel upon which thread is wound," so that the two words from the same root lead both to "hole" and "spindle."

The technical term for sending the ball through the aperture seems to have been in Nahuatl *petla*, for this verb means "to throw oneself through the ranks of the enemy, make a breach," while *petlaua* is "to take away the clothes," which is the forfeit the spectators had to pay to the winning party. But the same root has some other, totally different connotations. Thus *petlani* means "to shine," *petlania* "to make an object shine," and *petlatl* is "the mat" on which the Indians sat and slept. It would seem impossible to connect these meanings, which, however, are found side by side in the Mande languages. There is a universal Semitic root *fitil* "wick, cord." We have Assyrian *pitiltu* "cord, loop," Hebrew פָּתִל *pāṭil* "cord," which leads to Arabic فتيلة *faṭilah* "wick." But we have also Egyptian *petr* "cord, thread, wick of a lamp." In north-east Africa, in Soho, we have *fatal* "to plait, weave." In the Sudanese languages the word is universally in use. Hausa has *fatilla*, *fitilla* "lamp" and Songay has *fitila* "lamp" and *fitina*, which has nothing to do with this word and is from Arabic فتن *faṭn*, with the meaning "war, rebellion." In Bambara the two have become confused, and *fitne* means "lamp, war, rebellion." The meaning "to weave," found in Soho, is very old, for we have, outside of the Semitic languages, Persian *patil* "mat " In Nahuatl we have both "mat," and the same confusion as in Bambara, namely *petla* "to make a warlike onrush" and *petlaua* "to shine," from the meaning "lamp." The Nahuatl *petla* produced Kiche *petel* "spindle," which is found in most of the Maya languages. We have Kekchi *petet*, Pokonchi *pitejt*, Maya *pechech* "spindle," but in Maya we also have *pechatah* "to crush with the feet," *pech'* "crushed, oppressed, flattened," *pet* "circle," *petelpet* "flat, round things," hence *peten* "island." This idea of a flat round thing in Maya is apparently derived from the flat round stone, through the hole of which the ball had to pass. In any case, already Arabic فتل *fiṭila* means "to turn in a circle."

The resemblance of the American ball game to the African, its semi-religious significance in both continents, its celebration during the vernal equinox or at the beginning of the New Year, whether it fell in March or January, the identity of the nomenclature connected with the game, in Mexico and in Africa, preclude all chance development: the African civilization was not transferred to America piecemeal but as an organic whole.

CHAPTER XIV

CONCLUSIONS.[1]

1. It is yet too early to write the history of the advance of civilization from its incipiency to the present time. We do not possess sufficient data to assert whether the trend of civilization was from east to west or from west to east, but within historic times it appears that most cultural influences proceeded from east to west, from a central region in Asia towards Egypt and Europe. While some such influences began very early in the dimness of time, other benefits of civilization proceeded with extraordinary slowness, not merely centuries, but whole millenniums being consumed in the establishment of practices essential to the life of the eastern nations. It is useless to expatiate on such differences,—we can only ascertain the facts. Thus cotton, known to Assyria and India long before the VII. century, imported into Egypt and, possibly, into Greece before the beginning of the Christian era, never roused the peoples that received the valuable products by commerce to introduce the plant at home. Iron, which the European nations knew since earliest times, remained a rare article along the Nile, and the best steel, long in use in India and China, and imported into Rome together with the eastern products, was almost totally unknown to the metallurgists along the Mediterranean until the arrival of the Arabs. (II. 2–32, III. 1–18.)

2. The Arabs had unquestionably been acquainted with the use of cotton before their westward move-

[1] The references are to the volumes and pages of this work.

ment, but the fact that one of the names for "cotton" is derived from an Egyptian, or, rather, Coptic word for "religious purification" indicates that the Egyptian treatment of the dead, which must have descended in substance to the Copts, determined an intensive use of this material in the religious observances of the Arabs, and the extensive distribution of this "purification" word for "cotton" through the northern part of Africa shows that it was chiefly its ritualistic use which led to the cultivation of cotton throughout the Sudan region. Wherever the "purification" word was not adopted, as in the Mande languages, it shows once more that the Sudan owes the cultivation of cotton for industrial purposes to the Arabs. The cotton plant was chiefly not native to Africa, for not a single reference to it or representation of it on Egyptian monuments has been discovered. (II. 18–22.)

3. It is possible that the Bantu peoples knew the use of iron even in antiquity, but of this no proof exists. The new impetus to the iron industry in Africa was given by the Arabs, who popularized the Hindu and Chinese methods of hard steel manufacture in the west. The ancient alchemy, which was concerned with the production of mineral compounds and metallic objects for industrial purposes, did not advance much, if any, beyond the traditions established for ages by the metal-workers of Egypt and Greece. The Arabs, in inheriting the science, enriched it at once by new processes observed in their wide commercial ventures in the Indian seas and in China. The result of this semi-scientific interest of the Arabs may be observed in the extremely large number of alchemistic expressions and concepts which have entered into the languages of Europe. The effect of this activity, to a lesser extent, is seen in Africa in the greater use of iron among the Sudanic tribes in the Middle Ages. (III.1–53.)

4. The most remarkable westward movement of civilization may be observed in the enormous extension of shell-money. Known to China and India in the dimmest antiquity, but almost entirely unknown to Europe and western continental Asia, the cowrie industry and trade, bearing in the vocabulary the direct evidence of its Arabic initiative, in the Middle Ages reaches the shores of Guinea, is recorded in the Malli kingdom, and takes a firm footing off the shores of Angola. The direct relation of the African cowrie currency to its Asiatic prototype is unmistakable. The ancient Chinese and Hindu double standard of white and blue cowries dominates the African trade at Angola and in Guinea, and leads to the predominance of the blue currency, hence to the adulteration of shell-money by Chinese and Venetian glass-blowers, who thus establish the unprecedented popularity of blue beads and aggries in the Sudan. (II. 203–248.)

5. We possess no satisfactory account of the trade routes that converged at the bend of the Niger River, though we have much indirect evidence, especially in the vocabularies of the Sudanic peoples, to show the probable caravan routes over which the gold mines lying between the Mande and the Asante nations and the pepper-bearing regions were reached since Arabic occupation of the northern part of Africa. The same routes which the Hausas still use in their trading expeditions from Egypt and Tripoli were traveled over by the Arab merchants and their Negro servants in ancient times. The Berber element in the Mande languages is of the Zenaga type in the extreme west of Africa, whence it appears that either land routes or sea lanes hugged the shore about Cape Bajador. But the most intimate intercourse lay from the Magreb, that is, from Morocco and Algiers, over the Sahara and the Arabic oases and settlements in the neighbor-

hood of Lake Chad. The very considerable linguistic element of the Hassania Arabic in most of the languages of the Western Sudan is proof of the close relationship between the Magreb Arabs and the peoples of the Niger plateau. (II. & III., *Philology*, in *Word Index*.)

6. Since the foundation of the Gana state in the VII. or VIII. century until modern times several more or less powerful states arose in the Western Sudan, the Malli, Songay, Soso, Peul, Benin, Asante, Hausa kingdoms, some of them giving evidence of considerable cultural ability, though seldom rising above a bloody autocracy. The information we have about their histories is scanty in the extreme, but certain facts stand out prominently enough to admit of historical deductions. In the first half of the VII. century the Hindu Zotts, who had for some time lived in Persia as musicians, received certain privileges from the Arabs for their acceptance of Islam, and with their buffalo herds began a westward movement through Africa, ultimately reaching the bend of the Niger, where they settled, and, in all probability, formed the substratum of the lighter-colored Negroized Peuls of later times. They brought with them the combined Hindu and Syrian traditions of civilization, and introduced the agricultural habits, for which the Peuls are known even to-day. (III. 111.)

7. In the midst of these Zotts were the blacksmithing Hindu Gypsies, who moved westward with them, and from Egypt, in the middle of the VII. century, began their penetration of Europe and of Africa. Being nomads, blacksmiths, and cheats, they typified the Biblical descendants of Tubal Cain and of the Egyptians, upon whom was a curse that made of them "slaves of slaves," neither servants nor again free men. It is not unlikely that the Hindu low caste which they represented had something to do with the formation

of the low caste pariahs, as which they appear throughout northern Africa. Thus we have the anomaly that,
although the blacksmiths were respected for their
craft, they were in the contemptible class politically,
and Sudanic society developed, side by side with the
native free man and the slave, also the caste of the
griots, the Gypsies without a political and social
status, without privileges and without duties, hence
more nearly akin to the free men than to the slaves,
and frequently as wealthy and as powerful as the
upper class. (III. 78–100.)

8. The pariah condition of the griots is, if not
originally, yet preëminently the result of Arabic legislation. According to Islamic law not only were
criminals dealt with severely, but individuals and
classes that were likely to develop criminal tendencies
were visited with premonitory punishments. The
name of the griots in the Sudan, more especially among
the Mandingos, not only means "cheat, musician,"
but also "tarred," unquestionably from the punishment meted out to the Gypsies. But "tarring and
feathering," mentioned by Richard Coeur de Lion,
clearly as an eastern method of punishment, explains
the method of pasting feathers about the head and
appearing with a bird mask, adopted by the griots as
their distinctive mark, as which the bard and dancer
before the king of Malli is by Ibn-Batutah described
in the middle of the XIV. century. The griots are the
preservers of the ceremonial and religious dance, the
bards and parasites at court, the fortune-tellers and
medical quacks, the executors of Islamic rites, the
blacksmiths and metal-workers, in short everything
that characterizes them as Gypsies. It is not impossible that some of the fetishistic practices, not
definitely derived from Arabic sources, are, through
the griots, of Hindu origin. In any case, the griots

are the mediators, if not the originators and priests, of what is known as Sudanic fetishism. (III. 100–107, 213–217.)

9. Many cultural influences were carried by the Arabic merchant, the *targumān*, the interpreter who penetrated the interior, not only along the northern trade routes, but also from Zanzibar and Moçambique. Unfortunately we have no records of the early activities of these merchants, but from the XVI. century references to the *tangomãos, tangomanes*, as which they were known to the Portuguese and Spaniards, it appears that they were composed of all kinds of western Europeans, renegades and outlaws, who infested the mouths of Guinea rivers, became thoroughly Negroized in their manner of life, surrounded themselves with black wives, often ascended a throne, and carried on extensive commercial enterprises in the interior, with the aid of Negro trusties and couriers. Their cultural influence upon their retinues and customers was always considerable. Being unable to trade with Europe, except as smugglers and traitors, they extended their operations to the western islands, whatever these may have been. They were chiefly instrumental in obtaining slaves, gold, ivory, in exchange for a few European articles, such as beads and iron staves, and transferring native articles from the interior to the islands of the west. (III. 99–113.)

10. More important, on account of their constant and intimate relation to the Sudanese people, were the religious teachers and fakirs, the *Marabuts*, who found their way from the Islamic countries and developed their fanatical activities among a wonder-loving and ignorant people. Timbuktu and other cities on the Niger and in Guinea attracted Moslem teachers and saints, who developed their activities, undisturbed by factional disputes and persecutions. They brought

with them the undercurrent of the Islamic religion, as tainted by gnosticism in Egypt and in the Berber countries. With this they frequently combined that art of the physician, where the physician's realm encroached upon that of the religious teacher, through the health-giving amulet. This activity of the *Marabut* was still more direct in those cases where the Negroes formally became Mohammedans, but even the heathen Bambaras were strongly affected by the Moslem saints and teachers, although they did not subscribe to the precepts of the Islamic faith as such. (III. 130, 144–150, 163–179.)

11. The chief phylactery of the *Marabut* was the piece of paper or leather with some Koranic verses and apocryphal injunctions written upon it, hence the case in which the amulet was placed, the paper or leather itself, the ink with which the verses were written became "medicine" and "religion." This led to an enormous multiplication of fetishes in the sense of "amulets" and "phylacteries." The names of most of these in the Sudan are of Arabic origin. The most important amulets were those which had mystic words, the names of the constellations, the guardian angels, astrological and astronomical speculations written in squares variously constructed and known as *ǧaḍwals*. (I. 107–110, III. 268–280.)

12. The medical practices introduced by the *Marabut* were confined to the simple remedies that had become the stock in trade of the itinerant quack, such as cupping and cure of colds, toothache, distempers, etc. by fumigation, but in all such cases the medical practice became inseparable from the magical amulets, and the whole assumed a religious, fetishistic aspect. The cupping is simplified to suction with the lips, the magician claiming supernatural powers and surreptitiously introducing an object into his mouth, which he

claims to be the cause of the trouble. The fumigation may be external or, as in Gracco-Arabic medicine, may be taken through a pipe into the mouth, in which case the *tabbaq*, the styptic, glutinous substance used in such fumigations, reduces itself to the particular glutinous plant of Africa adapted for styptic purposes, the *Nicotiana tabacum* and *rustica*, the sovereign remedy *par excellence*. In those cases where the Arabic quack meets the European quack, the European name *bitumen*, equally used for such a substance, may prevail, but such is not the case in the Sudan. (II. 85–134.)

13. The vast amount of fetishistic beliefs which the *Marabut* has helped to spread through the Sudan may be roughly classified into two divisions, one being the direct result of Islamic teachings and practices, the second being an undigested mass of gnostic ideas, some of them of pre-Arabic, Berber or Egyptian provenience, some of them possibly of Negro origin, but all of them incorporated into the gnostic observances of African Moslems, and frequently resting on nothing more than philological calculations. The limits between the two are ephemeral, and the whole mass of fetishism is eclectic and syncretic, varying not only from nation to nation, but frequently also within the linguistic group from village to village. Through all the maze of conflicting and disjointed cosmogonic or folkloristic stories which refer to the Sudanic fetishism the fundamental concepts, all of them of Arabic origin, remain undimmed through the ages and aid us in bringing order out of chaos and rearranging the religious motifs into orderly Islamic sequences. (III. 116 ff., *et passim*.)

14. The chief Sudanic religious concept, which underlies a vast number of specific fetish worships as well as the larger worship of the invisible god or gods, is based

on the evolution of the Islamic Allah in the Sudan. From the start he is confused with the heavens, the sky, where he is naturally placed in Moslem thought. Hence the Arabic words for "sky," that are more tangible to the untutored mind, have everywhere taken the place of the invisible Allah. Arabic *ǧannāh* "paradise, the abode of recompense" on the one hand leads to the identification of God with heaven, and on the other leads to the identification with *ǧān* "the serpent." Throughout the Sudan, in Timne, Mande, Yoruba, Nupe, Bornu, Songay, Hausa, *ǧannāh* or *al-ǧannāh* forms the word for "heaven, sky," and in Yoruba a derivative from this means "God." (III. 172–174.)

15. In the Mande languages Arabic *samā* "heaven," *suman* "rain" leads to the "heaven, rain, year, season" words, which in Malinke and Bambara are apocopated to *san, sã, sa,* and the latter also meaning "serpent," *sa* "the serpent" also became the equivalent of Allah. But in the Mande languages *s* and *k* are interchangeable, wherefore we also find the forms *kā, kan, kali* for "serpent, above," which through Wolof *dyan* are clearly derived from Arabic *ǧannāh* "paradise," *ǧān* "serpent." But here a confusion has arisen with another Arabic word for "hoe," hence in Malinke and Bambara we have also *ka, kan, kana* "he cut with a sickle." Thus we have here also a confusion of "heaven" with "serpent" and "hoe." The relation of the whole group of these words to the same "paradise" words in the previous paragraph is made clear from the Asante language, where the words derived from the same Arabic *samā*, *suman* lead to the concept of the "abode of the blessed, abode of the departed spirits, spirit." (III. 174–177.)

16. The untutored Negroes stood in greater awe of the evil spirits of the Islamic mythology than of the beneficent *ǧinn*, hence the Arabic *ḥabbal* "a malicious

ǵinn, Satan" has led to the legion of the Sudanic *boli* or *bori*, the chief elements of the northern fetishism. Just as the Arabic *habbal* is connected with the idea of obsession, so the African *boli* is closely associated with obsession and epilepsy, and leads to practices generally connected with these, such as mad dances and delirious prophetic utterances. The *boli* becomes the essence of fetishism and is identified with "amulet" and "medicine," hence the *bolitigi* "the master of the *boli*" assumes the role of priest and doctor, and occupies an important place in the religious conceptions of the Sudanese peoples. (III. 142–162.)

17. To the Negroes the Moslem preacher was just such a superior person who lived on a familiar footing with the world of spirits and possessed all the knowledge of amulets and "medicine," hence the Arabic *qurra*' "holy man, devotee," *qara*' "to recite the Koran" have led in Africa to an enormous mass of words signifying "reading, sooth-saying, call upon a fetish," and "the master of the *boli*" also becomes "the possessor of the *kara*," which may be wisdom or "medicine," or a spirit, a ghost. With many of the nations such a person is distinctly connected with the Moslem religion, as in Asante *Krāmo* "Mohammedan," Peul *karamoko* "reader of the Koran." (III. 163–166, 190–193.)

18. A "naive Moslem theology," influenced, no doubt, by Christian ideas, is responsible in the Sudan for the invisible triune divinity, consisting of the male, fecundating principle, representing the Sun or Heaven, the female, generating principle, identified with the earth, and their eldest child, variously conceived. There seems to be in this an Arabic astrological speculation, as preserved in a Mossi tradition, that the invisible god had to restrain the sun from burning up the world by shutting it up at night and placing it in charge of nine of his children. (III. 293–296.)

19. Similar astrological considerations, as applied to the calendar, have preserved in northern Africa the divisions of the solar year, according to which the 360 days are followed by five "useless" days, while the Arabic lunar mansions have led among the Berbers to the 28 zodiacal periods of 13 days each, whereas in western Africa we find the matter reversed, the zodiac being divided into 13 parts, obviously of 28 days each. (III. 270 f., 326–331.)

20. The New Year generally began in March, and its celebration was confused with that of the vernal equinox, which comes two weeks later. Thus the tenth day of the month of Muharam, the Arabic ʿašūra, was identified among the Berbers and elsewhere in northern Africa with the New Year, and the ball game or polo, formerly played by Persian kings in the beginning of spring, gained religious significance in Africa, as it did in Europe. The Berber name of the ball, tašurt, from this same ʿašūra, shows that it was intimately connected with the Arabic word, which, from its connotations "companion, pot," must have led to a number of speculations upon these terms. (III. 279 280, 286–293, 334–344.)

21. Similar speculations upon similar connotations of the same root referring to a mythological concept, and a confusion of similar roots referring to religious ideas have led in the Sudan to fetishistic worships. Thus, from the Arabic terms duwaʿ "a species of owl, the handsomest bird of all" and duʿaʾ "blessing, crying for aid or succor" arises the Mandingo duga, which combines both connotations, and leads to their "redoubtable bird of omen " (III. 315 f.)

22. Far more interesting is the double confusion of Arabic nabī "prophet" with ʾamān "faith," and the latter with ʿāmir "hyena," from which arises the famous Sudanic Naba-Nama worship, where the fetish is

identified with an old hyena, and the *Namatigi*, the master of the *Nama*, among the Mandingos is considered to be the chief sorcerer, the holder of wisdom. (III. 160–162, 249–252.)

23. It is not always possible to get at the Arabic prototype of a particular worship among the Mandingos, as we possess but fragments of the original beliefs, but in some cases there seems to be a substratum of Arabic medicine that has led to fetishistic worships. Such is, no doubt, the case with Mandingo *ñaña* "the itch, or syphilis," possibly from Arabic *nagila* "the itch," and the related Bambara *manyan* "the itch," "a fetish whose pyramidal altar, in Hausa called *dakali*, may be seen near the villages." (III. 285 f.)

24. It is similarly difficult to trace the precise origin of the *dasiri* worship, which consists in sacrifices under a tree, upon which the *dasiri* stays, and beneath which is placed a bowl to receive the libations; nor can we locate the origin of the connection of the long-beaked Nama with bee-culture, though we may surmise that in the latter case we have, as in the case of the syphilis god, a faint medical recollection, honey having been considered in the Koran as a sovereign remedy. (III. 146–150, 252, 264.)

25. A very powerful Arabic influence in the Sudan was exerted by the astrological *ǵaḍwal*, a phylactery, in which the encysted graphic signs written in columns do not represent phonetic elements, but are intended for astrological sentences of augury, arising from the casting of sticks in geomancy. Such signs may be seen in the rock inscriptions photographed by Desplagnes. The signs themselves have distinct names and in the Sudan the leading ones among them have come to mean "tale, story." From the connotations "to chant the Koran" and "spider," for the root *raṭlah*, has similarly arisen Bambara *n'tale* "story, spider,"

and this has led throughout the Sudan to a mythical valuation of the spider in Negro stories and beliefs. (III. 271–278.)

26. Many fetishistic practices are derived from Sufi associations, since Sufi sectarians were entrenched at Timbuktu and elsewhere in the Sudan. To this influence may be ascribed the African ecstatic dances and self-castigation, which form an important part of Sudanic secret celebrations and initiations. At the same time the secret organizations bear evidence of being fashioned in the manner of the Moslem brotherhoods. (III. 163–179.)

27. Outside the religious influences, the Arabs exerted also powerful influences in the political and social orders of the Sudanic states. In the political order we find the name of the kingly power, *mansa*, derived from the Arabic *manša*, while the royal dignity found its outward expression in the Arabic stool, the Arabic *ṭaḫt*, *ṭuḫuṭ*, best preserved in the Asante *dufŭā*, Soninke *takhade*. The Arabic conical hat, *qub'* and *gifārah*, associated with the Magi, is at the base of all the "hat" names in the Sudan, and, apparently, was originally restricted to the kingly power. The priestly power, with which the conical hat was originally associated, received for its insignia the Arabic *mitraqah*, the rattle, which, through a homonym which in Arabic means "gourd" and "religious wisdom," was made from a gourd. (III. 192 f., 218 f., 318–321.)

28. Among the Bambaras the Arabic *nišan*, the distinction of nobility or the king, became as *n'tene* a mere totemic sign for a family or tribe. The Mandingos preserved the Arabic social distinction of free men and slaves, to which were added "the slaves of slaves," the griots, whose chief occupation was music. Though the Mandingos did not adopt the Arabic habiliments, those that they wore bore names derived

from the Arabic *šimlah*, *mai'zar*, *gifārah*, *lagām*, *lābis*, *bandārīah*, *kisa'*. (III. 219–221, 230–239, 318–321.)

29. The presence of Negroes with their trading masters in America before Columbus is proved by the representation of Negroes in American sculpture and design, by the occurrence of a black nation at Darien early in the XVI. century, but more specifically by Columbus' emphatic reference to Negro traders from Guinea, who trafficked in a gold alloy, *guanin*, of precisely the same composition and bearing the same name, as frequently referred to by early writers in Africa. (I. 33 f., 174 f., 159–161, II. 116–119, 262 f., 265–270.)

30. There were several foci from which the Negro traders spread in the two Americas. The eastern part of South America, where the Caraibs are mentioned, seems to have been reached by them from the West Indies. Another stream, possibly from the same focus, radiated to the north along roads marked by the presence of mounds, and reached as far as Canada. The chief cultural influence was exerted by a Negro colony in Mexico, most likely from Teotihuacan and Tuxtla, who may have been instrumental in establishing the city of Mexico. From here their influence pervaded the neighboring tribes, and ultimately, directly or indirectly, reached Peru.

31. That the Negro civilization was carried chiefly by the trader is proved not only by Columbus' specific reference, but also by the presence of the African merchant, the *tangoman*, as *tiangizman* in Mexico, hence Aztec *tiangiz* "market," and by the universality of the blue and white shell-money from Canada to La Plata, and the use of shells as a coin in the Peru-Guatemala trade. The exceptional position of the merchants in Mexico, with the chief worships directly attributed to them, similarly testifies to the importance of the trader in the

pre-Columbian, Africa-America relations. (II. 249 270, III. 230 f., 239–245, 259 f.)

32. The African penetration in religion and civic life and customs was thorough and, to judge from the survival of the Arabic words in a Malinke or Soninke form in America, especially among the Caraibs and Aztecs, proceeded almost exclusively from the Mandingos, either the ancestors of the present Malinkes, or a tribe in which the Soninke language had not yet completely separated from its Malinke affinities.

33. In Mexico we have the same confusion of "god," "rain," and "serpent" as among the Mandes, and the same root *coa* in Aztec, *can* in Maya-Kiche, as in the Mande, leads to a confusion of the three concepts in Aztec, where *coa* has also the meaning "sickle," as in Mande. (III. 307–314.)

34. Just as in Mande, so throughout America, the Arabic *ḥabal*, in forms derived from Mande *boli*, represents the idea of spirit or anything related to religion or medicine. In America, too, the *bolitigi*, the master of the *boli*, appears as *boratio* and a large number of forms linguistically derived from this, with the identical powers as in Africa and wielding the gourd rattle, the *mitraqah*, in Tupi and other South-American languages denominated *maraca*. The Mande *tigi* in the sense of "master" is also separately represented in many American languages and in the appellation *cacique*, formed by the early voyagers. (III. 158, 222–227, 228–230.)

35. The Asante *kara* "religious wisdom," Asante *Krãmo* "Mohammedan" were similarly applied in South America and the West Indies to the fetishist, leading to the Tupi *carai, caraiba* "the foreign sorcerer," by Columbus, through an identification with Cambalu, in China changed to *canibal*, and applied to the race, which apparently practised religious canni-

balism, as in some regions of the Sudan, and where the African rites seem to have taken firm root. (III. 180–198, 218–221.)

36. As in the Sudan, we have in Mexico the concept of the male and female divinity, forming with their descendant a kind of trinity, and designated, as in the Sudan, the "old" divinities. The detailed resemblance of the two trinities is shown in the case of the identification of the male principle with the sun, which, in the Mexican belief, as among the Mossi in the Sudan, is restrained by the nine guardians of the night. (III. 296–302.)

37. Similar astrological considerations, derived from the Arabic source, have led in Mexico to a calendar year, as in Africa, of thirteen months of twenty-eight days each or twenty-eight months of thirteen days each. But just as in Africa the old Coptic calendar of 360 days has survived, so in Mexico the year of 360 days is followed by the same "useless" days as in the Coptic and Berber calendar. (III. 270 f., 333 f., 344–351.)

38. Just as the Arabic ʿašūra was in Africa identified with the New Year, which began in March, and was celebrated by ball games, so the Mexican *Xolotl*, philologically derived from ʿašūra, was identified with the New Year and the ball game, which assumed a religious significance. The same philological speculations as in Arabic led to the identification of *Xolotl* with twins and as boiling in a pot. The ball game itself in Mexico uses the same terms for the grounds in which it was played, and the ball with which it was played, as in Africa. (III. 279–286, 344–351.)

39. The African bird of omen, from the Arabic *ḍuwaʿ* "a species of owl, the handsomest bird of all," led to Aztec *uactli* from *touactli*, for which we find the popularized *toluactli* "the Mexican bird of omen," but we also have for the owl *tecolotl*, Mayan *tunculuchu*,

from Malinke *duga*. The feathers of the handsomest
bird are in Mexican called *quetzalli*, related to a Sudanic "owl" word, and the relation of the *quetzalli* to
the Sudanic owl is seen in the fact that the region
where the feathers are found is called "Owl-land."
(III. 314–316.)

40. The Sudanic confusion of "prophet," "faith,"
and "hyena" is found over a large territory in America
where the Arabic *nabī* lies at the foundation of "Nagual" words, while *'amān* "faith" produces, parallel
to the Sudanic *Namatigi*, the Aztec *amanteca*, Kechua
amauta, Caraib *omeoto*, the wise man *par excellence*.
The confusion with the hyena, which in Mande leads
to *namakoro* "the old hyena," leads in Mexico to
Ueuecoyotl "the old coyote" and *Coyotlinaualli* "the
coyote wizard," where we once more have the Arabic
nabī. (III. 241–255, 296.)

41. The Mandingo "itch" or "syphilis," *ñaña*, and
Bambara *manyan* "a fetish whose pyramidal altar
may be seen near the villages" leads in Mexico to the
god of syphilis, *Nanauatzin*, to whom a pyramidal
altar, called *tzaqualli*, was erected, and this *tzaqualli*
is identical with Hausa *dakali* "a pagan altar." (III.
280–286.)

42. The Mexican picture-writing resembles the rock
inscriptions in the Sudan, which are unquestionably
of *ġadwal* astrological origin. The importance of the
spider in connection with such *ġadwals* in Africa, which
is of universal significance in the Sudan, appears in a
large number of Mound-builder gorgets in America
with the *ġadwal* cross in the middle. (III. 263–267,
273 f.)

43. The Sufi element of the ecstatic dance and self-
castigation are important elements of many American
religious ceremonials, and the name for the dance and

the refrains of the songs accompanying it are identical with those in Africa. (III. 199–212.)

44. The external representation of the royal dignity by means of a stool, generally of one piece of wood, called in the Sudan by its Arabic name *taht, tuhut*, was found among the Caraibs with the identical name, *duho*. The conical hat, representing royalty or high dignity in Mexico, among the Huastecans, and elsewhere, and in Aztec known as *copilli*, is linguistically identical with the "hat" words in Africa derived from Arabic *gifārah, gufārah*. (III. 218 f., 321 f.)

45. The Mande totemic *n'tene*, originally a sign of distinction, is preserved in Caraib *nitaino* "man of distinction," and the Sudanic identification of the griot with the musician has led in Mexico to an identity of name for "slave" and "musician." The Arabic designations of wearing-apparel are preserved in Mexico for the identical garments as in the Sudan. The *šimlah* appears here as *chimalli* and *tilmatli*, the *mai'zar* as *maxtli*, the *gifārah* as *copilli*, the *lābis* as *tlauiztli*, the *bandārīah* as *pantli*, the *kisa'* as *quachtli*, and the *logam* is found among the Caraibs as *nagua*. (III. 220 f., 230–239, 318–322.)

46. The identity of the spiritual civilizations, down to minutest details in the Sudan and in Mexico and elsewhere in America, leads to the assumption that other cultural elements, identical in both continents and frequently bearing the same names, are of African origin. This is preëminently the case with cotton, which in Africa has a religious purification significance, and the presence of which in America before Columbus outside of its religious use in connection with burials cannot be proved from documentary evidence. (II. 1–82.)

47. The great resemblance of agricultural methods in America to those in Africa leads to the conclusion

that tobacco and the bread roots of America, some of which are conceded by the early writers to be of African origin, owe their origin to the advanced Arabic agriculture, which may be traced in the Sudan, to judge from philological considerations. (I. 102–268, II. 83–200.)

48. A thorough investigation of the archaeological remains in the Western Sudan, coupled with a further painstaking philological study of the Arabic influences in Africa, may reveal other African elements that are the prototypes of similar conditions in the civilization of America.

WORD INDEX

'aṯr, Arabic, 11 f.
aveugle, French, 20.
awsin, Kurd, 10.
ἀξίνη, Greek, 10.
āya, Kannada, 4.
ayas, Sanskrit, 4.
ayi, Asante, 209.
ayō, Avestan, 4.
ayya, Kannada, 3.
'aza'r, Arabic, 78.
'aẓmaʾ, Arabic, 170.

bàa-en-pet, Egyptian, 7.
babara, Sumerian, 17.
bairhtjan, Gothic, 23.
bairhts, Gothic, 23.
bakal, Tagalog, 8.
balamo, Gypsy, 68.
balamu, Gypsy, 68.
balant, Arabic, 19.
balaqu, Assyrian, 34.
balaur, Arabic, 19.
balīm, Syriac, 68.
balluca, Latin, 34.
baluce, Latin, 34.
balūqah, Arabic, 34.
balur, Arabic, 19.
banḍ, Persian, 238.
banḍārīyah, Arabic, 238.
βάνδον, Greek, 238.
bankarey, Songay, 238.
bante, Hausa, 238.
bar, Sumerian, 6.
bara', Arabic, 172.
bara, Songay, 230.
băra, Asante, 171.
baraka, Berber, 332.
barand, Persian, 25.
baranḍ, Arabic, 25.
bāraq, Hebrew, 23.
baraqa, Arabic, 23.
barika, Bambara, 332.
barka, Bambara, 332.
barot, Coptic, 21.
bărqḍ, Syriac, 24.
barqṭā, Talmudic, 24.
barr, Arabic, 172.
barzĕl, Hebrew, 7.
basĕi, Čam, 7.
basnet, Coptic, 10.
batel, Spanish, 348.
batey, Taino, 348.
behique, Cuba, 226.

bĕl, Coptic, 65.
bele, Fernandian, 134.
bĕlīm, Hebrew, 68.
beorht, ASaxon, 23.
beornan, ASaxon, 26.
bere, Vei, 233.
beredž, Persian, 21.
beremo, Vei, 234.
berhta, OHGerman, 22.
bert, Ethiopic, 21.
besi, Malay, 7.
besnat, Coptic, 10.
bhraç, Sanskrit, 23.
bibrantia, LLatin, 24.
bieri, Fan, 158.
bieti, Fan, 158.
bila, Malinke, 172, 233.
bilānā, Hindustani, 65.
bilanó, Gypsy, 65.
bilaňov, Gypsy, 65.
bilaṭi, Syriac, 21.
biri, Bambara, 235.
birindž, Persian, 21.
birr, Arabic, 172.
biti, Malinke, 235.
bilīnkā, Malinke, 235.
bitta, Mandingo, 235.
bjartr, ONorse, 23.
bla, Bambara, 172, 233.
blam, Syriac, 68.
blind, German, 21.
blm, Hebrew, 68.
blns, Arabic, 18.
blnz, Arabic, 18.
boa, Mandingo, 159.
boatio, Mandingo, 159.
bo džeň, Akra, 174.
bohique, Taino, 226.
bohuti, Taino, 223.
bōl, Coptic, 65.
boli, Bambara, 142.
boratio, Venezuela, 223.
bori, Hausa, 154.
borom alale, Wolof, 230.
borome, Wolof, 230.
boviti, Taino, 223.
boye, Caraib, 226.
bra, Asante, 171.
bractea, Latin, 23.
brand, ASaxon, 25.
brandeum, LLatin, 24.
brandir, OFrench, 25.
brandisium, LLatin, 22.
brando, LLatin, 24.

SUBJECT INDEX

Abyssinia, gypsies in, 95 f.

Africa, its fetishism chiefly of Arabic origin, 131.

AFRICAN FETISHISM AND TOTEMISM, 116-141.

'Aǧūz of the Arabs, and the "old woman," 325 ff.; among the Berbers, 326 ff.

Akra "spirit" words, and Arabic *qara'*, 164; and Arabic "amulet," 177 f.

Alchemy, and the seven metals, 18; and the Arabs, 40.

Altar, three-pointed, of the Habbes triune god, 295 f.

Amanteca, confusion of the mythical, with the artisans, 245 f.

Amantecatl, history of the word, 241 f.

Amauta, Peruvian, the *amantecatl* of the Mexicans, 241.

Amulet words, African, from the Arabic, 129 ff.

Ancestor worship in Africa and the bori, 159.

Arabs, their metallurgy in Europe, 40; their words for "gypsy," 78 ff.; gypsies among the, 85 ff.; their week among the Mandingos, 127; their "amulet" words in Africa, 129 ff.; their "medicine" words in Bantu, 131 ff.; Arabic "tree" as foundation for African "medicine" words, 133 ff.; their medicine and African fetishism, 136; their blazonry in Africa, 141; their *ṣadaqah* and Bambara sacrifice, 145; their "religion" and Malinke *nama*, 160; their "reading" and Sudanic fetishism, 163 f.; their festivals among the Asantes, 168 f.; their "heaven" and Sudanic "spirit" words, 175 ff.; their "amulet" and Sudanic "spirit" words, 178 f.; Arabic *qara'* in America as *Caraib*, 190 ff.; Arabic *'istiḥārah*, and imprecation in Africa and America,

196 ff.; and interpretation of dreams, 197; their sword play and African gun firing, 206; their *šaiḫ* in America, 228 f.; their *šimlah*, in America, 231 f.; in the Sudan, 232; their *mai'zar*, in America, 232 f.; in Africa, 233; their *gafr*, in Africa, 233; in America, 234; their *laǧam* in Africa and America, 234; their *labisu* in Africa, 235 f.; their *kisa'* in Africa and America, 239; their *tarǧamān* in America, 239 f.; their *ḍabbar* in Africa, 240; their *naba* and American nagualism, 249; their *ṣubḥ* in the Nama worship, 252; their use of honey as medicine in the Sudan, 252; history of their *ǧadwal*, 268 ff.; their geomancy in Africa, 277 f.; their theology among the Mossis, 295; their *baraka* and the eating of porridge at New Year, 332; brought ball game to Europe, 342.

A REYTO, THE, 199-212.

A reyto, history of the, 199 ff.; and eulogy of the dead, 201.

A rtin Pacha on Arabic blazonry, 141, 236 ff.

Asante fetishism and sufism, 164 ff.; "spirit" words and Arabic *qara'*, 164; festivals and Arabic greater and lesser festivals, 169 f.; "dynamic force" and Arabic *bara'*, 171; "spirit" words and Arabic "heaven," 175 ff.

A thinganoi as gypsies, 66 f.; see *Touch-me-nots*.

Avicenna on steel, 11 f.

Bacabs, Plate of the, and Brinton, 266; and Cyrus Thomas, 267 f.; and the Arabic *ǧadwal*, 269 f.; and the Mound-builder gorgets, 273 f.

Ball game and *baraka* among the Berbers, 334 ff.; in Persia, 340; in Byzantium, 340 ff.; brought to

Made in the USA
Coppell, TX
04 March 2023

13751489R00282